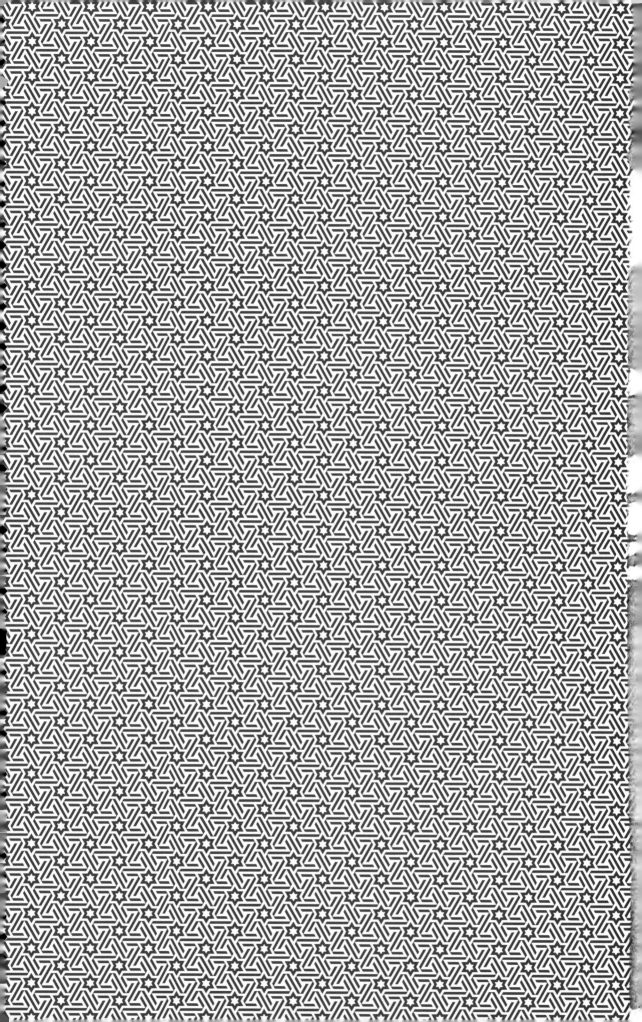

THE
LEBANESE
KITCHEN

✶

SALMA HAGE

Φ

Fäviken

Magnus Nilsson

- An exclusive insight into one of the world's most interesting restaurants, Fäviken Magasinet, and its remarkable head chef Magnus Nilsson

- Contains recipes for simple basics such as pickles and bread, as well as the dishes created by Nilsson and served at Fäviken restaurant

- Reveals Nilsson's natural and intuitive approach to working with the produce available in the environment around him, and how he creates a seasonal cycle of menus based on it

290 × 214 mm
272 pp, 150 col illus.
Hardback 978 0 7148 6470 9

Cookbooks

**Order today from
www.phaidon.com**

For sample recipes, videos
and exclusive interviews log
on to www.phaidon.com

PHAIDON

The Lebanese Kitchen
Salma Hage

- The definitive book on Lebanese home cooking, featuring 500 authentic and delicious recipes that are simple to create at home

- Lebanese food is the most enticing and varied of the increasingly popular Middle Eastern cuisines, perfect for cooking and entertaining for family and friends

- Additional recipes from guest chefs provide a unique glimpse into the kitchens of some of the world's finest Lebanese restaurants

- Salma Hage has over 50 years' experience cooking traditional Lebanese meals

270 × 180 mm
512 pp, 200 col illus.
Hardback 978 0 7148 6480 8

The Art of the Restaurateur
Nicholas Lander

- Reveals the hidden stories behind some of the world's best restaurants, which celebrate the complex but unrecognised art of the restaurateur

- Every restaurateur's story is fascinating, and has something different to tell about the creation of a successful restaurant

- The first book by renowned Financial Times restaurant critic, Nicholas Lander

- An accessible, engaging read for anyone who is interested in food, restaurants or creativity in business

245 × 172 mm
352 pp, 40 b&w illus.
Hardback 978 0 7148 6469 3

A BRIEF HISTORY OF LEBANESE CUISINE

There are more Lebanese outside Lebanon today than there are living in this smallest of countries. The diaspora left seeking refuge from a culture that had been destabilized by many years of occupations by the Ottomans, the French, and others, only to find itself amid its own 15-year civil war from 1975–1990. Yet the challenges of Lebanon's history have translated into culinary opportunity, as the many influences of those who have occupied the country have become a part of the way the Lebanese cook and eat.

Lebanon's diverse and fertile landscape has always been in high demand. Its many climates—the warm coastal plain on the Mediterranean sea, the cool mountains of fresh rain and snowfall, the fecund orchards and vineyards of the Bekaa Valley—all in such a narrow, compact space, have long made Lebanon a playground for the wealthy and a thoroughfare for commerce and business.

The European flair that took root in Lebanon as Arab culture mingled with French, when Lebanon was a protectorate of France from the 1920s until the 1940s, earned Beirut its reputation as a cosmopolitan city, the "Paris of the Middle East." While much of the beauty of the city's architecture has been damaged or destroyed by civil war and the fallout of political turmoil, the discord has not destroyed the soul of Lebanon. On the contrary, adversity has instilled the resolve and fun-loving resilience that are hallmarks of the Lebanese spirit.

The culinary scene in Lebanon is a mix of the earthy, hearty traditional peasant dishes that come from the country's many mountain villages and the cutting edge, contemporary cuisine found in Beirut and other cities, influenced by the mixture of cultures, both of the Levant and Europe, that have called Lebanon home throughout its history.

The preservation of foods when they are abundant and in season, called *mouneh*, was born out of necessity but has over the centuries become a true art for the Lebanese. They grew their own olives, made olive oil, and sold both in the local market or bartered with it. The traditional diet is rich in fruit, vegetables, legumes, and grains and it was important to preserve the abundant harvests of these crops, so that they could be eaten in the harsher months, when fresh fruit and vegetables was scarce. They would also preserve meats, which were otherwise eaten infrequently because of their expense and because of the lack of refrigeration.

Traditional Lebanese food is based on the rhythm of the seasons and locally available produce—a natural way of life that many of us now strive to get back to in our desire for sustainability. The abundance of produce available to the Lebanese cook, combined with the unique culinary heritage of the country, combine to form a cuisine that bears the challenges of its country's history and has translated them into culinary opportunity, incorporating the many influences of those who have occupied Lebanon into the way the Lebanese cook and eat.

SALMA'S STORY

Salma learned the secrets of Lebanese cuisine whilst growing up in her enormous Lebanese family on their farm in *Mazraat Et Toufah*, Lebanon, which translated means "apple hamlet" because of the fruit that is abundant in the area. The eldest of 12 siblings, Salma became her mother's right hand from a young age. *I learned quite a bit from my grandmother as I spent a lot of time with her when I was growing up. My mother had her hands full with so many children. Then I learned a lot from my mother-in-law and from my sisters-in-law. I had five sisters-in-law who were all wonderful cooks. I learned so much from them.*

Salma's father was a Maronite priest, who started out in life as a carpenter making doors and pews for churches while he studied. Salma remembers her excitement as a young child when her father was paid for making a cabinet for a man in the village with a jar of molasses. *My brother and I were so excited we couldn't sleep. It was such a luxury. We never had anything like chocolate from the shop. We waited and waited and waited for my dad to come home, but in the end we fell asleep. Next morning we woke up and saw it there in the middle of the room—a copper pot with a handle!*

Salma learned all the facets of a well-kept kitchen from her elders. There were no recipes, just conversation and a reliance on the senses. Like most great cooks, Salma learned some of the finer points of Lebanese cuisine from her grandmother, and she recalls how each spring her grandmother would raise one sheep to slaughter a week before Lent (meat was forbidden during Lent): *We used to fry the meat with its fat to preserve it. It would last until after lent had finished, and then we would take a spoon of the meat and fat and cook with it. It keeps for a surprisingly long time—a couple of months easily.*

Salma, her husband Heni, and their son Joe emigrated from Lebanon to England in 1967 and soon assimilated into their new life in London. Lebanese food continued to have important associations for them, especially because they now were so far away from their family and culture. Food also became their livelihood. Salma started as a kitchen hand when she first came to London in her mid-20s, then worked her way up to the role of head chef for a large catering organization, learning to appreciate English cuisine while bringing the flavors of home, of Lebanon, to share with others wherever she cooked. *I'm a professional English cook. I went to college and worked for over 30 years as a cook, but at home… I cook Lebanese*, Salma says.

Annual visits to Mazraat Et Toufah keep Salma deeply connected to her roots. She and her husband spend a couple of months in Lebanon each year and stay at their family home, high up in the hills with a beautiful view over the valley. All of their family members who have left Lebanon for distant shores, such as England or Canada, still return to see one another and remember the life they once lived together there.

THE LEBANESE PANTRY AND GARDEN

Anyone who cooks at home develops a pantry of ingredients that are always stocked, ready for cooking and eating at any time. Salma maintains a traditional Lebanese pantry and garden at her home in London, with an array of ingredients that are integral to her food.

Seasonality is the underlying element of freshness that influences the Lebanese way of cooking, which Salma learned from her youth growing up in the village and surrounded by farmers and people growing their own food. The profusion of all manner of produce in Lebanon is the result of soil enriched by a varied and seasonal climate.

Much of what Salma does on a daily basis in her kitchen is not just the preparation of dishes to serve her family and friends, but also keeping up her pantry and garden. Her way of life is geared toward the table, toward how to bring out the best in all that she cooks by using the finest ingredients she can find and making time to take care of the many small gestures that make her food so good, like mixing her special seven-spice blend or preparing fresh *laban*—Lebanese yogurt—each week.

The staples that Salma keeps in her pantry are the ingredients that her mother kept in her pantry in Mazraat Et Toufah. Lebanese cuisine is steeped in a culinary tradition that may enjoy tweaks and flights of the cook's fancy over generations, but that fundamentally stays the same.

Here are some of the items that feature in Salma's pantry and are grown in her garden. Don't worry about developing a pantry this extensive. Those who are city dwellers will know that space is often at a premium, and that gardens can simply be something that other people have. As you attempt some of the recipes in this book, you will find that you already have many ingredients on hand but that you're using them in new and exciting ways—ingredients, such as cinnamon as a savory spice or yogurt as a basis for soup.

SPICES

The spices that flavor Lebanese cuisine are many. So often when Salma cooks for friends a meal like Lebanese chicken and *hashweh*, a buttery, deeply satisfying dish of chicken, rice, ground beef or lamb, and toasted nuts seasoned with cinnamon, they find it difficult to name what exactly the delicious seasoning is that they taste, because they have not encountered a spice like cinnamon used in such a savory way before.

Salma often uses her Lebanese seven spice seasoning in her cooking. It is typical for a Lebanese family to have its own combination of seven spices that is traditional for that family. The seven spice blend is in certain regards like the family name—a source of pride, a distinguishing element. Salma's heady blend includes allspice, cinnamon, clove, ginger, black pepper, nutmeg, and fenugreek, and the recipe can be found on page 26.

Za'atar, a mixture of dried sumac, thyme, and sesame seeds, is another essential spice mix in the Lebanese pantry. Za'atar tastes of bold, citrus notes. Sesame gives za'atar its toasty nuttiness, the sumac its sourness. Za'atar can be an acquired taste, but like many acquired tastes—raw oysters, blue cheese, scotch on the rocks—the acquisition is well worth having and keeping. Combined with olive oil, za'atar makes a topping for savory rounds of thick Lebanese bread, typically eaten for breakfast. You can find za'atar at Middle Eastern grocery stores and many other supermarkets. It's also possible to make za'atar at home by carefully roasting fresh thyme (or purchasing dried thyme), toasting sesame seeds, and mixing them with sumac and some coarse salt.

Cumin and cardamom are also typical spices used in Lebanese cooking. Salma uses cardamom to give coffee a refreshing flavor and also to season meat dishes, such as lamb and chicken.

GRAINS AND LEGUMES

One of the reasons that the Lebanese way of cooking and eating is so healthy is the inclusion of whole grains in so many of its dishes. Harvested in the summer months in Lebanon, the abundance of grains and legumes are dried and used as the foundation for good eating, and in turn for good health, throughout the year. *We always grew our own beans*, says Salma of her family in Lebanon. *When they were fresh in summer, we would sew them together with needle and thread like necklaces, and hang them up to dry. When you need them again in winter, you drop them in hot water and they come up like new again.* The preparation of lentils, chickpeas, beans, rice, and cracked wheat is at heart Lebanese peasant food—food that is economical and provides the nutrients needed in a diet that is low in animal protein. Extensive use of grains and legumes raised the significance of their preparation and gives them exceptional flavor. Salma talks about lentils, beans and pulses as the mainstay of her diet as a child in Mazraat Et Toufah, primarily because they were the main ingredient available to them. This was due in large measure to the remote location of many Lebanese villages, including *Mazraat Et Toufah*, situated due east of Tripoli. Early on there was no transportation there, so trips to the souk, the big markets of Tripoli, were a significant event, all on foot until roads were built that reached up to the villages. *There was only one person in our village with a car*, Salma recalls, remembering with amusement how many of the villagers would try to squeeze in to it at one time for a trip to the markets.

The first dish Salma made as a girl of nine years old was *mujadara*, a staple of lentils, rice, and caramelized onions. Her work garnered the praise of her parents, and she ties her memory of her father's love for her to their time together in the kitchen. *I remember my father, God rest his soul*, Salma says. *He said to me, "that is wonderful darling, I'm so pleased you can cook."* Salma is like many Lebanese daughters who adore their doting fathers and cook for them as the proverbial road to their hearts.

My father always encouraged me with my cooking, Salma says. *Whatever I cooked, even if it wasn't edible, he'd say it was lovely and praise me. Dad said to me as a young girl, "you're going to be a great cook!" And thankfully he was right.*

OLIVES AND OLIVE OIL

Salma's husband Heni grew up in Sebhel, a Lebanese village famous for its olives. The Hage family property is graced with more than 1000 olive trees from which olives are harvested every September and oil is made. Antique presses once used on the farm are still kept in the basement of the family home there, held in nostalgia for an era that has passed. It was over the harvesting of olives that Salma met her future husband as a young girl. *We spoke to each other and got on well*, Salma remembers. *A few weeks later I eloped from my village to his. No messing about! My father thought I was a little too young, but we had his blessing. And that was it.*

The many, ancient olive groves on Heni's family property contribute to a mainstay of the Lebanese style of eating. Once brined and stored, green and black olives offer the addictive, salty flavor that no meal would be complete without.

Lebanon's olive oil, which is the primary fat used in Lebanese cooking, is highly prized by the Lebanese. Its flavor can be fruity or peppery, and its health benefits are renowned. Olive oil is delicious drizzled on vegetables, grains, meats, and salads or used as a dip with za'atar for Lebanese flatbreads or pita.

NUTS AND SEEDS

The Lebanese use a vast array of nuts in their cooking in ways that elevate dishes to greatness. Pine nuts, pistachios, walnuts, almonds, and cashew nuts are the most common nuts found in Lebanese cuisine, along with sesame and anise seeds.

Salma cooks with many different types of nut, with an emphasis on the traditional Lebanese pine nuts. She fries nuts by sautéing them in a little butter and salt until they are deep golden brown, and then uses them in a multitude of ways, such as to top open-faced meat pies, hummus, or as a garnish for rice. Green nuts are not uncommon at the Lebanese table. The green almonds and walnuts, which are ready to eat in the spring in Lebanon, are considered a fleeting delight, since they must be eaten right away.

Tahini is a paste made of ground sesame seeds, harvested in August in Lebanon, and is the basis for *hummus bi tahini*—chickpeas with tahini—and many other dips. Salma's tahini specialties include tahini sauce, combining the paste with lemon juice and garlic and whipping the mixture to a light, smooth consistency.

HERBS AND GRAPE (VINE) LEAVES

Mint, or *na'na*, is one of the essential flavors in Lebanese cuisine. Dried and fresh, mint brightens *laban khiyar*, yogurt cucumber salad, as well as the very traditional tomato salad with mint, scallions (spring onions), and olive oil. Mint is also the basis of Lebanese *tabbouleh* salad, which holds the essence of summer with its flavors of mint, parsley, tomato, and cracked wheat seasoned with olive oil and lemon juice. Salma offers a word to the wise about growing mint in your garden: the more you pick it, the more it grows, which is great until the mint takes over all available space in the garden. Mint can be controlled by planting it on its own, either in a planter or a special section of the garden that is cordoned off from the rest.

Few people are lucky enough to grow grape leaf vines in their yards and the majority have to hunt for wild vines that can be foraged, or in the absence of that, rely on jarred grape (vine) leaves. Salma picks the small, tender leaves, washes and dries them, then freezes them in packs to be used throughout the year for delectable grape leaf rolls. The rolls are stuffed with a mixture of rice and ground beef or lamb, or a vegetarian stuffing with chickpeas, and cooked with lemon juice until they are meltingly tender.

When Salma planted her grape vines from plants she and her son Joe bought, she was careful to select smaller plants. *I wanted to watch them grow up*, she says. In other words, Salma wants to be *with* her garden, and cultivating it is just as important to her as harvesting it.

FRUIT

While the Lebanese do have a tradition of pastry, of sweet treats, somewhat influenced by the French occupation of the last century, the emphasis after a meal is often on fruit. A platter of fresh apples, grapes, apricots, oranges, figs, dates, and pomegranates is almost always presented to guests after dinner. Salma's village in Lebanon was named for its abundant apples, which are cultivated along with much of the fruit in Lebanon at high elevations. Dates and citrus are grown on the coast near the Mediterranean sea, while apricots, cherries, peaches, and plums are grown at a higher elevation. In the foothills, particularly the Bekaa Valley, are the grapes that supply Lebanon's remarkable winemaking industry, as well as figs.

The fruit at home is unbelievable, Salma says. *Every morning I used to collect figs–I could fill a bowl every day. We had apples, grapes, peaches, lemons, all from small trees, all right outside the back door!* It's no wonder that the practice of preserving foods is alive and strong among the Lebanese, in an effort to hold onto the abundance of summer to enjoy throughout the year. Salma shares with us in *The Lebanese Kitchen* the many recipes she has developed making use in particular of fruit, which are such a part of her life in Lebanon. The apple recipes that originate from her apple-laden Lebanese village include apple jam, apple upside down cake, and delicate apple bundles in layers of phyllo (filo) dough.

Salma has always enjoyed the flavor of fresh tomatoes from her own land because they grew so many at home in her village. Tomato paste (puree) was made in huge batches, and was so integral to the family pantry that Salma never knew, until she was much older, that the puree could be purchased, jarred or canned. *We just never realized you could buy it!* Salma says. *And even so, we still make our own puree at home today.* Salma's simple recipe for tomato paste (purée) can be found on page 27.

ROSE WATER AND ORANGE BLOSSOM WATER
While Salma loves to cook savory cuisine, and did cook professionally for many years, her great passion in the kitchen is pastry and sweets of any kind. She shares with us her recipes for phyllo and nut baklawa and ma'amoul cookies, along with many other traditional pastries. Many of these include the fragrant essences of roses and orange blossoms, perhaps the most distinctive of all of the items in the Lebanese pantry. Rose water and orange blossom water are made from the distillation of the petals of the flowers in water. The waters are found in many supermarkets and online.

PICKLES AND PRESERVES
On the Lebanese table for most meals are homemade pickles. Their piquant flavor comes from the vinegar brine in which they are soaked. Vegetables of every kind are pickled in Lebanon, and in Salma's kitchen in England, at the height of their ripeness in the summer and fall (autumn) months— carrots, cauliflower, bell peppers and the ubiquitous bright pink turnips, or *lifft*, colored with a beet (beetroot) in the brine. Fruit preserves also have their allotted place on the Lebanese pantry shelf, bringing the taste of summer to the table all year. Salma loves to recall how Heni's sister, who emigrated to Australia, gave her the most unusual preserved fruit she'd ever eaten. *She took me to her fridge and she gave me something to try that was unbelievable*, she says. *It was crystallized jam pieces made from watermelon, but not the flesh. You take off the green skin and use the part between the skin and the red flesh. This was really like nothing I'd ever tasted before.*

Salma has an endless fascination with all facets of the Lebanese pantry, garden, kitchen, and table. She goes to the supermarket every other day to stock up for her daily cooking. She likes to get up early in the morning so she can go outside and water her garden, wash the kitchen floor, wash the fish, and mix the spices or boil the milk for laban. Every day at Salma's includes this kind of rhythm, her way of taking care of her own.

A LEBANESE MEAL

A typical Lebanese lunch or dinner menu, when family and friends are gathered—as they often are—is extensive. The appetite is piqued with traditional Lebanese *mezze*, or small-plate appetizers, such as *labneh, baba ganoush,* and *tabbouli* salad. These plates will stay at the table throughout the meal, to be scooped up with flatbread or cabbage leaves and add another dimension to a bite of vegetables, grains, meat, or fish.

Main dishes include platters of broiled (grilled) and roasted meats, such as lamb and chicken, fresh fish with tahini sauce, stuffed zucchini (courgettes) and grape (vine) leaves, and the showstopper of the meal, Lebanon's national dish of *kibbeh*. Ultralean ground (minced) beef or lamb is combined with onion and bulghur wheat, then eaten either raw (*kibbeh nayeh*), baked (*kibbeh sinyeh*), or fried in torpedo-shape balls. Salma makes a hundred kibbeh balls at once and freezes them so she always has kibbeh on hand. She can take out a few and place them straight from the freezer into hot oil. Even with the influences on Lebanese cuisine from the Turks and the French, dishes like Lebanese kibbeh remain proudly untouched.

There are always grains on the table, cooked with remarkable depth of flavor, and a dish of homemade pickles to enliven the palate. Vegetables are typically eggplants (aubergines), green beans, okra, and leafy greens, such as watercress and Swiss chard. Dessert will be a beautiful fruit plate, along with one of the many Lebanese sweet treats flavored with rose and orange blossom water.

Every Lebanese meal ends with, and every visit is punctuated by, cups of Lebanese coffee, *qahweh arabi*. Also known as Turkish coffee, it is dark, earthy, incredibly potent and not for the faint of heart! The coffee is served in demitasse cups and is sometimes sweetened with sugar or flavored with cardamom, but never lightened with cream.

BASIC RECIPES

*

وصفات اساسية

CHICKEN STOCK

—

مرق الدجاج

Preparation time: 10 minutes
Cooking time: 30 minutes
Makes 1 pint/600 ml

1 uncooked chicken carcass
1 carrot, chopped
1 celery stalk, chopped
1 onion, chopped
1 bay leaf
8 black peppercorns
4 thyme sprigs

Put the chicken into a large pot and pour in water to cover. Bring to a boil over a medium heat and skim off any scum that has formed on the surface. Add the remaining ingredients and bring back to a boil. Skim again, then reduce the heat and simmer for 30 minutes. Strain and store in a airtight container in the refrigerator for up to 3 days.

Brown chicken stock
For brown chicken stock, simply replace the raw chicken carcass with a leftover cooked one and simmer for 4 hours. Strain and store in the refrigerator for up to 3 days.

LEBANESE SEVEN SPICES SEASONING

—

خلطة البهارات السبعة

Preparation time: 5 minutes
Makes 7 oz/175 g

5 tablespoons ground allspice
3½ tablespoons pepper
3½ tablespoons ground cinnamon
5 tablespoons ground cloves
4 tablespoons ground nutmeg
4 tablespoons ground fenugreek
4 tablespoons ground ginger

Mix the spices together thoroughly and store in an airtight container in a dark place.

ZA'ATAR SEASONING

PHOTO PAGE 31

—

زعتر

Preparation time: 5 minutes
Makes 7 oz/175 g

5 tablespoons olive oil
7 tablespoons za'atar
2 teaspoons dried thyme
1 teaspoon marjoram
3 tablespoons sesame seeds, toasted

Mix all the ingredients together and store in a plastic container.

TOMATO PASTE

معجون الطماطم

Preparation time: 15 minutes
Cooking time: 1 hour 30 minutes
Makes ¾ cup (7 oz/200 g)

3¼ lb/1.5 kg tomatoes, chopped

Put the tomatoes into a large saucepan, cover, and cook for 10 minutes. Uncover the pan and cook for another 1 hour 20 minutes. Remove from the heat and pass the tomatoes through a fine strainer (sieve) into a bowl to remove the skins and seeds. Spoon the paste (purée) into an airtight container and store in the refrigerator.

TOMATO SAUCE

صلصة الطماطم

Preparation time: 10 minutes
Cooking time: 10–15 minutes
Serves 2

2 tablespoons olive oil
1 onion, diced
1 teaspoon seven spices seasoning
5 tablespoons tomato paste (purée)
salt and pepper

Heat the oil in a small saucepan, add the onion and seasoning, and cook over low heat, stirring occasionally, for 5 minutes until softened. Stir in the tomato paste (purée) and ⅔ cup (5 fl oz/150 ml) water and cook, stirring occasionally, for another 5 minutes. Season to taste with salt and pepper.

SPICY TOMATO SAUCE

صلصة الطماطم الحارة

Preparation time: 15 minutes
Cooking time: 35–40 minutes
Serves 4

2¼ lb/1 kg tomatoes, cut into quarters
3 garlic cloves, peeled
1 red chile, coarsely chopped
pinch of sugar
2–3 tablespoons olive oil
salt and pepper

Preheat the oven to 375°F/190°C/Gas Mark 5. Put the tomatoes, garlic, and chile on a baking sheet, sprinkle with sugar, and drizzle with the olive oil. Bake for 35–40 minutes until the tomatoes are soft. Remove from the oven, transfer the mixture to a food processor, and process until combined. Scrape into an ovenproof dish, season to taste with salt and pepper, and keep warm until ready to serve.

TOMATO AND OLIVE SAUCE

صلصة الطماطم بزيت
الزيتون

Preparation time: 10 minutes
Cooking time: 1 hour
Serves 4

2 tablespoons olive oil
3 garlic cloves, crushed
28 oz/800 g canned tomatoes
8 thyme sprigs
scant 1 cup (3½ oz/100 g) olives, pitted (stoned) and coarsely
    chopped
2 teaspoons salt
1 teaspoon pepper

Heat the olive oil in a saucepan, add the garlic, and cook over low heat, stirring occasionally, for 1 minute. Add the tomatoes, thyme leaves, olives, salt, and pepper and simmer for 1 hour.

PINE NUT SAUCE

صلصة الصنوبر

Preparation time: 2 minutes
Cooking time: 2–3 minutes
Serves 4

1 cup (4 oz/120 g) pine nuts
juice of 1 lemon
½ teaspoon salt
2 garlic cloves

Dry-fry the pine nuts in a small skillet or frying pan over low heat, stirring frequently, for a few minutes until golden. Remove from the heat and let cool, then put into a food processor. Add the remaining ingredients and generous ¾ cup (6½ fl oz/185 ml) water and process to combine.

HOMEMADE YOGURT

الزبادي المنزلي

Preparation time: 5 minutes, plus cooling time
Cooking time: 45 minutes
Makes 9 cups (4½ lb/2 kg)

10 cups (4 pints/2.3 litres) whole (full-fat) milk
¾ cup (6 oz /175 g) plain naturally set yogurt

Pour the milk into a saucepan, cover, and bring to a boil over very low heat, stirring occasionally. This may take up to 45 minutes. Remove the pan from the heat and let cool until the milk is tepid. Stir in the yogurt. Cover the pan with a lid and let stand overnight, covered with a clean towel, in a warm dark place. It is very important not to move the pan or remove the towel. The following day, stir the yogurt once and then put it in the refrigerator for 2 days before eating.

GARLIC AND ROSEMARY DRESSING

PHOTO PAGE 31

—

تتبيلة الثوم واكليل الجبل

Preparation time: 15 minutes
Cooking time: 30 minutes
Makes scant 1 cup (7 fl oz/200 ml)

2 garlic bulbs
scant 1 cup (7 fl oz/200 ml) olive oil, plus extra for drizzling
3 rosemary sprigs, chopped
salt and pepper

Preheat the oven to 375°F/190°C/Gas Mark 5. Put each garlic bulb on a square of foil, drizzle with olive oil, and wrap the foil around them to enclose. Put them into a small ovenproof dish and roast for about 30 minutes until the garlic is soft. Remove from the oven and let cool. Meanwhile, pour the olive oil into a small saucepan, add the rosemary sprigs, and heat gently for 10 minutes to steep (infuse) the oil with the herb. Remove the pan from the heat and set aside. Remove and discard the rosemary from the oil. Cut the bottom of the garlic bulbs and squeeze out the soft cloves into a bowl. Mash to a pulp and add to the olive oil. Alternatively, squeeze out the garlic into a small food processor, add the oil, and process until combined. Season with salt and pepper.

LEMON DRESSING

PHOTO PAGE 31

—

تتبيلة عصير الليمون

Preparation time: 5 minutes
Makes generous ⅔ cup (5½ fl oz/160 ml)

finely grated zest and juice of 1 lemon
2 teaspoons white wine vinegar
6 tablespoons olive oil
1½ oz/40 g preserved lemon (optional)
salt and pepper

Mix together the lemon zest and juice, vinegar, and olive oil in a bowl and season with salt and pepper. Quarter the preserved lemon, if using, then remove and discard the flesh. Finely chop the rind and add to the dressing, together with a pinch of salt.

GARLIC AND MINT DRESSING

PHOTO PAGE 31

—

تتبيلة الثوم والنعناع

Preparation time: 10 minutes
Makes scant 1 cup (7 fl oz/200 ml)

1 garlic clove, crushed
1 tablespoon red wine vinegar
scant 1 cup (8 fl oz/250 ml) extra virgin olive oil
3 tablespoons chopped fresh mint
pinch of superfine (caster) sugar
salt and pepper

Whisk together all the ingredients in a bowl and season to taste with salt and pepper.

WALNUT DRESSING

PHOTO PAGE 31

تتبيلة الجوز

Preparation time: 10 minutes
Makes 5 tablespoons

½ cup (2 oz/50 g) shelled walnuts
1 tablespoon white wine vinegar
3 tablespoons walnut oil
1 tablespoon sunflower oil
salt and pepper

Dry-fry the walnuts in a heavy skillet or frying pan, stirring frequently, for a few minutes until golden. Remove from the pan and chop finely. Whisk together the vinegar and walnut and sunflower oils in a bowl, season with salt and pepper, and stir in the nuts.

POMEGRANATE DRESSING

PHOTO PAGE 31

تتبيلة دبس الرمان

Preparation time: 5 minutes, plus resting time
Makes generous ⅔ cup (5½ fl oz/160 ml)

2 teaspoons red wine vinegar
2 tablespoons pomegranate molasses
5 tablespoons extra virgin olive oil
1 garlic clove, crushed
pinch of sugar
juice of ½ an orange
2 tablespoons pomegranate seeds
salt and pepper

Whisk together all the ingredients in a bowl and season to taste with salt and pepper. Store in the refrigerator for 2 days before eating.

BASIC PIE DOUGH

عجينة الفطائر الهشة

Preparation time: 10 minutes
Makes 1¾ lb/800 g

4 cups (1 lb 2 oz/500 g) all-purpose (plain) flour
2¼ sticks (9 oz/250 g) unsalted butter, chilled and diced
2 egg yolks
2 tablespoons water

Sift the flour into a bowl, add the butter, and rub in with your fingertips until the mixture resembles fine breadcrumbs. (This can also be done in a food processor.) Add the egg yolks and mix to a smooth dough, add 1–2 tablespoons water, if necessary. Wrap in plastic wrap (clingfilm) and chill in the refrigerator for 1 hour before using.

ZA'ATAR SEASONING AND A SELECTION OF DRESSINGS

ALMOND PIE DOUGH

—

عجينة اللوز

Preparation time: 10 minutes
Makes 1¾ lb/800 g

2½ cups (11 oz/300 g) all-purpose (plain) flour
1¾ sticks (7 oz/200 g) unsalted butter, chilled and diced
⅓ cup (2½ oz/65 g) superfine (caster) sugar
1 cup (4 oz/120 g) ground almonds
1 egg

Sift the flour into a bowl, add the butter, and rub in with your fingertips until the mixture resembles fine breadcrumbs. (This can also be done in a food processor.) Stir in the sugar and ground almonds, then add the egg and mix to a smooth dough, adding 2–3 tablespoons water, if necessary. Wrap in plastic wrap (clingfilm) and chill in the refrigerator for 1 hour before using.

SWEET PIE DOUGH

—

عجينة الفطائر المحلاة

Preparation time: 10 minutes
Makes 14 oz/400 g

1¼ cups (5 oz/150 g) all-purpose (plain) flour
pinch of salt
6 tablespoons (3 oz/80 g) unsalted butter, chilled and diced
¾ cup (3 oz/80 g) confectioners' (icing) sugar
grated zest of ½ lemon
1 egg yolk

Sift together the flour and salt into a bowl, add the butter, and rub in with your fingertips until the mixture resembles fine breadcrumbs. (This can also be done in a food processor.) Stir in the sugar and lemon zest, then add the egg yolks and mix to a smooth dough, adding 1 tablespoon water, if necessary. Wrap in plastic wrap (clingfilm) and chill in the refrigerator for 1 hour before using.

SUGAR SYRUP

شراب السكر (القطر)

Preparation time: 5 minutes
Cooking time: 10 minutes
Makes 3 cups (1¼ pints/750 ml)

1¾ cups (12 oz/350 g) sugar
2 lemon leaves
juice of 1 lemon
2 tablespoons orange flower water

Put the sugar into a saucepan, pour in 3 cups (1¼ pints/750 ml) water, and stir over medium heat until the sugar has dissolved. Add the lemon leaves and juice, increase the heat to high, and bring to a boil. Boil without stirring until syrupy. Remove the pan from the heat and let cool, then remove the lemon leaves and add the orange flower water. Store the sugar syrup in a sterilized glass jar in the refrigerator for up to 3 months and use when needed.

MEZZE

★

المقبلات

HUMMUS

PHOTO PAGE 41

—

حمص

Preparation time: 5–10 minutes
Serves 6–8

28 oz/800 g canned chickpeas
3 garlic cloves, peeled
4 tablespoons tahini
juice of 2 lemons
2 teaspoons sea salt
extra virgin olive oil, for drizzling
½ cup (2 oz/50 g) pine nuts, toasted

Drain the chickpeas, reserving ¼ cup (2 fl oz/50 ml) of the can juices, and rinse. Put the chickpeas into a food processor, add the garlic cloves and tahini, and process for a few minutes. Add the reserved can juices, followed by half the lemon juice and the sea salt, and process until smooth. Taste and add more lemon juice, if you like. Scrape the hummus into a dish, drizzle generously with olive oil, sprinkle with the toasted pine nuts, and serve.

HUMMUS WITH PINE NUTS

PHOTO PAGE 41

—

حمص مع الصنوبر

Preparation time: 5–10 minutes
Serves 6–8

28 oz/800 g canned chickpeas
3 garlic cloves, peeled
4 tablespoons tahini
juice of 2 lemons
2 teaspoons sea salt
extra virgin olive oil, for drizzling
½ cup (2 oz/50 g) pine nuts, toasted

Drain the chickpeas, reserving ¼ cup (2 fl oz/50 ml) of the can juices, and rinse. Put the chickpeas into a food processor, add the garlic cloves and tahini, and process for a few minutes. Add the reserved can juices, followed by half the lemon juice and the sea salt, and process until smooth. Taste and add more lemon juice, if you like. Scrape the hummus into a dish, drizzle generously with olive oil, sprinkle with the toasted pine nuts, and serve.

HUMMUS WITH LAMB AND PINE NUTS

PHOTO PAGE 41

حمص مع لحم الغنم
والصنوبر

Preparation time: 10 minutes
Cooking time: 10 minutes
Serves 6–8

28 oz/800 g canned chickpeas
3 garlic cloves, peeled
4 tablespoons tahini
juice of 2 lemons
2 teaspoons sea salt
extra virgin olive oil, for drizzling

For the lamb and pine nut topping:
½ teaspoon olive oil
3½ oz/100 g ground (minced) lamb
¼ teaspoon seven spices seasoning
⅓ cup (1½ oz/40 g) pine nuts, toasted
salt and pepper

First, make the lamb and pine nut topping. Heat the oil in a skillet or frying pan, add the lamb, and cook over medium heat for 5–6 minutes until evenly browned. Add the seven spice seasoning and season to taste with salt and pepper. Stir in the toasted pine nuts and remove the pan from the heat. Drain the chickpeas, reserving ¼ cup (2 fl oz/50 ml) of the can juices, and rinse. Put the chickpeas into a food processor, add the garlic cloves and tahini, and process for a few minutes. Add the reserved can juices, followed by half the lemon juice and the sea salt, and process until smooth. Taste and add more lemon juice, if you like. Scrape the hummus into to a serving dish, drizzle generously with olive oil, top with the lamb and pine nuts, and serve.

HUMMUS WITH BEET

PHOTO PAGE 41

حمص مع الشمندر

Preparation time: 10 minutes
Serves 6–8

28 oz/800 g canned chickpeas, drained and rinsed
¼ cup (2 fl oz/50 ml) beet (beetroot) juice
3 garlic cloves, peeled
4 tablespoons tahini
3 cooked beets (beetroots)
juice of 2 lemons
2 teaspoons sea salt
extra virgin olive oil, for drizzling

Put the chickpeas, beet (beetroot) juice, garlic cloves, tahini, and beets (beetroots) into a food processor and process for a few minutes. Add half the lemon juice and the sea salt and process until smooth. Taste and add more lemon juice, if you like. Scrape the hummus into a serving dish, drizzle generously with olive oil, and serve.

HUMMUS
WITH
CHILI OIL

PHOTO PAGE 41

حمص حار

Preparation time: 5 minutes
Serves 6–8

28 oz/800 g canned chickpeas
3 garlic cloves, peeled
4 tablespoons tahini
juice of 2 lemons
2 teaspoons sea salt
2 tablespoons steeped (infused) chili oil

Drain the chickpeas, reserving ¼ cup (2 fl oz/50 ml) of the can juices, and rinse. Put the chickpeas into a food processor, add the garlic cloves and tahini, and process for a few minutes. Add the reserved can juices, followed by half the lemon juice and the sea salt, and process until smooth. Taste and add more lemon juice, if you like. Scrape the hummus into to a serving dish, drizzle with the chili oil, and serve.

HUMMUS
WITH
PUMPKIN
AND
CILANTRO

PHOTO PAGE 41

حمص مع الكزبرة
واليقطين

Preparation time: 5 minutes
Cooking time: 30 minutes
Serves 6–8

1½ cups (7 oz/200 g) peeled, seeded, and diced pumpkin
extra virgin olive oil, for drizzling
14 oz/400 g canned chickpeas
4 garlic cloves, peeled
4 tablespoons tahini
juice of 2 lemons
2 teaspoons sea salt
2 tablespoons chopped fresh cilantro (coriander)

Preheat the oven to 400°F/200°C/Gas Mark 6. Put the pumpkin into a roasting pan, drizzle with a little oil, and roast for 30 minutes or until tender. Remove from the oven and let cool completely. Drain the chickpeas, reserving ¼ cup (2 fl oz/50 ml) of the can juices, and rinse. Put the chickpeas into a food processor, add the garlic cloves, tahini, and pumpkin, and process for a few minutes. Add the reserved can juices, followed by half the lemon juice and the sea salt, and process until smooth. Taste and add more lemon juice, if you like. Scrape the hummus into to a serving dish, drizzle generously with olive oil, sprinkle with the cilantro (coriander), and serve.

A SELECTION OF HUMMUS

HUMMUS WITH RED BELL PEPPER

PHOTO PAGE 41

—

حمص مع الفلفل
الاحمر

Preparation time: 10 minutes
Serves 6–8

14 oz/400 g canned chickpeas
2 garlic cloves, peeled
2 tablespoons tahini
2 red bell peppers in oil, drained
juice of 1 lemon
1 teaspoons sea salt
extra virgin olive oil, for drizzling

Drain the chickpeas, reserving ¼ cup (2 fl oz/50 ml) of the can juices, and rinse. Put the chickpeas into a food processor, add the garlic cloves, tahini, and bell peppers, and process for a few minutes. Add the reserved can juices, followed by half the lemon juice and the sea salt, and process until smooth. Taste and add more lemon juice, if you like. Scrape the hummus into to a serving dish, drizzle generously with olive oil, and serve.

HUMMUS WITH FAVA BEANS

PHOTO PAGE 41

—

حمص مع الفول

Preparation time: 10 minutes
Serves 6–8

14 oz/400 g canned chickpeas
4 garlic cloves, peeled
4 tablespoons tahini
¾ cup (3½ oz/100 g) frozen fava (broad) beans, skinned
juice of 2 lemons
2 teaspoons sea salt
1 tablespoon steeped (infused) chili oil

Drain the chickpeas, reserving ¼ cup (2 fl oz/50 ml) of the can juices, and rinse. Put the chickpeas into a food processor, add the garlic cloves, tahini, and beans, and process for a few minutes. Add the reserved can juices, followed by half the lemon juice and the sea salt, and process until smooth. Taste and add more lemon juice, if you like. Scrape the hummus into to a serving dish and serve with the chili oil.

LABNEH

—

لبنة

Preparation time: 3 hours, plus yogurt making time
Serves 4–6

1 quantity Homemade yogurt (see page 28)
olive oil, for drizzling
paprika, for dusting
salt

Line a strainer (sieve) with a double thickness of cheesecloth (muslin) and set over a large bowl. Pour in the homemade yogurt and let stand for about 3 hours until all the liquid has drained off. Season with salt, then spread out on a plate. Drizzle with olive oil and dust with paprika before serving.

GARLIC DIP

صلصة الثوم

Preparation time: 5 minutes, plus chilling time
Makes ⅔ cup (¼ pint/150 ml)

4 garlic cloves
½ teaspoon sea salt
juice of ½ lemon
⅔ cup (¼ pint/150 ml) thick plain (natural) yogurt
pinch of ground sumac

Crush the garlic with the sea salt in a mortar with a pestle. Add the lemon juice and mix well. Stir the mixture into the yogurt in a small serving bowl, then chill in the refrigerator for 20 minutes. Just before serving, add a pinch of sumac.

EGGPLANT AND GARLIC DIP

وصفة جدة سلمى
للباذنجان بالثوم

Preparation time: 10 minutes
Cooking time: 50 minutes
Serves 6–8

2 eggplants (aubergines)
2 small garlic cloves
extra virgin olive oil, for drizzling
pita breads, to serve

Preheat the oven to 400°F/200°C/Gas Mark 6. Put the eggplants (aubergines) on a baking sheet and bake for 50 minutes, turning them halfway through the cooking time. Remove from the oven and let stand until cool enough to handle, then carefully peel off the skins and discard. Chop the eggplants in half and soak up some of the liquid with paper towels. Put the eggplants into a bowl and mash with fork. Crushed the garlic cloves with a little salt and add to the mashed eggplant. Mix well and drizzle with extra virgin olive oil before serving with pita breads.

JIBNEH CHEESE

PHOTO PAGE 49

جبنة

Preparation time: 20 minutes, plus resting time
Cooking time: 20 minutes
Makes 2 medium rounds

14¾ cups (6 pints/3.5 liters) whole (full-fat) milk
¼ rennet tablet
salt
flatbread, to serve

Pour the milk into a large pan and heat until lukewarm, then remove from the heat. Dissolve the rennet tablet in a small bowl of cold water and add to the milk. Add a pinch of salt and stir. Cover the pan and let stand for 3 hours. Spoon the cheese into the middle of a cheesecloth (muslin) square and squeeze out the excess liquid. Roll the cheese into rounds and serve with flatbread.

TAHINI DIP

TAHINI DIP

PHOTO PAGE 44

—

صلصة الطحينة

Preparation time: 5 minutes
Makes ¾ cup (6 fl oz/175 ml)

1 garlic clove
¼ teaspoon sea salt
juice of ½ lemon
scant ½ cup (3½ fl oz/100 ml) mayonnaise
5 tablespoons tahini
pepper

Pound the garlic with the sea salt in a mortar with a pestle, then add the lemon juice and mix well. Spoon the mayonnaise into a small bowl and stir in the tahini and garlic mixture. Season with pepper.

ZUCCHINI AND BULGUR WHEAT WITH PARSLEY AND LEMON SALAD

—

برغل بالكوسا مع عصير الليمون والبقدونس

Preparation time: 15 minutes, plus soaking time
Makes ¾ cup (6 fl oz/175 ml)
Serves 4

Generous 1 cup (7 oz/200 g) bulgur wheat
2 zucchini (courgettes), cut into cubes
3 scallions (spring onions), sliced
½ small bunch of fresh parsley, chopped
½ small bunch of fresh mint, chopped
3–4 arugula (rocket) leaves, torn
2 cups (4 oz/120 g) alfafa sprouts
2 tablespoons pomegranate seeds
¼ cup (1 oz/25 g) shelled walnuts, chopped

For the dressing
2 tablespoons extra virgin oil
grated zest and juice of 1 lemon
¼ teaspoon Dijon mustard
salt and pepper

Put the bulgur wheat into a bowl, pour in hot water to cover, and let soak for 10–15 minutes. Drain in a strainer lined with cheesecloth (muslin), squeezing out the excess moisture. Tip the bulgur wheat into a bowl. Add the zucchini (courgettes), scallions (spring onions), parsley, mint, arugula (rocket), alfalfa sprouts, pomegranate seeds, and walnuts and toss well. Whisk together all the dressing ingredients in a small bowl, pour the dressing over the salad, and serve immediately.

BABA GANOUSH

PHOTO PAGE 47

بابا غنوج

Preparation time: 10–15 minutes, plus cooling time
Cooking time: 1 hour
Serves 6–8

3 eggplants (aubergines)
2 small garlic cloves
2 tablespoons tahini
juice of ½ lemon
olive oil, for drizzling
pomegranate seeds, for sprinkling
salt and pepper

Preheat the oven to 400°F/200°C/Gas Mark 6. Put the eggplants (aubergines) on a baking sheet and bake for about 1 hour until soft. Remove from the oven and let stand until cool enough to handle, then peel off the skins and discard. Let cool completely. Pound the garlic with a pinch of salt in a mortar with a pestle. Add the tahini and lemon juice and mix well. Finely chop the eggplant flesh and put it into a bowl. Stir in the garlic and tahini mixture and season to taste with salt and pepper. Serve with a drizzle of olive oil and a sprinkling of pomegranate seeds. Wrap in plastic wrap (clingfilm) and chill in the refrigerator for 1 hour before using.

FREEKEH, FIG, FETA, AND CARAMELIZED ONION SALAD

سلطة الفريكة والتين مع جبنة الفيتا والبصل المحمر

Preparation time: 20 minutes
Cooking time: 20–30 minutes
Serves 4

4 tablespoons olive oil
2 red onions, thinly sliced
1½ cups (9 oz/250 g) whole grain green wheat freekeh,
½ teaspoon ground allspice
2 teaspoons dried mint
3 ½ oz/100 g feta cheese, crumbled
4 dried figs, diced
2 tablespoons chopped mint,
4 fresh figs, quartered
1 tablespoon sugar
salt

Heat half the olive oil in a heavy skillet or frying pan over medium heat, add the onions, and cook, stirring occasionally, for about 15 minutes until browned and caramelized. Meanwhile, put the freekeh into a pan, pour in 2½ cups (1 pint/600 ml) water, add a pinch of salt, and bring to a boil over medium heat. Reduce the heat and simmer for 15–20 minutes until the water has been absorbed and the freekeh is cooked. Stir in the remaining olive oil, the allspice, dried mint, feta, dried figs, and fresh mint and season to taste with salt. Heat a ridged grill (griddle) pan over high heat. Coat the fig quarters in the sugar, add to the pan, and cook for 2–3 minutes on each side. Serve the salad garnished with the grilled figs.

BABA GANOUSH

SHANKLISH CHEESE WITH ZA'ATAR

شنكليش
(كرات الجبن بالزعتر)

Preparation time: 1–2 hours, plus yogurt making time
Cooking time: 15 minutes
Makes 5 balls

½ quantity Homemade Yogurt (see page 28)
1 teaspoon paprika
5 tablespoons za'atar
½ teaspoon chili flakes
2 tablespoons chopped rosemary,
salt
Lebanese bread, to serve

Set a pan with the yogurt over a very low heat and add 1 cup (8 fl oz/250 ml) water. Stir only once and heat until the whey separates from the curds. Line a strainer (sieve) with a double layer of cheesecloth (muslin) and set over a bowl. Spoon the yogurt into it and let drain until the cheese becomes dry. Tip the cheese into a bowl, add the paprika, and season with salt. Then with clean wet hands, take a golf ball-size piece of cheese and shape into a smooth ball. Repeat this with the remaining mixture. Mix together the za'atar, chili flakes, and rosemary on a plate and carefully roll the cheese balls in the mixture to coat. Put the balls on a plate lined with paper towels and chill in the refrigerator until set. Serve with Lebanese bread.

COUSCOUS AND CHICKPEA SALAD

سلطة الكسكس
والحمص

Preparation time: 15 minutes
Cooking time: 25 minutes
Serves 4–6

12 cherry tomatoes, halved
3 tablespoons olive oil
generous 2 cups (18 fl oz/500 ml) vegetable stock
⅔ cup (4 oz/120 g) giant couscous
14 oz/400 g canned chickpeas, drained and rinsed
1 onion, chopped
2 tablespoons ground cumin
2 tablespoons ground coriander
1 teaspoons ground ginger
3 tablespoons chopped fresh cilantro (coriander)
3 tablespoons chopped fresh parsley
juice of ½ lemon
salt and pepper

Preheat the oven to 400°F/200°C/Gas Mark 6. Put the tomatoes onto a baking sheet, drizzle with 1 tablespoon of the olive oil, and season with salt and pepper. Bake for 20–25 minutes until soft. Meanwhile, pour the vegetable stock into a small pan and bring to a boil. Add the couscous and simmer for 10 minutes until tender. Strain, tip into a bowl, and add the chickpeas. Heat the remaining olive oil in a skillet or frying pan, add the onion, and cook over low heat for 5 minutes until softened. Stir in the spices and cook for another 1 minute. Remove from the heat and stir the spiced onion into the couscous and chickpea mixture. Add the chopped cilantro (coriander), parsley, and tomatoes and season with salt and pepper and a squeeze of lemon.

SHANKLISH CHEESE WITH CHILI AND ROSEMARY

PHOTO PAGE 51

—

شنكليش مع الفلفل الحار
واكليل الجبل

Preparation time: 1–2 hours, plus yogurt making time
Cooking time: 15 minutes
Makes 5 balls

½ quantity Homemade Yogurt (see page 28)
pinch of paprika
5 tablespoons za'atar
1 tablespoon sumac
Lebanese bread, to serve

Set the yogurt over very low heat, add 1 cup (8 fl oz/250 ml) water, stir only once, and leave until the water separates from the yogurt. Line a strainer (sieve) with a double layer of cheesecloth (muslin) and set over a bowl. Spoon the yogurt cheese into it and let drain until the cheese becomes dry. Tip the cheese into a bowl, add the paprika, and season with salt. Then with clean wet hands take a golf ball-size piece of cheese and shape into a smooth ball. Repeat this with the remaining mixture to make 5 balls. Mix together the za'atar and sumac on a plate and carefully roll the cheese balls in the mixture to coat. Put the balls on a plate lined with paper towels and chill in the refrigerator until set. Serve with Lebanese bread.

BROCCOLI QUINOA SALAD

—

سلطة القرنبيط
الاخضر والكينوا

Preparation time: 15 minutes
Cooking time: 10–15 minutes
Serves 4

generous 1 cup (7 oz/200 g) quinoa
4 tablespoons olive oil
2 cups (5 oz/150 g) broccoli florets, cooked
4 garlic cloves, crushed
2 cups (5 oz/150 g) raw broccoli florets
juice of ½ lemon
3½ oz/100 g feta cheese, crumbled
3 tablespoons chopped fresh mint
3 tablespoons chopped fresh parsley
½ cup (2 oz/50 g) pine nuts, toasted
salt and pepper

Cook the quinoa in a large pan of salted boiling water for 10–15 minutes until tender but still with some bite. Drain and set aside in a large serving bowl. Heat the olive oil a large skillet or frying pan, add the cooked broccoli and garlic, and cook, stirring occasionally, for several minutes until it starts to disintegrate. Add the raw broccoli and a splash of water and cook for a few minutes until the florets are cooked but still crunchy. Remove the pan from the heat, add the broccoli to the quinoa, and mix well. Stir in the lemon juice, feta, mint, and parsley and season to taste with salt and pepper. Sprinkle with the toasted pine nuts and serve immediately.

SHANKLISH WITH CHILI AND ROSEMARY

MINT SALAD

سلطة النعناع

Preparation time: 10 minutes
Cooking time: 10 minutes
Serves 4–6

2 red bell peppers, seeded and quartered
1 tablespoon extra virgin olive oil
juice of ½ lemon
2 garlic cloves
½ teaspoon salt
3½ oz/100 g purslane or spinach
1 cucumber, diced
½ cup (2 oz/50 g) pitted black olives
½ cup (1 oz/25 g) chopped fresh mint

Preheat the broiler (grill). Put the bell peppers, skin side uppermost, on a baking sheet and broil (grill) for 10 minutes or until the skin blackens and blisters. Remove with tongs, put in a plastic bag, tie the top, and let cool. Meanwhile, combine the olive oil, lemon juice, garlic, and salt in a small bowl. When the bell peppers are cool enough to handle, remove from the bag and peel off the skins. Put the bell peppers, purslane, or spinach, cucumber, olives, and mint in a bowl, drizzle with the dressing, and serve.

BROILED HALLOUMI WITH MINT AND GARLIC

PHOTO PAGE 52

جبنة حلوم مشوية مع النعناع

Preparation time: 10 minutes, plus marinating time
Cooking time: 8–10 minutes
Serves 2–4

1 small bunch of fresh mint, chopped
1 garlic clove, finely chopped
4 tablespoons olive oil
juice of 1 lemon
3½ oz/100 g halloumi or mozzarella cheese, sliced
2 tablespoons pomegranate seeds
salt and pepper

Preheat the broiler (grill) to hot. Mix together the mint, garlic, olive oil, and lemon juice in a bowl and season with salt and pepper. Put the slices of cheese into a shallow ovenproof dish, pour the mint mixture over them, and let stand for 10 minutes. Put the dish under the broiler and cook the cheese for 4 minutes on each side. Remove the cheese from the heat, garnish with pomegranate seeds, and serve immediately.

FAVA BEANS IN OIL AND GARLIC

—

فول بالزيت والثوم

Preparation time: 15 minutes
Cooking time: 5 minutes
Serves 4

1 tablespoon olive oil
1 onion, finely chopped
2 cups (11 oz/300 g) frozen fava (broad) beans, skinned
juice of 1 lemon
pinch of sugar
2 tablespoons chopped fresh cilantro (coriander)
salt and pepper
Lebanese bread, to serve

Heat the oil in a skillet or frying pan, add the onion, and cook over low heat, stirring occasionally, for 5 minutes until soft but not colored. Add the beans and 5 tablespoons boiling water and cook until they are soft. Stir in the lemon juice and sugar and season to taste with salt and pepper. Add the cilantro (coriander) and serve with Lebanese bread.

TABBOULI

PHOTO PAGE 55

—

تبولة

Preparation time: 20 minutes, plus soaking time
Serves 6

20 cherry tomatoes, finely chopped
1¼ cups (6 oz/175 g) fine bulgur wheat
1 large bunch of fresh parsley, finely chopped
1 cucumber, diced
4 scallions (spring onions), finely chopped
1 green bell pepper, seeded and finely chopped
3 fresh mint sprigs, finely chopped
juice of 1 lemon
2 teaspoons salt
scant ½ cup (3½ fl oz/100 ml) olive oil

Put the tomatoes into a strainer (sieve) to drain off any juices. Put the bulgur wheat in a bowl, pour in hot water to cover, and let soak for 15 minutes. Drain the wheat in a strainer lined with cheesecloth (muslin), pressing out as much liquid as possible. Mix together the parsley, cucumber, scallions (spring onions), and bell pepper in a bowl. Add the mint and bulgur wheat, then tip in the tomatoes. Whisk together the lemon juice, salt, and olive oil in a bowl, then pour the dressing over the tabbouli and mix well.

TABBOULI

WINTER TABBOULI

WINTER TABBOULI

PHOTO PAGE 56

تبولة الشتاء

Preparation time: 25 minutes, plus soaking time
Serves 6

scant 1½ cups (7 oz/200 g) coarse bulgur wheat
1 cup (8 fl oz/250 ml) hot vegetable stock
1 red onion, finely diced
1 fennel bulb, thinly sliced
½ celeriac, peeled and sliced into thin strips
1 bunch of fresh parsley, finely chopped
1 bunch of fresh mint, finely chopped
⅔ cup (¼ pint/150 ml) extra virgin olive oil
juice of 1 lemon
2 tablespoons pomegranate syrup
2 tablespoons pomegranate seeds
½ cup (2 oz/50 g) shelled walnuts, coarsely chopped
salt and pepper

Put the bulgur wheat into a bowl, pour the hot stock over it, cover, and let stand for 5–10 minutes or until the liquid has been absorbed. Drain in a strainer lined with cheesecloth (muslin), squeezing out as much liquid as possible. Put it into a bowl and fluff up the grains with a fork. Add the onion, fennel, and celeriac and mix well, then add the parsley and mint. Whisk together the olive oil, lemon juice, and pomegranate syrup in a bowl, season with salt and pepper, and pour the dressing over the tabbouli. Sprinkle with the pomegranate seeds and walnuts.

WILD THYME AND ZA'ATAR SALAD

سلطة الزعتر والزعتر البري

Preparation time: 10 minutes
Serves 2

1 bunch of fresh wild thyme, picked
1 small shallot, finely chopped
juice ½ lemon
2 tablespoons olive oil
¼ teaspoon salt
¼ teaspoon pepper
1 tablespoon za'atar

Pick off the thyme leaves and put them into a bowl, add the shallot, lemon juice, olive oil, salt, and pepper, and mix well. Sprinkle with the za'atar and serve.

LEBANESE MIXED SALAD

PHOTO PAGE 59

—

سلطة لبنانية مشكلة

Preparation time: 10 minutes
Serves 4–6

1 romaine or cos lettuce, shredded
1 cucumber, seeded and diced
2 tomatoes, diced
1 tablespoon finely chopped fresh mint
1 tablespoon finely chopped fresh flat-leaf parsley,
½ red onion, thinly sliced
juice of ½ lemon
1 tablespoon extra virgin olive oil
salt and pepper

Put the lettuce, cucumber, tomatoes, herbs, and onion into a bowl. Drizzle with the lemon juice and olive oil, season with salt and pepper, and toss well.

CHICKPEAS AND SWISS CHARD

—

حمص مع السلق

Preparation time: 10 minutes
Cooking time: 2 minutes
Serves 4

2 tablespoons olive oil
28 oz/800 g canned chickpeas, drained and rinsed
3 teaspoons harissa paste
1 red onion, sliced
6 cherry tomatoes
½ bunch of Swiss chard, leaves shredded
juice of 1 lemon
bunch of fresh parsley, chopped

Heat the oil in a pan, add the chickpeas and harissa, and cook, stirring occasionally, for a few minutes, then add the onion and tomatoes. Cook for another 2 minutes or until the cherry tomatoes start to blister. Add the Swiss chard leaves and cook for a few minutes until slightly wilted. Transfer the mixture to a dish, add the lemon juice and parsley, and serve hot or cold.

LEBANESE MIXED SALAD

FATTOUSH

—

فتوش

Preparation time: 20 minutes
Serves 4

3 cups (3 oz/80 g) finely chopped leafy greens, such as baby
    spinach and Swiss chard
1 large bunch of fresh parsley, finely chopped
1 bunch of fresh mint, finely chopped
½ cucumber, diced
16 cherry tomatoes, finely chopped
½ green bell pepper, seeded and finely chopped
1 small onion, finely chopped
juice of 1 lemon
1 tablespoon white wine vinegar
scant ½ cup (3½ fl oz/100 ml) olive oil
1 tablespoon ground sumac
2 garlic cloves, crushed
1 piece of Lebanese flatbread, toasted
salt and pepper

Mix together the greens, parsley, mint, cucumber, tomatoes,
bell pepper, and onion in a large bowl. Lightly whisk together
the lemon juice, vinegar, and olive oil in a small bowl. Add the
sumac and garlic and season with salt and pepper. Tear the
toasted bread into small pieces and add to the salad bowl. Pour
the dressing over the salad and toss well. Serve immediately.

CARROT AND GOLDEN RAISIN SALAD

—

سلطة الجزر والزبيب

Preparation time: 15 minutes
Serves 6

5 long carrots, grated
¾ cup (3½ oz/100 g) golden raisins (sultanas)
3 tablespoons chopped fresh cilantro (coriander)
2 teaspoons grated fresh ginger
3 scallions (spring onions), sliced
balsamic vinegar, for drizzling
1 tablespoon sesame seeds, toasted

Mix together the carrots, golden raisins (sultanas), cilantro
(coriander), ginger, and scallions (spring onions) in a large
bowl. Drizzle with balsamic vinegar and sprinkle with the
sesame seeds.

EGGPLANT
AND
POMEGRANATE
SALAD

سلطة الباذنجان بدبس
الرمان

Preparation time: 10 minutes, plus cooling time
Cooking time: 1 hour
Serves 4

2 eggplants (aubergines)
olive oil, for drizzling
1 garlic clove, crushed
1 Boston (little gem) lettuce
2 tablespoons pomegranate seeds

Preheat the oven to 375°F/190°C/Gas Mark 5. Prick the eggplants (aubergines) all over with a skewer and put them on a baking sheet. Bake for about 1 hour until soft, then remove from the oven and let cool. When the eggplants are cool enough to handle, peel off and discard the skins and put the flesh into a bowl. Drizzle with olive oil, add the garlic, and mash until smooth. Serve with the lettuce and pomegranate seeds.

BEET SALAD

سلطة الشمندر

Preparation time: 10 minutes
Serves 2

4 cooked beets (beetroots), sliced
2 red onions, sliced
red wine vinegar, for drizzling
olive oil, for drizzling

Put the beet (beetroot) slices into a dish and top with the red onion slices. Drizzle with red wine vinegar and olive oil and let stand for 10 minutes before serving.

ARTICHOKE AND FAVA BEANS WITH LEMON DRESSING

ARTICHOKE AND FAVA BEANS WITH LEMON DRESSING

PHOTO PAGE 62

ارضي شوكي مع الفول
بتتبيلة عصير الليمون

Preparation time: 20 minutes
Cooking time: 40–45 minutes
Serves 2

1 globe artichoke
juice of 2 lemons
2 tablespoons olive oil
1 rosemary sprig
3 garlic cloves, lightly crushed
6 cherry tomatoes
1⅓ cups (7 oz/200 g) frozen fava (broad) beans, skinned
2 sage leaves, finely shredded
salt and pepper

For the dressing
grated zest and juice of 1 lemon
2 tablespoons extra virgin olive oil
1 teaspoons balsamic vinegar

Preheat the oven to 400°F/200°C/Gas Mark 6. Break off the artichoke stem and pull off the tough outer leaves. If necessary, remove and discard the choke and cut the artichoke into slices. Put them into a roasting pan and immediately pour the lemon juice over them to prevent discoloration. Do not discard the lemon. Drizzle the oil over them and add the rosemary sprig and garlic. Roast for 20 minutes, then remove the pan from the oven and add the cherry tomatoes. Return to the oven and roast for another 20 minutes. Put the beans and squeezed lemon wedges into a steamer and cook for 2 minutes. Whisk together all the dressing ingredients in a small bowl. When the artichoke is tender and tomatoes are roasted, remove the pan from the oven. Add the beans and lemon wedges, pour the dressing over the vegetables, and toss well. Transfer to a serving dish, add the sage, and serve at room temperature.

ORANGE AND RED ONION SALAD

سلطة البرتقال والبصل
الاحمر مع الرمان

Preparation time: 10 minutes
Serves 4

4 oranges, peeled and pith removed
¼ red onion, thinly sliced
½ fennel bulb, thinly sliced
½ cup (3½ oz/100 g) pomegranate seeds
2 garlic cloves, crushed
2 teaspoons red wine vinegar
1 tablespoon olive oil

Slice the oranges, put them into a bowl, and add the onion and fennel slices. Mix together the garlic, vinegar, and olive oil in a small bowl and drizzle the dressing over the salad. Sprinkle with the pomegranate seeds.

WATERMELON
WITH LABNEH AND
MINT

PHOTO PAGE 65

—

البطيخ الاحمر مع اللبنة
والنعناع

Preparation time: 10 minutes
Serves 2

½ watermelon, peeled, seeded, and cut into cubes
scant 1 cup (3½ oz/100 g) strawberries, hulled and halved
1 labneh za'atar ball, torn
1 tablespoon lemon juice
1 small bunch of fresh mint, leaves torn
¼ cup (1 oz/25 g) shelled almonds, toasted

Mix together the watermelon cubes and strawberries in a large bowl, add the pieces of labneh, the lemon juice and torn mint leaves. Finally, add the toasted almonds and combine. Serve immediately.

TOMATO
AND
ONION
SALAD

—

سلطة الطماطم
والبصل

Preparation time: 10 minutes
Serves 2

3 large beefsteak (beef) tomatoes, thickly sliced
1 red onion, thinly sliced
1 red endive (chicory), cored
3½ oz/100 g feta cheese
3 tablespoons extra virgin olive oil
1 tablespoon red wine vinegar
juice of ½ orange
2 tablespoons chopped fresh parsley
salt and pepper

Lay the tomato slices on a large serving dish and sprinkle the red onion over the top. Cut the red endive (chicory) lengthwise into thick slices, separate the leaves, and add to the dish. Crumble the feta over the salad and season with salt and pepper. Whisk together the oil, vinegar, and orange juice in a small bowl and pour the dressing over the salad. Toss well and garnish with chopped parsley.

THYME
AND
TOMATO
SALAD

—

سلطة الزعتر والطماطم

Preparation time: 10 minutes
Serves 2

6 tomatoes, finely diced
½ red onion, finely chopped
3 fresh thyme sprigs
1 tablespoon white wine vinegar
2 teaspoons olive oil
salt and pepper

Mix together the tomatoes and red onion in a bowl and add the thyme leaves. Drizzle with the vinegar and olive oil and season with salt and pepper.

WATERMELON WITH LABNEH AND MINT

GRAPEFRUIT AND ONION SALAD

GRAPEFRUIT AND ONION SALAD

PHOTO PAGE 66

—

سلطة الغريفون مع
البصل الاحمر

Preparation time: 5 minutes
Serves 4

4 pink grapefruit, peeled and pith removed
¼ red onion, thinly sliced
2–3 fresh mint sprigs
extra virgin olive oil, for drizzling
salt

Hold a grapefruit in one hand and remove the segments by cutting down on each side of the membranes with a sharp knife. Cut out the segments from the remaining grapefruit. Arrange the grapefruit segments on a serving plate, sprinkle with the red onion rings and mint leaves, drizzle with the olive oil, and season with salt.

SPICY TOMATOES AND CUMIN

—

سلطة الطماطم الحارة
بالكمون

Preparation time: 10 minutes
Cooking time: 5–10 minutes
Serves 4

1 teaspoon cumin seeds
½ teaspoon coriander seeds
2 tablespoons olive oil
1 small onion, diced
3 garlic cloves, crushed
2 inch/5 cm piece of fresh ginger, grated
16 cherry tomatoes
1 bunch of fresh cilantro (coriander), chopped
salt and pepper

Dry-fry the cumin and coriander seeds in a small skillet or frying pan, shaking the pan occasionally, for a few minutes until they release their aroma. Remove from the heat and grind coarsely in a spice grinder or in a mortar with a pestle. Heat the olive oil in a skillet or frying pan, add the onion, garlic, and ginger, and cook over low heat, stirring occasionally, for 5 minutes. Stir in the spices, add the tomatoes, and cook until the tomatoes start to blister. Season well with salt and pepper, add the cilantro (coriander), and serve.

CUCUMBER AND YOGURT SALAD

—

سلطة الزبادي بالخيار

Preparation time: 10 minutes
Serves 2

½ cucumber, quartered lengthwise and sliced
1 tablespoon chopped fresh mint
1 tablespoon chopped fresh cilantro (coriander)
1 garlic clove, crushed
1 cup (8 fl oz/250 ml) plain (natural) yogurt
Lebanese bread, to serve

Put all the ingredients into a bowl and toss well. Serve with the Lebanese bread.

SMOKED EGGPLANTS AND POMEGRANATE SEEDS

PHOTO PAGE 69

—

باذنجان مدخن مع حبوب
الرمان

Preparation time: 10 minutes
Cooking time: 30–40 minutes
Serves 4

2 eggplants (aubergines)
½ teaspoon coriander seeds
2 garlic cloves, coarsely chopped
juice of 1 lemon
½ teaspoon salt
2 tablespoons tahini
2 teaspoons pomegranate molasses
3 tablespoons pomegranate seeds
chopped fresh parsley, to garnish

Put the eggplants (aubergines) on an open gas flame and cook, turning frequently with long-handled tongs, for 30–40 minutes, until the skins are charred and blistered. Alternatively, put them on a baking sheet and cook under a hot broiler (grill), turning frequently, until charred and blistered. Meanwhile, dry-fry the coriander seeds in a small skillet or frying pan, stirring frequently, for a few minutes until they release their aroma. Remove from the heat and then grind to powder in a mortar with a pestle. When the eggplants are soft, peel off and discard the skins. Put the flesh into a food processor, add the garlic, lemon juice, salt, tahini, and pomegranate molasses, and process until smooth. Scrape the mixture into a dish, dust with the ground coriander, and sprinkle with the pomegranate seeds and chopped parsley.

YOGURT FATTOUSH

—

فتوش الزبادي

Preparation time: 15 minutes
Cooking time: 15–20 minutes
Serves 6–8

Lebanese flatbread or 2 pita breads, torn into pieces
2 tablespoons olive oil
scant ½ cup (3½ fl oz/100 ml) plain (natural) yogurt
2 garlic cloves, crushed
1 tablespoon dried mint
1 tablespoon sumac
3 tomatoes, chopped
½ cucumber, chopped
1 green bell pepper, seeded and chopped
5 radishes, sliced
2 cups (2 oz/50 g) arugula (rocket)
1 romaine or cos lettuce, shredded
2 tablespoons chopped fresh parsley
salt and pepper

Preheat the oven to 375°F/190°C/Gas Mark 5. Spread out the pieces of bread on a baking sheet. Mix together the olive oil and sumac in a bowl and season lightly with salt and pepper. Drizzle the mixture over the bread and bake for 15–20 minutes until golden. Meanwhile, mix together the yogurt, garlic, and mint in a salad bowl, season with salt and pepper, and set aside. When ready to serve, add all the remaining ingredients to the salad bowl and toss well. Top with sumac croutons and serve immediately.

MEZZE

SMOKED EGGPLANTS AND POMEGRANATE SEEDS

OLIVE SALAD

—

سلطة الزيتون

Preparation time: 15 minutes
Cooking time: 15–20 minutes
Serves 2

3½ oz/100 g new potatoes, halved
⅓ cup (1½ oz/40 g) green and black pitted (stoned) olives, halved
⅓ cup (¾ oz/20 g) sun-dried tomatoes
1 red onion, sliced
scant ½ cup (3½ oz/100 g) Lebanese soft cheese, diced
1 bunch of parsley, chopped
4–5 arugula (rocket) leaves, torn
1 teaspoon ground sumac
extra virgin olive oil, for drizzling
juice of 1 lime
salt and pepper

Cook the potatoes into a pan of salted boiling water for 15–20 minutes until tender. Drain and refresh under cold running water. Put them into a large serving bowl, add the olives, sun-dried tomatoes, onion, cheese, parsley, arugula (rocket), and sumac, and mix gently. Drizzle the olive oil and lime juice over the salad and season well with salt and pepper.

SFIHA YOGURT BREAD

—

صفيحة اللبنة

Preparation time: 20 minutes, plus resting time
Cooking time: 10–15 minutes
Makes 14

1½ cups (7 oz/200 g) hard (strong) whole wheat (wholemeal) bread flour
1⅓ cups (6 oz/175 g) all-purpose (plain) flour, plus extra for dusting
½ envelope active dry (fast-action) yeast
1½ teaspoons salt
1 tablespoon extra virgin olive oil, plus extra for brushing
1¼ cups (½ pint/300 ml) lukewarm water
9 oz/250 g Labneh (see page 42)

Mix together both types of flour, the yeast, and salt in a large bowl, add the oil, then gradually stir in the water to form a dough. (You may need a little less or more water to bring the dough together.) Turn out and knead for 10 minutes, then return the dough to the bowl and lightly dust with flour. Cover the bowl with plastic wrap (clingfilm) and let stand for 1 hour in a warm, dark place until risen. Meanwhile, preheat the oven to 450°F/230°C/Gas Mark 8. Brush 2 baking sheets with oil. Turn out the dough, punch down (knock back), and knead again for a few minutes. Take golf ball-size pieces of dough, roll into balls, and lightly dust with flour. Thinly roll out each dough ball into a circle. Spread the labneh cheese over the circles and put them onto greased baking sheets. Bake for 10–15 minutes and serve warm.

APPLE
AND
WALNUT SALAD

سلطة التفاح والجوز

Preparation time: 10 minutes
Serves 2

2 apples, cored and diced
3 celery stalks, chopped
juice of ½ lemon
½ cup (2 oz/50 g) shelled walnuts
3 tablespoons mayonnaise

Put all the ingredients into a bowl and toss well. Cover with plastic wrap (clingfilm) and store in the refrigerator until ready to serve.

STUFFED
CARROTS
WITH LAMB
AND
PINE NUTS

محشي الجزر بلحم الغنم
والصنوبر

Preparation time: 15 minutes
Cooking time: 30–40 minutes
Serves 2

5 large carrots
9 oz/250 g ground (minced) lamb
1 small onion, finely chopped
1 teaspoon seven spices seasoning
1 teaspoon salt
½ teaspoon pepper
2 teaspoons ground cumin
½ teaspoon ground cinnamon
¾ cup (3 oz/80 g) pine nuts, toasted
1 bunch of fresh parsley, chopped
1¼ cups (½ pint/300 ml) hot chicken stock
3 tablespoons (1½ oz/40 g) butter
½ small bunch of fresh mint, chopped

Trim the carrots to the same length, put them into a steamer, and cook for 10–15 minutes until nearly tender. Refresh under cold water and let cool. Meanwhile, heat a pan, then add the lamb and cook over medium heat, stirring frequently, for 5–8 minutes until evenly browned. Add the onion and seven spices seasoning and cook, stirring occasionally, for 5 minutes until softened. Stir in the salt, pepper, cumin, and cinnamon and cook for another 5 minutes. Pour in scant 1 cup (7 fl oz/ 200 ml) boiling water to cover and bring back to a boil. Reduce the heat, cover, and simmer, stirring occasionally, for 20 minutes until the liquid has been absorbed. Meanwhile, preheat the oven to 400°F/200°C/Gas Mark 6. Stir the pine nuts and parsley into the lamb mixture and remove the pan from the heat. When the carrots are cool enough to handle, carefully remove the center of each carrot with an apple corer and fill the cavity with the lamb mixture. Put the stuffed carrots into an ovenproof dish, pour the hot stock over them, and dot with the butter. Bake for 10 minutes, then remove from the oven, sprinkle with the mint, and serve.

CABBAGE
SALAD

—

سلطة الملفوف

Preparation time: 10 minutes
Serves 6

Chinese cabbage (leaves), chopped
1⅓ cups (7 oz/200 g) frozen peas, cooked
2 carrots, grated
2 tablespoons mayonnaise
salt and pepper

Put the Chinese cabbage (leaves), cooked peas, and grated carrots into bowl and mix well. Add the mayonnaise and toss, then season with salt and pepper.

—

POTATO
SALAD
WITH
TAHINI

—

سلطة البطاطا مع
الطحينة

Preparation time: 10 minutes
Cooking time: 15–20 minutes
Serves 4

2 large potatoes, cubed
juice of 1 lemon
5 tablespoons tahini
1 green bell pepper, seeded and chopped
2 scallions (spring onions), chopped
1 garlic clove
1 tablespoon chopped fresh parsley

Put the potatoes into a pan, pour in water to cover, add 1 teaspoon salt, and bring to a boil. Reduce the heat, cover, and cook for 15–20 minutes until tender. Remove the pan from the heat, drain the potatoes, and put them in a bowl. Let cool. Meanwhile, stir the lemon juice into the tahini in a small bowl until it becomes thicker. Stir in 5 tablespoons water until the dressing becomes smooth and paler. Pour the dressing over the cooled potatoes, add the bell pepper, scallions (spring onions), garlic, and parsley and mix gently.

—

TOASTED
HONEY
AND
SOY TOASTED
SEEDS

—

حبوب الصويا المحمصة
بالعسل

Preparation time: 2 minutes
Cooking time: 1 minute
Serves 4

2 tablespoons peanut (groundnut) oil
scant 1 cup (3½ oz/100 g) pumpkin seeds
¾ cup (3½ oz/100 g) sunflower seeds
1 tablespoon clear honey
1 tablespoon soy sauce

Heat the oil in a non-stick skillet or frying pan, add the pumpkin and sunflower seeds, and cook until the seeds are lightly toasted. Remove from the heat, stir in the honey and soy sauce, and return to the heat for 1 minute. Spread out the seeds on a non-stick baking sheet and let cool. When cool, store in an airtight container.

MINI FLATBREADS TOPPED WITH CRAB, SALMON, AND TAHINI SAUCE

خبز صغير مسطح مع السلطعون وصلصة الطحينة

Preparation time: 15 minutes
Cooking time: 8–10 minutes
Serves 2

1 x 7 oz/200 g salmon fillet, skinned
7 oz/200g crabmeat
grated zest and juice of 1 lemon
1 tablespoon chopped chervil
1 tablespoon chopped parsley
1 tablespoon chopped cilantro (coriander)
½ teaspoon ground sumac
½ teaspoon cayenne pepper

For the dressing
5 tablespoons plain (natural) yogurt
1 tablespoon tahini
½ teaspoon tomato paste (purée)
1 tablespoon lemon juice
salt and pepper

To serve
small flatbreads
cayenne pepper
watercress
¼ teaspoon black sesame seeds

Heat a pan of water just to boiling point, reduce the heat so that the surface is barely simmering, add the salmon fillet, and poach for 7–8 minutes. Transfer the fish to a plate with a spatula (fish slice) and let cool, then flake into large pieces and put in a bowl. Add the crabmeat, lemon juice, herbs, sumac, and cayenne pepper and mix gently. Mix together all the dressing ingredients in a bowl and season to taste with salt and pepper. Serve the crab and salmon on a flatbread, drizzle with the sauce, and garnish with a pinch of cayenne pepper, watercress, and black sesame seeds.

BEET AND BELGIAN ENDIVE SALAD

سلطة الشمندر والهندباء

Preparation time: 10 minutes
Serves 2

4 cooked beets (beetroots), sliced
4 Belgian endive (chicory) heads, leaves separated
½ red onion, sliced
olive oil, for drizzling
red wine vinegar, for drizzling
salt and pepper

Put the vegetables into a bowl and drizzle with the olive oil and red wine vinegar. Season with salt and pepper, then serve.

MINI FLATBREADS TOPPED WITH SPICED LAMB AND ANCHOVIES

خبز صغير مسطح مع لحم
الغنم والانشوفي

Preparation time: 15 minutes
Cooking time: 40 minutes
Serves 2

2 small flatbreads
½ teaspoon olive oil
7 oz/200 g ground (minced) lamb
1 small onion, chopped
3 canned anchovies, drained and finely chopped
1 teaspoon seven spices seasoning
1 teaspoon ground cumin
½ teaspoon ground cinnamon
¼ teaspoon ground allspice
3 tablespoons chopped fresh mint
juice of ½ lemon
salt and pepper

For the dressing
3 tablespoons plain (natural) yogurt
1 teaspoon grated lemon zest
1 tablespoon chopped fresh mint
pepper

Heat a ridged grill (griddle) pan and, when it is hot, add the flatbreads. Warm through, turning once, until lightly charred on both sides. Set aside. Heat the oil in a non-stick skillet or frying pan, add the lamb, and cook over medium heat, stirring frequently, for 5–8 minutes until evenly browned. Add the onion and anchovies, reduce the heat to low, and cook, stirring occasionally, for another 10 minutes. Stir in all the spices, add a little water if the pan seems too dry, and simmer for 20 minutes. Stir in the mint and lemon juice and season with salt and pepper. Remove the pan from the heat. Spoon the lamb mixture onto the warm flatbreads. Mix all the dressing ingredients together in a small bowl, season with a pinch of pepper, and spoon the dressing over the lamb.

FAVA BEAN FALAFEL

فلافل بالفول

Preparation time: 30 minutes, plus chilling time
Cooking time: 2 minutes
Makes 20

scant ½ cup (3½ oz/100 g) dried chickpeas, soaked overnight
    in water to cover, then drained and rinsed
⅔ cup (3½ oz/100 g) frozen fava (broad) beans,
    thawed and peeled
2 tablespoons chickpea (gram) flour
2 garlic cloves
1 small onion, chopped
1 tablespoon chopped fresh cilantro (coriander)
1 tablespoon chopped fresh parsley
1 tablespoon ground cumin
½ teaspoon pepper
½ teaspoon salt
1 teaspoon dried mint
1 teaspoon ground coriander
corn oil, for frying

Put the chickpeas, beans, flour, garlic, onion, cilantro
(coriander), parsley, cumin, pepper, salt, mint, and ground
coriander into a food processor and process until smooth
and thoroughly combined. Tip the mixture into a dish and
press down with the back of a spoon. Cover with plastic wrap
(clingfilm) and chill in the refrigerator for a few hours or
overnight. Use a falafel mold to make 20 falafels, cleaning
it each time with hot water. If you don't have a mold, take
walnut-size pieces of the mixture and shape into small patties
with your hands. Heat the corn oil in a deep pan. Add the
falafel, in batches, and cook until golden brown. Remove with a
slotted spoon, drain on paper towels, and keep warm while you
cook the remaining batches. Serve hot.

MINI FLATBREAD TOPPED WITH HALLOUMI, AVOCADO, AND PARSLEY SALAD

PHOTO PAGE 79

خبز صغير مسطح مع
الافوكادو وجبنة حلوم

PARSLEY AND FAVA BEAN FALAFEL

فلافل بالفول
والبقدونس

Preparation time: 5–10 minutes
Cooking time: 5–10 minutes
Serves 2

2 small flatbreads
9 oz/250 g halloumi cheese, cut into ¼ inch/5 mm slices
1 teaspoon extra virgin oil
1 tablespoon za'atar
2 ripe avocados, peeled and pitted (stoned)
juice of 1 lemon
1 bunch of fresh parsley, leaves only
⅓ cup (2 oz/50 g) shelled peas, cooked
¾ cup (2 oz/50 g) snow peas (mangetouts), blanched
1 tablespoon micro herb basil
salt and pepper

Heat a ridged grill (griddle) pan and, when it is hot, add the flatbreads. Warm through, turning once, until lightly charred on both sides. Set aside. Brush the slices of cheese with olive oil and sprinkle with a little za'atar. Put the slices in the grill pan and cook each side for a few minutes or until lightly charred marks appear. Remove from the heat. Thinly slice the avocados and toss lightly with the lemon juice to prevent discoloration. Put the slices of cheese and avocado on top of the flatbreads and garnish with parsley leaves, peas, snow peas (mangetouts), and tiny basil leaves. Season with pepper and serve.

Preparation time: 30 minutes, plus chilling time
Cooking time: 2 minutes
Makes 20

scant ½ cup (3½ oz/100 g) dried chickpeas, soaked overnight in water to cover, drained and rinsed
⅔ cup (3½ oz/100 g) fava (broad) beans, peeled
2 tablespoons chickpea (gram) flour
2 garlic cloves
2 scallions (spring onions), chopped
3 tablespoons chopped fresh parsley
1 tablespoon ground cumin
½ teaspoon pepper
½ teaspoon salt
1 teaspoon dried mint
corn oil, for frying

Put the chickpeas, beans, flour, garlic, scallions (spring onions), parsley, cumin, pepper, salt, and mint into a food processor and process until smooth. Tip into a dish and press down with the back of a spoon. Cover with plastic wrap (clingfilm) and chill in the fridge for a few hours or overnight. Use a falafel mold to make 20 falafels. If you don't have a mold, take walnut-size pieces of the mixture and shape into small patties with your hands. Heat the corn oil in a deep pan. Add the falafel, in batches, and cook until golden. Remove with a slotted spoon, drain on paper towels, and keep warm while you cook the remaining batches. Serve hot.

MINI FLAT BREAD TOPPED WITH HALLOUMI, AVOCADO, AND PARSLEY SALAD

FALAFEL

FALAFEL

PHOTO PAGE 82

فلافل

Preparation time: 30 minutes, plus chilling time
Cooking time: 2 minutes
Makes 20

scant 1 cup (7 oz/200 g) dried chickpeas, soaked overnight
    in water to cover, drained and rinsed
2 garlic cloves
1 small onion, chopped
1 tablespoon chopped fresh cilantro (coriander)
1 tablespoon chopped fresh parsley
1 tablespoon ground cumin
½ teaspoon pepper
½ teaspoon salt
1 teaspoon dried mint
1 teaspoon ground coriander
½ teaspoon baking soda (bicarbonate of soda)
corn oil, for frying

Put the chickpeas, garlic, onion, cilantro (coriander), parsley,
cumin, pepper, salt, mint, ground coriander, and baking soda
(bicarbonate of soda) into a food processor and process until
smooth and thoroughly combined. Tip the mixture into a dish
and press down with the back of a spoon. Cover with plastic
wrap (clingfilm) and chill in the refrigerator for a few hours
or overnight. Use a falafel mold to make 20 falafels, cleaning
it each time with hot water. If you don't have a mold, take
walnut-size pieces of the mixture and shape into small patties
with your hands. Heat the corn oil in a deep pan. Add the
falafel, in batches, and cook until golden brown. Remove with a
slotted spoon, drain on paper towels, and keep warm while you
cook the remaining batches. Serve hot.

CARROT AND CUMIN FALAFEL

فلافل بالجزر والكمون

Preparation time: 30 minutes, plus chilling time
Cooking time: 2–3 minutes
Makes 20

scant ½ cup (3½ oz/100 g) dried chickpeas, soaked overnight
    in cold water to cover, then drained and rinsed
1 cup (3½ oz/100 g) grated carrot
2 tablespoons chickpea (gram) flour
2 garlic cloves
1 small onion, chopped
2 tablespoons chopped fresh cilantro (coriander)
1 tablespoon ground cumin
1 teaspoon dried mint
½ teaspoon pepper
½ teaspoon salt
1 teaspoon ground coriander
corn oil, for frying

Put the chickpeas, carrot, flour, garlic, onion, cilantro (coriander), cumin, mint, pepper, salt, and ground coriander into a food processor and process until smooth and thoroughly combined. Tip into a dish and press down with the back of a spoon. Cover with plastic wrap (clingfilm) and chill in the refrigerator for a few hours or overnight. Use a falafel mold to make 20 falafels, cleaning it each time with hot water. If you don't have a mold, take walnut-size pieces of the mixture and shape into small patties with your hands. Heat the corn oil in a deep pan. Add the falafel, in batches, and cook until golden brown. Remove with a slotted spoon, drain on paper towels, and keep warm while you cook the remaining batches. Serve hot.

GREEN BEANS WITH LEMON AND GARLIC

فاصولياء خضراء مع
الليمون والثوم

Preparation time: 5 minutes
Cooking time: 10 minutes
Serves 4

4 cups (14 oz/400 g) green beans, trimmed
3 garlic cloves
juice of ½ lemon
3 tablespoons olive oil
salt and pepper

Cook the green beans in a pan of lightly salted boiling water for 10–15 minutes until tender. Drain, rinse under cold running water, and drain again. Crush the garlic cloves with a pinch of salt in a mortar with a pestle. Mix together the crushed garlic, lemon juice, and olive oil in a small bowl, pour the dressing over the beans, and toss well. Season to taste with salt and pepper and serve.

ZUCCHINI AND CUMIN FALAFEL

فلافل بالكوسا والكمون

Preparation time: 30 minutes, plus chilling time
Cooking time: 2–3 minutes
Makes 20

scant ½ cup (3½ oz/100 g) dried chickpeas, soaked overnight in water to cover, then drained and rinsed
generous ½ cup (3½ oz/100 g) grated zucchini (courgette), squeezed dry
4 tablespoon chickpea (gram) flour
2 garlic cloves
1 small onion, chopped
1 tablespoon chopped fresh cilantro (coriander)
1 tablespoon chopped fresh parsley
1 tablespoon ground cumin
1 teaspoon dried mint
½ teaspoon pepper
½ teaspoon salt
1 teaspoon ground coriander
corn oil, for frying

Put the chickpeas, zucchini (courgette), flour, garlic, onion, cilantro (coriander), parsley, cumin, mint, pepper, salt, and ground coriander into a food processor and process until smooth. Tip into a dish and press down with the back of a spoon. Cover with plastic wrap (clingfilm) and chill in the fridge for a few hours or overnight. Use a falafel mold to make 20 falafels. If you don't have a mold, take walnut-size pieces of the mixture and shape into small patties with your hands. Heat the corn oil in a deep pan. Add the falafel, in batches, and cook until golden. Remove, drain on paper towels, and keep warm while you cook the remaining batches. Serve hot.

GREEN BEANS WITH TOMATOES AND CRANBERRY BEANS

فاصولياء خضراء مع الطماطم واللوبياء

Preparation time: 10 minutes
Cooking time: 30–35 minutes
Serves 4

14 oz/200 g canned chopped tomatoes
1 tablespoons olive oil
3 small onions, finely chopped
3 garlic cloves, crushed
6 cups (1 lb 5 oz/600 g) green beans, trimmed and halved
½ teaspoon seven spices seasoning
400 g/14 oz cranberry (borlotti) beans, drained and rinsed
salt and pepper

Put the tomatoes into a pan, add 2½ cups (1 pint/600 ml) water, and cook over low heat, stirring occasionally, for 15 minutes. Heat a large skillet or frying pan, add the oil, onions, and garlic and cook over low heat, stirring occasionally, for 5–8 minutes, until the onions are softened and translucent. Add the green beans and seven spices seasoning, season with salt and pepper, and cook, stirring occasionally, for another 5 minutes. Scrape the green bean mixture into the tomato sauce and add the cranberry (borlotti) beans. Stir well and cook for another few minutes until heated through, then serve.

BELL PEPPER AND CHILE FALAFEL

فلافل بالفلفل الاحمر
والفلفل الحار

Preparation time: 30 minutes, plus chilling time
Cooking time: 2–3 minutes
Makes 20

scant 1 cup (7 oz/200 g) dried chickpeas, soaked overnight in
    cold water, then drained and rinsed
1 red bell pepper in oil, drained and coarsely chopped
4 tablespoons chickpea (gram) flour
2 garlic cloves
1 teaspoon dried mint
1 small onion, chopped
2 tablespoons chopped fresh cilantro (coriander)
1 red chile, seeded and chopped
½ teaspoon pepper
½ teaspoon salt
1 teaspoon ground coriander
corn oil, for frying

Put the chickpeas, bell pepper, flour, garlic, mint, onion,
cilantro (coriander), chile, pepper, salt, and ground coriander
into a food processor and process until smooth and thoroughly
combined. Tip into a dish and press down with the back of
a spoon. Cover with plastic wrap (clingfilm) and chill in the
refrigerator for a few hours or overnight. Use a falafel mold to
make 20 falafels, cleaning it each time with hot water. If you
don't have a mold, take walnut-size pieces of the mixture and
shape into small patties with your hands. Heat the corn oil in
a deep pan. Add the falafel, in batches, and cook until golden
brown. Remove with a slotted spoon, drain on paper towels,
and keep warm while you cook the remaining batches. Serve hot.

ROASTED ZUCCHINI IN GARLIC

كوسا مشوي بالثوم

Preparation time: 10 minutes
Cooking time: 30 minutes
Serves 4

3 zucchini (courgettes), halved lengthwise
2 tablespoons olive oil
3 garlic cloves
1 rosemary sprig
juice of ½ lemon

Preheat the oven to 375°F/190°C Gas Mark 5. Put the zucchini
(courgette) halves into a roasting pan and pour the olive
oil over them. Add the garlic and rosemary and roast for 30
minutes. Remove the pan from the oven, squeeze the juice of
½ a lemon over the zucchini, and serve.

CILANTRO
AND
GREEN
CHILE
FALAFELS

فلافل بالكزبرة والفلفل
الاخضر الحار

Preparation time: 30 minutes, plus chilling time
Cooking time: 2–3 minutes
Makes 20

scant 1 cup (7 oz/200 g) dried chickpeas, soaked overnight in
    cold water, then drained and rinsed
2 tablespoons chickpea (gram) flour
2 garlic cloves
1 small onion, chopped
2 tablespoons chopped fresh cilantro (coriander)
1 green chile, seeded and coarsely chopped
1 tablespoon ground cumin
½ teaspoon pepper
½ teaspoon salt
1 teaspoon ground coriander
1 teaspoon dried mint
corn oil, for frying

Put the chickpeas, flour, garlic, onion, cilantro (coriander),
chile, cumin, pepper, salt, ground coriander, and mint into
a food processor and process until smooth and thoroughly
combined. Tip into a dish and press down with the back of
a spoon. Cover with plastic wrap (clingfilm) and chill in the
refrigerator for a few hours or overnight. Use a falafel mold to
make 20 falafels, cleaning it each time with hot water. If you
don't have a mold, take walnut-size pieces of the mixture and
shape into small patties with your hands. Heat the corn oil in
a deep pan. Add the falafel, in batches, and cook until golden
brown. Remove with a slotted spoon, drain on paper towels, and
keep warm while you cook the remaining batches. Serve hot.

GRILLED
ZUCCHINI
AND
MINT

كوسا مشوي مع النعناع

Preparation time: 10–15 minutes
Cooking time: 5 minutes
Serves 2–4

4 zucchini (courgettes), halved and cut into chunks
2 tablespoons olive oil
½ teaspoon cumin seeds
juice of 1 lemon
1 bunch of fresh parsley, chopped
1 bunch of fresh mint, chopped
¼ cup (1 oz/25 g) slivered (flaked) almonds, toasted
salt and pepper

Put the zucchini (courgette) chunks into a bowl, add the olive
oil and cumin seeds, and toss well with your hands. Heat a
ridged grill pan (griddle) until it is hot, add the zucchini, in
batches, and cook, turning frequently, for 5 minutes. When
all the zucchini are cooked, put them into a bowl and add the
lemon juice and chopped herbs. Season with salt and pepper,
sprinkle with the toasted almonds, and serve.

FRIED GREEN BEANS AND TOMATOES

فاصولياء خضراء عريضة
مقلية مع الطماطم

Preparation time: 10 minutes
Cooking time: 10–15 minutes
Serves 4

1½ cup (5 oz/150 g) green beans, trimmed
1 tablespoon olive oil
juice of 1 lemon
½ teaspoon seven spices seasoning
6 cherry tomatoes, halved
1 small bunch of fresh cilantro (coriander), chopped
salt and pepper

Cook the beans in a pan of salted boiling water for about 10 minutes until tender, then drain. Heat the oil in a skillet or frying pan, add the beans, lemon juice, and seven spices seasoning, and cook over high heat for a few minutes. Add the cherry tomatoes and cook for 1 minute more. Tip the mixture into a dish, season to taste with salt and pepper, sprinkle with chopped cilantro (coriander), and serve.

RED CABBAGE AND POMEGRANATE

ملفوف احمر مع الرمان

Preparation time: 15 minutes
Cooking time: 1 hour 30 minutes
Serves 6–8

1 tablespoon olive oil
1 tablespoon butter
2 red onions, sliced
1 red cabbage, cored and shredded
1 cinnamon stick
½ teaspoon ground allspice
2 tablespoons red wine vinegar
3 tablespoons brown sugar
1 apple, peeled and grated
juice of ½ orange
4 tablespoon pomegranate syrup
scant ½ cup (2 oz/50g) raisins

Put all the ingredients into a heavy pan and mix well. Cover and cook over low heat, stirring occasionally, for 1½ hours. Serve immediately.

CABBAGE PARCELS

لفائف الملفوف
المحشية

Preparation time: 30 minutes
Cooking time: 30 minutes
Serves 8–10

1 white cabbage, leaves separated and coarse stems removed
1 cup (7 oz/200 g) basmati rice, soaked and drained
½ green bell pepper, seeded and finely chopped
4 scallions (spring onions), finely chopped
3 fresh mint sprigs, finely chopped
1 small onion, finely chopped
1 tomato, finely chopped
4 tablespoons finely chopped parsley
14 oz/400 g canned chickpeas, drained and rinsed
1 teaspoon seven spices seasoning
2 garlic cloves, crushed
juice of 1 lemon
2 tablespoons olive oil, plus extra for drizzling
Salt and pepper

Blanch the cabbage leaves in a large pan of boiling water for 1–2 minutes, then drain. Mix together the rice, bell pepper, scallions (spring onions), mint, onion, tomato, parsley, chickpeas, and seven spices seasoning in a bowl. Season with salt and pepper and drizzle with a little olive oil. Reserve 3–4 cabbage leaves and put 3–4 more on the bottom of a pan. Spread out the remaining leaves on a work surface and divide the rice and vegetable filling among them. Roll up carefully, tucking in the sides. Squeeze the parcels to remove any excess liquid, then put them into the pan, and season. Cover with the reserved cabbage leaves and put a plate on top. Pour in hot water, cover the pan and cook for 30 minutes. Meanwhile, mix together the garlic, lemon juice and olive oil in a bowl. When the cabbage parcels are tender, lift them out of the pan onto a serving dish. Pour the dressing over them and serve.

FRIED CAULIFLOWER

قرنبيط مقلي

Preparation time: 10 minutes
Cooking time: 2–3 minutes
Serves 6

1 cauliflower, divided into florets
4 tablespoons all-purpose (plain) flour
4 tablespoons cornstarch (cornflour)
scant 1 cup (7 fl oz/200 ml) sparking mineral water, chilled
½ teaspoon smoked paprika, plus extra for serving
6¼ cups (2½ pints/1.5 liters) sunflower oil for deep-frying
salt

Cook the cauliflower florets in a pan of salted boiling water for 5–10 minutes until tender. Drain well and pat dry with paper towels. Sift together the flour and cornstarch (cornflour) into a bowl and whisk in the sparkling water. Season with salt and add the paprika. Heat the oil in a deep-fryer to 350°F/180°C or until a cube of bread browns in 30 seconds. Working in batches, dip the cauliflower florets into the batter, drain off the excess, and add to the hot oil. Cook until crispy and golden. Remove and drain on paper towels. Sprinkle with paprika and serve immediately.

UPSIDE DOWN EGGPLANTS

PHOTO PAGE 91

مقلوبة الباذنجان

Preparation time: 30–40 minutes
Cooking time: 1 hour
Serves 12

2 large eggplants (aubergines), cut lengthwise
    into ¼ inch/5 mm thick slices
1 tablespoon olive oil, plus extra for brushing
1 lb 2 oz/500 g ground (minced) lamb
1 onion, sliced
½ teaspoon ground cinnamon
½ teaspoon ground allspice
½ teaspoon ground cumin
1 tablespoon tomato paste (purée)
2½ cups (1 pint/600 ml) hot vegetable stock
1 cup (7 oz/200 g) basmati rice, rinsed
1 cinnamon stick
¼ cup (1 oz/25 g) pine nuts, toasted
¼ cup (1 oz/25 g) slivered (flaked) almonds, toasted
Salt and pepper

Preheat the oven to 375°F/190°C/Gas Mark 5 and heat a ridged grill (griddle) pan. Brush each eggplant (aubergine) slice with olive oil, put them in the hot grill pan, in batches, and cook for a few minutes on each side or until slightly golden and stripy. Once they have all been cooked, put them on a plate, season with salt and pepper, and set aside. Heat the oil in a skillet or frying pan, add the lamb, and cook over medium heat, stirring frequently, for 8–10 minutes until evenly browned. Add the onion, reduce the heat, and cook, stirring occasionally, for another 5 minutes until softened. Stir in the cinnamon, allspice, cumin, and tomato paste (purée) and season with salt and pepper. Pour in scant 1 cup (7 fl oz/200 ml) of the hot stock, mix well, and simmer over low heat for 10 minutes. Remove the pan from the heat and set aside. Meanwhile, put the rice into a pan, pour in 1¼ cups (½ pint/300 ml) of the remaining hot stock, and add the cinnamon stick. Bring to a boil over medium heat, then reduce the heat, cover, and simmer for 10 minutes or until all the stock has been absorbed and the rice is tender. Remove the pan from the heat and discard the cinnamon stick. Line the bottom and sides of an 8 inch/20 cm round cake pan with some of the eggplant slices. Add half the lamb, followed by half the rice. Add another layer of eggplant slices, then the remaining lamb, followed by the remaining rice. Pour in the remaining stock and cover the top with eggplant slices. Cover the cake pan with foil, put it onto baking sheet, and bake for 20 minutes. Remove the foil, return the cake pan to the oven, and bake for another 10 minutes. Remove the pan from the oven and let cool for 10 minutes, then turn out onto a serving plate. (Put plate upside down over the cake pan and, holding them together, invert them.) Sprinkle with the pine nuts and almonds and serve.

UPSIDE DOWN EGGPLANTS

FRIED EGGPLANT WITH POMEGRANATE MOLASSES AND CHICKPEAS

—

باذنجان مقلي مع دبس
الرمان والحمص

Preparation time: 10 minutes
Cooking time: 10–15 minutes
Serves 2

1 eggplant (aubergine), cut into cubes
½ teaspoon salt
2 tablespoons olive oil
2 garlic cloves, crushed
2 teaspoons cumin seeds
14 oz/400 g canned chickpeas, drained and rinsed
2 tablespoons pomegranate molasses
2 tablespoons red wine vinegar
2 tablespoons pomegranate seeds
1 red onion, sliced
2 tablespoons chopped fresh parsley

Sprinkle the eggplant (aubergine) cubes with the salt. Heat the oil in a pan over medium heat, add the eggplant, and cook, shaking the pan occasionally, for 5–10 minutes until evenly golden. Add the garlic and cumin seeds and cook for 1 minute, then add the chickpeas, pomegranate molasses, and red wine vinegar. Cook for another few minutes, then remove from the heat and transfer to a serving dish. Top with the pomegranate seeds, red onion slices, and chopped parsley and serve.

EGGPLANTS COATED IN ZA'ATAR BREADCRUMBS

PHOTO PAGE 93

—

باذنجان مغلف بالبقسماط
والزعتر مع غموس
الشطة الحارة

Preparation time: 2 minutes
Cooking time: 20–30 minutes
Makes 8–10

2 eggplants (aubergines), thickly sliced lengthwise
5 tablespoons olive oil, plus extra for brushing
1 rosemary sprig
1 teaspoon sea salt
4 cups (7 oz/200 g) fresh breadcrumbs
1 tablespoon za'atar
2 tablespoons grated Parmesan cheese
pinch of cracked black pepper
4 tablespoons sweet chili sauce

Preheat the oven to 375°F/190°C/Gas Mark 5. Spread out the eggplant (aubergine) slices on a baking sheet, drizzle with 1 tablespoon olive oil, add the rosemary, and sprinkle with the salt. Bake for 20 minutes, turning the slices halfway through the cooking time. Meanwhile, mix together the breadcrumbs, za'atar, Parmesan, and pepper in a bowl. Remove the eggplants from the oven and brush with olive oil, then coat both sides of the slices with the breadcrumbs mixture. Heat the remaining olive oil in a skillet or frying pan, add the eggplant slices, in batches, and cook over medium heat for 3–5 minutes on each side until the coating is golden and crispy. Remove from the pan and drain on paper towels. Serve warm with sweet chili sauce.

EGGPLANTS COATED IN ZAʹATAR BREADCRUMBS

EGGPLANT ROLLS

EGGPLANT
ROLLS

PHOTO PAGE 94

—

لفائف الباذنجان

Preparation time: 15 minutes
Cooking time: 50 minutes–1 hour
Makes 8–10

⅓ cup (2½ oz/65 g) instant (easy cook) rice, rinsed
2 large eggplants (aubergines), cut lengthwise into
    ¼ inch/5 mm slices
1 tablespoon olive oil, for brushing
9 oz/250 g ground (minced) lamb
1 small onion, finely chopped
1 teaspoon seven spices seasoning
1 teaspoon salt
2 teaspoons ground cumin
½ teaspoon pepper
½ teaspoon ground cinnamon
¾ cup (3 oz/80 g) pine nuts, toasted
1 bunch of fresh parsley, chopped
14 oz/400 g canned chopped tomatoes
2 garlic cloves, crushed
1 teaspoon brown sugar
4 tablespoons grated Parmesan cheese
Salt and pepper

Preheat the oven to 375°F/190°C/Gas Mark 5. Prepare the rice according to the package instructions. Brush the eggplant (aubergine) slices with olive oil, put them onto a baking sheet, and roast for 10 minutes or until slightly golden. Remove from the oven and let cool. Meanwhile, heat the oil in a pan, add the lamb, and cook over medium heat, stirring frequently, for 5–8 minutes until evenly browned. Add the onion and seven spices seasoning and cook for 5 minutes, then stir in the salt and pepper. Drain the rice, add it to the lamb, stir well, and add the cumin and cinnamon. Cook for another 5 minutes, then pour in 1⅔ cups (14 fl oz/400 ml) boiling water. Bring back to a boil, reduce the heat, cover, and simmer, stirring occasionally, for 20 minutes until the liquid has been absorbed. Stir in the pine nuts and parsley and remove the pan from the heat. Put the tomatoes, garlic, and sugar in a separate pan and cook over medium heat, stirring occasionally, for 20 minutes until thickened and reduced. Remove the pan from the heat and pour the sauce into a flameproof dish. Preheat the broiler (grill). Put a spoonful of lamb filling at the end of an eggplant slice and carefully roll it up. Put the roll on top of the tomato sauce in the dish. Continue making rolls in this way until all the eggplant slices have been used, putting them into the dish. Sprinkle the rolls with the Parmesan and put the dish under the broiler for 2 minutes until the cheese has melted. Serve warm.

EGGPLANT FATTEH

PHOTO PAGE 97

—

فتة الباذنجان

Preparation time: 15 minutes
Cooking time: 30–40 minutes
Serves 4

4–5 tablespoons vegetable oil
1 eggplant (aubergine), cut into cubes
1 lb 2 oz/500 g ground (minced) lamb
2 onions, chopped
2 garlic cloves, sliced
1 teaspoon seven spices seasoning
dash of Worcestershire sauce
2 tomatoes, chopped
2 pita breads
scant ¾ cup (2¾ oz/70 g) pine nuts, toasted in oil
salt and pepper

For the yogurt
1 cup (8 fl oz/250 ml) plain (natural) yogurt
2 garlic cloves, crushed
3 tablespoons chopped fresh mint,

Preheat the oven to 400°F/200°C/Gas Mark 6. Pour enough oil into an ovenproof dish to cover the bottom and put it into the oven to warm. Add the eggplant (aubergine) cubes and roast, shaking the dish occasionally, for about 30 minutes until golden. Meanwhile, put the lamb into a saucepan and cook over medium-low heat, stirring occasionally, for 5–8 minutes until evenly browned. Add the onions and sliced garlic and cook, stirring occasionally, for 5 minutes. Stir in the seven spices seasoning, Worcestershire sauce, and tomatoes and season well with salt and pepper. Add scant ½ cup (3½ fl oz/100 ml) water and simmer for 20 minutes. Put the pita breads into the oven to warm for a few minutes until crispy, then remove and cut into squares. Mix together the yogurt, garlic, and mint. Remove the eggplant cubes from the oven and stir them into the lamb mixture, then transfer to a serving dish. Top with the yogurt mixture, sprinkle with the pine nuts, put the crispy bread squares around the side, and serve.

EGGPLANT FATTEH

WALNUT AND CAYENNE DIP

HUMMUS FATTEH

—

فتة الحمص

Preparation time: 15 minutes
Cooking time: 5 minutes
Serves 4

2 pita breads
28 oz/800 g canned chickpeas, drained and rinsed
scant ¾ cup (2¾ oz/70 g) pine nuts, toasted in oil
salt and pepper

For the yogurt
1 cup (8 fl oz/250 ml) plain (natural) yogurt
2 garlic cloves, crushed
3 tablespoons chopped fresh mint
pinch of paprika

Preheat the oven to 400°F/200°C/Gas Mark 6. Put the pita breads into the oven to crisp for a few minutes, then remove and cut in squares. Cook the chickpeas in a boiling water, then drain. Mix together the yogurt, garlic, and mint. Put the chickpeas into a dish, top with the yogurt mixture, and sprinkle it with a pinch of paprika. Put the crispy bread squares around the side of the yogurt mixture and serve.

WALNUT AND CAYENNE DIP

PHOTO PAGE 98

—

غموس الجوز والشطة

Preparation time: 10 minutes
Cooking time: 5 minutes
Serves 4

½ Lebanese flatbread
½ teaspoon cayenne pepper
1 red bell pepper preserved in oil, peeled and seeded
¼ teaspoon smoked chili powder
1¼ cups (5 oz/150 g) chopped walnuts
1 tablespoons pomegranate syrup
juice of ½ lemon
1 tablespoon plain (natural) yogurt
1 tablespoon chopped fresh parsley
2 tablespoons pine nuts, soaked in water for 20 minutes
    and drained
salt and pepper

Preheat the oven to 400°F/200°C/Gas Mark 6. Put the bread on a baking sheet and toast in the oven for 5 minutes until golden and crispy. Transfer to a food processor or blender and process to fine breadcrumbs. Tip out the breadcrumbs, put 4 tablespoons of them into a dish, and add the cayenne pepper. Pour scant ½ cup (3½ fl oz/100 ml) water in to the food processor or blender and add the red bell pepper, chili powder, walnuts, pomegranate syrup, and lemon juice. Add the breadcrumb and cayenne mixture and process until fine. Transfer the mixture to a bowl, season with salt and pepper, and stir in the yogurt, chopped parsley, and pine nuts.

BULGUR WHEAT SALAD WITH GREENS AND FRIED ONIONS

BULGUR WHEAT SALAD WITH GREENS AND FRIED ONIONS

PHOTO PAGE 100

—

سلطة البرغل
مع الخضراوات والبصل
المقلي

Preparation time: 15 minutes
Cooking time: 10–15 minutes
Serves 4

4 tablespoons olive oil
3 onions, sliced
scant 1½ cup (7 oz/200 g) coarse bulgur wheat, rinsed
juice of 1 lemon
1¼ cups (½ pint/300 ml) hot vegetable stock
1 green cabbage, shredded
¼ cup (1 oz/25 g) toasted whole almonds
salt

For the dressing
5 tablespoons extra virgin olive oil
juice of ½ lemon
salt and pepper

Heat half the olive oil in a skillet or frying pan, add the onions, and cook over medium-low heat, stirring occasionally, for about 10 minutes until golden and slightly crisp. Remove from the pan and drain on paper towels. Put the bulgur wheat, remaining olive oil, and the lemon juice into a pan, pour in the hot vegetable stock, and bring to a boil. Reduce the heat and simmer, stirring frequently, for 10 minutes or until the wheat is tender. Drain off any liquid that has not been absorbed, fluff up the grains with a fork, and let cool. Meanwhile, cook the shredded cabbage in a separate pan of salted boiling water for 3–4 minutes, then drain, rinse under cold running water, and drain again. Put the cooled bulgur wheat into a serving bowl, add the cabbage, and toss lightly. To make the dressing, whisk together the olive oil and lemon juice in a small bowl and season to taste with salt and pepper. Pour the dressing over the salad, sprinkle with the toasted almonds and top with the fried onions.

CREAM OF LENTILS

—

كريم العدس

Preparation time: 10 minutes
Cooking time: 1 hour 45 minutes
Serves 2

1 tablespoon olive oil
1 onion, chopped
2 garlic cloves
scant 1 cup (7 oz/200 g) lentils
1 teaspoon seven spices seasoning
1 teaspoon pepper
½ teaspoon ground coriander
¼ teaspoon grated nutmeg
½ cup (4 fl oz/120 ml) heavy (double) cream

Heat the oil in a large pan, add the onion and garlic, and cook over low heat, stirring occasionally, for 5 minutes until softened but not colored. Add the lentils and pour in 3¾ cups (1½ pints/850 ml) water. Bring to a boil over medium heat, then reduce the heat and simmer for about 1 hour until the lentils are tender. Use an immersion (stick) blender to process the lentils to a purée, then stir in all the spices. Simmering for another 45 minutes, then stir in the cream and serve.

RICE AND VERMICELLI

PHOTO PAGE 103

—

ارز بالشعيرية

Preparation time: 5 minutes
Cooking time: 10–12 minutes
Serves 4

scant 1½ cups (10 oz/275 g) basmati rice, rinsed
2 tablespoons olive oil
2¾ oz/70 g vermicelli
2 teaspoons ground cumin
3 teaspoons salt

Put the rice into a heatproof bowl, pour in hot water to cover, and let soak for 10 minutes, then drain. Heat the oil in a saucepan, add the vermicelli, and cook, stirring occasionally, for a few minutes until golden. Add the rice, cumin, and salt and continue to cook, stirring constantly, for 2 minutes. Pour in generous 2 cups (18 fl oz/500 ml) hot water and stir, then cover and cook for 10 minutes until all the liquid has been absorbed. Serve immediately.

BULGUR WHEAT, CHICKPEAS AND LEEKS

برغل بالحمص
والكراث

Preparation time: 30 minutes, plus soaking time
Serves 4

¾ cup (3½ oz/100 g) bulgur wheat
⅔ cup (¼ pint/150 ml) hot vegetable stock
14 oz/400 g canned chickpeas, drained and rinsed
juice of ½ lemon
½ teaspoon ground cumin
½ teaspoon ground cinnamon
½ teaspoon ground coriander
4 scallions (spring onions), chopped
3 tomatoes, seeded and diced
1 bunch of fresh parsley, chopped
1 tablespoon butter
1 tablespoon olive oil
1 leek, sliced
14 oz/400 g canned chopped tomatoes
2 garlic cloves, crushed
1 teaspoon brown sugar
¼ cup (1 oz/25 g) sliver (flaked) almonds, toasted
salt and pepper

Put the bulgur wheat into a bowl and pour the hot stock over it. Cover with plastic wrap (clingfilm) and let stand for 10 minutes or until all the liquid has been absorbed. Fluff up the grains with a fork, then stir in the chickpeas. Add the lemon juice and spices and mix well, then fold in the scallions (spring onions), tomatoes, and most of the parsley. Season to taste with salt and pepper. Melt the butter with the oil in a skillet or frying pan, add the leek, and cook over low heat, stirring occasionally, for 7–8 minutes until softened. Add the tomatoes, garlic, and sugar and cook, stirring occasionally, for 15 minutes. Stir in the bulgur wheat mixture and heat through for 5 minutes. Season to taste with salt and pepper, transfer to a serving dish, add the remaining chopped parsley and the almonds, and serve.

HOT LEBANESE SALAD

سلطة لبنانية حارة

Preparation time: 10 minutes
Serves 4-6

1 cucumber, chopped
1 romaine or cos lettuce, shredded
2 tomatoes, quartered
1 garlic clove, crushed
juice of ½ lemon
2 tablespoons extra virgin olive oil
1 green chile, chopped
salt

Put the cucumber, lettuce, and tomatoes into a bowl. Whisk together the garlic, lemon juice, olive oil, chile, and a pinch of salt in a small bowl, pour the dressing over the salad, mix well, and serve.

FRIED LEEKS
AND
BULGUR WHEAT
—

كراث مقلي مع البرغل

Preparation time: 15 minutes, plus soaking time
Cooking time: 30 minutes
Serves 4

2 tablespoons (1 oz/25 g) butter
2 tablespoons olive oil
6 leeks, coarsely chopped
3 onions, chopped
generous 1 cup (5 oz/150 g) coarse bulgur wheat,
    soaked in boiling water
½ teaspoon seven spices seasoning
½ teaspoon pepper
salt

Melt the butter with the oil in a large skillet or frying pan,
add the leeks and onions, and cook over low heat, stirring
occasionally, for about 8 minutes until tender but not colored.
Tip in the bulgur wheat with the remaining soaking liquid and
add the seven spices seasoning, pepper, and a generous pinch
of salt. Toss well, cover the pan, and cook for 20 minutes. Taste
and adjust the seasoning, if necessary, and serve.

GREEN STEM
AND
TAHINI SALAD
—

سلطة اضلاع السلق مع
الطحينة

Preparation time: 5 minutes
Cooking time: 2–3 minutes
Serves 4

stems of Lebanese greens
2 garlic cloves
2 tablespoons tahini
juice of ½ lemon
dash of olive oil
sea salt

Cook the stems in a pan of boiling water for a few minutes until
tender, then drain, and rinse under cold running water. Drain
again, squeeze out the excess water, and put into a serving dish.
Crush the garlic with a little salt in a mortar with a pestle, stir
in the tahini, lemon juice, and olive oil, and mix together.
Pour the dressing over the stalks and toss well before serving.

ENDIVE
IN OIL

PHOTO PAGE 107

هندباء بالزيت

Preparation time: 10–15 minutes
Cooking time: 5–10 minutes
Serves 4

4 tablespoons olive oil
1 onion, diced
2 garlic cloves, crushed
2 heads red endive (chicory), leaves separated
2 heads green endive (chicory), leaves separated
juice of 1 lemon
1 tablespoon chopped tarragon
½ cup (2 oz/50 g) shelled walnuts, toasted and chopped
salt and pepper
Garlic Dip (see page 43), to serve

Heat half the oil in a large skillet or frying pan, add the onion, and cook over low heat, stirring occasionally, for 5 minutes until softened. Add the garlic and cook for another minute, then add the endive (chicories), the remaining oil, and the lemon juice and cook over low heat until the leaves start to wilt a little. Transfer to a serving plate, season with salt and pepper, add the tarragon and walnuts, and serve with the garlic dip.

WARM
SPINACH
AND
RICE
SALAD

سلطة السبانخ والارز مع
الكزبرة والقرفة

Preparation time: 10 minutes
Cooking time: 15–20 minutes
Serves 4

1 teaspoon fennel seeds
1 teaspoon olive oil
1 onion, finely chopped
1 teaspoon ground coriander
generous 1 cup (8 oz/225 g) basmati rice, rinsed
1¼ cups (½ pint/300 ml) hot vegetable stock
pinch of saffron threads, lightly crushed
1 tablespoon butter
9 oz/250 g baby spinach leaves
pinch of ground cinnamon
salt and pepper

Dry-fry the fennel seeds in a skillet or frying pan, shaking the pan occasionally, for a few minutes until they release their aroma. Remove from the heat, tip onto a plate, and set aside. Add the oil to the pan and heat. Add the onion and cook over low heat, stirring occasionally, for 5 minutes until softened but not colored. Return the fennel seeds to the pan, add the ground coriander, and cook for a few minutes. Put the rice into a pan, pour in the hot vegetable stock, and add the saffron and onion mixture, then bring to a boil. Cover the pan, turn off the heat, and let stand for 10 minutes or until all the liquid has been absorbed. Melt the butter in a skillet or frying pan, add the spinach and cinnamon, and cook, turning once or twice, for a few minutes until wilted. Add the spinach to the cooked rice and mix gently. Transfer to a serving dish and serve warm.

ENDIVE IN OIL

LEEKS IN OIL

كراث بالزيت

Preparation time: 10 minutes
Cooking time: 10–15 minutes
Serves 4

1 tablespoon butter
4 tablespoons olive oil
3 leeks, sliced
2 bay leaves
1 teaspoon fresh thyme, leaves picked
1 teaspoon sugar
3 tablespoons chopped fresh parsley,
grated zest and juice of ½ lemon
salt and pepper

Melt the butter with the oil in a large pan, add the leeks, bay leaves, and thyme, and cook over low heat, stirring occasionally, for 5–8 minutes until the leeks are softened. Add the sugar and cook, stirring constantly, for another 5 minutes. Remove from the heat and let cool slightly. Remove and discard the bay leaves and add the parsley and the lemon zest and juice. Season with salt and pepper and serve.

FOUTER MOUKALA AND CORIANDER

فطر مُقلّى (فطر مقلي وكزبرة)

Preparation time: 10 minutes
Cooking time: 10 minutes
Serves 2

1 tablespoon butter
1 tablespoon olive oil
3⅔ cups (9 oz/250 g) cremini (chestnut) mushrooms, quartered
scant 1½ cups (3½ oz/100 g) white (button) mushrooms,
3 garlic cloves, crushed
1 teaspoon chopped fresh thyme leaves
½ teaspoon chopped fresh rosemary leaves,
2 tablespoons chopped fresh cilantro (coriander)
Grated zest and juice of ½ lime
1 tablespoon plain (natural) yogurt
salt and pepper
Lebanese flatbread, to serve

Melt the butter with the oil in a large skillet or frying pan, add all the mushrooms and the garlic, and cook for a few minutes. Add the thyme and rosemary, season well with salt and pepper, and cook over low heat, stirring frequently, for 5 minutes until the mushrooms have cooked down. Add the cilantro (coriander) and lime zest and juice and mix well. Warm the Lebanese flat bread and serve the mushrooms on top with a spoonful of yogurt.

FRIED LEEKS IN TOMATO ARAK WITH ALMONDS

—

كراث مقلي مع الطماطم
والعرق واللوز

Preparation time: 10 minutes
Cooking time: 25 minutes
Serves 2–4

1½ teaspoons (¼ oz/10 g) butter
1 leek, sliced
2 garlic cloves, crushed
2 tablespoons arak
14 oz/200 g canned tomatoes
1 teaspoon brown sugar
⅓ cup (1½ oz/40 g) slivered (flaked) almonds
2 tablespoons chopped fresh cilantro (coriander)

Melt the butter in a large skillet or frying pan, add the leek, and cook over low heat, stirring occasionally, for 6–8 minutes until softened but not colored. Add the garlic, arak, and tomatoes and cook for 10–15 minutes until the tomatoes are pulpy and the mixture has thickened. Stir in the sugar and season to taste with salt and pepper. Dry-fry the almonds in a small skillet or frying pan over low heat, shaking the pan frequently, until golden, then add them to the vegetables. Transfer to a serving dish, sprinkle with the chopped cilantro (coriander), and serve.

FRIED BELL PEPPERS AND BROCCOLI

—

قرنبيط اخضر وفلفل
رومي مقلي

Preparation time: 10 minutes, plus resting time
Cooking time: 3–4 minutes
Serves 4

1 egg
scant ½ cup (3½ fl oz/100 ml) warm milk
scant ½ cup (3½ fl oz/100 ml) warm water
1½ cups (6 oz/175 g) all-purpose (plain) flour
½ packet active dry (rapid-rise) yeast
1 small head of broccoli, cut into florets
1 red bell pepper, seeded and sliced
1 yellow bell pepper, seeded and sliced
corn oil, for deep-frying

Light beat the egg in a large bowl, then gradually whisk in the warm milk and water. Sift the flour into the bowl, add the yeast, and whisk to a batter. Cover and let stand in a warm place for 30 minutes. Meanwhile, blanch the broccoli florets in a pan of boiling water for a few minutes, then drain. Heat the corn oil in a deep-fryer to 350°F/180°C or until a cube of bread browns in 30 seconds. Stir the batter, then dip the bell pepper slices and broccoli florets into it, shaking off the excess, and add to the hot oil in batches, if necessary. Deep-fry until golden, then remove with a slotted spoon, and drain on paper towels. Serve immediately.

FRIED POTATOES AND ONIONS

بطاطس مقلية مع البصل

Preparation time: 10 minutes
Cooking time: 30–40 minutes
Serves 4

2 large potatoes, cut into cubes
3 tablespoons olive oil
1 large onion, sliced
½ teaspoon seven spices seasoning
½ teaspoon ground cumin
3 tablespoons chopped fresh cilantro (coriander)
sea salt and pepper

Put the potatoes into a pan, add water just to cover and a pinch of salt, and bring to a boil. Reduce the heat and cook for 15 minutes, until tender. Drain well, return to the pan, and set over very low heat for a few minutes to dry out. Heat 2 tablespoons of the olive oil in a skillet or frying pan, add the onion, and cook over low heat, stirring occasionally, for 20–30 minutes until golden and caramelized. Transfer the onion to a plate and set aside. Add of the remaining olive oil to the pan and heat. Add the potatoes and cook, turning occasionally, for 5–7 minutes until golden and crispy on all sides. Return the onions to the pan and season with sea salt and pepper. Gently stir in the seven spices seasoning and cumin, transfer to a serving dish, sprinkle with chopped cilantro (coriander), and serve.

SAUTÉED POTATOES

بطاطس سوتيه

Preparation time: 10 minutes
Cooking time: 25 minutes
Serves 4

3 firm-fleshed potatoes, cut into ¾-inch/2-cm cubes
olive oil, for frying
salt and pepper
Cucumber and Yogurt Salad (see page 67), to serve

Cook the potatoes in a pan of boiling water for 10 minutes until nearly tender. Drain well and pat dry with paper towels. Season well with salt and pepper. Pour oil into a wide sauté pan, skillet, or frying pan to a depth of ¼ inch/5 mm and heat. Add the potatoes and cook over medium to low heat, gently shaking the pan frequently. Cook for 10–15 minutes until the potatoes are golden and crisp on the outside with a tender center. Remove with a slotted spoon and drain on paper towels. Serve warm with the cucumber and yogurt salad.

CUMIN
MASHED
POTATO
—

بطاطس مهروسة مع
الكمون

Preparation time: 10 minutes
Cooking time: 15–20 minutes
Serves 4

4 firm-fleshed potatoes, chopped
1 teaspoon cumin seeds
5 tablespoons (2½ oz/65 g) butter, melted
5 tablespoons heavy (double) cream
salt and pepper
chopped fresh parsley, to garnish

Put the potatoes into a pan, pour in water to cover, and add a pinch of salt. Bring to a boil and cook over medium heat for 10–15 minutes until tender. Drain well, return to the pan, and set over very low heat for a few minutes to dry. Dry-fry the cumin seeds in a small skillet or frying pan, shaking the pan occasionally, until they release their aroma. Remove from the heat and grind in a spice grinder or in a mortar with a pestle. Add the cumin, melted butter, and cream to the potatoes, season with salt and pepper, and mash well. Transfer to a serving dish, top with some chopped parsley, and serve warm.

ROAST
POTATOES
WITH GREEN
AND RED
CHILI
SAUCE
—

طماطم مقلية مع
الصلصة الحارة

Preparation time: 10 minutes
Cooking time: 25 minutes
Serves 2

2 firm-fleshed potatoes, diced
2 sweet potatoes, diced
sunflower oil, for drizzling
1 green chile, seeded and finely chopped
1 red chile, seeded and finely chopped
3 tablespoons extra virgin oil
3 tablespoons chopped fresh cilantro (coriander)

Preheat the oven to 400°F/200°C/Gas Mark 6. Put both types of potatoes in a roasting pan, drizzle generously with sunflower oil, and toss to coat. Roast, turning once or twice, for 25 minutes or until evenly crisp and golden. Meanwhile, mix together the green and red chiles and extra virgin oil in a small bowl, then add the cilantro (coriander). Serve the roast potatoes with the chili sauce.

POTATO, RICE, AND SEVEN SPICE

ارز مع البطاطس بخلطة
السبعة بهارات

Preparation time: 10 minutes
Cooking time: 20 minutes
Serves 4–6

1 cup (7 oz/200 g) basmati rice, rinsed
2 tablespoons olive oil
1 onion, finely diced
4 (1 lb/2 oz/500 g) potatoes, cut into cubes
1 teaspoon seven spices seasoning
½ teaspoon ground cumin
½ teaspoon ground allspice
½ bunch of fresh parsley, chopped
salt and pepper

Put the rice into a pan, pour in 1¼ cups (½ pint/300 ml) boiling water, and bring to a boil. Reduce the heat, cover, and simmer for 10–15 minutes until all the water has been absorbed. Heat the oil in a skillet or frying pan, add the onion and potato cubes, and cook over high heat, tossing the pan frequently, for 8–10 minutes until the potatoes are evenly crisp. Reduce the heat, add the seven spices seasoning, cumin, and all spice, cover, and cook for another 10 minutes or until the potatoes are tender. When the rice is cooked, add it to the pan of cooked potatoes and mix gently. Season to taste with salt and pepper, sprinkle with the chopped parsley, and serve.

ROASTED VEGETABLES

خضار مشوية

Preparation time: 20 minutes
Cooking time: 30–40 minutes
Serves 4

1 red bell pepper, halved, seeded, and cut into wedges
1 yellow bell pepper, halved, seeded, and cut into wedges
1 orange bell pepper, halved, seeded, and cut into wedges
2 baby zucchini (courgettes), sliced lengthwise
1 eggplant (aubergine), cut into cubes
1 red onion, cut into wedges
5 tablespoons olive oil
2 rosemary sprigs
2 thyme sprigs
14 oz/400 g canned chickpeas, drained and rinsed
½ teaspoon paprika
½ bunch of fresh cilantro (coriander), chopped
salt and pepper

Preheat the oven to 400°F/200°C/Gas Mark 6. Put the bell peppers, zucchini (courgettes), eggplant (aubergine), and red onion into a bowl, pour in the oil, and toss well. Tip the vegetables into a roasting pan, add the herb sprigs, and roast for 30 minutes. Mix the chickpeas with the paprika in a bowl, then add the mixture to the roasting pan, return it to the oven, and roast for another 10 minutes. Remove the roasting pan from the oven and discard the herb sprigs. Transfer the vegetables to a serving dish, season with salt and pepper, sprinkle with chopped cilantro (coriander), and serve.

BATATA HARRA

بطاطس حارة

Preparation time: 10 minutes
Cooking time: 20 minutes
Serves 4

3 firm-fleshed potatoes, cut into ¾ inch/2 cm dice
1 teaspoon cumin seeds
1 teaspoon coriander seeds
¼ teaspoon ground turmeric
4–5 tablespoons vegetable oil
salt and pepper
Cucumber and Yogurt Salad (see page 67), to serve

Rinse the potatoes and then dry on paper towels. Dry-fry the cumin and coriander seeds in a small skillet or frying pan over low heat, shaking the pan occasionally, for a few minutes until they give off their aroma. Remove from the heat and grind coarsely in a spice mill or in a mortar with a pestle. Tip them into a bowl, stir in the turmeric, and season with salt and pepper. Pour the oil into a skillet or frying pan to a depth of about ¼ inch/5 mm and heat. Dust the potatoes with the spices, add them to the hot oil, and cook over medium to low heat, tossing the pan frequently, until they are golden and crisp with a tender center. Serve warm the cucumber and yogurt salad

SWEET POTATO, CUMIN, AND CHILI OIL

بطاطس حلوة مع كمون
وخلطة الزيت بالفلفل
الحار

Preparation time: 10 minutes
Cooking time: 1 hour
Serves 4

3 sweet potatoes
1 teaspoon cumin seeds
2 tablespoons (1 oz/25 g) butter
½ small red chile, seeded and finely chopped
3 tablespoons extra virgin olive oil
1 teaspoon ground coriander
¼ teaspoon sesame seeds, toasted
salt and pepper

Preheat the oven to 425°F/220°C/Gas Mark 7. Prick the potatoes all over with a fork, put them on a baking sheet, and bake for 45–60 minutes until soft and tender. Meanwhile, dry-fry the cumin seeds in a small skillet or frying pan over low heat, stirring frequently, for a few minutes until they release their aroma. Remove from the heat and grind in a spice grinder or in a mortar with a pestle. Remove the potatoes from the oven and let stand until cool enough to handle. Halve the potatoes and scoop out the flesh into a bowl. Add the cumin and butter, season with salt and pepper, and mash well.Mix together the chile, olive oil, coriander, and sesame seeds in a small bowl. Spoon the mashed sweet potato into a serving dish and make a dip with the back of the spoon. Pour in the chili oil and serve.

MUSHROOM AND SPINACH GRAPE LEAVES

—

ورق العنب مع الفطر
والسبانخ

Preparation time: 30 minutes, plus soaking time
Cooking time: 1 hour
Makes 12

22 grape (vine) leaves
1 tablespoon butter
4 tablespoons olive oil
5⅔ cups (14 oz/400 g) chopped cremini
    (chestnut) mushrooms
2 garlic cloves, crushed
½ teaspoon salt
1 teaspoon seven spices seasoning
½ teaspoon ground cumin
3½ oz/100 g baby spinach
¼ cup (1 oz/25 g) pine nuts, toasted
pepper

If using fresh leaves, bring a pan of salted water to a boil, add the leaves, and blanch for 3 minutes. Remove from the pan and put them on a wire rack to cool. If using leaves preserved in brine, soak them in hot water for 30 minutes, then drain, rinse thoroughly, and pat dry with paper towels. Melt the butter with 1 tablespoon of the oil in a skillet or frying pan, add the mushrooms, garlic and salt, and cook over medium-low heat, stirring occasionally, for 5–7 minutes until softened. Stir in the seven spices seasoning and cumin and cook another minute. Add the spinach, cover the pan, and cook for a few minutes until it has wilted. Remove the pan from the heat and let cool, then add the pine nuts. Lay 1 grape (vine) leaf flat on a work surface, put a spoonful of the filling on top, and carefully roll up the leaf into a cigar shape. Repeat with the remaining leaves and filling until 12 leaves have been used. Put the remaining leaves in the bottom of a large pan and put the grape leaf rolls on top. Drizzle with the remaining olive oil and season with salt and pepper. Position a plate snuggly on top of the leaves and pour in enough boiling water to cover. Bring back to a boil, then reduce the heat and simmer for 50–60 minutes. Carefully lift out the grape leaf rolls with a slotted spoon and serve warm.

BUTTERNUT SQUASH WEDGES AND TAHINI SAUCE

PHOTO PAGE 119

—

قرع محمص مع صلصة الطحينة

Preparation time: 10 minutes
Cooking time: 40–45 minutes
Serves 2

1 butternut squash, cut into wedges
5 tablespoons olive oil
1 thyme sprig
1 rosemary sprig
½ teaspoon smoked crushed chiles
1 teaspoon sea salt
4 tablespoons tahini
1 garlic clove, crushed
juice of ½ lemon

Preheat the oven to 375°F/190°C/Gas Mark 5. Put the squash wedges into a roasting pan, drizzle with 4 tablespoons of the olive oil, add the thyme sprig and rosemary sprig, and sprinkle with the crushed chiles and sea salt. Roast for 40–45 minutes or until tender. Meanwhile, make the sauce. Mix together the tahini, garlic, remaining olive oil, lemon juice, and 5 tablespoons water in a bowl. Remove the squash from the oven, transfer the wedges to a serving dish; and serve with the tahini sauce.

ROASTED PUMPKIN AND CHICKPEAS WITH TAHINI DRESSING

—

يقطين مشوي مع الحمص

Preparation time: 15 minutes
Cooking time: 30 minutes
Serves 2

1 pumpkin, peeled, seeded, and cut into cubes
1 onion, sliced
3 garlic cloves, crushed
3 tablespoons olive oil
1 rosemary sprig
½ teaspoon sea salt
14 oz/400 g canned chickpeas, rinsed and drained
pinch of chili flakes
juice of 1½ lemons
5 tablespoons tahini
2 tablespoons extra virgin oil
1 bunch of fresh parsley, chopped
1 bunch of fresh mint, chopped
salt and pepper

Preheat the oven to 375°F/190°C/Gas Mark 5. Put the pumpkin, onion, and garlic into a large roasting pan, drizzle with the oil, and toss well. Add the rosemary sprig and sprinkle with the sea salt. Roast for 30 minutes, shaking the pan halfway through the cooking time. Remove the roasting pan from the oven, add the chickpeas, chili flakes, and 4 tablespoons lemon juice, return to the oven, and cook for another 10 minutes. Meanwhile, mix together the tahini, extra virgin olive oil, and remaining lemon juice in a bowl and season to taste with salt and pepper. Transfer the pumpkin and chickpea mixture to a serving dish, stir in the parsley and mint, and serve with the tahini dressing.

BUTTERNUT SQUASH WEDGES AND TAHINI SAUCE

STUFFED GRAPE LEAVES

STUFFED GRAPE LEAVES

PHOTO PAGE 121

ورق عنب

Preparation time: 45 minutes, plus soaking time
Cooking time: 1 hour
Serves 8–10

50 grape (vine) leaves
1 cup (7 oz/200 g) long-grain rice, rinsed
2 small tomatoes, diced
1 onion, finely chopped
½ yellow bell pepper, seeded and finely chopped
14 oz/400 g canned chickpeas, drained and rinsed
1 tablespoon finely chopped fresh mint
1 tablespoon finely chopped fresh parsley
1 teaspoon seven spices seasoning
olive oil, for drizzling
salt and black pepper

If using fresh leaves, bring a pan of salted water to a boil, add the leaves, and blanch for 3 minutes. Remove from the pan and put them on a wire rack to cool. If using leaves preserved in brine, soak them in hot water for 30 minutes, then drain, rinse thoroughly, and pat dry with paper towels. Mix together all the other ingredients, except the olive oil, in a bowl and season with salt and pepper. Lay 1 grape (vine) leaf flat on a work surface, put a spoonful of the filling on top, and carefully roll up the leaf into a cigar shape. Repeat with the remaining leaves and filling until 40 leaves have been used. Put the remaining leaves in the bottom of a large pan and put the grape leaf rolls on top. Drizzle with olive oil and season with salt and pepper. Position a plate snuggly on top of the leaves and pour in enough boiling water to cover. Bring back to a boil, then reduce the heat and simmer for 50–60 minutes. Carefully lift out the grape leaf rolls with a slotted spoon and serve warm.

KADAIFI PASTRY PIE WITH ZUCCHINI AND ZA'ATAR

PHOTO PAGE 123

—

فطائر الكوسا والزعتر
بعجينة الكنافة

Preparation time: 30 minutes
Cooking time: 30–35 minutes
Serves 12

14 oz/400 g kadaifi pastry
1¼ sticks (5 oz/150 g) butter, melted
3 tablespoons olive oil
4 zucchini (courgettes), diced
4 scallions (spring onions), sliced
1 red chile, finely chopped
1 small bunch of fresh mint leaves, chopped
1 tablespoon za'atar
4 eggs, lightly beaten
4 tablespoons grated Parmesan cheese
salt and pepper

Preheat the oven to 350°F/180°C/Gas Mark 4. Put the kadaifi pastry into a food processor and pulse 5–6 times to break it up slightly because this will make it easier to work with. Tip it into a bowl and pour the melted butter over it. Mix well, then divide the mixture in half. Press half the pastry over the bottom and up the sides of a 9½-inch/24-cm tart pan, then set aside while you make the filling. Heat the oil in a skillet or frying pan, add the zucchini (courgettes), scallions (spring onions), and chile, and cook over low heat, stirring occasionally, for 5 minutes. Add the mint and season with salt and pepper. Spoon this mixture evenly into the tart pan, then cover with the remaining pastry, pressing it down firming. Mix the za'atar with the lightly beaten eggs, pour the mixture over the top of the pie, and sprinkle with the Parmesan. Put the pan into the oven and bake for 30–35 minutes, until golden and crisp.

KADAIFI PASTRY PIE WITH ZUCCHINI AND ZA'ATAR

SPINACH AND CHEESE TURNOVERS

PHOTO PAGE 124

فطائر السبانخ

Preparation time: 30–35 minutes, plus resting time
Cooking time: 10–15 minutes
Makes about 20

1½ cups (7 oz/200 g) hard (strong) whole wheat (wholemeal)
    bread flour
1½ cups (6 oz/175 g) all-purpose (plain) flour,
    plus extra for dusting
½ envelope active dry (fast-action) yeast
1½ teaspoons salt
2 teaspoons extra virgin olive oil
1¼ cups (½ pint/300 ml) hot water
butter for greasing
1 egg lightly beaten with 2 tablespoons water

For the spinach and cheese filling
9 oz/250g spinach, coarse stems removed, shredded
1 onion, chopped
juice of ½ lemon
scant 1 cup (3½ oz/100 g) grated mozzarella cheese
salt and pepper

Sift together both kinds of flour into a bowl, then tip in the
bran from the sifter (sieve), and add the yeast and salt. Make a
well in the middle of the dry ingredients and add the oil, then
gradually add the water and mix to a dough. You may need a
little less or more water to bring the dough together. Knead for
10 minutes, then return the dough to the bowl, and dust lightly
with flour. Cover the bowl with plastic wrap (clingfilm) and let
stand in a warm place for 1 hour. Meanwhile, make the filling.
Mix together the spinach, onion, lemon juice, and mozzarella
in a bowl and season with salt and pepper. Preheat the oven to
450°F/230°C/Gas Mark 8. Grease 2 baking sheets with butter.
Punch down (knock back) the dough and knead again for a few
minutes. Use your hands toa make golf ball-size dough balls
and dust them lightly with flour. Thinly roll out each dough ball
into a circle, put a little of the spinach filling into the middle,
dampen the edges of the dough, and bring up the sides to seal
to form a turnover. Put the turnovers onto the prepared baking
sheets and brush with the egg wash. Bake for 10–15 minutes
until golden. Serve immediately.

PARSLEY PANCAKES

عجة البقدونس

Preparation time: 15 minutes
Cooking time: 6 minutes
Makes 6–8

2 extra large (UK large) eggs
⅔ cup (¼ pint/150 ml) milk
5 tablespoons (2½ oz/65 g) butter, melted
scant 1 cup (3½ oz/100 g) self-rising flour
1 teaspoon baking powder
2 scallions (spring onions), chopped
1 bunch of fresh parsley, chopped
¼ teaspoon fennel seeds
olive oil, for brushing
juice of 1 lime
salt and pepper
arugula (rocket), to serve

Lightly beat the eggs with the milk in a small bowl, then pour in the melted butter. Sift together the flour and baking powder into a separate bowl, pour in the milk mixture, and mix to a smooth paste. Add the scallions (spring onions), parsley, and fennel seeds and season with salt and pepper. Heat a non-stick skillet or frying pan, brush generously with oil, add 2 tablespoons of the pancake batter, and let spread. Cook for about 2 minutes on each side until golden. Depending on the size of the pan, cook no more than 2–3 pancakes at a time. Remove the pancakes from the pan, drain on paper towels, and keep warm while you cook the next batch. Continue to cook the pancakes in this way, brushing with more oil when needed, until all the batter has been used. Serve the pancakes with a squeeze of lime juice and handful of arugula (rocket) leaves.

SCALLION AND CHILE PANCAKES

عجة البصل الاخضر مع
الفلفل الحار

Preparation time: 15 minutes
Cooking time: 4 minutes
Makes 8

2 extra large (UK large) eggs
⅔ cup (¼ pint/150 ml) milk
5 tablespoons (2½ oz/65 g) butter, melted
scant 1 cup (3½ oz/100 g) self-rising flour
1 teaspoon baking powder
2 scallions (spring onions), chopped
1 red chile, seeded and finely diced
½ teaspoon sumac
1 small bunch of fresh cilantro (coriander), chopped
olive oil, for brushing
juice of 1 lime
salt and pepper
salad greens (leaves), to serve

Lightly beat the egg with the milk in a small bowl, then pour in the melted butter. Sift together the flour and baking powder into a separate bowl, pour in the milk mixture, and mix to a smooth paste. Stir in the scallions (spring onions), chile, sumac, and cilantro (coriander), and season with salt and pepper. Heat a non-stick skillet or frying pan, brush generously with oil, add 2 tablespoons of the pancake batter, and let spread. Cook for about 2 minutes on each side until golden. Depending on the size of the pan, cook no more than 3–4 pancakes at a time. Remove the pancakes from the pan, drain on paper towels, and keep warm while you cook the next batch. Continue to cook pancakes in this way, brushing with more oil when needed, until all the batter has been used. Serve the pancakes with a squeeze of lime juice and handful of salad greens (leaves).

ZUCCHINI PANCAKES

عجة الكوسا

Preparation time: 15 minutes
Cooking time: 4 minutes
Makes 8–10

2 extra large (UK large) eggs
⅔ cup (¼ pint/150 ml) milk
5 tablespoon (2½ oz/65 g) butter, melted
scant 1 cup (3½ oz/100 g) self-rising flour
1 teaspoon baking powder
1 zucchini (courgette)
2 scallions (spring onions), chopped
1 green chile, seeded and finely chopped
½ teaspoon ground coriander
1 small bunch of fresh cilantro (coriander), chopped
olive oil, for brushing
juice of 1 lime
salt and pepper
baby spinach, to serve

Lightly beat the egg with the milk in a small bowl, then pour
in the melted butter. Sift together the flour and baking powder
into a separate bowl, pour in the milk mixture, and mix to
a smooth paste. Grate the zucchini (courgette), squeeze
out any excess liquid in a clean dish towel, and add to the
batter with the scallions (spring onions), chile, and ground
coriander. Season with salt and pepper. Heat a non-stick skillet
or frying pan, brush generously with oil, add 2 tablespoons
of the pancake batter, and let spread out. Cook for about 2
minutes on each side until golden. Depending on the size of
the pan, cook no more than 3–4 pancakes at a time. Remove
the pancakes from the pan, drain on paper towels, and keep
warm while you cook the remaining batches. Continue to cook
pancakes in this way, brushing with more oil when needed,
until all the batter has been used. Serve the pancakes with a
squeeze of lime juice and baby spinach.

GARLIC
AND
MINT
OMELET

عجة الثوم والنعناع

Preparation time: 5 minutes
Cooking time: 5–10 minutes
Serves 2

1 teaspoon olive oil
2 garlic cloves, finely chopped
2 tablespoons chopped fresh mint
3 eggs, lightly beaten
Salt and pepper

Preheat the broiler (grill). Heat the oil in a skillet or frying pan with a flameproof handle, add the garlic, and cook over low heat, stirring frequently, for 2–3 minutes. Stir the mint into the eggs and season with salt and pepper. Pour the mixture into the pan and cook over low to medium heat for 5 minutes until the eggs are set on the underside. Put the pan under the hot broiler for a few minutes until the top of the omelet is cooked. Slide the omelet onto a plate, folding it in half. Cut in half and serve immediately.

SCRAMBLED
EGG
WITH
SMOKED
SALMON, BEET,
AND
SUMAC

بيض مخلوط مع سمك
السلمون المدخن والشمندر
والسماق

Preparation time: 5 minutes
Cooking time: 5–10 minutes
Serves 2

2 small flatbreads
4 eggs
2 tablespoons milk
2 teaspoons sumac
1 tablespoon butter
3 oz/80 g smoked salmon, cut into bite-size pieces
1 cooked beet (beetroot), diced
2 tablespoons chopped fresh parsley
salt and pepper

Preheat the oven to 375°F/190°C/Gas Mark 5. Put the flatbreads into the oven for 5 minutes until crisp. Meanwhile, lightly beat the eggs with the milk and sumac in a bowl and season with salt and pepper. Melt the butter in a skillet or frying pan, pour in the egg mixture, and cook over medium-low heat, stirring with decreasing energy with a wooden spoon, until just set. Tip the scrambled egg into a bowl and gently stir in the smoked salmon and beet (beetroot). Put a crisp flatbread on each of the 2 plates and divide the scrambled egg mixture between them. Sprinkle with the parsley and serve immediately.

SCRAMBLED EGGS WITH SUMAC AND TOMATO

—

بيض مخلوط مع السماق والطماطم

Preparation time: 5 minutes
Cooking time: 5–10 minutes
Serves 2

1 tomato, halved
4 eggs, lightly beaten
3 tablespoons skimmed milk
2 teaspoons sumac
2 tablespoons (1 oz/25 g) butter
2 slices of rustic (farmhouse) bread, toasted
2 tablespoons chopped fresh parsley
salt and pepper

Preheat the broiler (grill), then broil (grill) the tomato halves for 5 minutes. Sprinkle with salt and set aside. Beat the eggs with the milk and sumac in a small bowl and season with salt and pepper. Heat a skillet or frying pan, add the butter, and, when it has melted, pour in the egg mixture. Cook over medium-low heat, stirring with decreasing energy with a wooden spoon, for 2 minutes or until just setting. Put a slice of toasted bread on each of 2 individual plates and divide the scrambled egg between them. Sprinkle with the parsley, put a tomato half on the side, and serve immediately.

SCRAMBLED EGGS WITH LAMB AND PINE NUTS

—

بيض مخلوط مع لحم الغنم والصنوبر

Preparation time: 10 minutes
Cooking time: 25 minutes
Serves 2

1 tablespoon olive oil
3½ oz/100 g ground (minced) lamb
¼ onion, chopped
1 garlic clove, crushed
1 teaspoon seven spices seasoning
pinch of ground cumin
2 fresh mint sprigs, chopped
1½ tablespoons (¾ oz/20 g) butter
4 eggs
1 tablespoon milk
Salt and pepper
toasted pine nuts, to garnish

Heat the oil in a skillet or frying pan, add the lamb, and cook over medium-low heat, stirring frequently, for 7–8 minutes until browned. Add the onion, garlic, and spices, reduce the heat to low, and cook, stirring occasionally, for 20 minutes. Season to taste with salt and pepper and stir in the chopped mint. Melt the butter in another skillet or frying pan. Lightly beat the eggs with the milk in a bowl and pour the mixture into the pan. Cook over medium-low heat, stirring with decreasing energy with a wooden spoon, until beginning to set. Add the lamb, mix well, and remove from the heat. Taste and adjust the seasoning, if necessary, divide between individual plates, sprinkle with toasted pine nuts, and serve immediately.

BAKED EGG WITH SPINACH AND SUMAC

BAKED EGG WITH SPINACH AND SUMAC

PHOTO PAGE 133

—

بيض مشوي مع السبانخ والسماق

Preparation time: 10 minutes
Cooking time: 20 minutes
Serves 2

2 tablespoons butter, melted
1 tablespoon olive oil
2 garlic cloves, crushed
7 oz/200g baby spinach, coarse stems removed
3 tablespoons light (single) cream
pinch of freshly grated nutmeg
2 eggs
1 teaspoon sumac
salt
flatbread, to serve

Preheat the oven to 350°C/180°C/Gas Mark 4. Brush 2 ramekins with melted butter. Heat a skillet or frying pan, add the olive oil and garlic, and cook for 1 minute. Add the spinach and 1–2 tablespoons water, cover, and cook for 3–5 minutes. Tip into a colander and squeeze out any excess water, then chop the spinach and put it into a bowl. Stir in the cream and nutmeg and divide the mixture between the ramekins. Crack an egg on top of the spinach in each ramekin, sprinkle with the sumac and salt, and put the ramekins on a baking sheet. Bake for 20 minutes, until the egg is set. Serve immediately with flatbread.

BUTTERNUT SQUASH AND CILANTRO KIBBEH

—

كبة القرع والكزبرة

Preparation time: 15–20 minutes
Cooking time: 1 hour 15 minutes
Serves 8

1 butternut squash, peeled, seeded, and cubed
4 tablespoons (2 oz/50 g) butter
1 onion, grated
3¼ cups (1 lb/450 g) bulgur wheat, soaked in water for 10 minutes and squeezed out in cheesecloth (muslin)
1¾ cups (7 oz/200 g) all-purpose (plain) flour
1 teaspoon ground coriander
1 teaspoon seven spices seasoning
1 teaspoon pepper
2 tablespoons dried mint
1 bunch of fresh cilantro (coriander), chopped
3 teaspoons salt
olive oil, for brushing and drizzling

Put the butternut squash in a steamer set over a pan of simmering water, cover, and cook for 20–30 minutes until tender. Tip into a bowl and mash well with the butter. Add the onion, bulgur wheat, flour, ground coriander, seven spices seasoning, pepper, mint, cilantro (coriander), and salt mix well until thoroughly combined. Preheat the oven to 400°F/200°C/Gas Mark 6. Brush a 12 inch/30 cm round cake pan with a little oil and put it into the oven to warm for 5 minutes. Firmly press the mixture into the prepared pan, score the top into 8 portions, drizzle with olive oil, and bake in the oven for 40 minutes. Slice and serve warm.

BOILED EGGS WITH ZA'ATAR SOLIDERS

PHOTO PAGE 135

—

بيض مسلوق مع
اعواد الهيليون المغلفة
بالزعتر

Preparation time: 5 minutes
Cooking time: 1 minute
Serves 1

2 extra large (UK large) eggs
4 asparagus spears, trimmed
olive oil, for brushing
1 tablespoon za'atar
1 tablespoon butter
salt and black pepper
Lebanese flat bread, to serve

Bring a small pan of water to a boil, gently lower the eggs into the pan, and cook for 4 minutes. Meanwhile, heat a ridged grill pan. Brush the asparagus spears with olive oil, put them on the hot griddle, and cook, turning occasionally, for a few minutes until they start to char. Sprinkle with the za'atar, add the butter, and cook until the butter has melted. Serve the eggs with asparagus and a piece of flatbread.

—

PUMPKIN KIBBEH

—

كبة اليقطين

Preparation time: 30 minutes, plus soaking time
Cooking time: 1 hour 45 minutes
Serves 8

2½ lb/1.2 kg pumpkin, peeled, seeded, and chopped
2½ cups (12 oz/350 g) bulgur wheat, soaked in water for 10
    minutes and squeezed out in cheesecloth (muslin)
1 teaspoon ground coriander
2 tablespoons chopped fresh parsley
½ teaspoon dried basil
1 teaspoon pepper
1 teaspoon salt
6 tablespoons all-purpose (plain) flour
1 tablespoon olive oil, plus extra for brushing and drizzling
2 onions, sliced
scant 1 cup (3½ oz/100 g) macadamia nuts

Put the pumpkin into a steamer set over a pan of simmering water, cover, and cook for 30 minutes until very tender. Tip into a bowl and mash until smooth. Add the bulgur wheat, ground coriander, parsley, basil, pepper, salt, and flour and mix well until thoroughly combined. Heat the oil in a frying pan or skillet, add the onions, and cook over low heat, stirring occasionally, for 15 minutes until lightly caramelized. Meanwhile, dry-fry the nuts in a small skillet or frying pan for a few minutes, then remove from the heat. Preheat the oven to 400°F/200°C/Gas Mark 6. Brush a 12 inch/30 cm round cake pan with oil. Spoon half the pumpkin mixture into the prepared pan, pressing it down firmly, add the onions and nuts, and cover with the remaining pumpkin mixture. Smooth the top, score into 8 portions, and make a ¾-inch/2-cm hole in the center. Drizzle with as little oil and bake for 1 hour. Transfer to a serving dish and serve warm.

BOILED EGGS WITH ZA´ATAR SOLIDERS

LARGE SWEET POTATO KIBBEH WITH MOZZARELLA AND TOMATO

PHOTO PAGE 137

—

كبة البطاطس الحلوة
مع جبن الموزاريلا
والطماطم

Preparation time: 30 minutes, plus soaking time
Cooking time: 2 hours
Serves 8

2¼ lb/1 kg sweet potatoes
1 onion, grated
1 teaspoon paprika
1 teaspoon pepper
2 teaspoons salt
4 tablespoons all-purpose (plain) flour
2½ cups (12 oz/350 g) bulgur wheat, soaked in water for 10
    minutes and squeezed out in cheesecloth (muslin)
2¼ cups (9 oz/250 g) grated mozzarella cheese
scant 1 cup (3½ oz/100 g) drained sun-dried tomatoes, chopped
1 bunch of fresh basil, chopped
1 bunch of fresh parsley, chopped
olive oil, for brushing and drizzling

Preheat the oven 400°F/200°C/Gas Mark 6. Prick the sweet
potatoes all over with a fork and bake for 45–60 minutes until
tender. Remove from the oven and let cool slightly, then halve,
scoop out the flesh, and put it into a bowl. Add the onion,
paprika, pepper, salt, flour, bulgur wheat, mozzarella, sun-dried
tomatoes, basil, and parsley and mix well until thoroughly
combined. Brush a 12-inch/30-cm round cake pan with oil.
Put the mixture into the prepared pan, pressing it down firmly.
Score the top into 8 portions and make a ¾ inch/2 cm hole in
the center. Drizzle with oil and bake for 1 hour. Remove from
the oven and let cool before cutting.

RAW KIBBEH

—

كبة نية

Preparation time: 15 minutes
Serves 6

14 oz/400 g boneless leg of lamb, cut into cubes
½ onion, chopped
1 teaspoon dried mint
1 teaspoon pepper
1 teaspoon ground cumin
½ teaspoon seven spices seasoning
1 teaspoon salt
2 tablespoons chopped fresh mint
generous 1 cup (5 oz/150 g) bulgur wheat, soaked in water for
    10 minutes and squeezed out in cheesecloth (muslin)
olive oil, for drizzling
mint leaves, to garnish

Put the lamb into a food processor and process until finely
ground (minced), then tip into a bowl. Put the onion, dried
mint, pepper, cumin, seven spices seasoning, salt, and fresh
mint into the food processor and process until finely chopped
and combined. Add the spice and herb mixture to the lamb and
knead well, then add the bulgur wheat and continue to knead
until thoroughly combined. Tip onto a plate, drizzle with olive
oil, garnish with mint leaves, and serve.

LARGE SWEET POTATO KIBBEH WITH MOZZARELLA AND TOMATO

POTATO
AND
WALNUT
KIBBEH

كبة البطاطس
والجوز

Preparation time: 20 minutes, plus soaking time
Cooking time: 1 hour 40 minutes
Serves 8

2 cups (14 oz/400 g) dried chickpeas
1 teaspoon baking soda (bicarbonate of soda)
6 potatoes, unpeeled
1 onion, grated
2 ½ cups (12 oz/350 g) bulgur wheat, soaked in water for 10
    minutes and squeezed out in cheesecloth (muslin)
2 cups (8 oz/225 g) all-purpose (plain) flour
2 tablespoons chopped fresh parsley
2 tablespoons chopped fresh cilantro (coriander)
1 teaspoon dried mint
½ teaspoon ground cumin
1 teaspoon seven spices seasoning
1 tablespoon olive oil, plus extra for brushing and drizzling
4 onions, sliced
scant 1 cup (3½ oz/100 g) chopped walnuts
salt and pepper

Put the chickpeas into a bowl, pour in hot water to cover, stir in the baking soda (bicarbonate of soda), and let soak overnight. Drain and rinse the chickpeas and spread them out on a clean dish towel, fold it over them, and gently roll a rolling pin over the cloth to remove the skins. Put the chickpeas into a pan, pour in water to cover, and scoop out and discard the skins as they separate from the chickpeas. Boil the unpeeled potatoes for 20–25 minutes until tender, then drain and, when cool enough to handle, peel of the skins. Put them into a bowl and mash, then season with salt and pepper. Add the grated onion, bulgur wheat, flour, parsley, cilantro (coriander), mint, cumin, and seven spices seasoning, season with salt and pepper, and mix well until thoroughly combined. Heat the oil in a skillet or frying pan, add the sliced onions, and cook over low heat, stirring occasionally, for 5 minutes until softened but not colored. Stir in the walnuts and remove from the heat. Preheat the oven to 400°F/200°C/Gas Mark 6. Brush a 12 inch/30 cm round cake pan with a little oil and put it into the oven to warm for 5 minutes. Divide the potato mixture in half and firmly press one half into the prepared pan. Add the onion and walnut mixture, then cover with the remaining potato mixture, pressing firmly. Score the top into 8 portions, drizzle with oil, and bake for 1 hour. Serve immediately.

POTATO KIBBEH WITH SPICES AND PARSLEY

كبة بطاطس بالتوابل مع البقدونس

Preparation time: 20–30 minutes, plus soaking time
Cooking time: 1 hour 30 minutes
Serves 8

2¼ lb/1 kg potatoes, quartered
olive oil, for brushing and drizzling
1 onion, grated
1 bunch of fresh parsley, chopped
½ teaspoon paprika
½ teaspoon seven spices seasoning
½ teaspoon pepper
½ teaspoon salt
½ teaspoon ground cumin
2 tablespoons all-purpose (plain) flour
2½ cups (12 oz/350 g) bulgur wheat, soaked in water for
     10 minutes and squeezed out in cheesecloth (muslin)

Boil the potatoes in salted water for 25 minutes until very tender, then drain, return to the pan, and let dry for 10 minutes in a warm place. Press the potatoes through a ricer into a large bowl. Preheat the oven to 400°F/200°C/Gas Mark 6. Brush a 12 inch/30 cm cake pan with oil. Add the onion, parsley, paprika, seven spices seasoning, pepper, salt, cumin, flour, and bulgur wheat to the potatoes and mix well until thoroughly combined. Put the mixture into the prepared pan, pressing it down firmly. Score the top into 8 portions, make a ¾ inch/2 cm hole in the center, drizzle with oil, and bake for 1 hour. Let cool before serving.

LARGE CHICKEN KIBBEH WITH APRICOTS

كبة دجاج مع المشمش

Preparation time: 20 minutes, plus soaking time
Cooking time: 20–30 minutes
Serves 8

1 large onion
2¼ lb/1 kg skinless boneless chicken breasts
generous 2 cups (11 oz/300 g) bulgur wheat, soak in water for
     10 minutes and squeezed out in cheesecloth (muslin)
1 teaspoon seven spices seasoning
2 teaspoons ground cumin
2 teaspoons pepper
¾ cup (3½ oz/100 g) dried apricots, chopped
2 beets (beetroots), grated
olive oil, for brushing and drizzling
salt

Put the onion and chicken into a food processor and process until finely ground (minced), then tip into a bowl. Add the bulgur wheat, seven spices seasoning, cumin, pepper, apricots, and beets (beetroots), season well with salt, and knead until thoroughly combined. Preheat the oven to 400°F/200°C/Gas Mark 6. Brush a 12 inch/30 cm round cake pan with a little oil and put it into the oven to warm for 5 minutes. Firmly press the chicken mixture into the prepared pan, score the top into 8 portions, and drizzle with oil. Bake for 20–30 minutes.

CHICKEN KIBBEH OVALS WITH LAMB FILLING

كبة الدجاج البيضوية
المحشية بلحم غنم

Preparation time: 1 hour, plus soaking and chilling time
Cooking time: 15–20 minutes
Make 10-12

2¼ lb/1 kg skinless, boneless chicken breasts, coarsely chopped
½ onion
2 teaspoons dried oregano
1 teaspoon pepper
2 teaspoons ground cumin
1 teaspoon seven spices seasoning
2 teaspoons salt
2 tablespoons chopped fresh parsley
generous 2 cups (11 oz/300 g) bulgur wheat, soaked in water for
    10 minutes and squeezed out in cheesecloth (muslin)

For the filling
1 teaspoon olive oil
9 oz/250 g ground (minced) lamb
1 onion, chopped
⅓ cup (1½ oz/40 g) pine nuts, toasted
1 teaspoon seven spices seasoning
1 teaspoon pepper
2 teaspoon chopped sage

Put the chicken into a food processor and process until finely ground (minced), then tip it into a bowl. Put the onion, oregano, pepper, cumin, seven spices seasoning, salt, and parsley into the food processor and process until finely ground. Add the onion mixture to the chicken and knead well, then add the bulgur wheat and continue to knead until thoroughly combined. Make the filling. Heat the oil in a skillet or frying pan, add the lamb, and cook over medium heat, stirring frequently, for 8–10 minutes until evenly browned. Reduce the heat, add the onion, and cook, stirring occasionally, for another 5 minutes. Stir in the pine nuts, seven spices seasoning, and pepper and cook for a few more minutes. Remove from the heat, add the sage, and let cool. Preheat the oven to 350°F/180°C/Gas Mark 5. Line a baking sheet with wax (greaseproof) paper. Lay a piece of plastic wrap (clingfilm) on the work surface. With dampened hands, shape a golf ball-size portion of the chicken mixture into a patty that is slightly bigger than an oval kibbeh mold and is about ¼ inch/5 mm thick. Put the patty on the plastic wrap. Line the mold with plastic wrap. Shape another handful of the chicken mixture into a patty to fit into the mold with the same thickness as the base. Spoon 2 teaspoonfuls of the filling on top of the base patty, put the mold over the top, and push down tightly. Remove the mold and carefully take away the plastic wrap. Trim the edge to create a smooth finish and put the kibbeh ovals onto the prepared baking sheet. Repeat until all the mixture has been used. Brush with olive oil and bake for 15–20 minutes.

CHICKEN KIBBEH OVALS

—

كبة الدجاج البيضوية

Preparation time: 1 hour, plus soaking and chilling time
Cooking time: 15–20 minutes
Make 10-12

2¼ lb/1 kg skinless, boneless chicken breasts
½ onion, grated
2 teaspoons dried oregano
1 teaspoon pepper
2 teaspoons ground cumin
1 teaspoon seven spices seasoning
1 teaspoon salt
2 tablespoons chopped fresh parsley
generous 2 cups (11 oz/300 g) bulgur wheat, soaked in water for
    10 minutes and squeezed out in cheesecloth (muslin)

For the filling
1 tablespoon olive oil
1 onion, chopped
½ cup (2 oz/50 g) pine nuts, toasted
½ cup (2 oz/50 g) walnuts, chopped
⅓ cup (2 oz/50 g) dried apricots, chopped
1 heaping teaspoon ground sumac

Put the chicken into a food processor and process until finely
ground (minced), then tip it into a bowl. Put the onion,
oregano, pepper, cumin, seven spices seasoning, salt, and
parsley into the food processor and process until finely ground.
Add the onion mixture to the chicken and knead well, then
add the bulgur wheat and continue to knead until thoroughly
combined. Chill in the refrigerator for 1 hour. Preheat the
oven to 350°F/180°C/Gas Mark 5. Line a baking sheet with wax
(greaseproof) paper. Make the filling. Heat the oil in a skillet
or frying pan, add the onion, and cook over low heat, stirring
occasionally, for 10 minutes until lightly browned. Stir in the
nuts, apricots, and sumac and cook for another 2 minutes.
Dampen your hands with a little water and shape a handful of
the chicken mixture into an oval to fit the palm of your hand.
Use your index finger to make a hole in the top, then gradually
make a hollow, working around with your finger to create a thin
wall. Add a tablespoonful of the filling, seal with a pinch, and
reshape into an oval. Repeat this until all the chicken mixture
has been used. Put the kibbeh on the prepared baking sheet
and bake for 15–20 minutes or until cooked through.

CHICKEN KIBBEH OVALS WITH GOAT CHEESE FILLING

—

كبة دجاج مع جبن الماعز

Preparation time: 1 hour, plus soaking time
Cooking time: 30 minutes
Make 10–12

2¼ lb/1 kg skinless, boneless chicken breasts
½ onion
2 teaspoons dried oregano
1 teaspoon pepper
2 teaspoons ground cumin
2 teaspoons seven spices seasoning
2 teaspoons salt
2 tablespoons chopped fresh parsley
generous 2 cups (11 oz/300 g) bulgur wheat, soaked in water for
    10 minutes and squeezed out in cheesecloth (muslin)
olive oil, for drizzling

For the filling
1¼ cups (5 oz/140 g) sun-dried tomatoes, chopped
7 oz/200 g goat cheese, sliced
½ teaspoon pepper

Put the chicken into a food processor and process until finely ground (minced), then tip into a bowl. Put the onion, oregano, pepper, cumin, seven spices seasoning, salt, and parsley into the food processor and process until finely ground. Add the onion mixture to the chicken and knead well, then add the bulgur wheat and continue to knead until thoroughly combined. Preheat the oven to 350°F/180°C/Gas Mark 4. Line a baking sheet with wax (greaseproof) paper. Lay a piece of plastic wrap (clingfilm) on the work surface. With dampened hands, shape a golf ball-size portion of the chicken mixture into a patty that is slightly bigger than a crescent-shaped kibbeh mold and is about ¼ inch/5 mm thick. Put the patty on the plastic wrap. Line the mold with plastic wrap. Shape another handful of the chicken mixture into a patty to fit into the mold with the same thickness as the base. Put a tablespoonful of chopped tomatoes and a piece of goat cheese on top of the base patty, put the mold over the top, and push down tightly. Remove the mold and carefully take away the plastic wrap. Trim the edge to give a smooth finish and put onto the prepared baking sheet. Repeat until all the mixture has been used. Drizzle lightly with olive oil and bake for 30 minutes

LARGE LAMB KIBBEH

اقراص كبة لحم
الغنم

Preparation time: 30 minutes, plus soaking time
Cooking time: 1 hour 30 minutes
Serves 8

1 x 1¾ lb/800 g half leg of lamb
1 large onion, coarsely chopped
1 teaspoon seven spices seasoning
1 teaspoons ground cumin
1 teaspoon pepper
1 teaspoon dried mint
3⅓ cups (1¼ lb/570 g) bulgur wheat, soaked in water for
    10 minutes and squeezed out in cheesecloth (muslin)
olive oil, for brushing and drizzling

For the filling
1 teaspoon olive oil
1 lb 2 oz/500 g ground (minced) lamb
2 onions, chopped
¾ cup (3 oz/80 g) pine nuts, toasted
1 teaspoon seven spices seasoning
1 teaspoon pepper
1 teaspoon salt
1 teaspoon ground coriander
1 teaspoon ground cinnamon

First make the filling. Heat the oil in a skillet or frying pan, add the lamb, and cook over medium heat, stirring frequently for 8–10 minutes until evenly browned. Reduce the heat, add the onions, and cook, stirring occasionally for another 5 minutes. Stir in the pine nuts, seven spices seasoning, pepper, salt, ground coriander, and cinnamon and cook for a few more minutes. Remove the pan from the heat. Trim the fat from the lamb, then cut the meat off the bone. Put it into a food processor with the onion and process until finely ground (minced). Tip it into a bowl, add the seven spices seasoning, cumin, pepper, mint, and bulgur wheat, knead until thoroughly mixed. Preheat the oven to 400°F/200°C/Gas Mark 6. Brush a 12 inch/30 cm round cake pan with a little oil and put it into the oven to warm for 5 minutes. Divide the mixture in half and firmly press one half into the prepared pan. Add the filling, then cover with the remaining lamb and bulgur wheat mixture, pressing firmly. Score the top into 8 portions, drizzle with oil, and bake for 50 minutes. Serve immediately.

FRIED LAMB KIBBEH

FRIED LAMB KIBBEH

PHOTO PAGE 144

كبة لحم الغنم
المقلية

Preparation time: 1 hour, plus soaking and chilling time
Cooking time: 10 minutes
Serves 4–6

1 large onion
1 lb 5 oz/600 g boneless leg of lamb, diced
2½ cups (12 oz/350 g) bulgur wheat, soak in water for 10
    minutes and squeezed out in cheesecloth (muslin)
1 teaspoon seven spices seasoning
1 teaspoon ground cumin
1 teaspoon pepper
1 teaspoon dried mint
sunflower oil, for deep-frying

For the filling
1 tablespoon olive oil
7 oz/200 g ground (minced) lamb
1 onion, chopped
⅓ cup (1½ oz/40 g) pine nuts, toasted
½ teaspoon seven spices seasoning
½ teaspoon pepper
½ teaspoon salt
½ teaspoon ground coriander
½ teaspoon ground cinnamon

First, make the filling. Heat the oil a skillet or frying pan, add
the lamb, and cook over medium heat, stirring frequently, for
8–10 minutes until evenly browned. Reduce the heat, add the
onion, and cook, stirring occasionally, for another 5 minutes.
Add the pine nuts, seven spices seasoning, pepper, salt,
coriander, and cinnamon and cook for a few more minutes.
Remove the pan from the heat and set aside. Put the onion
and lamb into a food processor and process until finely ground
(minced). Tip into a bowl, add the bulgur wheat, seven spices
seasoning, cumin, pepper, and mint, and knead well until
thoroughly combined. Dampen your hands with a little water,
take a handful of the mixture, and mold into an oval to fit the
palm of your hand. Use your index finger to make a hole in the
top, then gradually make a hollow, working around with your
finger to create a thin wall. Add a tablespoonful of the filling,
seal with a pinch, and reshape into an oval. Repeat this to until
all the lamb and bulgur mixture has been used. Put the kibbeh
onto a baking sheet and chill in the refrigerator for 1 hour.
Heat the sunflower oil in a deep-fryer to 350°F/180°C or until a
cube of bread browns in 30 seconds. Carefully add the kibbeh
to the hot oil, in batches, and cook for 10 minutes. Drain on
paper towels and serve warm.

BAKED LAMB KIBBEH

كبة لحم الغنم
المشوية

Preparation time: 1 hour, plus soaking and chilling time
Cooking time: 30 minutes
Serves 4–6

1 large onion
1 lb 5 oz/600 g boneless leg of lamb, diced
2½ cups (12 oz/350 g) bulgur wheat, soak in water for 10 minutes and squeezed out in cheesecloth (muslin)
1 teaspoon seven spices seasoning
1 teaspoon ground cumin
1 teaspoon pepper
1 teaspoon dried mint
olive oil for brushing

For the filling
1 tablespoon olive oil
7 oz/200 g ground (minced) lamb
1 onion, chopped
⅓ cup (1½ oz/40 g) pine nuts, toasted
½ teaspoon seven spices seasoning
½ teaspoon pepper
½ teaspoon salt
½ teaspoon ground coriander
½ teaspoon ground cinnamon

First make the filling. Heat the oil in a skillet or frying pan, add the lamb, and cook over medium heat, stirring frequently, for 8–10 minutes until evenly browned. Reduce the heat, add the onion, and cook, stirring occasionally, for another 5 minutes. Stir in the pine nuts, seven spices seasoning, pepper, salt, coriander, and cinnamon and cook for a few more minutes. Remove from the heat and set aside. Put the onion and lamb into a food processor and process until finely ground (minced). Tip into a bowl and add the bulgur wheat, seven spices seasoning, cumin, pepper, and mint, and knead well until thoroughly combined. Dampen your hands with a little water, take a handful of the mixture, and mold into an oval to fit the palm of your hand. Use your index finger to make a hole in the top, then gradually make a hollow, working around with your finger to create a thin wall. Add a tablespoonful of the filling, seal with a pinch, and reshape into an oval. Repeat this until all the lamb and bulgur mixture has been used. Brush a baking sheet with oil, put the kibbeh onto it, and chill in the refrigerator for 1 hour. Preheat the oven to 400°F/200°C/Gas Mark 6. Brush the kibbeh with oil and bake for 30 minutes or until cooked and golden.

MINI LAMB KIBBEH AND YOGURT

الكبة اللبنية

Preparation time: 40–45 minutes, plus soaking and chilling time
Cooking time: 40 minutes
Serves 4–6

1 large onion
1 lb 5 oz/600 g boneless leg of lamb, diced
2½ cups (12 oz/350 g) bulgur wheat, soak in water for 10
    minutes and squeezed out in cheesecloth (muslin)
1 teaspoon seven spices seasoning
2 teaspoons ground cumin
1 teaspoon pepper
1 teaspoon dried mint
generous 2 cups (18 fl oz/500 ml) plain (natural) yogurt
1 tablespoon cornstarch (cornflour)
½ cup (3½ oz/100 g) basmati rice, rinsed
1 teaspoon olive oil
3 garlic cloves, chopped
2 tablespoons chopped fresh mint

For the filling
1 tablespoon olive oil
7 oz/200 g ground (minced) lamb
1 onion, chopped
⅓ cup (1½ oz/40 g) pine nuts, toasted
½ teaspoon seven spices seasoning
½ teaspoon pepper
½ teaspoon salt
½ teaspoon ground coriander
½ teaspoon ground cinnamon

First, make the filling. Heat the oil in a skillet or frying pan, add the lamb, and cook over medium heat, stirring frequently, for 8–10 minutes until evenly browned. Reduce the heat, add the onion, and cook, stirring occasionally, for another 5 minutes. Stir in the pine nuts, seven spices seasoning, pepper, salt, coriander, and cinnamon and cook for a few more minutes. Remove the pan from the heat. Put the onion and lamb into a food processor and process until finely ground (minced). Tip into a bowl, add the bulgur wheat, seven spices seasoning, half the cumin, the pepper, and dried mint, and knead until thoroughly incorporated. Dampen your hands with a little water, take a handful of the mixture, and mold into an oval to fit the palm of your hand. Use your index finger to make a hole in the top, then gradually make a hollow, working around with your finger to create a thin wall. Add a tablespoonful of the filling, seal with a pinch, and reshape into an oval. Repeat this to until all the lamb and bulgur mixture has been used. Put the kibbeh onto a baking sheet and chill in the refrigerator for 1 hour. Meanwhile, pour the yogurt into a large pan and add 1⅔ cups (14 fl oz/400 ml) water, then whisk in the cornstarch (cornflour) and bring to a boil, whisking constantly. Add the rice, then add the kibbeh, reduce the heat, and simmer for 30 minutes. Heat the oil in a skillet or frying pan, add the garlic, and cook over low heat, stirring frequently, for a few minutes until lightly golden. Add the garlic to the kibbeh, then add the fresh mint and remaining cumin. Season well with salt and pepper and serve.

LAMB KIBBEH OVALS

PHOTO PAGE 149

كبة لحم غنم هلالية

Preparation time: 1 hour, plus soaking time
Cooking time: 50 minutes
Make 10-12

2¼ lb/1 kg boneless leg of lamb, chopped
½ onion
2 teaspoons dried mint
1 teaspoon pepper
2 teaspoons ground cumin
1 teaspoon seven spices seasoning
1 teaspoon salt
2 tablespoons chopped mint
generous 2 cups (11 oz/300 g) bulgur wheat, soaked in water for
    10 minutes and squeezed out in cheesecloth (muslin)
olive oil, for brushing and drizzling

For the filling
½ teaspoon olive oil
9 oz/250 g ground (minced) lamb
1 onion, chopped
⅓ cup (1½ oz/40 g) pine nuts, toasted
¼ teaspoon seven spices seasoning
½ teaspoon pepper

Put the lamb into a food processor and process until finely ground (minced), then tip into a bowl. Put the onion, dried mint, pepper, cumin, seven spices seasoning, salt, and fresh mint into the food processor and process until finely ground. Add the onion mixture to the lamb and knead well, then add the bulgur wheat, and knead until thoroughly combined.
Make the filling. Heat the oil in a skillet or frying pan, add the lamb, and cook over medium heat, stirring frequently, for 8–10 minutes until evenly browned. Reduce the heat, add the onion, and cook, stirring occasionally, for another 5 minutes. Stir in the pine nuts, seven spices seasoning, and pepper and cook for a few more minutes. Remove from the heat and let cool.
Preheat the oven to 350°F/180°C/Gas Mark 4. Brush a baking sheet with olive oil. Lay a piece of plastic wrap (clingfilm) on the work counter. With dampened hands, shape a golf ball-size portion of the lamb and bulgur wheat mixture into a patty that is slightly bigger than a crescent-shaped kibbeh mold and is about ¼ inch/5 mm thick. Put the patty on the plastic wrap. Line the mold with plastic wrap. Shape another handful of the lamb and bulgur wheat mixture into a patty to fit into the mold with the same thickness as the base. Spoon 2 teaspoonfuls of the filling on top of the base patty, put the mold over the top, and push down tightly. Remove the mold and carefully take away the plastic wrap. Trim the edge to create a smooth finish and put onto the prepared baking sheet. Repeat until all the mixture has been used. Put the kibbeh onto the prepared baking sheet, drizzle lightly with olive oil, and bake for 50 minutes.

LAMB KIBBEH OVALS

CHICKEN FATTEH

فتة الدجاج

Preparation time: 20 minutes
Cooking time: 50–55 minutes
Serves 4

1 cinnamon stick
6 cardamom seeds
4 cloves
3 skinless, boneless chicken breasts
1 tablespoon olive oil
1 onion, sliced
2 garlic cloves, crushed
1 teaspoon paprika
¾ cup (3 oz/80 g) pine nuts, toasted
2 pita breads, toasted
salt and pepper

For the yogurt sauce
1 cup (8 fl oz/250 ml) plain (natural) yogurt
2 garlic cloves, crushed
2 tablespoons chopped mint
2 tarragon sprigs, chopped

Bring a pan of water to a boil and add the cinnamon stick, cardamom seeds, and cloves. Reduce the heat so that the surface of the water is barely bubbling, add the chicken, and poach for 45 minutes or until very tender. Lift out the chicken with a slotted spoon and let cool, then shred into bite-size pieces. Heat the oil in a skillet or frying pan, add the onion, and cook over low heat, stirring occasionally, for 5 minutes until softened. Add the garlic and cook for another minute, then stir in the shredded chicken and paprika and season well with salt and pepper. Cook for a few minutes until heated through, then transfer to a warm serving dish. Mix together all the ingredients for the yogurt sauce and spoon it over the chicken. Sprinkle with the pine nuts. Cut the toasted pita breads into squares, put them on top of the dish, and serve.

HOMEMADE SPICY LAMB SAUSAGE

سجق لحم الغنم
بالبهارات الحارة

Preparation time: 10 minutes, plus chilling time
Cooking time: 10 minutes
Makes 4

14 oz/400 g ground (minced) lamb
2 garlic cloves, crushed
1½-inch/4-cm piece of fresh ginger, grated
½ teaspoon ground cinnamon
1 teaspoon ground cumin
1 teaspoon ground coriander
½ teaspoon ground allspice
½ teaspoon ground cloves
½ tsp paprika
1 teaspoon salt
1 teaspoon pepper
3 tablespoons fresh orange juice
5 tablespoons olive oil
Lebanese Mixed Salad (see page 58), to serve

Using your hands, mix together the lamb, garlic, ginger, cinnamon, cumin, coriander, allspice, cloves, paprika, salt, and pepper in a bowl until thoroughly combined. Gradually add the orange juice and 2 tablespoons of the olive oil and knead the mixture for 3–4 minutes. Cover the bowl with plastic wrap (clingfilm) and chill in the refrigerator overnight until firm. The following day, shape finger-like sausages from the lamb mixture. Heat a skillet or frying pan and add the remaining oil. Add the sausages to the pan, in batches, and cook over medium heat, turning frequently, for 10 minutes. Serve hot with a Lebanese salad.

HOMEMADE CHICKEN SAUSAGE

سجق الدجاج

Preparation time: 20 minutes
Cooking time: 10 minutes
Makes 4

4 skinless, boneless chicken breasts, coarsely chopped
2 garlic cloves, crushed
1 tablespoon za'atar
¼ teaspoon chili flakes
1 teaspoon salt
1 teaspoon pepper
3 tablespoons lemon juice
5 tablespoons olive oil
Lebanese Mixed Salad (see page 58), to serve

Put the chicken into a food processor and process until finely ground (minced). Tip it into a bowl, add the garlic, spices, salt, pepper, lemon juice, and 2 tablespoons of the olive oil, and knead well for 3–4 minutes until thoroughly combined. Cover the bowl with plastic wrap (clingfilm) and chill in the refrigerator overnight until firm. The following day, make finger-like sausages from the mixture. Heat a skillet or frying pan and add the remaining oil. Add the sausages to the pan, in batches, and cook over medium heat, turning frequently, for 10 minutes. Serve the sausages hot with a Lebanese salad.

CHICKEN LIVERS WITH GARLIC AND LEMON SAUCE

كبدة الدجاج مع الثوم
والليمون

Preparation time: 10 minutes
Cooking time: 15 minutes
Serves 4

14 oz/400 g chicken livers, diced
½ teaspoon salt
2 tablespoons olive oil

For garlic and lemon sauce
4 garlic cloves
⅔ cup (¼ pint/150 ml) extra virgin olive oil
juice ½ lemon
salt and pepper

Put the chicken livers into a dish, sprinkle with the salt, and toss well. Heat the olive oil a skillet or frying pan, add the chicken livers, and cook over medium heat, stirring frequently, for 15 minutes. Meanwhile, make the sauce. Crush the garlic with a pinch of salt in a mortar with a pestle. Add the oil olive and lemon juice and stir well. Season with salt and pepper. Pour half the sauce over the liver and remove the pan from the heat. Transfer the liver mixture to a warm serving dish and serve immediately with the remaining sauce on the side.

CHICKEN SHAWARMA

لفة شاورما الدجاج

Preparation time: 10 minutes, plus marinating time
Cooking time: 30 minutes
Serves 2

2 skinless boneless chicken breasts, sliced
2 garlic cloves, crushed
1 tablespoon olive oil
1 teaspoon seven spices seasoning
½ teaspoon sea salt
¼ teaspoon chili flakes
juice of 1 lemon
¼ iceberg lettuce, shredded
1 tablespoon chopped fresh parsley
1 tablespoon chopped fresh cilantro (coriander)
8 cherry tomatoes, halved
lemon juice, to taste
2 Lebanese flatbreads, warmed
2 tablespoons Hummus (see page 38)
salt and pepper

Put the chicken, garlic, olive oil, seven spices seasoning, 1 teaspoon pepper, sea salt, chili flakes, and lemon juice into a bowl, mix well, and let marinate for 1 hour. Meanwhile, put the lettuce, parsley, cilantro (coriander), and tomatoes in another bowl and season with salt and pepper. Heat a large skillet or frying pan, add all the chicken and marinade, and cook over medium heat, stirring frequently, for 10–15 minutes until the chicken is cooked through. Add a squeeze of lemon juice and remove the pan from the heat. Lay out the warm flatbreads out and divide the salad between them. Spoon the chicken on top, add a spoonful of hummus to each, and roll up tightly. Serve immediately.

EGGPLANT
MEAT
ROLLS

—

لفائف الباذنجان
واللحم

Preparation time: 20 minutes
Cooking time: 1 hour 10 minutes
Makes 4

3 eggplants (aubergines), cut into ¼-inch/5-mm slices
olive oil, for brushing
3 cups (12 oz/350 g) grated mozzarella cheese
sea salt

For the filling
12 oz/350 g ground (minced) lamb
5 oz/150 g ground (minced) beef
1 onion, finely chopped
2 garlic cloves, crushed
14 oz/400 g canned chopped tomatoes
½ teaspoon ground cinnamon
1 teaspoon ground cumin
1 teaspoon ground coriander
1 teaspoon paprika
2 thyme sprigs, chopped
1 teaspoon dried rosemary
Salt and black pepper

Heat a ridged grill pan. Brush the eggplant (aubergine) slices
with olive oil on both sides and season generously with sea salt.
Put them on the pan and cook for 5 minutes on each sides or
until softened and cooked through. Using tongs, transfer them
to a wire rack and let cool while you make the filling. Heat a
large skillet or frying pan, add the lamb and beef, and cook over
medium heat, stirring frequently, for 8–10 minutes until evenly
browned. Reduce the heat, add the onion and garlic, and cook,
stirring occasionally, for 5 minutes. Add the tomatoes, refill
the can with water, and add to the pan. Add all the spices and
herbs and simmer, stirring occasionally, for 45 minutes. Season
with salt and pepper to taste and remove the pan from the heat.
Preheat the broiler (grill). Put a spoonful of the filling on the
wider end of an eggplant slice and roll up. Put the roll on a
baking sheet with the seam underneath. Continue making rolls
in this way until all the eggplant slices have been used.
Sprinkle the rolls with grated mozzarella and season with
pepper. Put the baking sheet under the broiler and cook for 2–3
minutes or until the cheese has melted. Serve immediately.

LAMB SHAWARMA

—

لفة شاورما لحم الغنم

Preparation time: 20 minutes, plus marinating time
Cooking time: 10 minutes
Serves 4

12 oz/350g lamb tenderloin (fillet), sliced
2 garlic cloves, crushed
2 tablespoons olive oil
1 teaspoon seven spices seasoning
¼ teaspoon ground cinnamon
½ teaspoon ground cumin
1 teaspoon pepper
½ teaspoon sea salt
2 teaspoons dried mint
pinch of paprika
juice of ½ lemon
¼ iceberg lettuce, shredded
1 tablespoon chopped fresh parsley
1 tablespoon chopped fresh mint
8 cherry tomatoes, halved
lemon juice, to taste
2 Lebanese flatbreads, warmed
2 tablespoons Garlic Dip (see page 43)
salt and pepper

Put the lamb, garlic, olive oil, seven spices seasoning,
cinnamon, cumin, pepper, sea salt, dried mint, paprika, and
lemon juice into a bowl, mix well, and let marinate for 1 hour.
Meanwhile, put the lettuce, parsley, fresh mint, and tomatoes
in another bowl and season with salt and pepper. Heat a large
skillet or frying pan, add the lamb and marinade, and cook over
medium heat, stirring frequently, for 10–15 minutes until the
meat is cooked through. Add a squeeze of lemon and remove
the pan from the heat. Lay out the warm flatbreads on a work
surface and divide the salad between them. Spoon the lamb
on top, add a spoonful of garlic dip to each, and roll up tightly.
Serve immediately.

FISH SHAWARMA

—

لفة شاورما السمك

Preparation time: 15 minutes
Cooking time: 12 minutes
Serves 2

14 oz/400 g cod loin
2 tablespoons olive oil
½ teaspoon sea salt
½ teaspoon pepper
pinch of paprika
1 tablespoon salted capers, rinsed
¼ iceberg lettuce, shredded
1 tablespoon chopped fresh parsley
1 tablespoon chopped fresh dill
1 tablespoon snipped chopped fresh chives
8 cherry tomatoes, halved
2 Lebanese flatbreads, warmed in the oven or under the
    broiler (grill) for a few minutes
juice of ½ lemon
2 tablespoons Garlic Dip (see page 43)
salt and pepper

Rub the cod loin with the olive oil, sea salt, ½ teaspoon pepper, and the paprika. Heat a skillet or frying pan, add the cod and capers, and cook for 5–6 minutes on each side or until the flesh flakes easily. Remove the pan from the heat, lift out the cod with a spatula (fish slice), and flake the flesh into large pieces. Set aside with the capers and pan juices. Put the lettuce, parsley, dill, chives, and tomatoes into a bowl and season with salt and black pepper. Lay out the flatbreads on a work surface and divide the salad between them. Top with the fish, capers, and a spoonful of garlic dip on each. Squeeze the lemon juice over the top and roll up tightly. Serve immediately.

LAMB TONGUE AND TOMATO STEW

PHOTO PAGE 157

—

لسانات غنم مع يخني
الطماطم

Preparation time: 15 minutes
Cooking time: 5 hours
Serves 4

1¾ lb/800 g lamb tongue
2 bay leaves
1 teaspoon salt
1 tablespoon olive oil
1 brown onion, sliced
1 red onion, sliced
3 tablespoons tomato paste (purée)
1 teaspoon dried basil
½ teaspoon ground cumin
½ teaspoon seven spices seasoning
1 teaspoon pepper
Lebanese bread, to serve

Put the tongue, bay leaves, and salt into a large pan, pour in boiling water to cover, and bring to a boil over medium heat. Reduce the heat, cover, and simmer for 4½ hours or until the tongue is very tender. Remove the pan from the heat, then drain the tongue and let cool. Carefully peel off the skin from the tongue and discard. Cut the meat into chunks. Heat the oil in a large pan, add the onions, and cook over medium-low heat, stirring frequently, for about 8 minutes until softened and lightly browned. Add the meat, tomato paste (purée), basil, and all the spices and stir well. Pour in boiling water to cover and bring back a boil, then reduce the heat and simmer for another 20 minutes until the tomato sauce has reduced and thickened. Serve immediately with Lebanese bread.

LAMB TONGUE AND TOMATO STEW

LAMB
MANAKISH

بيتزا باللحوم

Preparation time: 30 minutes, plus resting time
Cooking time: 30–35 minutes
Makes 2 large pizzas

1¾ cups (7 oz/200 g) hard (strong) whole wheat (wholemeal)
    bread flour
1⅓ cups (6 oz/175 g) all-purpose (plain) flour,
    plus extra for dusting
½ envelope active dry (fast-action) yeast
½ tablespoon salt
2 teaspoons extra virgin olive oil, plus extra for brushing
1¼ cups (½ pint/300 ml) lukewarm water

For the topping
14 oz/400 g ground (minced) lamb
2 garlic cloves, crushed
1 teaspoon dried mint
1 teaspoon ground cumin
1 teaspoon seven spices seasoning
4 tablespoons tomato paste (purée)
1 red onion, sliced
3 oz/85 g spicy sausage, sliced
2 tablespoons chopped fresh mint
salt and pepper

First, make the dough. Mix together both types of flour, the
yeast, and salt in a bowl, then add the oil and gradually stir
in the lukewarm water until a dough forms. You may need a
little less or more water to bring the dough together. Knead
the dough for 10 minutes, then shape it into a ball, return it to
the bowl, and dust with a little flour. Cover tightly with plastic
wrap (clingfilm) and leave for 1 hour in a warm, dark place to
rise. Meanwhile, make the topping. Heat a heavy pan, add the
lamb, and cook over medium heat, stirring frequently, for 8–10
minutes until evenly browed. Reduce the heat, add the garlic,
mint, spices, and scant ½ cup (3½ fl oz/100 ml) water, and
simmer, stirring occasionally, for 20 minutes. Remove from the
heat and season well with salt and pepper. Preheat the oven
450°F/230°C/Gas Mark 8. Brush 2 baking sheets with oil.
Turn out the dough onto a lightly floured surface and punch
down (knock back), then divide it in half with your hands.
Roll out each piece of dough on a lightly floured surface to a
circle and then place on the prepared baking sheets. Spread
the tomato paste (purée) evenly over both dough bases. Divide
the lamb mixture between them and spread to the edges
of the dough. Top with the onion and sausage and bake for
10–15 minutes or until the bases are crispy. Remove the pizzas
from the oven, season with salt and pepper, and sprinkle with
chopped mint. Cut the pizzas into slices and serve immediately.

COD GOUJONS WITH GARLIC DIP

شرائح سمك القد
وغموس الثوم

Preparation time: 15 minutes
Cooking time: 8–10 minutes
Makes 18

12 oz/350 g cod fillet, skinned
3 slices (3 oz/80 g) wheat (brown) bread, crusts removed
2 tablespoons snipped chives
pinch of paprika
4 tablespoons all-purpose (plain) flour
1 egg
3 tablespoons milk
sunflower oil, for deep-frying
salt and pepper
Garlic Dip (see page 43) and salad greens (leaves), to serve

Cut the fish into strips and set aside. Put the bread into a food processor and process to fine breadcrumbs. Tip the breadcrumbs onto a plate and stir in the chives and paprika. Put the flour onto another plate, season with salt and pepper, and mix well. Lightly beat the egg with the milk in a shallow dish. Heat the oil in a deep-fryer to 350°F/180°C or until a cube of bread browns in 30 seconds. Meanwhile, dip the fish strips in the flour, shaking off any excess, then in the egg mixture, and, finally, in the breadcrumbs. Add the fish strips to the hot oil, in batches, and fry for 8–10 minutes, until golden. Remove with a slotted spoon and drain on paper towels. Pile the goujons into a warm serving dish and serve immediately with garlic dip and salad greens (leaves).

PAN-FRIED SARDINES

سمك ساردين مشوي

Preparation time: 10 minutes
Cooking time: 4–5 minutes
Serves 4

8 large sardines, scaled, cleaned, and head and fins removed
4 garlic cloves
½ teaspoon salt
3 tablespoons olive oil
juice of 1 lemon
salad greens (leaves), to serve

Open out the sardines like a book and place on a work surface skin side uppermost. Press firmly along the backbone of each fish with your thumb. Turn the fish over and carefully remove the backbones, snipping with scissors at the tail end. Trim the sides of the sardines and set aside in a dish. Crush the garlic with the salt in a mortar with a pestle. Stir in the olive oil and lemon juice, then pour the mixture over the sardines and rub in on both sides. Heat a heavy skillet or frying pan, add the sardines, skin side down, and cook for 2–3 minutes, then turn, and cook for another minute. Transfer the fish, skin side uppermost, to individual plates and serve immediately with salad greens (leaves).

FRIED SEA BASS ON A TAHINI AND CURRY SAUCE

FRIED SEA BASS ON A TAHINI AND CURRY SAUCE

PHOTO PAGE 160

—

سمك القاروص المقلي
مع صلصة
الطحينة والكاري

Preparation time: 10 minutes
Cooking time: 10 minutes
Serves 2

4 sea bass fillets
1 tablespoon butter
1 teaspoon sesame seeds, toasted
2 tablespoons chopped cilantro (coriander)
salt and black pepper
squeeze of lemon juice, to serve

For the sauce
6 tablespoons tahini
1 teaspoon salt
juice of 1 lemon
1 teaspoon hot curry powder
120ml water

Preheat the oven to 350°F/180°C/Gas Mark 4. Mix together all sauce ingredients in a bowl and stir in ½ cup (4 fl oz/120 ml) water. Pour the sauce into an ovenproof dish and put in the oven to warm. Cut each fish fillet in half, score the skin with 2 slashes, and season with salt and pepper. Heat a skillet or frying pan, add the butter, and when it has melted, add the fish, skin side down. and cook for about 2 minutes until the skin is golden and crispy. Turn the fillets over and cook for another 1–2 minutes until the flesh flakes easily. Remove the dish from the oven, add the fish to the sauce, and sprinkle with the sesame seeds. Return the dish to the oven for 5 minutes. Remove from the oven, sprinkle the fish with chopped cilantro (coriander), add a squeeze of lemon juice, and serve immediately.

SOUPS

*

الحساء

CARROT
AND
CELERY SOUP

—

حساء الجزر والكرفس

Preparation time: 15 minutes
Cooking time: 20 minutes
Serves 4

3 tablespoons olive oil
1 onion, chopped
6 celery stalks, chopped
5 carrots, chopped
1 vegetable bouillon (stock) cube
salt and pepper

Heat the oil in a large saucepan, add the onion, celery, and
carrots, and cook over low heat, stirring occasionally, for
5 minutes until softened. Crumble in the vegetable bouillon
(stock) cube and pour in water to cover. Increase the heat to
medium and cook for 15–20 minutes or until the vegetables
are tender. Remove the pan from the heat, ladle the soup into
a blender or food processor, and process until smooth. Season
to taste with salt and pepper and serve immediately.

MONK SOUP

—

حساء الراهب

Preparation time: 30 minutes
Cooking time: 45 minutes
Serves 6–8

1 cup (8 oz/225 g) dried green lentils, rinsed
3 teaspoons salt
1¼ cups (6 oz/175 g) bulgur wheat, soaked in hot water
   for 20 minutes and drained
1¾ cups (6 oz/175 g) all-purpose (plain) flour
14 oz/400 g canned chickpeas, drained and rinsed
1 onion, grated
2 teaspoons ground cumin
1 teaspoon pepper
3 teaspoons salt
3 tablespoons chopped fresh parsley, plus extra to garnish
4 garlic cloves, crushed
5 tablespoons olive oil
juice of 1 lemon

Put the lentils into a large saucepan, pour in 8½ cups
(3½ pints/2 liters) boiling water, and bring back to a boil over
medium heat. Reduce the heat, cover, and simmer for about
20 minutes until tender. Meanwhile, combine the bulgur
wheat, flour, and chickpeas in a bowl then add the grated
onion, cumin, pepper, salt, and parsley, and mix well. Scoop
out walnut-size pieces of the mixture and roll them into balls
between the palms of your hands. There will be about 40. When
the lentils are nearly tender, add the chickpea balls to the pan,
replace the lid, and simmer for another 15 minutes. Combine
the crushed garlic, olive oil, and lemon juice. Pour this mixture
into the pan and simmer for another few minutes. Ladle
the soup and chickpea balls into warm bowls, garnish with
chopped parsley, and serve immediately.

SWEET ONION SOUP

حساء البصل الحلو

Preparation time: 20 minutes
Cooking time: 1 hour
Serves 2

1 tablespoon (½ oz/15 g) butter
1 tablespoon olive oil
3 onions, sliced
2 tablespoons balsamic vinegar
1 tablespoon brown sugar
generous 2 cups (18 fl oz/500 ml) hot beef stock
1 rosemary sprig
1 bay leaf
1 teaspoon Worcestershire sauce
juice of ½ lemon
salt and pepper

Melt the butter with the olive oil in a medium saucepan, add the onions, vinegar, and sugar, and cook over medium heat, stirring occasionally, for 25–30 minutes until the onions are very soft and caramelized. Pour in the stock, add the rosemary, bay leaf, and Worcestershire sauce, and simmer for 25 minutes until the soup has thickened. Remove and discard the herbs. Stir in the lemon juice, season with salt and pepper to taste, and serve immediately.

PEA AND FLAX SEED SOUP

حساء البازلاء وبذور الكتان

Preparation time: 10 minutes
Cooking time: 15 minutes
Serves 4

1 tablespoon olive oil
1 onion, chopped
1 vegetable bouillon (stock) cube
4 tablespoons ground flax seeds (linseeds)
1¾ cups (9 oz/250 g) frozen peas
1½ cups (5 oz/150 g) chopped snow peas (mangetouts)
   and sugar snaps
2 tablespoons chopped fresh mint
salt and pepper

Heat the oil in a large saucepan, add the onion, and cook over low heat, stirring occasionally, for 5 minutes until softened. Crumble in the bouillon (stock) cube, add the flax seeds (linseeds), and pour in 3¾ cups (1½ pints/900 ml) water. Increase the heat to medium and bring to a boil. Add the peas, snow peas (mangetouts), and sugar snaps and cook over medium heat for 10 minutes or until the vegetables are tender. Remove the pan from the heat, pour the soup into a blender or food processor, add the mint, and process until smooth. Season to taste with salt and pepper and serve immediately.

LENTIL
AND
GREENS SOUP

—

حساء العدس مع
الخضار الورقية اللبنانية

Preparation time: 15 minutes
Cooking time: 30 minutes
Serves 4

5 garlic cloves
4 tablespoons olive oil
1 onion, finely chopped
1¼ cups (10 oz/275 g) dried green lentils, rinsed
2 bunches Lebanese greens, stems removed, shredded
1 teaspoon seven spices seasoning
salt and pepper

Thinly slice 2 of the garlic cloves. Heat 1 tablespoon of the oil in a large saucepan, add the onion, and cook over low heat, stirring occasionally, for 5 minutes until soft but not browned. Add the garlic and cook for another minute. Add the lentils and pour in enough boiling water to cover. Cover the pan and cook for 20 minutes until the lentils are tender. Add the shredded greens and seven spices seasoning and cook for another 2 minutes. Crush the remaining garlic cloves with a little salt in a mortar with a pestle. Stir in the remaining olive oil, pour the mixture into the soup, and season with pepper. Serve immediately.

—

VEGETABLE
AND
LENTIL SOUP

—

حساء العدس والخضار

Preparation time: 15 minutes
Cooking time: 1 hour 10 minutes
Serves 6

1 tablespoon olive oil
2 onions, chopped
3 garlic cloves, sliced
5 carrots, chopped
1 parsnip, chopped
1 leek, sliced
1 rutabaga (swede), cubed
½ teaspoon seven spices seasoning
1 vegetable bouillon (stock) cube
scant 1 cup (7 oz/200 g) split peas, soaked in hot water
    for 5 minutes and drained
salt and pepper
chopped fresh parsley, to garnish

Heat the oil in a saucepan, add the onions, and cook over low heat, stirring occasionally, for 5 minutes or until softened but not browned. Add the garlic and cook for another few minutes. Add all the vegetables and the seasoning, crumble in the bouillon (stock) cube, cover, and cook for 5 minutes. Add the split peas to the pan and pour in boiling water to cover. Replace the lid and simmer for 1 hour, then remove the pan from the heat. Process the soup in a blender or purée with an immersion (stick) blender until smooth, adding more hot water if necessary. Pour the soup into a tureen, season to taste with salt and pepper, garnish with chopped parsley, and serve.

VEGETABLE
AND
BEAN SOUP

—

حساء الخضار والفاصولياء

Preparation time: 15 minutes
Cooking time: 35–40 minutes
Serves 4

3 tablespoons olive oil
1 onion, finely chopped
3 garlic cloves, crushed
4 carrots, sliced
1 cup (7 oz/200 g) dried split peas, rinsed
14 oz/400 g canned cranberry (borlotti) beans,
    drained and rinsed
3 cups (1¼ pints/750 ml) vegetable stock
3 tablespoons heavy (double) cream
salt and pepper

Heat the oil in a large saucepan, add the onion, and cook over low heat, stirring occasionally, for 5 minutes. Add the garlic and cook for another minute, then add the carrots and cook, stirring occasionally, for 5 minutes. Meanwhile, put the split peas in another pan, pour in boiling water to cover, and cook for 5 minutes. Drain and rinse the peas. Add the split peas to the pan of carrots and onion, then stir in the beans. Pour in the stock and simmer for 20 minutes. Season to taste, stir in the cream, and serve.

HEARTY
WINTER
WARMER ALL
BEAN SOUP

—

حساء الحبوب للشتاء البارد

Preparation time: 20 minutes, plus soaking time
Cooking time: 1 hour 30 minutes
Serves 4

¾ cup (6 oz/175 g) dried chickpeas, soaked overnight in water,
    then drained and rinsed
¾ cup (6 oz/175 g) dried green lentils
14 oz/400 g canned cranberry (borlotti) beans,
    drained and rinsed
11 oz/300 g canned sweet corn kernels, drained and rinsed
3 cups (1¼ pints/750 ml) vegetable stock
1 tablespoon olive oil
2 onions, finely chopped
4 garlic cloves, sliced
3 teaspoons salt
1 teaspoon pepper
1½ teaspoons seven spices seasoning
4 tablespoons ground flax seeds (linseeds)

Put the chickpeas into a large pan, pour in 4¼ cups (1¾ pints/ 1 liter) water, and bring to a boil. Reduce the heat, cover, and simmer for 45 minutes. Add the lentils and cook for another 25 minutes. Add the cranberry (borlotti) beans and sweet corn. Bring the stock to a boil in another pan. Gradually add the hot stock to the bean mixture, letting each addition be absorbed before adding the next. Meanwhile, heat the olive oil in a skillet, add the onions and garlic, and cook over medium-low heat for 7–8 minutes until softened. Stir the onion mixture into the beans, then the salt, pepper, seven spices seasoning, and ground flax seeds (linseeds). Cover and simmer for 10 minutes. Serve immediately.

ROASTED BUTTERNUT SQUASH SOUP WITH CHILI AND ALMONDS

PHOTO PAGE 171

—

حساء القرع المشوي مع الفلفل
الحار واللوز

Preparation time: 15 minutes
Cooking time: 45 minutes
Serves 4

1 butternut squash, peeled and cubed
2 tablespoons olive oil, plus extra for drizzling
1 onion, chopped
3 garlic cloves, crushed
¼ teaspoon smoked chili flakes, plus extra to garnish
½ teaspoon cumin seeds
3¾ cups (1½ pints/900 ml) chicken stock
2 apples, peeled and grated
scant ½ cup (3½ fl oz/100 ml) plain (natural) yogurt
3 tablespoons slivered (flaked) almonds, toasted
salt and freshly ground white pepper

Preheat the oven to 375°F/190°C/Gas Mark 5. Spread out the butternut squash in an ovenproof dish, drizzle with olive oil, and roast for 30–35 minutes. Meanwhile, heat the olive oil in a saucepan, add the onion, and cook over low heat, stirring occasionally, for 5 minutes until softened. Add the garlic, chili flakes, and cumin seeds and cook for another 2–3 minutes. Pour in the chicken stock, add the grated apple, and bring to a boil. Remove the butternut squash from the oven once it is tender and add to the pan. Using an immersion (stick) blender, purée the mixture until smooth. Stir in the yogurt and season well with salt and white pepper. Ladle into warm bowls and serve immediately sprinkled with toasted almonds and a pinch of chili flakes.

RED LENTIL AND CUMIN SOUP

—

حساء العدس الاحمر والكمون

Preparation time: 15 minutes
Cooking time: 30–35 minutes
Serves 4

1 tablespoon cumin seeds
2 tablespoons olive oil
1 onion, chopped
2 garlic cloves, crushed
1 teaspoon cayenne pepper
14 oz/400 g canned chopped tomatoes
4¼ cups (1¾ pints/1 liter) hot chicken stock
⅔ cup (5½ oz/160 g) dried red lentils
2 tablespoons plain (natural) yogurt
2 tablespoons chopped fresh cilantro (coriander)
salt and pepper

Dry-fry the cumin seeds in a skillet or frying pan for a few minutes until they release their aroma, then set aside. Heat the oil in a large pan, add the onion, and cook over low heat, stirring occasionally, for 5 minutes until softened. Add the garlic and cook for another 2 minutes. Add the cumin seeds, cayenne pepper, and chopped tomatoes, pour in the chicken stock, and bring to a boil over medium heat. Add the lentils, reduce the heat, and cook for 20 minutes. Stir in the yogurt and season with salt and pepper. Transfer the soup to a tureen, garnish with the chopped cilantro (coriander), and serve immediately.

ROASTED BUTTERNUT SQUASH SOUP WITH CHILI AND ALMONDS

SPICY TOMATO SOUP WITH VERMICELLI

PHOTO PAGE 173

—

حساء الطماطم بالبهارات مع
الشعيرية

Preparation time: 20 minutes
Cooking time: 50 minutes
Serves 4

2 tablespoons olive oil
1 onion, finely chopped
3 garlic cloves, crushed
1 carrot, diced
6 tomatoes, chopped
1 red bell pepper, halved, seeded, and diced
½ Scotch bonnet red chile, seeded and chopped
1 bay leaf
1 rosemary sprig
3 cups (1¼ pints/750 ml) vegetable stock
2 oz/50 g vermicelli
pinch of sugar
salt and pepper

Heat the oil in a large pan, add the onion, and cook over low heat, stirring occasionally, for 5 minutes until softened. Add the garlic and carrots and cook for another 5 minutes until the carrot starts to soften. Add the tomatoes, bell pepper, and chile and cook for a few minutes. Add the bay leaf and rosemary, pour in the stock, increase the heat to medium, and bring to a boil. Reduce the heat, cover, and simmer for 30 minutes. Remove the pan from the heat. Remove the bay leaf and rosemary sprig and ladle the soup into a blender or food processor. Pulse until smooth, then pour the soup back into the pan and bring back to a boil. Add the vermicelli, breaking it up as you work, and cook for 10 minutes. Season with a pinch of sugar and salt and pepper to taste and serve immediately.

CHICKPEA AND FLAX SEED SOUP

—

حساء الحمص وبذور الكتان

Preparation time: 15 minutes
Cooking time: 40 minutes
Serves 4–6

2 tablespoons olive oil,
1 onion, finely chopped
2 carrots, diced
1½ tablespoons whole flax seeds (linseeds)
½ teaspoon seven spices seasoning
½ teaspoon ground cumin
¼ teaspoon pepper
14 oz/400 g canned chickpeas, drained and rinsed
1 vegetable bouillon (stock) cube
1 teaspoon salt
chopped fresh cilantro (coriander), to garnish

Heat the oil in a large pan, add the onion, carrots, flax seeds (linseeds), seven spices seasoning, cumin, and pepper, and cook over low heat for 5–8 minutes until softened but not browned. Add the chickpeas and cook for a few minutes, then crumble in the bouillon (stock) cube and pour in 5 cups (2 pints/1.2 liters) boiling water. Increase the heat to medium and bring back to a boil. Reduce the heat and simmer for 30 minutes. Serve immediately garnished with chopped cilantro (coriander).

SPICY TOMATO SOUP WITH VERMICELLI

GARLIC, ALMOND, AND POMEGRANATE SOUP

GARLIC, ALMOND, AND POMEGRANATE SOUP

PHOTO PAGE 174

—

حساء الثوم واللوز

Preparation time: 20 minutes
Cooking time: 1 hour
Serves 4

1 garlic bulb
2 tablespoons olive oil, plus extra for drizzling
1 onion, chopped
3 celery stalks, chopped
¾ cup (3 oz/80 g) blanched almonds
2½ cups (1 pint/600 ml) chicken stock
1 bay leaf
scant ½ cup (3½ fl oz/100 ml) whole (full-fat) milk
2 tablespoons heavy (double) cream
1 tablespoon snipped fresh chives
1 tablespoon pomegranate seeds
1 tablespoon slivered (flaked) almonds, toasted
salt and freshly ground white pepper

Preheat the oven to 375°F/190°C/Gas Mark 5. Cut off the top of the garlic bulb and remove the loose papery skin. Put it in the middle of a square of foil, drizzle with olive oil, and wrap it up. Put it in the oven and roast for 30–40 minutes until soft. Meanwhile, heat the oil in a large saucepan, add the onion and celery, and cook over low heat, stirring occasionally, for 5 minutes until softened. Add the almonds, pour in the chicken stock, and bring to a boil. Remove the garlic, unwrap it, and let stand until cool enough to handle. Squeeze the garlic cloves into the pan, add the bay leaf, and simmer for 10 minutes. Remove the pan from the heat and remove and discard the bay leaf. Pour the soup into a blender or food processor and process until smooth. Return the soup to the pan, stir in the milk and cream, and heat through gently. Season well with salt and white pepper and just before serving, top with the chives, pomegranate seeds, and almonds.

KISHK SOUP

—

حساء الكشك

Preparation time: 5 minutes
Cooking time: 15–20 minutes
Serves 2

1 tablespoon olive oil
2 garlic cloves, crushed
8 oz/225 g kishk
bread, to serve

Heat the olive oil in a saucepan, add the garlic, and cook, stirring frequently, for 2 minutes. Pour in 2½ cups (1 pint/600 ml) water and whisk in the kishk. Simmer over low heat for 15 minutes, then serve with bread.

SHELLFISH AND FENNEL SOUP

PHOTO PAGE 177

—

حساء المحار والشومر

Preparation time: 30 minutes
Cooking time: 30 minutes
Serves 4–6

12 oz/350 g uncooked jumbo shrimp (king prawns)
1 lb 2 oz/500 g live mussels
1 teaspoon fennel seeds
1½ tablespoons (¾ oz/20 g) butter
2 tablespoons olive oil
1 leek, finely chopped
2 garlic cloves, crushed
⅔ cup (¼ pint/150 ml) white wine
1 fennel bulb, thinly sliced
4 tomatoes, chopped
1 bay leaf
3 cups (1¼ pints/750 ml) warm fish stock
pinch of saffron threads, lightly crushed
2 tarragon sprigs, chopped
2 tablespoons chopped fresh parsley
salt and freshly ground white pepper

Pull off the heads from the shrimp (prawns) and peel off the shells. Using a sharp knife, make a deep cut along the back of each shrimp, remove the black vein with the point of the knife, and discard. Scrub the mussels under cold running water and discard any with broken or damaged shells or that do not shut immediately when sharply tapped. Dry-fry the fennel seeds in a skillet or frying pan for a few minutes until they release their aroma, then tip onto a plate and set aside. Melt the butter with the olive oil in a large saucepan, add the leek, and cook over low heat, stirring occasionally, for 8–10 minutes until softened. Add the garlic and cook for another minute, then pour in the wine and cook until it has been absorbed. Add the fennel and tomatoes and cook for 2 minutes, then add the bay leaf and pour in the warm fish stock. Bring to a boil, add the saffron, and simmer for 10 minutes. Add the fennels seeds, shrimp, and mussels, cover, and cook for about 5 minutes until the mussels have opened and the shrimp are cooked through. Discard any mussels that remain shut. Stir in the tarragon and parsley, season to taste with salt and white pepper, and serve immediately.

SHELLFISH AND FENNEL SOUP

LAMB MEATBALL SOUP

PHOTO PAGE 179

حساء كرات لحم الغنم

Preparation time: 20 minutes
Cooking time: 30–40 minutes
Serves 4

9 oz/250 g ground (minced) lamb
I onion, grated
I½ tablespoons all-purpose (plain) flour
I teaspoon seven spices seasoning
14 oz/400 g canned chopped tomatoes
4¼ cups (1¾ pints/I liter) vegetable stock
I tablespoon brown sugar
II oz/300 g canned sweet corn kernels, drained and rinsed
salt and pepper

Combine the lamb, grated onion, and flour in a bowl. Add the seven spices seasoning, season well with salt and pepper, and mix thoroughly. Dampen your hands, take 2 tablespoons of the mixture, and roll into a small ball between your palms. Continue making meatballs in this way until all the mixture has been used. Pour the tomatoes and vegetable stock into a large saucepan and stir in the sugar. Bring to a boil and simmer for 15 minutes. Add the meatballs and simmer for another 15–20 minutes until the meat is cooked through. Add the sweet corn and heat through for 2 minutes. Taste and adjust the seasoning, if necessary, and serve immediately.

LENTIL AND LAMB SOUP

حساء العدس ولحم الغنم

Preparation time: 20 minutes
Cooking time: I hour
Serves 4

3 tablespoons olive oil
I onion, chopped
2 garlic cloves, chopped
I lb 2 oz/500 g stewing lamb, cut into small cubes
7½ cups (3 pints/1.75 liters) hot chicken stock
I bay leaf
2 thyme sprigs
I rosemary sprig
⅔ cup (5 oz/150 g) dried green lentils
I cup (2 oz/50 g) chopped sun-dried tomatoes
2 cups (2 oz/50 g) baby spinach
2 tablespoons chopped fresh mint
salt and pepper

Heat the oil in a large saucepan, add the onion and garlic, and cook over low heat, stirring occasionally, for 5 minutes until softened. Add the lamb, increase the heat to medium, and cook, stirring frequently, for 8–10 minutes until evenly browned. Pour in the hot stock and add all the herbs. Bring to a boil, add the lentils, reduce the heat, and simmer for 40–50 minutes until the lentils and lamb are tender. Add extra water during cooking, if necessary. Remove and discard the bay leaf, thyme, and rosemary sprigs. Stir the sun-dried tomatoes, spinach, and mint into the soup, season with salt and pepper, and serve immediately.

LAMB MEATBALL SOUP

CHICKEN
AND
YOGURT SOUP
WITH
CHILI AND
LEMON
—

حساء الدجاج والزبادي مع التوابل
الحارة والليمون

Preparation time: 20 minutes
Cooking time: 30–35 minutes
Serves 6

1½ tablespoons (¾ oz/20 g) butter
2 tablespoons olive oil
1 leek, sliced
2 garlic cloves, crushed
1 bay leaf
5 cups (2 pints/1.2 liters) hot chicken stock
1 lb 2 oz/500 g skinless, boneless chicken breasts, cut in strips
1 teaspoon cornstarch (cornflour)
⅔ cup (¼ pint/150 ml) plain (natural) yogurt
7 oz/200 g canned chickpeas, drained and rinsed
¼ teaspoon chili flakes
juice of 1 lemon
2 tablespoons chopped fresh cilantro (coriander)
pinch of paprika
salt and pepper

Melt the butter with the oil in a large saucepan, add the leek, and cook over low heat for 8–10 minutes. Add the garlic and bay leaf and cook for another minute. Increase the heat, pour in the stock, and bring to a boil. Add the chicken, reduce the heat, and simmer for 15 minutes. Remove the chicken from the pan and set aside. Mix the cornstarch (cornflour) to a paste with a little water and add to the pan. Bring back to a boil, and cook until thickened. Stir in the yogurt and chickpeas and return the chicken to the pan. Add the chili flakes and lemon juice and season. Add the cilantro (coriander) and paprika, and serve.

CHICKEN
SOUP
—

حساء الدجاج

Preparation time: 15 minutes
Cooking time: 25 minutes
Serves 4

2 tablespoons olive oil
1 onion, finely chopped
1 celery stalk, finely chopped
4 tablespoons tomato paste (purée)
1 teaspoon seven spices seasoning
1 cinnamon stick
3 cups (1¼ pints/750 ml) hot chicken stock
¾ cup (5½ oz/160 g) long grain rice, rinsed
2 cooked skinless, boneless chicken breasts, shredded
salt and pepper
large handful chopped fresh parsley, to garnish

Heat the oil in a large pan, add the onion and celery, and cook over low heat, stirring occasionally, for 5 minutes until softened. Add the tomato paste (purée), seven spices seasoning, and cinnamon stick and cook for another minute. Add the stock and rice. Bring to a boil and cook for 15 minutes until the rice is nearly tender, then add the chicken, and cook for 5 minutes more. Season, remove the cinnamon stick, pour the soup into a tureen, garnish with parsley, and serve.

CREAMY CHICKEN AND VERMICELLI SOUP

حساء كريما الدجاج بالشعيرية

Preparation time: 20 minutes
Cooking time: 35–40 minutes
Serves 4–6

2 tablespoons olive oil
1 onion, chopped
1 carrot, diced
1 celery stalk, chopped
3 thyme sprigs
1 bay leaf
4¼ cups (1¾ pints/1 liter) chicken stock
4 skinless chicken thighs and 4 skinless chicken drumsticks
3 oz/80 g vermicelli
1 cup (8 fl oz/250 ml) plain (natural) yogurt
3 tablespoons chopped fresh parsley
2 tarragon sprigs, chopped
salt and pepper

Heat the oil in a large pan, add the onion, carrot, celery, and thyme, and cook over medium heat for 5 minutes. Add the bay leaf and stock, and bring to a boil. Add the chicken, cover, and simmer for 25 minutes. When the chicken is cooked remove it from the pan, shred the meat from the bones, and set aside. Remove the thyme and bay leaf. Add the vermicelli to the pan and cook for 8 minutes until tender. Return the chicken to the pan, stir in the yogurt, parsley and tarragon, season and serve.

RABBIT SOUP

حساء لحم الارنب

Preparation time: 30 minutes
Cooking time: 1 hour 30 minutes
Serves 6

1½ tablespoons (¾ oz/20 g) butter
2 tablespoons olive oil
1 onion, chopped
1 leek, sliced
2 celery stalks, diced
1 carrot, diced
4¼ cups (1¾ pints/1 liter) chicken stock
1 x 1 lb 10 oz/750 g rabbit, cut into pieces
scant ¾ cup (5 oz/150 g) basmati or long grain rice
4 tablespoons tomato paste (purée)
1 tablespoon brown sugar
1 teaspoon seven spices seasoning
2 tablespoons chopped fresh parsley
2 tarragon sprigs, chopped
salt and pepper

Melt the butter and oil in a pan, add the onion and leek, and cook over low heat for 5 minutes. Add the celery and carrot and cook for a few minutes more. Add the stock and rabbit and simmer, covered, for 1 hour. Lift out the rabbit. Add the rice, tomato paste (purée), brown sugar, and seven spices seasoning and cook for 20 minutes. Meanwhile, shred the rabbit meat and discard the bones. Return the meat to the pan, season, and add the parsley and tarragon. Serve immediately.

FISH

✦

السمك

ف السمك

FISH
RAGOUT

يخني السمك

Preparation time: 20 minutes
Cooking time: 30–40 minutes
Serves 4

3 tablespoons olive oil
1 onion, chopped
2 celery stalks, chopped
1 fennel bulb, sliced
1 red bell pepper, seeded and sliced
2 garlic cloves, crushed
⅔ cup (¼ pint/150 ml) white wine
3 cups (1¼ pints/750 ml) fish stock
1 bay leaf
14 oz/400 g canned chopped tomatoes
2 tablespoons tomato paste (purée)
1 lb/450 g monkfish fillet, cut into chunks
7 oz/200 g cod fillet, skinned and cut into chunks
14 oz/400g canned lima (butter) beans, drained and rinsed
2 tablespoons chopped fresh cilantro (coriander)
salt and pepper

Heat the olive oil in a large saucepan, add the onion, and cook over low heat, stirring occasionally, for 5 minutes until softened but not browned. Add the celery, fennel, bell pepper, and garlic and cook, stirring occasionally, for another 10 minutes. Pour in the white wine, increase the heat to medium-high, and cook until it has been absorbed. Pour in the fish stock, add the bay leaf, tomatoes, and tomato paste (purée), and bring to a boil. Add the fish, reduce the heat, cover, and simmer for 10 minutes. Add the beans, stir well, replace the lid, and simmer for another 5 minutes. Remove and discard the bay leaf. Season well with salt and pepper, sprinkle with the cilantro (coriander), and serve.

FISH PIE

فطيرة السمك

Preparation time: 20 minues
Cooking time: 30–40 minutes
Serves 4–6

1 lb 10 oz/750 g potatoes, diced
3 cups (1¼ pints/750 ml) whole (full-fat) milk
6 tablespoons (3 oz/80 g) butter, melted
2 teaspoons dried thyme
2 tablespoons chopped fresh parsley
grated zest of 1 lemon
12 oz/350 g cod or salmon fillet
12 oz/350g smoked white fish fillet
4 black peppercorns
1 bay leaf
4 tablespoons (2 oz/50 g) butter
½ cup (2 oz/50 g) all-purpose (plain) flour
1½ cups (6 oz/175 g) grated cheddar cheese
7 oz/200 g small cooked shrimp (prawns), peeled
5 tablespoons dried breadcrumbs
salt and pepper

Put the potatoes in a large saucepan, add a pinch of salt, and pour in water to cover. Bring to a boil and cook for about 20 minutes, until very tender. Meanwhile, heat 5 tablespoons of the milk in a small saucepan until warm, then remove from the heat. Drain the potatoes, return to the pan and mash with the butter and warm milk. Add the thyme, parsley, and lemon zest and season with salt and pepper. Put both types of fish into a wide saucepan, pour in the remaining milk, add the black peppercorns and bay leaf and bring just to a boil. Reduce the heat so that the surface of the liquid barely bubbles and poach for 8–10 minutes, until the fish flakes easily. Remove the pan from the heat, lift out the fish with a spatula (fish slice) and let cool slightly. Strain the milk into a small bowl. When the fish is cool enough to handle, remove and discard the skin and flake the flesh. Melt the butter in a large saucepan, stir in the flour and cook, stirring constantly, for 1 minute. Remove the pan from the heat and gradually stir in the reserved milk. Return the pan to medium heat and bring just to a boil, stirring constantly. Stir until the sauce thickens, then remove the pan from the heat, stir in the grated cheese, and season with salt and pepper. Preheat the broiler (grill). Stir the flaked fish and shrimp (prawns) into the sauce, then spoon the mixture into a flameproof dish. Spoon the mashed potato evenly over the top and sprinkle with the dried breadcrumbs. Put the dish under the hot broiler and cook until the topping in golden and crisp. Serve immediately.

SAFFRON
AND
CILANTRO
FISH STEW

PHOTO PAGE 189

—

يخني السمك مع
الزعفران والكزبرة

Preparation time: 20 minutes
Cooking time: 15 minutes
Serves 4

3 tablespoons olive oil
1 onion, finely chopped
2 celery stalks, finely chopped
1 fennel bulb, sliced
4 tomatoes, chopped
2 red bell peppers, seeded and sliced
3¾ cups (1½ pint/900 ml) vegetable stock
1½ lb/700 g white fish, such as cod or haddock, cut into chunks
8 uncooked jumbo shrimp (king prawns), peeled and deveined
pinch of saffron threads
½ teaspoon ground turmeric
¼ teaspoon chili flakes
juice of 1 lemon
2 tablespoons chopped fresh cilantro (coriander)
salt and pepper
bread, to serve

Heat the oil in a large saucepan, add the onion, celery, and fennel, and cook over medium heat, stirring occasionally, for 5 minutes until softened but not browned. Add the tomatoes and bell peppers and cook for 1 minute more. Pour in the stock and bring to a boil. Add the fish, shrimp (prawns), and all the spices. Reduce the heat and simmer for 5–10 minutes until the fish is slightly opaque in the middle and flakes easily. Stir in lemon juice to taste and the cilantro (coriander). Season to taste with salt and pepper and serve in bowls with bread.

SAFFRON AND CILANTRO (CORIANDER) FISH STEW

FRIED COD
WITH
CARAMELIZED
ONIONS
AND
RICE

—

صيادية بسمك القد

Preparation time: 15–20 minutes
Cooking time: 30–40 minutes
Serves 2

2 tablespoons (1 oz/25 g) butter
1 tablespoon olive oil
2 onions, sliced
2 tablespoons brown sugar
scant ¾ cup (5 oz/150 g) basmati or long grain rice, rinsed
2 garlic cloves, finely chopped
3 tomatoes, seeded and diced
juice of 1 lemon
2 tablespoons capers, drained and rinsed
2 x 5 oz/150 g cod loin fillets, skinned
2 tablespoons chopped fresh parsley
salt and pepper

Melt half the butter with half the olive oil in a skillet or frying pan, add the onions and sugar, and cook over medium heat, stirring frequently, for 15–20 minutes until the onions start to caramelize. Meanwhile, put the rice into a saucepan, pour in boiling water to cover, and bring back to a boil. Reduce the heat, cover, and simmer for 10–12 minutes or until the water has been absorbed and the rice is tender. Stir the rice into the caramelized onions and set aside. Heat the remaining oil in another skillet or frying pan, add the garlic, and cook over low heat, stirring occasionally, for 1–2 minutes. Add the tomatoes, lemon juice, and capers and cook over medium heat for 10 minutes, then transfer the mixture to a bowl and keep warm. Melt the remaining butter in the skillet or frying pan, add the fish and cook for 3–4 minutes on each side until the flesh flakes easily. Season with salt and pepper and sprinkle with chopped parsley. To serve, divide the rice and onions between 2 individual plates, put a cod fillet on top, and spoon the tomato and caper sauce over them.

SMOKED HADDOCK AND RICE

سمك الحدوق المدخن
مع الارز

Preparation time: 20 minutes
Cooking time: 45 minutes
Serves 4

11 oz/300 g smoked haddock fillet
2 tablespoons olive oil
2 onions, chopped
2 carrots, chopped
3 cups (7 oz/200 g) sliced mushrooms,
2 tomatoes, chopped
scant 1 cup (6 oz/175 g) basmati or long grain rice, rinsed
¼ teaspoon seven spices seasoning
¼ teaspoon black pepper
¼ teaspoon ground cumin
1 teaspoon medium curry powder
1 teaspoon salt
½ cup (2 oz/50 g) pine nuts, toasted

Put the fish into a wide saucepan, pour in water to cover, and bring just to a boil. Reduce the heat so that the surface barely bubbles and poach the fish for about 10 minutes, until the flesh flakes easily. Lift out the fish with a spatula (fish slice) and reserve the cooking liquid. Heat the oil in a large saucepan, add the onions, and cook over low heat, stirring occasionally, for 5 minutes until softened. Add the carrots and mushrooms and cook for another few minutes, then add the tomatoes and cook for another 5 minutes. Remove and discard the skin from the smoked haddock, flake the flesh into bite-size pieces, and add to the vegetables. Add the rice, seven spices seasoning, pepper, cumin, curry powder, and salt, pour in 3½ cups (1¾ pints/800 ml) of the reserved cooking liquid, and bring to a boil. Reduce the heat, cover, and cook for 20–25 minutes until the rice is tender and all the liquid has been absorbed. Transfer to a warm serving dish, garnish with the pine nuts, and serve immediately.

HADDOCK
WITH
ONIONS, RICE,
AND
WALNUTS

—

سمك الحدوق مع البصل
والارز والجوز

Preparation time: 10 minutes
Cooking time: 30–40 minutes
Serves 4

1 cup (7 oz/200 g) basmati or long grain rice
2 haddock fillets
3 peppercorns
1 bay leaf
2 tablespoons olive oil
2 onions, thinly sliced
1 teaspoon ground cumin
1 teaspoon ground coriander
1 teaspoon curry powder
1 bunch of fresh cilantro (coriander), chopped
2 cups (2 oz/50 g) baby spinach
½ cup (2 oz/50 g) chopped walnuts
salt and pepper

Cook the rice in a large saucepan of salted boiling water for 15–20 minutes until tender, then drain, rinse with boiling water, and set aside. Meanwhile, bring a wide saucepan of water to a boil. Add the haddock, peppercorns, and bay leaf, reduce the heat so that the surface of the water is barely bubbling, and poach the fish for 8–10 minutes until the flesh flakes easily. Transfer the fish to a dish with a spatula (fish slice). Remove and discard the skin and flake the flesh into bite-size pieces. Heat the oil in a large pan, add the onions, and cook over low heat, stirring occasionally, for 10–15 minutes until golden. Stir in the cumin, ground coriander, and curry powder and cook for another few minutes. Add the rice and mix well, then add the haddock, cilantro (coriander), and spinach and mix again. Season well with salt and pepper, transfer to a warm serving dish, sprinkle with the walnuts, and serve.

SOLE FILLETS
WITH
TAHINI,
PAPRIKA
AND
PINE NUTS

—

شرائح سمك الصول مع الطحينة
والفلفل الحلو والصنوبر

Preparation time: 15–20 minutes
Cooking time: 6 minutes
Serves 4

1 tablespoon (½ oz/15 g) butter
1 tablespoon olive oil
4 lemon sole fillets, skinned
pinch of paprika
¾ cup (3 oz/80 g) pine nuts, toasted
salt and pepper

For the sauce
1 tablespoon olive oil
1 shallot, finely chopped
2 garlic cloves, crushed
5 tablespoons tahini
juice of 1 lemon

First make the sauce. Heat the oil in a small skillet or frying pan, add the shallot, and cook over low heat, stirring occasionally, for 4–5 minutes until softened but not browned. Add the garlic and cook for another minute. Add the tahini and lemon juice, stir until the mixture thickens to a paste, then whisk in 6 tablespoons water. Remove the pan from the heat and keep warm. Melt the butter with the oil in another skillet or frying pan. Season the fish fillets with salt and pepper, add to the pan, and cook gently for 3 minutes on each side. Pour the tahini sauce over the fish, sprinkle with paprika to taste and the toasted pine nuts, and serve immediately.

FLOUNDER COATED IN TAHINI AND BREADCRUMBS

—

سمك موسى مغلف بالطحينة
وفتات الخبز اليابس

Preparation time: 20 minutes
Cooking time: 2–3 minutes
Serves 2

2 slices of wheat (brown) bread, crusts removed
4 tablespoons grated Parmesan cheese
2 tablespoons chopped fresh parsley
pinch of paprika
2 flounder or plaice fillets
2 tablespoons tahini
all-purpose (plain) flour, for dusting
1 egg, lightly beaten
vegetable oil, for pan-frying
salt and pepper
Tabbouli (see page 54), to serve

Put the bread into a food processor or blender and process to fine crumbs, then tip into a bowl. Stir in the Parmesan, parsley, and paprika and season with salt and pepper. Brush both sides of the fish fillets with tahini, then dip them in the flour, beaten egg, and, finally, in the breadcrumb mixture. Heat the oil in shallow skillet or frying pan, add the fish, and cook for 2–3 minutes on each side until golden. Remove with a spatula (fish slice) and serve immediately with the Tabbouli.

SALMON WITH SUMAC CRUST, CORIANDER AND GINGER DRESSING

—

سلمون مغمس بالسماق مع
الكزبرة والزنجبيل

Preparation time: 10 minutes
Cooking time: 4 minutes
Serves 2

3 tablespoons sumac
1 teaspoon dill
3 tablespoons olive oil
sea salt
2 salmon fillets, skinned
salad greens (leaves), to serve

For the dressing
juice of ½ orange
3 tablespoons extra virgin olive oil
2 tablespoons minced fresh ginger
1 teaspoon coriander seeds, crushed
2 tablespoons chopped fresh cilantro (coriander)
salt and pepper

Mix together the sumac, dill, olive oil, and a pinch of sea salt in a small bowl, then rub the mixture all over the salmon fillets. Set aside. To make the dressing, mix together all the ingredients in a bowl and season with salt and pepper. Heat a skillet or frying pan, add the oil and, when it is hot, add the salmon fillets. Cook over medium-low heat for 2 minutes on each side. Transfer the fish to warm plates, drizzle with the dressing, and serve with salad greens (leaves).

SALMON
FISH CAKES
WITH
SESAME SEED
AND
SUMAC CRUMB

كعك سمك
السلمون مع السمسم
والسماق

Preparation time: 10 minutes, plus chilling time
Cooking time: 1 hour 15 minutes
Serves 2

350 g baking potatoes
2 x 5 oz/150 g salmon fillets, skinned
1 x 5 oz/150 g cod fillet, skinned
1 bay leaf
4 black peppercorns
3 tablespoons chopped parsley
1¼ cups (2½ oz/65 g) panko breadcrumbs
2 tablespoons sesame seeds, toasted
1 tablespoon sumac
all-purpose (plain) flour, for dusting
2 eggs, lightly beaten
4 tablespoons sunflower or vegetable oil
garlic dip, to serve

Preheat the oven to 400°F/200°C/Gas Mark 6. Prick the potatoes with a fork, put into the oven, and bake for 1 hour until tender. Remove the potatoes from the oven and let stand until cool enough to handle, then halve and scoop out the flesh into a bowl. Meanwhile, bring a wide saucepan of water to a boil, add the bay leaf and peppercorns, then add the salmon and cod. Reduce the heat so that the surface of the water is barely bubbling and poach the fish for 10–15 minutes until the flesh flakes easily. Lift out the fish with a spatula (fish slice) and flake the flesh, then mix it with the potato. Season well with salt and pepper and add the chopped parsley. Mix together the panko breadcrumbs, sumac, and sesame seeds on a plate. Spread out the flour on another plate. Divide the fish mixture into 4 equal pieces and shape each into a patty with your hands. Dust each fish cake with flour, then dip into the beaten eggs, and, finally, coat in the breadcrumb mixture. Put the fish cakes on a baking sheet and chill in the refrigerator for 1 hour. Heat the oil in a skillet or frying pan over medium heat, add the fish cakes, in batches if necessary, and cook for 5 minutes on each side until golden. Remove the fish cakes from pan and drain on paper towels, then transfer to 2 warm plates and serve immediately with a garlic dip.

SEA BASS FILLETS WITH FREEKEH AND CRISPY ONIONS

شرائح سمك القاروص
مع الفريكة والبصل
المقرمش

Preparation time: 25 minutes
Cooking time: 30 minutes
Serves 4

2 cups (12 oz/350 g) freekeh
1 teaspoon salt
3 tablespoons olive oil
2 tablespoons chopped fresh parsley
2 tablespoons chopped fresh mint
8–10 fresh mint leaves, torn
1 tablespoon capers, drained and rinsed
5 small sweet pickled cucumbers (gherkins), chopped
sunflower oil, for frying
2 onions, sliced
4 sea bass fillets
2 tablespoons (1 oz/25 g) butter
juice of 1 lemon
sea salt
1 lemon, cut into wedges, to garnish

Put the freekeh into a saucepan, pour in 5 cups (2 pints/1.2 liters) boiling water, add the salt and 2 tablespoons of the olive oil, and bring to a boil. Reduce the heat and simmer for 30 minutes until tender. Meanwhile, mix together all the herbs, the capers, and pickled cucumbers (gherkins) in a bowl. When the freekeh is tender, drain, rinse with cold water, and drain well again. Add to the herb mixture, toss well, and set aside. Pour sunflower oil into a shallow saucepan to a depth of ¾ inch/2 cm and heat. Add the onions and cook over medium-high heat, stirring occasionally, until crispy. Remove with a slotted spoon and drain on paper towels. Score the skin of the sea bass with 3 slashes, rub with sea salt and brush with the remaining olive oil. Heat a skillet or frying pan, add the butter, and when it has nearly melted, add the fish fillets skin side down. Cook for 3 minutes until the skin is crisp, then turn the fillets over and cook the other side for 2 minutes. Dress the freekeh salad with a lemon juice to taste and season well with salt and pepper, then divide among 4 individual plates. Put the fish fillets on top, sprinkle with the crispy onions, and serve immediately.

ROASTED SEA BASS AND TAHINI SAUCE

PHOTO PAGE 201

—

سمك القاروص المشوي مع صلصة
الطحينة

Preparation time: 15 minutes
Cooking time: 35–40 minutes
Serves 2

2 x 1 lb-2-oz/500 g sea bass spines trimmed, scaled, and cleaned
2 tablespoons olive oil
¼ cup (1 oz/25 g) pine nuts, toasted
2 tablespoons chopped fresh parsley

For the sauce
5 garlic cloves, peeled
pinch of salt
1 hot green chile, seeded (optional) and finely chopped
juice of 1 lemon
6 tablespoons tahini
½ teaspoon chili flakes
¼ teaspoon black pepper

Preheat the oven to 375°F/190°C/Gas Mark 5. Put the fish into a roasting pan. Gently heat the olive oil in a small saucepan or in the microwave until warm, then brush it over the fish. Roast for 15 minutes, then turn the fish over and roast for another 10 minutes. Meanwhile, make the sauce. Crush the garlic cloves with the salt in a mortar with a pestle. Add the chopped chile, lemon juice, and tahini, and mix well. Transfer to a bowl and stir in ½ cup (4 fl oz/120 ml) water, then add the chili flakes and black pepper. Remove the roasting pan from the oven and pour the sauce over the fish. Return to the oven and cook for another 5–10 minutes. Remove from the oven, sprinkle with toasted pine nuts and chopped parsley, and serve immediately.

ROASTED SEA BASS AND TAHINI SAUCE

SAMAK MESHWI

SAMAK MESHWI
(BROILED SEA BASS)

PHOTO PAGE 202

—

سمك مشوي

Preparation time: 10 minutes
Cooking time: 8–10 minutes
Serves 4

juice of 2 lemons
2 tablespoons olive oil
4 garlic cloves, crushed
4 small sea bass, fins trimmed, scaled, and cleaned
2 teaspoons salt
2 teaspoons pepper
4 teaspoons ground cumin
2 lemons, halved
ground sumac, for sprinkling

Mix together the lemon juice, olive oil, and garlic in a small bowl. Using a sharp knife, make 3 diagonal slashes on each side of each fish. Mix together the salt, pepper, and cumin in a small bowl and rub the mixture into the fish, inside and out. Brush one side of each fish with the lemon mixture and place them, brushed side down, on the grill of a hot barbecue. Grill for about 4 minutes, then brush the second side of each fish with the lemon mixture, turn them over and grill for another 4 minutes. Meanwhile, put the lemon halves, cut side down, on the grill. Transfer the fish to serving plates and sprinkle with a little sumac. Serve immediately with the grilled lemons for squeezing.

SAMAK MESHWI
(BAKED SEA BASS)

—

سمك مشوي

Preparation time: 20–25 minutes
Cooking time: 25 minutes
Serves 2

2 tablespoons olive oil, plus extra for brushing
1 green bell pepper, seeded and diced
3 scallions (spring onions), chopped
1 small bunch of fresh cilantro (coriander), chopped
2 x 1 lb 2-oz/500 g sea bass, fins trimmed, scaled, and cleaned
1 teaspoon salt
½ teaspoon seven spices seasoning
¼ teaspoon ground cinnamon
¼ teaspoon ground allspice
1 lemon, cut into wedges
green bean and garlic salad, to serve

Preheat the oven to 400°F/200°C/Gas Mark 6. Brush a baking sheet with oil. Heat the olive oil in a skillet or frying pan, add the bell pepper and scallions (spring onions, and cook over low heat, stirring occasionally, for 5–8 minutes until softened. Stir in the cilantro (coriander), remove from the heat, and set aside. Score the skin of the fish, then brush all over with olive oil and rub in the salt and spices. Divide the bell pepper and scallion mixture and half the lemon wedges between the cavities of the sea bass. Put the fish onto the prepared baking sheet and roast for 25 minutes until the flesh flakes easily. Transfer the fish to individual plates, garnish with the remaining lemon wedges, and serve warm with green bean and garlic salad.

SEA BASS WITH TAHINI AND CHILI SAUCE TOPPED WITH NUTS

سمك القاروص مع الطحينة
والصلصة الحارة

Preparation time: 20–25 minutes
Cooking time: 5–10 minutes
Serves 4

4 sea bass fillets
olive oil, for brushing
1 teaspoon sea salt
1 tablespoon (½ oz/15 g) butter
2 tablespoons fresh chopped cilantro (coriander)
1 lemon, cut into wedges

For the sauce
5 tablespoons tahini
juice of 1 lemon
1 teaspoon olive oil
3 garlic cloves, chopped
1 red chile, seeded and finely chopped
½ teaspoon chili powder
½ teaspoon cayenne pepper
1 small bunch fresh cilantro (coriander), chopped
3 tablespoons pine nuts, toasted
2 tablespoons chopped walnuts

Put the fish fillets on a board, skin side uppermost, and score the skin 3 times with a sharp knife. Brush olive oil all over the fish fillets, rub salt into the skin and flesh, and set aside. To make the sauce, whisk together the tahini, lemon juice, and 6 tablespoons water to a smooth paste in a bowl. Heat the oil in a skillet or frying pan, add the garlic, chopped chile, chili powder, and cayenne pepper, and cook for 1 minute. Add the pine nuts, walnuts, and tahini mixture. Cook, stirring, for about 1 minute until the sauce starts to thicken. Remove the pan from the heat, stir in the cilantro (coriander), set aside, and keep warm. Heat a heavy skillet or frying pan, then add the butter and, when it has melted, lay the fish fillets skin side down in the pan. Cook for 2–3 minutes until the skin is golden and crispy. Carefully turn the fillets over and cook the flesh side for another 2 minutes until the flesh is opaque and flakes easily. Transfer the fish fillets to warm individual plates. Drizzled with the tahini and chili sauce, sprinkle with the cilantro, and garnish with lemon wedges. Serve immediately.

SARDINES
AND
GARLIC

—

سردين مع الثوم وصلصة
الطحينة

Preparation time: 10 minutes
Cooking time: 5 minutes
Serves 4

8 sardines, about 1 lb-2-oz/500 g, scaled, cleaned,
    and heads removed
2 tablespoons olive oil
5 tablespoons tahini
4 garlic cloves, crushed
½ teaspoon salt
juice of 1 lemon
2 tablespoons chopped fresh parsley
salt
bread, to serve

Rub the sardines with salt. Heat the oil a large skillet or frying pan, add the sardines, and cook over medium heat, turning once, for about 5 minutes until crispy. Remove from the pan and drain on paper towels. Mix together the tahini, garlic, ½ teaspoon salt, and lemon juice in a bowl, whisk in 6 tablespoons water, and continue to whisk until smooth. Stir in the parsley. Put the crispy sardines on individual plates, spoon the sauce on the side, and serve immediately with bread.

SEA BREAM
WITH
ROASTED
EGGPLANT
AND
TOMATOES

—

شبوط مع الباذنجان المشوي
والطماطم

Preparation time: 20 minutes
Cooking time: 35 minutes
Serves 2

1 eggplant (aubergine), cubed
2 tomatoes, halved
3 garlic cloves, crushed
4 tablespoons olive oil, plus extra for brushing
2 teaspoons cumin seeds
2 rosemary sprigs
pinch of sea salt
2 sea bream fillets
olive oil
juice of 1 lemon
2 tablespoons chopped fresh parsley
salt and pepper

Preheat the oven to 400°F/200°C/Gas Mark 6. Put the eggplant (aubergine) cubes and tomatoes into a roasting pan, add the garlic cloves, and pour over the olive oil. Toss well, then add the cumin seeds, rosemary, and sea salt. Roast for 35 minutes, shaking the pan halfway through the cooking time. Meanwhile, brush the fish fillets with olive oil and season well with salt and pepper. Heat a skillet or frying pan, add the fish fillets skin side down, and cook for 3 minutes. Turn them over and cook the other side for another 2 minutes. Add lemon juice to taste and transfer to warm individual plates. Garnish with chopped parsley and serve with the roasted eggplant and tomatoes.

SAFFRON MONKFISH AND RICE

SAFFRON MONKFISH AND RICE

PHOTO PAGE 206

—

سمك الراهب بالزعفران والارز

Preparation time: 20 minutes
Cooking time: 25–30 minutes
Serves 2

1 x 7 oz/200 g monkfish fillet, cubed
2 tablespoons olive oil, plus extra for drizzling
1 tablespoon sumac
1 tablespoon (½ oz/15 g) butter
1 teaspoon cumin seeds
1 onion, sliced
½ teaspoon ground turmeric
pinch of saffron threads
¾ cup (5 oz/150 g) basmati or long grain rice, rinsed
scant 1 cup (7 fl oz/200 ml) warm fish stock
2 tablespoons chopped fresh parsley
salt and freshly ground white pepper

Put the monkfish into a bowl, drizzle with olive oil, sprinkle with the sumac, and toss gently to coat. Melt the butter in a skillet or frying pan, add the monkfish, and cook, turning frequently, for 3–4 minutes. Remove from the heat, set aside, and keep warm. Dry-fry the cumin seeds in a saucepan for a few minutes until they release their aroma. Add the olive oil and, when it is hot, add the onion. Cook over low heat, stirring occasionally, for 5 minutes until softened but not browned. Stir in the turmeric, saffron, and rice and to cook for another few minutes. Increase the heat, pour in the warm fish stock, and bring to a boil. Cover the pan, reduce the heat, and cook for 20–25 minutes until the rice is tender and the liquid has been absorbed. Stir in the parsley and season well with salt and white pepper. Transfer to a warm serving dish, top with the monkfish, and serve immediately.

FISH
WITH
PRESERVED
LEMON
AND
GARLIC

PHOTO PAGE 209

—

سمك السلطان ابراهيم مع
الليمون المحفوظ والثوم

Preparation time: 10 minutes
Cooking time: 20 minutes
Serves 2

olive oil, for brushing
2 x 8-10 oz/225-275 g red snapper or mullet,
    scaled and cleaned
1 preserved lemon, quartered
6 unpeeled garlic cloves, crushed
2 bay leaves
1 small bunch of fresh parsley
sea salt
rice or vermicelli, to serve

Preheat the oven to 400°F/200°C/Gas Mark 6. Brush the olive oil all over the fish and sprinkle with sea salt. Fill the cavities with the preserved lemon, garlic, bay leaves, and parsley. Put the fish in to a roasting pan and bake for 20 minutes. Remove from the oven, transfer to warm plates, and serve immediately with rice or vermicelli.

FISH
WITH
NUT FILLING

—

سمك السلطان ابراهيم محشي
بالمكسرات

Preparation time: 15 minutes
Cooking time: 30–40 minutes
Serves 2

2 x 8 oz/225 g red snapper or mullet, scaled and cleaned
2 tablespoons olive oil, plus extra for brushing
1 onion, chopped
scant 1 cup (6 oz/175 g) or long grain rice, rinsed
1½ cups (12 fl oz/350 ml) hot vegetable stock
3 tablespoons almonds, toasted
3 tablespoons pine nuts, toasted
1 teaspoon seven spices seasoning
2 tablespoons chopped fresh parsley
1 lemon, cut into wedges
salt and pepper

Preheat the oven to 400°F/200°C/Gas Mark 6. Put the fish on a baking sheet, brush them all with olive oil, and season generously with salt and pepper. Heat the oil in a skillet or frying pan, add the onion, and cook over low heat, stirring occasionally, for 5 minutes until softened. Add the basmati or long grain rice and cook, stirring. for a few minutes, then pour in the stock and increase the heat. Cover and bring to a boil, then reduce the heat and simmer for 10–12 minutes until the rice is nearly tender. Remove from the heat and drain off any liquid still remaining in the pan. Tip the rice into a bowl and fold in the nuts and seven spices seasoning. Season well with salt and pepper. Divide the rice mixture between the cavities of the fish. Cover with foil and bake for 20 minutes. Remove the fish from the oven and transfer to individual plates. Sprinkle with the parsley, garnish with the lemon wedges, and serve immediately.

FISH WITH PRESERVED LEMON AND GARLIC

RED SNAPPER WITH CHILI OIL

RED
SNAPPER
WITH
CHILI OIL

PHOTO PAGE 210

—

سمك السلطان ابراهيم مع
الزيت بخلطة الفلفل الحار

Preparation time: 10 minutes
Cooking time: 8–10 minutes
Serves 2

2 x 8 oz/225 g red snapper or mullet, scaled and cleaned
all-purpose (plain) flour, for dusting
1 teaspoon chili powder
1–2 tablespoons chili oil
juice of 1 lemon
salt and pepper
Lebanese flatbread, to serve

Make diagonal slashes in the skin of the fish and season inside
and outside with salt and pepper. Dust with flour, shake off any
excess. Sprinkle with the chili powder. Heat a skillet or frying
pan. When hot, add the chili oil, then add the fish and cook
for 4 minutes on each side. Add lemon juice to taste and serve
immediately with Lebanese flatbread.

RED
SNAPPER
IN
SESAME OIL

—

البوري الاحمر بزيت
السمسم

Preparation time: 10 minutes, plus marinating time
Cooking time: 12–15 minutes
Serves 2

2 x 8 oz/225 g red snapper or mullet, scaled and cleaned
8–10 parsley stems
1 red chile, seeded and finely chopped
2 garlic cloves, crushed
1 parsley sprig, finely chopped
1 tablespoon olive oil
2 tablespoons sesame oil
juice of 1 lemon
sea salt

Make 3 slashes on each side of the fish and put them into an
ovenproof dish. Stuff the cavities with the parsley stems.
Mix together the chile, garlic, chopped parsley, olive oil,
half the sesame oil, and a pinch of sea salt in a bowl. Brush
the mixture over the fish and let marinate for 30 minutes.
Meanwhile, preheat the oven to 400°F/200°C/Gas Mark 6.
Roast the fish for 12–15 minutes until the flesh flakes easily.
Remove from the oven, sprinkle with the remaining sesame oil
and lemon juice to taste, and serve immediately.

SUMAC CRUSTED TUNA WITH WATERMELON SALAD

PHOTO PAGE 213

—

سمك التونة بالسماق مع سلطة البطيخ الاحمر

Preparation time: 20 minutes
Cooking time: 2–4 minutes
Serves 2

2 x 6 oz/180 g tuna loin steak
olive oil, for brushing
1 tablespoon ground sumac

For the watermelon salad
¼ watermelon, seeded and cubed
2 shallots, thinly sliced
¾ cup (3 oz/80 g) pitted black olives
4 mint sprigs, picked
2 tablespoons chopped fresh parsley
2 teaspoons red wine vinegar
2 tablespoons olive oil
salt and pepper

Put all the ingredients for the watermelon salad into a large bowl, season with salt and pepper, and mix well. Set aside until ready to serve. Next, brush the tuna with olive oil and rub in the sumac. Heat a heavy skillet or frying pan and, when hot, add the tuna steaks and cook for 2–4 minutes on each side, according to your taste. Serve immediately with the watermelon salad on the side.

FRIED SMELT

—

السردين المقلي المقرمش

Preparation time: 5 minutes
Cooking time: 3 minutes
Serves 4

¾ cup (3 oz/80 g) all-purpose (plain) flour, for dusting
1 lb 2 oz/500 g smelt (whitebait)
2 teaspoons paprika
sunflower oil, for deep-frying
salt and pepper
lemon wedges and Tahini Sauce (see page 219), to serve

Put the flour in to a bowl and season with salt and pepper. Add the smelt (whitebait), in batches, and toss well to coat. Shake off any excess and put onto a plate. Sprinkle with half the paprika. Heat the sunflower oil in a deep-fryer to 375°F/180°C or until a cube of bread browns in 30 seconds. Add the fish, in batches, and cook for about 3 minutes until golden and crispy. Remove and drain on paper towels. Keep warm while you cook the remaining batches. Sprinkle with the remaining paprika and serve immediately with lemon wedges and Tahini Sauce.

SUMAC CRUSTED TUNA WITH WATERMELON SALAD

OCTOPUS WITH RED ONION AND LEMON SALAD

PHOTO PAGE 215

—

اخطبوط مع البصل الاحمر
وسلطة الليمون

Preparation time: 20 minutes
Cooking time: 45 minutes
Serves 4

2¼ lb/1 kg baby octopus, cleaned
500ml water
⅔ cup (4 fl oz/120 ml) red wine vinegar
1 red onion, thinly sliced
6 ripe tomatoes, cut into chunks
4 tablespoons olive oil
3 tablespoons chopped fresh parsley
juice of ½ lemon
salt and black pepper
crusty bread, to serve

Put the octopus into a pan, pour in water to cover, and add a generous pinch of salt. Reserve 2 teaspoons of the red wine vinegar and pour the remainder into the pan. Bring to a boil, then reduce the heat, cover, and simmer for 45 minutes, until the octopus is tender. Drain well. Add the onion, tomatoes, olive oil, and red wine vinegar and toss well. Add the parsley and lemon juice and season with salt and pepper. Serve with bread.

DEEP FRIED OCTOPUS WITH CORIANDER AND YOGURT SAUCE

—

اخطبوط مقلي مع الكزبرة
وصلصة الزبادي

Preparation time: 25 minutes
Cooking time: 8–10 minutes
Serves 2–4

1 lb/2 oz/500 g baby octopus, cleaned and cut into bite-sized pieces
½ cup (2 oz/50 g) cornstarch (cornflour)
½ cup (2 oz/50 g) all-purpose (plain) flour, plus extra for dusting
½ teaspoon baking soda (bicarbonate of soda)
scant ½ cup (3½ fl oz/100 ml) sparkling mineral water, chilled
2 teaspoons Thai fish sauce
juice of ½ lemon
pinch of chili flakes
pinch of freshly ground white pepper
sunflower oil, for deep-frying

For the sauce
5 tablespoons plain (natural) yogurt
finely grated zest and juice of ½ lime
2 tablespoons chopped cilantro (coriander)

Sift the cornstarch (cornflour), flour, and baking soda (bicarbonate of soda) into a bowl, then whisk in the mineral water, to make a smooth batter. Stir in the fish sauce, lemon juice, chili flakes, and white pepper. Mix all the ingredients for the sauce together in a bowl, cover, and chill. Heat sunflower oil in a deep-fryer to 350°F/180°C or until a cube of bread browns in 30 seconds. Dust the octopus pieces with flour, shake off the excess, then dip them into the batter. Deep-fry them, in batches, for 2 minutes until crispy and golden. Remove with a slotted spoon, drain on paper towels, and keep warm while you cook the remaining batches. Serve the octopus pieces in a warm dish with the sauce.

OCTOPUS WITH RED ONION AND LEMON SALAD

SQUID IN GARLIC AND CHILLI

حبار بالثوم والفلفل الحار

Preparation time: 20–25 minutes
Cooking time: 1–2 minutes
Serves 6–8

4 squid
½ cup (2 oz/50 g) cornstarch (cornflour)
½ cup (2 oz/50 g) all-purpose (plain) flour,
    plus extra for dusting
½ teaspoon baking soda (bicarbonate of soda)
scant ½ cup (3½ fl oz/100 ml) sparkling mineral water, chilled
4 garlic cloves, finely chopped
1 green chile, seeded and finely chopped
1 teaspoon za'atar
vegetable or sunflower oil for deep-frying
salt and pepper
chopped fresh cilantro (coriander), to garnish

For the dip
scant ½ cup (3½ fl oz/100 ml) plain yogurt
1 garlic clove, crushed
juice and grated zest of 1 lime

First, make the dip. Combine all the ingredients in a bowl and set aside. Rinse the squid thoroughly, then firmly pull the head from the body (the innards will come away with it). Cut off the tentacles from the head, then press out and discard the beak. Reserve the tentacles and discard the rest of the head. Remove and discard the quill from the body sac, remove any remaining membrane, and rinse well under cold running water. Peel off the skin. Prepare the remaining squid in the same way. Cut the body sacs into rings. Sift together the cornstarch (cornflour), flour, and baking soda (bicarbonate of soda) into a bowl, then gradually whisk in the mineral water, continuing to whisk until a smooth batter forms. Stir in the garlic, chile, and za'atar and season with salt and pepper. Heat the oil in a deep-fryer to 350°C/180°F or until a cube of bread browns in 30 seconds. Working in batches, dip the squid rings and tentacles into the batter, drain off any excess, and carefully add to the hot oil. Deep-fry for about 1 minute until golden and crispy. Remove with a slotted spoon, drain on paper towels, and keep warm while you cook the remaining batches. Pile the squid into a warm serving dish, sprinkle with cilantro (coriander), and serve immediately with the dip.

FRIED SQUID WITH CHILE AND SUMAC

حبار مقلي مع الفلفل
الحار والسماق

Preparation time: 10 minutes, plus marinating time
Cooking time: 2 minutes
Serves 4–6

2 squid, cleaned and cut into rings, or 12 oz/350 g squid rings
4 tablespoons olive oil
1 red chile, seeded and finely chopped
1 tablespoon sumac
juice of 1 lemon
½ cup (4 fl oz/120 ml) sunflower oil
1 tablespoon chili oil

Put the squid rings into a bowl, pour in the olive oil, add the chile and sumac, and mix well. Add the lemon juice, toss the squid rings, and let marinate for 30 minutes. Heat the oil in a deep skillet or frying pan. Add the squid rings and cook for 1–2 minutes on each side until golden. Transfer to a warm serving dish with a slotted spoon, season with salt, drizzle with chili oil and serve immediately.

PAN-FRIED SCALLOPS IN SUMAC

سكالوب مقلي بالسماق

Preparation time: 10 minutes
Cooking time: 4 minutes
Serves 2

16 small scallops, shucked
1 tablespoon sumac
4 tablespoons (2 oz/50 g) butter
1 tablespoon olive oil
2 garlic cloves, crushed
juice of 1 lemon
2 tablespoons finely chopped fresh parsley

Toss the scallops in the sumac. Melt the butter with the olive oil in a skillet or frying pan, add the scallops, and cook for 1–2 minutes until golden. Add the garlic, then turn the scallops over and cook for 1–2 minutes more. Add the lemon juice, sprinkle with the parsley, and serve immediately.

PAN-FRIED SCALLOPS IN GARLIC

PAN-FRIED SCALLOPS IN GARLIC

PHOTO PAGE 218

سكالوب مقلي بالثوم

Preparation time: 10 minutes
Cooking time: 2 minutes
Serves 4

12 scallops, shucked
4 tablespoons (2 oz/50 g) butter
1 tablespoons olive oil
2 garlic cloves, crushed
juice of 1 lemon
2 tablespoons finely chopped fresh parsley

Slice the scallops in half. Melt the butter with the olive oil in a skillet or frying pan, add the scallops and sear for about 1½ minutes until golden. Add the garlic, turn the scallops over, and cook for another minute. Add the lemon juice and parsley and serve immediately.

PAN-FRIED SCALLOPS AND TAHINI SAUCE

سكالوب مقلي بصلصة الطحينة

Preparation time: 10 minutes
Cooking time: 15 minutes
Serves 4

4 tablespoons (2 oz/50 g) butter
1 tablespoon olive oil
2 garlic cloves, crushed
16 scallops, shucked
1 teaspoons sesame seeds, toasted
3 tablespoons chopped fresh parsley

For the tahini sauce
1 teaspoon olive oil
1 shallot, finely diced
1 teaspoon curry powder
5 tablespoons tahini
juice of 1 lemon
salt and pepper

First, make the tahini sauce. Heat the olive oil in a small saucepan, add the shallot, and cook over low heat, stirring occasionally, for 4–5 minutes until softened. Stir in the curry powder and cook, stirring, for 2 minutes. Add the tahini, stir in the lemon juice, and cook until thickened to a paste, then whisk in 5 tablespoons water. Continue to whisk until smooth, then season with salt and pepper and cook for 5 minutes. Meanwhile, melt the butter with the olive oil in a skillet or frying pan, add the garlic and cook, stirring frequently, for 1 minute. Add the scallops and cook for about 2 minutes on each side, then add the sesame seeds. Pour the tahini sauce into a shallow dish, top with the scallops, sprinkle with the parsley and serve immediately.

FISH

JUMBO SHRIMP IN GARLIC

قريدس ملكي بالثوم

Preparation time: 10 minutes
Cooking time: 5 minutes
Serves 2

12 uncooked jumbo shrimp (king prawns)
4 tablespoons (2 oz/55 g) butter
1 tablespoon olive oil
3 garlic cloves, finely chopped
2 tablespoons chopped fresh cilantro (coriander)
salt and pepper

Pull off the heads of the shrimp (prawns) and peel off the body shells, leaving the tails intact. Make a cut along the backs of the shrimp and remove the black veins with the point of a knife. Melt the butter with oil in a skillet or frying pan, then add the garlic and cook, stirring frequently, for 1 minute. Add the shrimp and cook, stirring frequently, for 3–5 minutes until they have all turned pink. Add the cilantro (coriander), season with salt and pepper, and serve immediately.

DEEP-FRIED SHRIMP, RED SNAPPER, AND COD
IN A THYME BATTER

قريدس وسلطان
ابراهيم وسمك قد مقلي مع
خليط الزعتر

Preparation time: 15 minutes
Cooking time: 5 minutes
Serves 4–6

1¾ cups (8 oz/225 g) all purpose (plain) flour
3 teaspoons baking powder
1 teaspoon salt
1 teaspoon baking soda (bicarbonate of soda)
2 tablespoons fresh thyme leaves
2 red snapper or mullet fillets, skinned
1 cod fillet, skinned
16 uncooked jumbo shrimp (king prawns), peeled and deveined
sunflower oil, for deep-frying
sea salt
tahini dip, to serve

Sift together the flour, baking powder, salt, and baking soda (bicarbonate of soda) into a large bowl. Gradually whisk in 1¼ cups (½ pint/300 ml) water until a smooth batter is formed. Stir in the thyme leaves. Cut the fish into bite-size pieces. Dip the fish and shrimp (prawns) into the batter. Heat the sunflower oil in a deep-fryer to 350°F/180°C or until a cube of bread browns in 30 seconds. Add the fish and shrimp, in batches, and deep-fry for 5 minutes until golden. Drain the fish bites on paper towels, transfer to a warm serving dish, sprinkle with sea salt, and serve immediately with a tahini dip.

PHYLLO ROLLS
WITH FENNEL, CRAB, AND CHILI

رقائق ملفوفة بالسلطعون مع
الشومر والفلفل الحار

Preparation time: 20 minutes
Cooking time: 25 minutes
Makes 12

4 sheets of phyllo (filo) pastry
7 tablespoons (3½ oz/100 g) butter, melted
1 tablespoon fennel seeds, toasted

For the filling
14 oz/400 g crabmeat, thawed if frozen
2 scallions (spring onions), finely chopped
1 fennel bulb, thinly sliced
1 red chile, seeded and chopped
2 tablespoons chopped fresh cilantro (coriander)
juice of ½ lemon

Preheat the oven to 400°F/200°C/Gas Mark 6. Line a baking sheet with wax (greaseproof) paper. Put all the ingredients for the filling into a large bowl, mix well and set aside. Lay each sheet of phyllo (filo) on a work surface and brush with melted butter. Spoon the crab filling onto the bottom part of the pastry and roll up like a sausage, making sure it is tight. Brush with melted butter and sprinkle with the fennel seeds. Cut the roll into 12 pieces and put the on the prepared baking sheet. Bake for 25 minutes until lightly golden. Serve hot or cold.

JUMBO SHRIMP, SPICY SAUSAGE, AND LEBANESE BREAD

JUMBO SHRIMP, SPICY SAUSAGE, AND LEBANESE BREAD

PHOTO PAGE 222

—

القريدس الملكي مع السجق الحار
والخبز اللبناني

Preparation time: 10 minutes
Cooking time: 10–12 minutes
Serves 2

1 tablespoon olive oil
2 large shallots, finely chopped
4 garlic cloves, finely chopped
7 oz/200 g spicy sausage, sliced
scant ½ cup (3½ fl oz/100 ml) white wine
½ teaspoon chili flakes
1¾ lb/800 g jumbo shrimp (king prawns), peeled and deveined
1 bunch of parsley, chopped
2 Lebanese flatbreads
salt and pepper
Lebanese Salad (see page 59), to serve

Heat the olive oil in a large saucepan, add the shallots, and cook over low heat, stirring occasionally, for 4–5 minutes until softened but not browned. Add the garlic and cook for another minute. Add the sausage slices and cook until they release their oil. Add the white wine and cook for 1 minute, then stir in the chili flakes and add the shrimp (prawns). Cover the pan and cook, stirring occasionally, for about 5 minutes until all the shrimp have turned pink. Just before serving, add the chopped parsley and season well with salt and pepper. Tear the flat breads in to bite-size pieces and add to the pan. Stir again and serve immediately with the Lebanese Salad.

JUMBO SHRIMP COATED IN ZA'ATER AND CILANTRO

—

قريدس ملكي مغلف
بالزعتر والكزبرة

Preparation time: 5 minutes, plus marinating time
Cooking time: 5 minutes
Serves 2

12 uncooked jumbo shrimp (king prawns), peeled and deveined
3 tablespoons olive oil
2 tablespoons za'ater
juice of 1 lemon
2 tablespoons chopped cilantro (coriander)
salt

Put the shrimp (prawns), olive, and za'ater into a bowl and turn to coat. Let marinate for 20 minutes. Heat a large, heavy skillet or frying pan. When it is hot, add the shrimp and cook for 3–5 minutes until they have turned pink and are cooked through. Add the lemon juice and cilantro (coriander) and toss to mix. Season with salt and serve immediately.

RISOTTO
WITH
CRAB
AND
CILANTRO

ريزوتو السلطعون بالكزبرة

Preparation time: 20 minutes
Cooking time: 30–35 minutes
Serves 4

1 cooked crab or 5 oz/150 g white and brown crabmeat
1 teaspoon sumac
juice of 1 lemon
1 bunch of fresh cilantro (coriander), chopped
4¼ cups (1¾ pints/1 liter) hot fish stock
2 tablespoons olive oil
1 onion, chopped
2 cups (12 oz/350 g) risotto rice
½ cup (4 fl oz/120 ml) white wine
2 tablespoons tahini
salt and freshly ground white pepper

Remove all the crabmeat from the cooked crab, if using. Put the crabmeat into a bowl, add the sumac, lemon juice, and cilantro (coriander) and mix gently. Pour the stock into a saucepan and bring to a boil over medium-low heat. Heat the oil in another large saucepan, add the onion, and cook over low heat, stirring occasionally, for 5 minutes until softened but not browned. Add the rice and cook, stirring constantly with a wooden spoon, for 1–2 minutes until the rice start to turn opaque is coated with oil. Pour in the wine, increase the heat to high, and cook until it has been absorbed. Stir in a ladleful of the hot fish stock and cook, stirring constantly, until it has been completely absorbed. Continue adding the stock, a ladleful at a time, and stirring until each addition has been absorbed. This will take 18–20 minutes. Stir in the tahini and crab mixture and heat through for a few minutes. Season with salt and pepper and serve immediately.

SWEET POTATO FISH CAKES WITH ZA'ATER CRUMB

كعك السمك بالبطاطس الحلوة

Preparation time: 10 minutes, plus chilling time
Cooking time: 50 minutes
Serves 2

2 large sweet potatoes
7 oz/200 g crabmeat
1 onion, finely chopped
2 tablespoons finely chopped fresh cilantro (coriander)
dash of Tabasco sauce
5–6 slices of white bread, crusts removed
2 tablespoons za'ater
all-purpose (plain) flour for dusting
2 eggs, lightly beaten
4 tablespoons vegetable or sunflower oil
½ small bunch of arugula (rocket)
1 lemon, cut into wedges
sea salt and pepper

Preheat the oven to 400°F/200°C/Gas Mark 6. Prick the sweet potatoes with a fork, put them in the oven, and bake 45 minutes until tender. Remove the sweet potatoes from the oven, cut them in half, and scoop out the flesh into a bowl. Add the crabmeat, onion, cilantro (coriander) and Tabasco sauce to taste and mix well. Season well with salt and pepper. Put the slices of bread into a food processor and process to fine crumbs. Add half the breadcrumbs to the crabmeat mixture and mix well. Tip the remaining breadcrumbs onto a plate, stir in the za'ater, and season with salt and pepper. Spread out the flour on another plate. Divide the crabmeat mixture into 4 equal pieces and shape each into a patty with you hands. Dust the patties with flour, then dip into the beaten eggs, and, finally, coat in the spicy breadcrumbs. Put the fish cakes onto a baking sheet and chill in the refrigerator for 1 hour. Heat the oil in a skillet or frying pan over medium heat, add the fish cakes, in batches if necessary, and cook for 5 minutes on each side until golden. Serve immediately with arugula (rocket), lemon wedges, and a sprinkling of sea salt.

MEAT

*

اللحوم

LAMB
AND
EGGPLANT
STACK

مطبق الباذنجان
بلحم الغنم

Preparation time: 15 minutes
Cooking time: 1 hour 50 minutes
Serves 6

2 large eggplants (aubergines), cut into ¼ inch/5 mm thick slices
1 tablespoon olive oil, plus extra for brushing
1 lb 2 oz/500 g ground (minced) lamb
1 onion, chopped
2 garlic cloves, chopped
2 tablespoons tomato paste (purée)
28 oz/800 g canned chopped tomatoes
2 teaspoons dried thyme
1 bay leaf
2 teaspoons seven spices seasoning
2 teaspoons ground cumin
pinch of grated nutmeg
pinch of ground cinnamon
5 oz/150 g ricotta cheese
1 cup (4 oz/120 g) grated mozzarella cheese
3 tablespoons chopped fresh parsley
salt and pepper

Preheat the oven to 375°F/190°C/Gas Mark 5. Brush the
eggplant (aubergine) slices with olive oil and sprinkle with salt.
Put them onto a baking sheet and roast for 35 minutes, turning
halfway through the cooking time. Meanwhile, heat the olive oil
in a large saucepan, add the lamb, and cook over medium heat,
stirring frequently, for 8–10 minutes until evenly browned.
Reduce the heat, add the onion and garlic, and cook, stirring
occasionally, for 5 minutes. Stir in the tomato paste (purée) and
cook for another 5 minutes, then add the chopped tomatoes,
thyme, bay leaf, seven spices seasoning, cumin, nutmeg, and
cinnamon, and season with salt and pepper. Simmer for 1 hour.
Put a quarter of the eggplant slices in the bottom of a 12 x 6 x
2 inch/30 x 15 x 5 cm ovenproof dish. Cover with one-third of
the lamb mixture. Repeat these layers until all the ingredients
have used, ending with a layer of eggplant slices. Top with
spoonfuls of ricotta and sprinkle with the grated mozzarella.
Season with salt and pepper and bake for 25 minutes. Remove
the dish from the oven and let cool slightly, then sprinkle with
the chopped parsley, and serve.

EGGPLANT WITH LAMB AND RICE

لحم الغنم مع
الباذنجان والارز

Preparation time: 15 minutes
Cooking time: 2 hours
Serves 4

1 eggplant (aubergine), cut into cubes
3 tablespoons olive oil
1 onion, finely chopped
3 garlic cloves, crushed
1 lb 2 oz/500 g boneless lamb, diced
1 teaspoon seven spices seasoning
1 teaspoon pepper
1 cup (7 oz/200 g) basmati or quick-cook long grain rice, rinsed
salt

Preheat the oven to 400°F/200°C/Gas Mark 6. Put the eggplant (aubergine) cubes into a roasting pan, add 2 tablespoons of the olive oil to coat. Roast for 40 minutes. Meanwhile, heat the remaining oil in a large saucepan, add the onion and garlic, and cook over low heat, stirring occasionally, for 5 minutes until softened. Add the lamb, increase the heat to medium, and cook, stirring frequently, for 8–10 minutes until evenly browned. Pour in water to cover the lamb and add the seven spices seasoning, pepper, and a pinch of salt. Reduce the heat and simmer for 1 hour, then add the cooked eggplant and the rice. Cook for another 10 minutes or until the rice is tender, then serve.

SHOULDER OF LAMB WITH CRANBERRY BEANS

فاصولياء (كتف الغنم
مع الفاصولياء)

Preparation time: 30 minutes
Cooking time: 2 hours 30 minutes
Serves 4

1½ lb/700 g shoulder of lamb, boned and bone reserved
3 tablespoons olive oil
2 onions, chopped
4 garlic cloves
1 teaspoon seven spices seasoning
½ cup (5 oz/150 g) tomato paste (purée)
4 x 7 oz/400 g cans cranberry (borlotti) beans, drained and washed
5 cloves
1 cinnamon stick
4 cardamom pods
salt and pepper
chopped fresh mint, to garnish

Trim any visible fat from the lamb and dice the meat. Heat the oil in a large saucepan, add the onions and garlic, and cook over low heat, stirring occasionally, for 5 minutes until softened. Add the lamb, increase the heat, and cook, stirring frequently, for 8–10 minutes until evenly browned. Stir in the seven spices seasoning and cook for another few minutes. Pour in boiling water to cover and add the bone (to provide additional flavor). Reduce the heat, cover, and simmer for 2 hours. Stir in the tomato paste (purée), beans, cloves, cinnamon, and cardamom. Bring to a boil, then simmer for 10–15 minutes. Season to taste with salt and pepper, sprinkle with mint, and serve.

ZUCCHINI STUFFED WITH LAMB

محشي الكوسا بلحم الغنم

Preparation time: 30 minutes
Cooking time: 25 minutes
Serves 4

9 oz/250 g ground (minced) lamb
1 small onion, chopped
1 teaspoon seven spices seasoning
1 tablespoon dried mint
3 tablespoons chopped fresh parsley
⅓ cup (2 oz/60 g) long grain rice, rinsed
10 small Lebanese zucchini (courgettes), trimmed
1 tomato, chopped
salt and pepper

For the sauce
1 tablespoon olive oil
1 onion, chopped
4 tablespoons tomato paste (purée)
1 teaspoon salt
1 teaspoon pepper
1 teaspoon seven spices seasoning

Heat a skillet or frying pan, add the lamb, and cook over medium heat, stirring frequently, for 8–10 minutes until evenly browned. Add the onion and seven spices seasoning, reduce the heat, and cook, stirring occasionally, for 5 minutes until softened. Stir in the mint and parsley and season with salt and pepper. Remove the pan from the heat and stir in the rice. To make the sauce, heat the oil in a large saucepan, add the onion, and cook over low heat, stirring occasionally, for 5 minutes until softened. Stir in the tomato paste (purée), salt, pepper, and seven spices seasoning and cook for another minute. Pour in 1¼ cups (½ pint/300 ml) boiling water and bring to back to a boil, then reduce the heat. Meanwhile, using an apple corer, remove the flesh from the zucchini (courgettes) and stuff the cavities with the lamb and rice mixture. Put a piece of tomato at either the end to prevent the filling from falling out. Add the zucchini and any leftover rice to the to the sauce, cover the pan, and simmer gently for 25 minutes.

LAMB
AND
BEANS

—

لحم الغنم مع اللوبياء

Preparation time: 20 minutes
Cooking time: 3 hours
Serves 4

3 tablespoons olive oil
2 small onions, chopped
2 cloves garlic, lightly crushed
½ teaspoon ground allspice
1 teaspoon ground cumin
1 cinnamon stick
1 teaspoon ground coriander
1 lb/450 g boneless leg of lamb, diced and the bone reserved
⅓ cup (3½ oz/100 g) tomato paste (purée)
2 teaspoons salt
1 teaspoon pepper
1 teaspoon seven spices seasoning
3 x 7 oz/400 g cans cranberry (borlotti) beans, drained and washed

Heat 1 tablespoon of the oil in a saucepan, add the onions and garlic, and cook over low heat, stirring occasionally, for 5 minutes until the onions are softened but not browned. Stir in the allspice, cumin, cinnamon, and coriander and cook for another minute. Remove the onions and garlic from the pan and set aside. Add the remaining oil to the pan and increase the heat to medium. Add the lamb, in batches if necessary, and cook, stirring frequently, for 8–10 minutes until evenly browned. Return the onions to the pan and pour over enough water to cover—about 3 cups (1¼ pints/750 ml). Add the reserved bone for extra flavor. Reduce the heat, cover the pan, and simmer for 2 hours. Remove the bone from the pan. Stir in the tomato paste (purée), salt, pepper, seven spices seasoning, and borlotti beans and simmer for another 45 minutes until the sauce is reduced. Remove and discard the cinnamon stick before serving.

LAMB
CHOPS
WITH
SEVEN
SPICES

—

اضلع الغنم بالبهارات
السبعة

Preparation time: 5 minutes
Cooking time: 12 minutes
Serves 4

2 garlic cloves, crushed
1½ tablespoons seven spices seasoning
juice of 1 lemon
1 teaspoon salt
1 teaspoon black pepper
4 lamb chops
plain (natural) yogurt and lemon wedges, to serve

Mix together the garlic, seven spices seasoning, lemon juice, salt, and pepper in a bowl, add the lamb chops, and rub the mixture into the meat. Let marinate for 1½ hours. Cook over a hot barbecue or under a hot broiler (grill) for 4–6 minutes on each side. Serve with yogurt and a wedge of lemon.

LAMB-STUFFED CABBAGE

PHOTO PAGE 233

محشي ورق الملفوف
بلحم الغنم

Preparation time: 25 minutes
Cooking time: 1 hour
Serves 6

1 savoy cabbage, leaves separated
1 tablespoon olive oil
1 small onion, chopped
3½ oz/100 g ground (minced) lamb
scant ¾ cup (5 oz/150 g) long grain rice, rinsed
½ teaspoon salt
½ teaspoon pepper
1 teaspoon seven spices seasoning
4 tablespoons chopped fresh cilantro (coriander)
1 teaspoon ghee

Put the cabbage leaves into a large pan, pour in boiling water to cover, and cook for 10 minutes. Drain well and set aside to cool. Heat the oil in a skillet or frying pan, add the onion and lamb, and cook over medium heat, stirring frequently, for 8–10 minutes until the lamb is browned. Put the rice into a bowl, add the lamb mixture, salt, pepper, seven spices seasoning, and cilantro (coriander), and mix well. Then add the ghee. Put some of the cabbage leaves in the bottom of a pan. Put 2 teaspoons of the lamb mixture on top of each of the remaining leaves, then roll up like a cigar and set aside. Put the rolls into the pan and cover with a small plate. Cover with boiling water and simmer for 40 minutes with a lid on the pan, then serve.

LAMB, RICE AND FAVA BEANS

ارز بالفول مع
لحم الغنم

Preparation time: 20 minutes
Cooking time: 1 hour 30 minutes
Serves 4

1 tablespoon olive oil
14 oz/400g boneless lamb, diced
1 onion, chopped
1 celery stalk, diced
1 carrot, diced
2 garlic cloves, crushed
5 tablespoons red wine
generous 2 cups (18 fl oz/500 ml) hot beef stock
1 cinnamon stick
1 teaspoon seven spices seasoning
1 cup (7 oz/200 g) basmati or quick-cook long grain rice
¾ cup (3½ oz/100 g) frozen fava (broad) beans, thawed
salt and pepper

Heat the oil in a large saucepan, add the lamb, and cook over medium heat, stirring frequently, for 8–10 minutes until browned. Add the onion, celery, and carrot and cook, stirring occasionally, for 5 minutes. Add the garlic and cook for another minute. Pour in the wine and cook for 1 minute, then add the stock and spices, and bring to a boil. Reduce the heat, cover, and simmer for 1 hour. Add the rice, season, replace the lid, and cook for 5 minutes. Add the beans, replace the lid, and cook for another 5 minutes. Turn off the heat and let stand, covered, for 5 minutes before serving.

LAMB-STUFFED CABBAGE

STUFFED ZUCCHINI WITH LAMB AND PINE NUTS

—

محشي الكوسا بلحم
الغنم والصنوبر

Preparation time: 10 minutes
Cooking time: 1 hour 15 minutes
Serves 2

4 zucchini (courgettes), halved lengthwise
1 tablespoon olive oil, plus extra for brushing
9 oz/250 g ground (minced) lamb
1 onion, chopped
2 garlic cloves, crushed
1 teaspoon seven spices seasoning
½ teaspoon pepper
½ teaspoon salt
14 oz/400 g canned chopped tomatoes
½ cup (2 oz/50 g) pine nuts, toasted

Preheat the oven to 375°F/190°C/Gas Mark 5. Put the zucchini (courgettes) into a roasting pan, cut sides uppermost, and brush with olive oil. Roast for 30 minutes. Meanwhile, heat the oil in a saucepan, add the lamb, and cook over medium heat, stirring frequently, for 8–10 minutes until evenly browed. Reduce the heat, add the onion and garlic, and cook, stirring occasionally, for another 5 minutes. Stir in the seven spices seasoning, pepper, and salt and cook for another 10 minutes. Meanwhile, put the chopped tomatoes into another saucepan, add 2½ cups (600 ml/1 pint) water, and bring to a boil over medium heat. Reduce the heat and simmer for 20 minutes. Remove the zucchini from the oven but do not turn it off. Scoop out the zucchini flesh with a spoon and discard. Divide the lamb mixture among the zucchini halves, pour the tomato sauce over them, and sprinkle with the pine nuts. Cover the roasting pan with foil, return it to the oven, and cook for 40–45 minutes. Serve immediately.

LAMB CHOPS RUBBED WITH GARLIC

—

اضلع الغنم المفروكة
بالثوم

Preparation time: 5 minutes
Cooking time: 12 minutes
Serves 2

5 garlic cloves, very finely chopped
juice of 1½ lemons
2 teaspoons pepper
2 teaspoons paprika
2 teaspoons seven spice seasoning
2 teaspoons salt
1 tablespoon olive oil
4 lamb chops

Mix together the garlic, lemon juice, pepper, paprika, seven spice seasoning, salt, and olive oil in a large bowl, stir in 1½ cups (12 fl oz/350 ml) water, and add the lamb. Rub the marinade into the meat, cover the bowl with plastic wrap (clingfilm), and let marinate at room temperature for 1½ hours. Drain the lamb and grill over a hot barbecue or under a preheat broiler (grill) for 3–6 minutes on each side, depending on how well done you like your lamb. Serve immediately.

LAMB CHOPS, GRAPE LEAVES AND ZUCCHINI

—

اضلع اَلغنم مع ورق العنب والكوسا

Preparation time: 30 minutes
Cooking time: 1 hour 40 minutes
Serves 6

2 tablespoons olive oil
1 lb 2 oz/500 g lamb chops, trimmed
50 grape (vine) leaves
10 baby zucchini (courgettes)
1 tomato, chopped

For the filling
olive oil
7 oz/200 g ground (minced) lamb
1 onion, finely chopped
1¼ cups (9 oz/250 g) basmati or quick-cook long grain rice, rinsed
1 teaspoon seven spices seasoning
1 small bunch of fresh parsley, chopped
salt and pepper

Heat the olive oil a large saucepan, add the lamb chops, and cook over medium heat for 2 minutes on each side until evenly browned. Transfer to a plate and set aside. If using fresh grape (vine) leaves, bring a saucepan of salted water to a boil, add the leaves, and blanch for 30 seconds, then drain and set aside. If using leaves preserved in a salt solution (brine), soak them in hot water for 30 minutes, then drain, rinse thoroughly, and pat dry with paper towels. Meanwhile, make the filling. Heat the oil in the same pan used for the chops, add the ground (minced) lamb, and cook over medium heat, stirring frequently, for 8–10 minutes until evenly browed. Add the onion and cook for a few minutes until softened, then stir in the rice, seven spices seasoning, and parsley. Simmer for 2 minutes, then season with salt and pepper, remove from the heat, and set aside. Using an apple corer, remove and discard the flesh from each zucchini (courgette). Stuff the zucchini with the ground lamb filling and plug the end with a piece of chopped tomato to stop the filling from falling out. Lay out the grape leaves on a work surface, put a teaspoon of the filling in the middle of each, and carefully roll up into a cigar shape. Repeat this until you have made 40 rolls. Put the remaining grape leaves into a large saucepan, put the lamb chops on top, and add the grape leaf rolls and zucchini. Cover the zucchini with a plate that just fits in the pan. Pour in boiling water to cover, put a lid on the pan, and simmer gently for 40–50 minutes. Remove from the heat and serve immediately.

LAMB CHOPS IN TAHINI AND CURRY SAUCE

اضلع الغنم بصلصة
الطحينة والكاري

Preparation time: 15 minutes
Cooking time: 15 minutes
Serves 4

2 tablespoons olive oil
8 lamb chops
1 onion, chopped
2 tablespoons chopped fresh cilantro (coriander)
rice and vermicelli, to serve

For the tahini and curry sauce
3 garlic cloves, crushed
1 teaspoon salt
juice of 1 lemon
5 tablespoons Tahini Sauce (see page 200)
2 teaspoons medium curry powder

Preheat the oven to 400°F/200°C/Gas Mark 6. Crush the garlic with the salt in a mortar with a pestle. Stir in the lemon juice, tahini sauce, and 5 tablespoons water. Add the curry powder, mix well, and set aside. Heat the oil in a skillet or frying pan, and sear the chops for 1 minute on each side, then transfer to an ovenproof dish. Add the onion to the pan and cook for 5–8 minutes until softened. Spoon the onion over the lamb chops, then pour in the sauce. Bake for 15 minutes. Remove from the oven, sprinkle with the cilantro (coriander), and serve with rice and vermicelli.

LAMB HARISSA

هريسة لحم الغنم

Preparation time: 20 minutes
Cooking time: 2 hours 15 minutes
Serves 4

1 lb/450 g boneless leg of lamb, diced, and 1 lb/450 g lamb bones
3 cups (1¼ pints/750 ml) lamb stock
2 tablespoons olive oil
2 onions, chopped
1 teaspoon ground cumin
3 cardamom pods
1 cinnamon stick
1 teaspoon pepper
½ teaspoon ground cinnamon
1½ teaspoons salt
1 cup (7 oz/200 g) pearl barley
juice of ½ lemon
3 tablespoons chopped fresh parsley

Put the lamb and lamb bones into a large pan, cover with water, and bring to a boil, skimming off the scum. Drain, then put the lamb and bones into a clean pan with the stock. Bring to a boil, reduce the heat, cover, and simmer for 1½ hours. Meanwhile, heat the oil in another pan, add the onions, cumin, cardamom, cinnamon stick, pepper, ground cinnamon, and salt, and cook over low heat for 5 minutes until the onions have softened. Remove the pan from the heat. When the lamb has been cooking for 1½ hours, add the spiced onions and barley, and simmer for 45 minutes. Stir in the lemon juice and parsley and serve.

LAMB
AND
BULGUR
WHEAT

برغل بلحم الغنم

Preparation time: 20 minutes, plus soaking time
Cooking time: 1 hour 20 minutes
Serves 4

2½ cups (12 oz/350 g) bulgur wheat
2 teaspoons olive oil
2 small onions, finely chopped
4 garlic cloves, sliced
12 oz/350 g lamb leg cutlets, diced
3 cardamom pods
5 cloves
1 cinnamon stick
1 teaspoon seven spices seasoning
2 teaspoons salt
1 teaspoon pepper
⅓ cup (3 oz/80 g) tomato paste (purée)
1 teaspoon ground cumin
chopped fresh mint, to garnish

Put the bulgur wheat into a bowl, pour in water to cover, and let soak for 30 minutes. Meanwhile, heat half the olive oil in a deep skillet or frying pan, add the onions and garlic, and cook over low heat, stirring occasionally, for 7–8 minutes until softened and lightly golden, then transfer to a plate. Add the remaining oil to the pan and heat. Add the lamb, increase the heat to medium, and cook, stirring frequently, for 8–10 minutes until evenly browned. Return the onions and garlic to the pan and add the cardamom pods, cloves, and cinnamon stick. Pour in 3 cups (1¼ pints/750 ml) boiling water, add the seven spices seasoning, salt, and pepper, and bring to a boil. Reduce the heat, cover, and simmer for 1 hour. Drain the bulgur wheat. Spoon off any fat from the pan of lamb, then stir in the bulgur wheat, tomato paste (purée), and cumin, and continue to cook for 10 minutes. Serve garnished with chopped mint.

LAMB
WITH
SAFFRON
RICE
AND
WALNUTS

PHOTO PAGE 239

—

لحم الغنم مع الارز
بالزعفران والجوز

Preparation time: 20 minutes
Cooking time: 1 hour
Serves 4

8 lamb chops
2 tablespoons olive oil
scant 1 cup (3½ oz/100 g) shelled walnuts, chopped
2 teaspoons (clear) honey
¼ teaspoon chili flakes
1 teaspoon fennel seeds
1 onion, chopped
scant 1 cup (6 oz/175 g) basmati or quick-cook long grain rice,
    rinsed
2½ cup (1 pint/600 ml) hot vegetable stock
pinch of saffron threads, lightly crushed
½ teaspoon ground turmeric
⅔ cup (3½ oz/100 g) frozen peas, thawed
2 tablespoons chopped fresh mint
salt and pepper

Preheat the oven to 300°F/150°C/Gas Mark 2. Brush the chops
with 1 tablespoon of the olive oil and season with salt and
pepper. Heat a skillet or frying pan, add the chops, and cook
for 1 minute on each side. Transfer to a roasting pan and roast
for 1 hour, turning the chops halfway through the cooking time.
Meanwhile, dry-fry the walnuts in a ovenproof skillet or frying
pan for 1 minute, then stir in the honey and chili flakes. Put
the pan into the oven with the lamb and let dry for 10 minutes.
Remove from the oven and let cool slightly. Heat a saucepan,
add the fennel seeds, and dry-fry for 1 minute or until they
release their aroma. Tip the seeds onto a plate and return the
pan to the heat. Add the remaining olive oil, then add the onion
and cook over low heat, stirring occasionally, for 7–8 minutes
until the onion starts to color. Add the rice and cook, stirring
constantly, for 1 minute. Gradually stir in the hot vegetable
stock and season with salt and pepper. Return the fennel seeds
to the pan and stir in the walnuts, saffron, and turmeric. Bring
to a boil over medium heat, then reduce the heat, cover, and
simmer for 10–15 minutes or until the rice is tender and the
liquid has been absorbed. Stir in the peas and heat through,
then add the chopped mint. Serve the lamb chops with the
saffron rice and walnuts.

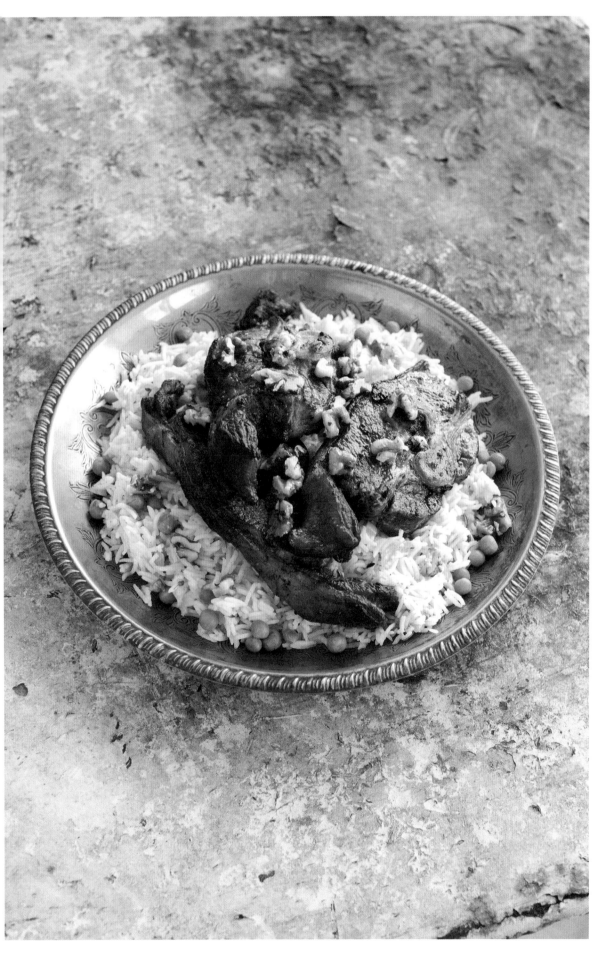

239   LAMB WITH SAFFRON RICE AND WALNUTS

LAMB, SPINACH AND RICE

لحم الغنم مع
السبانخ والارز

Preparation time: 20 minutes
Cooking time: 30 minutes
Serves 4

1 tablespoon olive oil
14 oz/400 g boneless lamb, diced
1 onion, chopped
2 celery stalks, diced
1 carrot, diced
2 garlic cloves, crushed
5 tablespoons red wine
generous 2 cups (18 fl oz/500 ml) hot beef stock
1 cinnamon stick
2 teaspoons seven spices seasoning
1 cup (7 oz/200 g) basmati rice, rinsed and soaked in boiling
water, or quick-cook long grain rice
5 cups (5 oz/150 g) baby spinach
salt and pepper

Heat the oil in a large saucepan, add the lamb, and cook over medium heat, stirring frequently, for 8–10 minutes until evenly browned. Add the onion, celery, and carrot and cook, stirring occasionally, for 6–8 minutes until lightly colored. Stir in the garlic and cook for 1 minute. Pour in the wine and cook for another minute, then pour in the hot stock, add the spices, and bring to a boil. Reduce the heat, cover, and simmer for 1 hour. Drain the rice and add it to the pan. Season with salt and pepper and cook for 10 minutes or until the rice is tender. Finally, stir in the spinach and cook for a few minutes until wilted. Serve immediately.

LAMB KEBAB

كباب لحم الغنم

Preparation time: 15 minutes, plus marinating time
Cooking time: 2–6 minutes
Serves 4

2¼ lb/1 kg boneless leg of lamb
1 tablespoon olive oil
juice of 1 lemon
1 tablespoon white wine vinegar
1 teaspoon salt
1 teaspoon pepper
3 garlic cloves, crushed
cucumber and mint yogurt salad and Lebanese bread, to serve

Trim off the fat from the lamb, cut the meat into strips, and put it into a dish. Pour in the olive oil, lemon juice, and vinegar, add the salt, pepper, and garlic, and toss well. Let marinate for 30 minutes. Heat a large skillet or frying pan until hot, then add the lamb and cook for 2–4 minutes, if you like your lamb rare, or 3–6 minutes, if you prefer it medium. Serve immediately with cucumber and mint yogurt salad and warm Lebanese bread.

LAMB
AND
SPINACH
FATTEH

—

فتة لحم الغنم
والسبانخ

Preparation time: 15 minutes
Cooking time: 35 minutes
Serves 4

3 tablespoons vegetable oil
1 lb 2 oz/500 g ground (minced) lamb
2 onions, chopped
2 garlic cloves, sliced
1 teaspoon seven spices seasoning
¼ teaspoon ground cinnamon
½ teaspoon ground cumin
2 tomatoes, chopped
2 pita breads
5 cups (5 oz/150 g) baby spinach
¾ cup (3 oz/80 g) pine nuts, toasted in oil
salt and pepper

For the yogurt
1 cup (8 fl oz/250 ml) plain (natural) yogurt
2 garlic cloves, crushed
2 tablespoons chopped fresh mint
salt and pepper

Preheat the oven to 400°F/200°C/Gas Mark 6. Heat the oil in a large saucepan, add the lamb, and cook over medium heat, stirring frequently, for 8–10 minutes until evenly browned. Add the onions and garlic, reduce the heat, and cook, stirring occasionally, for 5 minutes. Stir in the spices and tomatoes, season well with salt and pepper, add ⅔ cup (¼ pint/150 ml) water, and simmer for 20 minutes. Meanwhile, put the pita breads in the oven and warm through for a few minutes until crisp. Remove from the oven and cut into squares. Combine the yogurt, garlic, and mint in a bowl, season lightly with salt and pepper, and set aside. Stir the spinach into the lamb mixture and cook for a few minutes until wilted. Transfer the lamb mixture to a serving dish, top with the yogurt and pine nuts, put the crisp bread squares around the side, and serve.

MEATLOAF

—

رغيف لحم الغنم

Preparation time: 10 minutes
Cooking time: 1 hour 30 minutes
Serves 4

olive oil, for brushing
1 onion, grated
1 lb 2 oz/500 g ground (minced) lamb
1 cup (4 oz/120 g) all-purpose (plain) flour
2 tomatoes, chopped
2 eggs
¼ teaspoon grated nutmeg
½ teaspoon ground cinnamon
2 tablespoons chopped fresh parsley
2 tablespoons chopped fresh mint
salt and pepper

Preheat the oven to 400°F/200°C/Gas Mark 6. Line a large baking sheet with foil, shiny side down, and brush generously with oil. Put all the ingredients into a large bowl and mix together with your hands. Tip the mixture onto the prepared baking sheet and wrap the foil around the meatloaf to form a wide sausage shape. Bake in the oven for 1½ hours and serve immediately.

PHYLLO ROLLS STUFFED WITH LAMB AND MINT

—

لفائف رقائق العجين المحشوة
بلحم الغنم والنعناع

Preparation time: 40 minutes
Cooking time: 25 minutes
Makes 8–10

9 oz/250 g ground (minced) lamb
1 teaspoon seven spices seasoning
1 onion, finely chopped
½ red bell pepper, seeded and finely chopped
1 tomato, finely diced
dash of Worcestershire sauce
4 sheets of phyllo (filo) pastry
7 tablespoons (3½ oz/100 g) butter, melted
1 tablespoon za'atar
salt and pepper

Heat a skillet or frying pan, add the lamb, and cook over medium heat, stirring frequently, for 8–10 minutes until evenly browned. Stir in the seven spices seasoning and season with salt and pepper. Add the onion, bell pepper, tomato, and Worcestershire sauce, reduce the heat, and cook, stirring occasionally, for 10 minutes. Remove the pan from the heat and let cool completely. Preheat the oven to 400°F/200°C/Gas Mark 6. Line a baking sheet with wax (greaseproof) paper. Lay 1 sheet of phyllo (filo) pastry on the work surface and brush with melted butter, then lay a second sheet on top and brush with butter again. Repeat this with the remaining pastry. Spoon the lamb mixture onto the bottom half of the pastry from left to right, then carefully roll up tightly into a sausage shape. Brush again with melted butter and cut into 1½ inch/4 cm slices. Put them onto the prepared baking sheet and sprinkle with za'atar. Bake for 25 minutes or until golden. Remove from the oven, transfer to a wire rack to cool, and then serve.

LAMB
BURGERS

برغر لحم الغنم

Preparation time: 30 minutes
Cooking time: 10 minutes
Serves 4

1 lb 2 oz/500 g ground (minced) lamb
1 onion, grated
3 tablespoons breadcrumbs
2 tablespoons all-purpose (plain) flour
2 tablespoons chopped fresh parsley
2 teaspoons salt
1 teaspoon pepper
1 teaspoon ground cumin
1 teaspoon seven spices seasoning
1 teaspoon ground coriander
3–4 tablespoons corn oil
khobez bread, to serve

Put the lamb, onion, breadcrumbs, flour, parsley, salt, pepper, and spices in a bowl and mix well with your hands. Divide the mixture into 8 pieces and shape each into a patty. Heat 2 tablespoons of the oil in a skillet or frying pan, add half the lamb patties, and cook for 4–5 minutes on each side. Remove with a spatula (fish slice) and drain on paper towels. Keep warm while you cook the second batch of patties. Serve with flatbread.

LAMB
FREEKEH

فريكة لحم الغنم

Preparation time: 20 minutes
Cooking time: 30–40 minutes
Serves 4

2 tablespoons olive oil
14 oz/400 g boneless leg of lamb, cut into chunks
5 shallots, halved
1 tablespoon butter
generous 2 cups (18 fl oz/500 ml) chicken or vegetable stock
1½ cups (9 oz/250 g) freekah
1 teaspoon smoked paprika
1 teaspoon ground allspice
3–4 thyme sprigs, chopped
2 oz/50 g feta cheese, very thinly sliced
salt and pepper

Heat 1 tablespoon of the oil in a heavy saucepan over medium-high heat, add the lamb, and sear for 1 minute each side. Remove from the pan with a slotted spoon and set aside. Reduce the heat to low and add the shallots, butter, and a ladleful of the stock to the pan. Cook, stirring occasionally, for about 15 minutes until the shallots have softened and caramelized. Add the freekeh, paprika, allspice, thyme, the remaining olive oil, and the remaining stock, season with salt and pepper, and cook, stirring occasionally, until the liquid has been absorbed and the freekah is cooked through. A few minutes before the freekah is ready, return the lamb to the pan and cook to your liking. Serve warm with the slivers of feta.

LAMB MEATBALLS IN TOMATO SAUCE

LAMB
MEATBALLS
IN
TOMATO
SAUCE

PHOTO PAGE 244

—

كرات لحم الغنم
بصلصة الطماطم

Preparation time: 20–30 minutes, plus chilling time
Cooking time: 40–50 minutes
Serves 4 (makes 18–20)

For the meatballs
14 oz/400 g ground (minced) lamb
1 onion, finely grated
4 tablespoons white breadcrumbs
2 garlic cloves, crushed
2 teaspoons ground cumin
1 teaspoon ground cinnamon
1 egg
salt and pepper

For the sauce
1 tablespoon olive oil
1 onion, chopped
2 garlic cloves, crushed
3 thyme sprigs
2 bay leaves
14 oz/400 g canned chopped tomatoes
2 tablespoons tomato paste (purée)
1 cup (8 fl oz/250 ml) vegetable stock
pinch of sugar
1 bunch of fresh parsley, chopped
salt and pepper

Put all the ingredients for the meatballs into a bowl, season with salt and pepper, and knead together with your hands until combined. Roll walnut-sized pieces of the mixture into balls between the palms of your hands. Put the meatballs on a plate and chill in the refrigerator for 30 minutes. Meanwhile, make the sauce. Heat the oil in a saucepan, add the onion, and cook over low heat, stirring occasionally, for 7 minutes until softened and lightly colored. Stir in the garlic and cook for 1 minute, then add the herbs and chopped tomatoes. Stir in the tomato paste (purée) and vegetable stock, increase the heat, and bring to a boil. Add a pinch of sugar and season with salt and pepper. Add the meatballs to the sauce, reduce the heat to low, and simmer for 40 minutes until the sauce has thickened and the meatballs are cooked. Remove and discard the thyme sprigs and bay leaves, stir in the parsley, and serve immediately.

MEAT

ROLLED MEAT PACKAGES IN TOMATO SAUCE

PHOTO PAGE 247

—

لفافات اللحم بصلصة الطماطم

Preparation time: 1 hour 20 minutes
Cooking time: 10 minutes
Serves 2

4 x 6 oz/175 g lean lamb cutlets (steaks)
2 garlic cloves, crushed
1 quantity Tomato and Olive Sauce (see page 28)
2 small green chiles, chopped
1 teaspoon seven spices seasoning
olive oil, for brushing
salt and pepper

Preheat the oven to 350°F/180°C/Gas Mark 4. Beat the meat with a meat mallet to ¼ inch/5 mm thick. Crush the garlic in a mortar with a pestle, then stir in 2 tablespoons of the Tomato and Olive Sauce and the chiles. Spread a quarter of this mixture over each steak, roll up tightly, and tie with kitchen string. Sprinkle the rolls with the seven spices seasoning and season with salt and pepper. Brush a skillet or frying pan with oil, add the meat packages, and cook over medium-high heat, turning occasionally, for a few minutes until evenly browned. Transfer the packages to a sheet of foil, wrap them up, and seal tightly. Put the foil package into an ovenproof dish and bake for 5–10 minutes. Meanwhile, gently heat the remaining Tomato and Olive Sauce in a saucepan. Remove the dish from the oven and unwrap the meat packages. Transfer to a serving dish, pour the hot Tomato and Olive Sauce over them, and serve.

LAMB SKEWERS

—

كباب لحم الغنم

Preparation time: 10 minutes, plus marinating time
Cooking time: 3–4 minutes
Serves 4

2 tablespoons plain (natural) yogurt
2 tablespoons olive oil
2 tablespoons red wine vinegar
1 teaspoon salt
½ teaspoon black pepper
½ teaspoon white pepper
½ teaspoon ground cumin
1 lb 2 oz/500 g boneless leg of lamb, cut into cubes
12 small shallots, halved
2 large pita breads
2 tablespoons Tahini Sauce (see page 200)

Mix together the yogurt, olive oil, vinegar, salt, black pepper, white pepper, and cumin in a large bowl. Add the lamb, rub the marinade into the meat, and let marinate for 4 hours at room temperature or overnight in the refrigerator. Thread the pieces of meat onto skewers, alternating with the shallots, 6 pieces per skewer with a small gap in between. Grill over a hot barbecue or cook under a preheated broiler (grill) for 3–4 minutes on each side until the meat is cooked through. Meanwhile, warm the pitas in a preheated oven, 350°F/180°C/Gas Mark 4, for a few minutes. Pull off the cubes of lamb and the shallots into the pita bread, top with Tahini Sauce, and serve.

ROLLED MEAT PACKAGES IN TOMATO SAUCE

KOFTAS
WITH
TOMATO
SAUCE
AND
POTATOES

—

كفتة لحم الغنم مع
البطاطس والطماطم

Preparation time: 40–45 minutes
Cooking time: 1 hour
Serves 4

4 potatoes
olive oil, for brushing
chopped fresh parsley, to garnish

For the tomato sauce
2 tablespoons olive oil
2 small onions, sliced
1 teaspoon seven spices seasoning
3 garlic cloves, crushed
28 oz/800 g canned chopped tomatoes
2 tablespoons tomato paste (purée)
1 cinnamon stick
salt and pepper

For the koftas
1 lb 2 oz/500 g lean ground (minced) lamb
2 small onions, grated
2 garlic cloves, grated
⅓ cup (½ oz/40 g) all-purpose (plain) flour
1 egg, lightly beaten
1 cup (2 oz/50 g) chopped fresh parsley
1 teaspoon seven spices seasoning
½ teaspoon pepper
2 teaspoons dried mint
1 teaspoon sea salt
1 tablespoon olive oil

Put the unpeeled potatoes into a large saucepan, pour in water to cover, and bring to a boil. Cook for 20–30 minutes until nearly tender, then drain and let cool. When cool enough to handle, peel off the skins and cut the potatoes into ½ inch/ 1 cm slices. Lightly brush an ovenproof dish with oil and add the potato slices, flat side down in a single layer, then set aside. Make the tomato sauce. Heat the oil in a saucepan, add the onions and seven spices seasoning, and cook over low heat, stirring occasionally, for 5 minutes until softened but not colored. Add the garlic and cook for another minute. Increase the heat to medium, add the tomatoes, tomato paste (purée), 2½ cups (1 pint/600 ml) water, and the cinnamon stick, and season with salt and pepper. Bring to a boil, reduce the heat, cover, and simmer for 30 minutes. Remove the lid from the pan and simmer for another 30 minutes until slightly reduced. Preheat the oven to 400°F/200°C/Gas Mark 6. Make the koftas. Put the lamb, onions, garlic, flour, egg, parsley, seven spices seasoning, pepper, mint, and salt into a large bowl and mix well with a wooden spoon until thoroughly combined. Dampen your hands and shape golf ball-sized pieces of the mixture into patties (about 20). Heat the oil in a skillet or frying pan, add the koftas, in batches, and cook until browned on the underside, then turn. Put the browned koftas on top of the potato slices, overlapping them. Remove the cinnamon stick from the tomato sauce, pour the sauce over the koftas, and cover with foil. Bake for 1 hour. Serve immediately, sprinkled with parsley.

KOFTAS
AND
TAHINI
SAUCE

—

كفتة لحم الغنم
بصلصة الطحينة

Preparation time: 20 minutes
Cooking time: 1 hour
Serves 6

4 potatoes
olive oil, for brushing
chopped fresh parsley, to garnish
olive oil, for brushing and pan-frying
2 large potatoes, cur into ¼-inch/5-mm slices
flatbread, to serve

For the koftas
14 oz/400g lean ground (minced) lamb
2 small onions, grated
2 garlic cloves, grated
2 tablespoons all-purpose (plain) flour
1 egg yolk
1 cup (2 oz/50 g) chopped fresh parsley
1 teaspoon seven spices seasoning
½ teaspoon ground cinnamon
½ teaspoon pepper
1 teaspoon dried mint
½ teaspoon sea salt

For the tahini sauce
⅔ cup (¼ pint/150 ml) tahini
juice of 1 lemon
½ teaspoon sea salt

Preheat the oven to 375°F/190°C/Gas Mark 5. Brush an
8½ inch/22 cm round cake pan or ovenproof dish with oil.
Put all the ingredients for the koftas into a bowl and mix well.
Dampen your hands and shape golf ball-sized pieces of the
mixture into patty shapes. Repeat this until all the mixture is
used. Put the patties into the prepared pan or dish. Heat some
oil in a skillet or frying pan, add the potato slices, and cook
on both sides until golden. Remove the slices and drain on
paper towels. To make the sauce, mix the tahini with the lemon
juice, then gradually stir in 1¼ cups (½ pint/300 ml) warm
water. Pour the sauce over the koftas to cover, then top with
the potato slices in a single layer. Cover with foil and bake for
1 hour. Remove from the oven and let cool slightly before
serving with flatbread.

KOFTAS WITH TOMATO AND EGGPLANT

PHOTO PAGE 251

—

كفتة لحم الغنم مع
الباذنجان بصلصة
الطماطم

Preparation time: 1 hour 30 minutes
Cooking time: 1 hour
Serves 4

1 large eggplant (aubergine)
2 tablespoons olive oil, plus extra for frying
chopped fresh parsley, to garnish

For the tomato sauce
2 tablespoons olive oil
2 small onions, chopped
1 teaspoon seven spices seasoning
3 garlic cloves, crushed
28 oz/800 g canned chopped tomatoes
2 tablespoons tomato paste (purée)
1 cinnamon stick
pinch of sugar
salt and pepper

For the koftas
9 oz/250 g lean ground (minced) lamb
1 small onion, grated
2 garlic cloves, grated
2 tablespoons all-purpose (plain) flour
1 egg yolk
½ cup (1 oz/25 g) chopped fresh parsley
1 teaspoon seven spices seasoning
½ teaspoon pepper
1 teaspoon dried mint
½ teaspoon sea salt
1 tablespoon olive oil

Slice the eggplant (aubergine) into eight ¼ inch/5 mm thick circles and brush with the oil. Put them into an ovenproof dish in a single layer, sprinkle with salt, and roast for 35–40 minutes. Meanwhile, make the tomato sauce. Heat the oil in a saucepan, add the onions and seven spices seasoning, and cook over low heat, stirring occasionally, for 7–8 minutes until softened. Add the garlic and cook for 1 minute, then increase the heat, and stir in the tomatoes, tomato paste (purée), and 1¼ cups (½ pint/300 ml) water. Add the cinnamon stick and sugar, season well with salt and pepper, and bring to a boil. Reduce the heat and simmer for 1 hour. To make the koftas, put the lamb, onion, garlic, flour, egg yolk, parsley, seven spices seasoning, pepper, mint, and salt into a large bowl and mix well with a wooden spoon until combined. Shape golf ball-sized pieces of the mixture into patty shapes. Heat the oil in a skillet or frying pan, add the koftas, in batches if necessary, and cook until browned on the underside, then turn and cook until the second side is browned. You may need to do this in two batches so that the pan isn't overcrowded. Put the koftas on top of the eggplant slices without overlapping. Remove the cinnamon stick from the tomato sauce, pour the sauce over the top of the koftas, and cover with foil. Reduce the oven temperature to 350°F/180°C/Gas Mark 4 and cook the koftas for 1 hour. Remove the foil for the last 10 minutes of the cooking time. Serve immediately sprinkled with chopped parsley.

KOFTAS WITH TOMATO AND EGGPLANT

LAMB
KOFTAS

—

كفتة لحم الغنم

Preparation time: 30 minutes
Cooking time: 15 minutes
Makes 20

olive oil, for brushing
1 lb/2 oz/500 g lean ground (minced) lamb
2 small onions, grated and squeezed of excess liquid
2 garlic cloves, grated
⅓ cup (½ oz/40 g) all-purpose (plain) flour
1 egg, lightly beaten
1 cup (2 oz/50 g) chopped fresh parsley
1 teaspoon seven spices seasoning
½ teaspoon pepper
2 teaspoons dried mint
2 teaspoons sea salt

Generously brush a flameproof dish with oil. Put the lamb, onions, garlic, flour, egg, parsley, seven spices seasoning, pepper, mint, and salt into a large bowl and mix well. Dampen your hands and shape golf ball-sized pieces of the mixture into sausage shapes. Put them into the prepared dish, leaving a little space between each one. Preheat the broiler (grill). Broil (grill) the koftas for 15 minutes, turning them halfway through the cooking time, until they have cooked through.

GRILLED
KIBBEH
ON
SKEWERS

—

كباب مشوي على
السيخ

Preparation time: 15 minutes, plus soaking time
Cooking time: 10 minutes
Serves 4

1 cup (5 oz/150 g) fine bulgur wheat
14 oz/400 g lean finely ground (minced) lamb
1 onion, very finely chopped
1 garlic clove, crushed
3 teaspoons ground allspice
1½ teaspoons ground cinnamon
¼ teaspoon ground nutmeg
1 teaspoon chili powder
1 teaspoon salt
1 teaspoon pepper
4 tablespoons finely chopped fresh flat-leaf parsley
plain (natural) yogurt, salad, pita breads, and pickles, to serve

Put the bulgur wheat into a bowl, pour in water to cover, and soak for 1 hour, then drain. Meanwhile, prepare the meat. Put the lamb, onion, garlic, allspice, cinnamon, nutmeg, chili powder, salt, and pepper into a large bowl, add 2 tablespoons water, and knead until combined. Add the parsley and bulgur wheat and knead for another 10 minutes until the mixture has the texture of soft dough. Divide the mixture into 12–16 portions and roll them into balls. Thread a skewer through a ball, then squeeze out the kibbeh with your hands to form a sausage shape. Repeat with the remaining mixture. Grill over a hot barbecue or cook under a preheated broiler (grill), turning occasionally, for about 10 minutes until cooked through. Serve with yogurt spooned over, fresh salad, pita, and pickles.

LAMB SHANKS AND STUFFED GRAPE LEAVES

زند الغنم مع محشي
ورق العنب

Preparation time: 45 minutes
Cooking time: 2 hours
Serves 4

1 tablespoon olive oil
4 lamb shanks
1 onion, diced
2 garlic cloves, crushed
2 teaspoons ground cumin
1 teaspoon ground cinnamon
1 teaspoon ground allspice
28 oz/800 g canned chopped tomatoes
3 cups (1¼ pints/750 ml) chicken stock or water
2 tablespoons chopped fresh cilantro (coriander)
salt and pepper
Stuffed Grape Leaves (see p279)
plain (natural) yogurt, to serve

Heat the olive oil in a large, heavy saucepan, add the lamb shanks, and sear over medium-high heat for about 5 minutes on each side. Remove from the pan and set aside. Reduce the heat, add the onion to the pan, and cook, stirring occasionally, for 5 minutes until softened. Add the garlic and, cook, stirring for another minute. Stir in the cumin, cinnamon, and allspice and season with salt and pepper. Increase the heat to medium, stir in the tomatoes and stock, return the lamb to the pan, and bring to a boil. Reduce the heat to low, cover, and simmer, stirring occasionally, for 1 hour. Turn the lamb shanks once halfway through the cooking time. Uncover the pan and cook for another 20–30 minutes until the lamb is tender and cooked to your liking. Remove the lamb from pan, cover, and keep warm. Cook the sauce for another 10–15 minutes until reduced, then stir in the cilantro (coriander). Taste and adjust the seasoning, if necessary, and serve with Stuffed Grape (vine) Leaves and a spoonful of yogurt.

POTATO PATTIES STUFFED WITH LAMB

اقراص البطاطس المحشوة بلحم الغنم

Preparation time: 30–40 minutes, plus chilling time
Cooking time: 20–30 minutes
Makes 30

2¼ lb/1 kg potatoes, cubed
5 tablespoons (2½ oz/65 g) butter
¾ cup (3 oz/80 g) whole wheat (wholemeal) flour
6 eggs
2 teaspoons seven spices seasoning
1¼ cups (6 oz/175 g) bulgur wheat, soaked for 5 minutes and drained
2¼ cups (9 oz/250 g) all-purpose (plain) flour
5½ cups (11 oz/300 g) breadcrumbs
vegetable oil, for frying
salt and pepper

For the lamb
olive oil
12 oz/350 g ground (minced) lamb
2 small onions, chopped
2 garlic cloves, finely chopped
1 teaspoon seven spices seasoning
1½ tablespoons medium curry powder
1 teaspoon pepper
2 teaspoons salt

Cook the potatoes in a large saucepan of salted boiling water for 15 minutes until soft. Drain and mash with the butter, whole wheat (wholemeal) flour, and 1 egg. Season with 2 teaspoons salt, 1 teaspoon pepper, and the seven spices seasoning. Squeeze the water out of the bulgur wheat, add to the potato, and mix well until thoroughly combined. Chill in the refrigerator. Meanwhile, prepare the lamb. Heat the oil in a skillet or frying pan, add the lamb, and cook over medium heat, stirring frequently, for 8–10 minutes until evenly browned. Add the onions and garlic, reduce the heat, and cook, stirring occasionally, for 5 minutes until softened. Stir in the seven spices seasoning, curry powder, pepper, and salt and cook for another few minutes. Remove the pan from the heat and let cool to room temperature. Lightly beat the remaining eggs in a shallow dish and put the all-purpose (plain) flour and breadcrumbs into separate shallow dishes. Remove the potato mixture from the refrigerator and shape golf ball-sized pieces into circles. Dust with flour and put a heaping teaspoon of the lamb mixture into the middle of each circle. Carefully wrap the potato mixture around the lamb filling to form patties. Pour oil into a skillet or frying pan to a depth of about 1½ in/4 cm and heat. Dust each patty first in flour, then dip into the beaten egg, and, finally, coat in breadcrumbs. Place the patties on a tray as the process is completed. Carefully add 3–4 patties to the hot oil and cook until golden brown on both sides. Remove with a slotted spoon, drain on paper towels, and keep warm while you cook the remaining patties in batches of 3–4. Serve hot.

LEG OF LAMB STUFFED WITH APRICOTS

LEG OF LAMB STUFFED WITH APRICOTS

PHOTO PAGE 256

—

فخذة غنم مشوية
ومحشوة بالمشمش

Preparation time: 20 minutes
Cooking time: 50 minutes–1 hour 15 minutes
Serves 4–6

2½ lb/1.2 kg leg of lamb, boned
2 garlic cloves, sliced
2 rosemary sprigs
olive oil, for drizzling
sea salt and pepper

For the stuffing
½ onion, finely chopped
½ celery stalk, finely diced
1 cup (4 oz/120 g) finely chopped dried apricots
scant 1 cup (3½ oz/100 g) shelled walnuts, chopped
2 tablespoons chopped fresh mint
2 tablespoons chopped fresh parsley
¼ teaspoon ground cardamom
¼ teaspoon ground ginger
¼ teaspoon ground cinnamon
¼ teaspoon ground allspice
¼ teaspoon grated nutmeg
salt and pepper

To serve
2 tablespoons pomegranate seeds
2 tablespoons chopped fresh parsley

Preheat the oven to 350°F/180°C/Gas Mark 4. Put all the stuffing ingredients into a bowl, mix well, and season with salt and pepper. Lay the lamb flat on a board, skin side down, and season well with sea salt and pepper. Spoon the stuffing onto the lamb, roll up the meat, and tie securely with kitchen string. Season again with salt and pepper. Make slits in the skin of the lamb and slide the garlic slices into them. Put the lamb into a roasting pan, lay the rosemary sprigs on top, and drizzle with oil. Roast, basting halfway through the cooking time, for 50 minutes if you like your lamb rare or for 1 hour 10 minutes for medium. Remove the lamb from the oven, wrap in foil, and let rest for 10 minutes. Transfer the lamb to a serving dish, sprinkle with pomegranate seeds and chopped parsley, and serve immediately.

LEG
OF
LAMB

PHOTO PAGE 259

فخذة غنم بالفرن

Preparation time: 10 minutes
Cooking time: 2 hours 30 minutes
Serves 4

2½ lb/1.2 kg leg of lamb
4 garlic cloves, sliced
4 rosemary sprigs
salt and pepper
chopped fresh mint, to garnish

Preheat the oven to 350°F/180°C/Gas Mark 4. Pat the lamb dry with paper towels, then makes slits over the top. Stuff the garlic slices into the slits and put the rosemary sprigs on top. Season with salt and pepper and wrap the leg in foil. Put it into a roasting pan and roast for 2½ hours. Serve unwrapped and garnished with mint.

SUMMER
SQUASH
RINGS
WITH
LAMB

حلقات النخاع مع
لحم الغنم

Preparation time: 40–50 minutes
Cooking time: 1 hour 15 minutes
Serves 4–6

2 tablespoons olive oil
1 onion, finely chopped
2 garlic cloves, crushed
½ teaspoon seven spices seasoning
½ teaspoon dried basil
14 oz/400 g canned chopped tomatoes
1¾ lb/800 g summer squash (marrow),
    cut into ¾ inch/2 cm slices

For the lamb
9 oz/250 g ground (minced) lamb
1 onion, chopped
2 garlic cloves, crushed
½ teaspoon seven spices seasoning
dash of Worcestershire sauce
2 tablespoons tomato paste (purée)
salt and pepper

Heat the oil in a pan, add the onion, and cook over low heat for 5 minutes until softened. Add the garlic and cook for another minute, then stir in the seven spices seasoning, basil, and chopped tomatoes and increase the heat to medium. Pour in 1¼ cups (½ pint/300 ml) hot water and bring to a boil, then reduce the heat and simmer, stirring occasionally, for 20 minutes. Meanwhile, preheat the oven to 350°F/180°C/Gas Mark 4. Put the summer squash (marrow) slices into an ovenproof dish. Put the lamb into another pan and cook over medium heat, stirring frequently, until browned. Add the onion, garlic, and seven spices seasoning and cook for 5 minutes, then add a dash of Worcestershire sauce and the tomato paste (purée). Stir in ⅔ cup (¼ pint/150 ml) hot water and simmer for 15 minutes. Spoon the lamb mixture over the summer squash and spread evenly, then pour the tomato sauce over. Cover the dish with foil and bake cook for 1¼ hours.

OKRA AND LAMB

OKRA
AND
LAMB

PHOTO PAGE 260

بامياء بلحم الغنم

Preparation time: 20 minutes
Cooking time: 2 hours 15 minutes
Serves 4

2 tablespoons olive oil, plus extra for drizzling
2 small onions, finely chopped
5 garlic cloves, sliced
14 oz/400 g boneless lamb, diced
1 lb/450 g okra, trimmed
3 tablespoons tomato paste (purée)
½ teaspoon seven spices seasoning
salt and pepper

Preheat the oven to 375°F/190°C/Gas Mark 5. Heat the olive oil in a large skillet or frying pan, add the onions, and cook over low heat, stirring occasionally, for 5 minutes until softened but not colored. Add the garlic and cook for another minute. Add the lamb, increase the heat to medium, and cook, stirring frequently, for 8–10 minutes until evenly browned. Meanwhile, put the okra into a roasting pan, drizzle with a little olive oil, and roast for 30 minutes. Meanwhile, pour enough boiling water into the pan of lamb to cover and cook for 30 minutes. Stir in the tomato paste (purée), okra, and seven spices seasoning and continue to cook for 1 hour more or until the sauce has reduced and thickened and the lamb is tender. Season with salt and pepper and serve.

LIVER
CASSEROLE

طاجن كبدة الغنم

Preparation time: 20 minutes
Cooking time: 1 hour 50 minutes
Serves 4

1¼ cups (5 oz/150 g) all-purpose (plain) flour
1 teaspoon pepper
pinch of salt
1 lb 2 oz/500 g lambs liver or calf liver, sliced
1 onion, chopped
2 carrots, chopped
2¾ cups (7 oz/200 g) mushrooms, chopped
1 beef bouillon (stock) cube
2 teaspoons cornstarch (cornflour)
1 teaspoon paprika
chopped fresh parsley, to garnish

Preheat the oven to 350°F/180°C/Gas Mark 4. Mix the flour with pepper and salt in a shallow dish. Add the liver, in batches, and toss to coat. Shake off the excess and put it onto the prepared baking sheet. Put it into the oven and cook for 20 minutes. Remove the liver from the oven and transfer it to a casserole. Add the onion, carrots, and mushrooms, crumble in the bouillon (stock) cube, sprinkle with the cornstarch (cornflour), and pour in enough boiling water to cover. Add the paprika and season with pepper. Cover the casserole, put it into the oven, and cook for 1½ hours. This dish is best reheated, sprinkled with parsley, and eaten the next day.

LAMB SPAGHETTI WITH CASHEW NUTS AND SEVEN SPICE

—

مكرونة سباغيتي
بلحم الغنم مع البهارات
السبعة والكاجو

Preparation time: 20 minutes
Cooking time: 50 minutes–1 hour
Serves 2

7 oz/200 g spaghetti
1 cinnamon stick
salt

For the sauce
3 tablespoons olive oil
2 onions, finely chopped
3 garlic cloves, crushed
9 oz/250 g ground (minced) lamb
5 tablespoons tomato paste (purée)
1 teaspoon seven spices seasoning
½ teaspoon ground cinnamon
⅔ cup (2½ oz/65 g) cashew nuts, toasted

First make the sauce. Heat the oil in a large skillet or frying pan, add the onions, and cook over low heat, stirring occasionally, for 5 minutes until softened but not colored. Add the garlic and cook for another minute. Add the lamb, increase the heat to medium, and cook, stirring and breaking up the meat with a wooden spoon, for 5–8 minutes until evenly browned. Stir in the tomato paste (purée) and a splash of water, reduce the heat, and simmer for 30 minutes, adding more water if necessary. Meanwhile, bring a large saucepan of water to a boil and add a generous pinch of salt. Add the spaghetti and cinnamon stick, bring back to a boil, and cook for 8–10 minutes until tender but still firm to the bite. Stir the seven spices seasoning and cinnamon into the sauce, season with salt and pepper, and cook for another 5 minutes. Drain the spaghetti and tip it into a serving dish, discarding the cinnamon stick. Add the sauce and toss well, then sprinkle with toasted cashew nuts, and serve immediately.

RACK OF LAMB WITH A PARSLEY AND GARLIC CRUST

PHOTO PAGE 265

—

ريش الغنم المغلف بالبقدونس والثوم

Preparation time: 10 minutes
Cooking time: 20 minutes
Serves 2

12 oz/350 g rack of lamb, trimmed
1 tablespoon olive oil
1 tablespoon butter
1 bunch of fresh parsley
3 fresh mint sprigs
2 garlic cloves
4 tablespoons fresh breadcrumbs
2 tablespoons pomegranate molasses
salt and pepper

Preheat the oven to 350°F/180°C/Gas Mark 4. Rub the lamb with the olive oil and season with salt and pepper. Melt the butter in a skillet or frying pan, add the lamb, and cook over medium heat, turning frequently, for 2 minutes until browned on all sides. Transfer the lamb to a roasting pan and put it into the oven for 5 minutes, then remove and let rest. Meanwhile, make the crust. Put the parsley, mint, and garlic into a food processor and process until finely chopped and combined, then add the breadcrumbs, and pulse until combined. Tip out onto a plate. Brush the meat with the pomegranate molasses, then roll it in the herb and breadcrumb mixture. Return it to the oven and cook for another 10 minutes or a little longer if your prefer your meat well done. Remove from the oven and let rest for 10 minutes, then serve.

SHOULDER OF LAMB IN YOGURT

—

كتف الغنم بالزبادي

Preparation time: 20 minutes
Cooking time: 1 hour 30 minutes
Serves 4

14 oz/400g boneless shoulder of lamb, diced
2 tablespoons olive oil
1 onion, chopped
4 garlic cloves, sliced
generous 2 cups (18 fl oz/500 ml) plain (natural) yogurt
1 egg
½ teaspoon ground cumin
½ teaspoon pepper
½ teaspoon salt
generous ¼ cup (2 oz/50 g) basmati or long grain rice, cooked
1 teaspoon dried mint

Put the lamb into a saucepan, pour in water to cover, and bring to a boil. Remove from the heat, drain, and rinse. Heat the oil in another saucepan, add the onions and garlic, and cook over low heat, stirring occasionally, for 7–8 minutes, until softened and lightly colored. Add the lamb, pour in water to cover, and simmer for 1 hour until the liquid has reduced. Put the yogurt and egg into another saucepan, pour in generous 2 cups (18 fl oz/500 ml) water, and bring to a boil, whisking constantly. Add the lamb, cumin, pepper, salt, and rice and cook for 15 minutes. Stir in the mint and serve.

RACK OF LAMB WITH A PARSLEY AND GARLIC CRUST

LAMB SHAWARMA

شاورما لحم الغنم

Preparation time: 20 minutes, plus marinating time
Cooking time: 10 minutes
Serves 4

1 lb/450 g boneless leg of lamb
2 garlic cloves, crushed
4 tablespoons olive oil
juice of ½ lemon
pinch of grated nutmeg
pinch of ground cinnamon
salt and black pepper
Lebanese bread and salad, to serve

Cut off and discard any visible fat from the lamb and cut the meat into strips. Put it into a bowl, add the garlic, and pour half the olive oil and all of the lemon juice over it. Add the spices, season with salt and pepper, and toss well. Let marinate for 30 minutes. Heat with the remaining olive oil in a skillet or frying pan, add the lamb, and cook over medium heat, stirring frequently, for 10 minutes until evenly browned and cooked through. Serve immediately with Lebanese bread and salad.

LAMB AND CAULIFLOWER STEW

يخني القرنبيط مع لحم الغنم

Preparation time: 20–30 minutes
Cooking time: 1 hour
Serves 4

3 tablespoons olive oil
1 lb 2 oz/500 g lamb, diced
1 onion, chopped
3 garlic cloves, sliced
4 tablespoons tomato paste (purée)
3 cups (1¼ pints/750 ml) hot chicken stock
½ cauliflower, cut into florets
1 teaspoon seven spices seasoning
salt and pepper

Heat 2 tablespoons of the oil in a large deep skillet or frying pan, add the lamb, and cook over medium heat, stirring frequently, for 8–10 minutes until evenly browned. Transfer the meat to a plate and set aside. Add the remaining oil to the pan and heat, then add the onion and cook over low heat, stirring occasionally, for 5 minutes until softened but not colored. Increase the heat to medium, add the garlic, and return the meat to the pan, then stir in the tomato paste (purée). Pour in enough stock to cover and bring to a boil, then reduce the heat and simmer for 1 hour. Bring a saucepan of salted water to a boil, add the cauliflower, and cook for 5–8 minutes until nearly tender, then drain and add to the stew. Stir in the seven spices seasoning and season to taste with salt and pepper. Cook for a few more minutes and then serve.

LAMB STEW
WITH
POTATOES
AND
TOMATOES

—

يخني لحم الغنم مع البطاطس
والطماطم

Preparation time: 30–40 minutes
Cooking time: 2 hours 30 minutes
Serves 4

1 lb 2 oz/500 g boneless lamb, diced
2 tablespoons olive oil
1 onion, sliced
2 garlic cloves, chopped
1 teaspoon thyme leaves, chopped
1 teaspoon dried mint
1 bay leaf
scant ½ cup (3½ fl oz/100 ml) red wine
3 tablespoons tomato paste (purée)
14 oz/400 g canned chopped tomatoes
1 cups (14 fl oz/400 ml) beef stock
1 lb/450 g small potatoes, quartered
2 tablespoons chopped fresh mint
salt and pepper
flatbread, to serve

For the spice mixture
2 teaspoons pepper
1 teaspoon sea salt
1 teaspoon ground cinnamon
¼ teaspoon ground allspice
pinch of grated nutmeg
1 tablespoon all-purpose (plain) flour

Preheat the oven to 325°F/160°C/Gas Mark 3. First, make the spice mixture. Mix together all the spices in a large bowl and add the flour. Add the diced lamb to the bowl and toss to coat well. Heat a large flameproof casserole, add half the oil, then add the lamb, in batches, if necessary, and cook over medium heat, stirring frequently, for 8–10 minutes until evenly browned on all sides. Remove from casserole and set aside. Add the remaining oil to the casserole and heat. Add the onion and cook over low heat, stirring occasionally, for 7–8 minutes until softened and lightly colored. Add the garlic and herbs and cook for another minute. Pour in the red wine and cook for 2–3 minutes. Return the meat to the casserole, add the tomato paste (purée), and cook for 1 minute, then add the tomatoes and stock. Bring to a boil, cover, and transfer the casserole to the oven. Cook for 1½ hours. Remove the casserole from the oven, add the potatoes, and taste and adjust the seasoning. Replace the cover, return the casserole to the oven, and cook for another hour. Remove the casserole from the oven, stir in the chopped mint, and serve immediately with flatbread to soak up the juices.

LAMB SHANK AND OLIVE CASSEROLE

LAMB SHANK AND OLIVE CASSEROLE

PHOTO PAGE 268

—

طاجن زند الغنم مع
الزيتون

Preparation time: 30 minutes
Cooking time: 2 hours 30 minutes
Serves 8

8 lamb shanks, trimmed
2 tablespoons all-purpose (plain) flour
1 tablespoon olive oil
1 red onion, sliced
3 garlic cloves, lightly crushed
4 canned anchovy fillets, drained and chopped
2 teaspoons seven spices seasoning
scant 1 cup (7 fl oz/200 ml) red wine
scant 1 cup (7 fl oz/200 ml) hot beef stock
14 oz/400 g canned chopped tomatoes
1½ cups (5 oz/150 g) green olives
1 tablespoon pomegranate syrup
pinch of paprika
8 fresh basil leaves, torn
salt and pepper

Preheat the oven to 325°F/160°C/Gas Mark 3. Dust the lamb shanks with the flour and season with salt and black pepper. Heat the oil a large flameproof casserole, add the lamb shanks, and cook over medium heat, turning occasionally, for 8–10 minutes until evenly browned. Transfer the lamb shanks to a plate and add the onions and garlic to the casserole. Reduce the heat and cook, stirring occasionally, for 5 minutes until softened. Add the anchovies and seven spices seasoning and return the lamb shanks to the casserole. Pour in the red wine and cook for a few minutes, then add the hot stock and chopped tomatoes. Bring to a boil, cover, and transfer the casserole to the oven. Cook for 2 hours or until the lamb is very tender and falling off the bones, then remove from the oven. Return the casserole to the stove, add the olives, pomegranate syrup, and paprika, and simmer for 15 minutes. Stir in the basil, taste and adjust the seasoning, if necessary, and serve.

LAMB STEW WITH EGGPLANT

LAMB STEW WITH EGGPLANT

PHOTO PAGE 270

—

يخني الباذنجان مع
لحم الغنم

Preparation time: 30 minutes
Cooking time: 2 hours
Serves 4

1 large eggplant (aubergine), cut into 1½ inch/4 cm cubes
4 tablespoons olive oil
1 lb/2 oz/500 g lamb, cut into 1½ inch/4 cm cubes
1 tablespoon all-purpose (plain) flour
1 onion, sliced
2 garlic cloves, chopped
1 teaspoon chopped dried thyme
1 teaspoon dried mint
1 bay leaf
scant ½ cup (3½ fl oz/100 ml) red wine
3 tablespoons tomato paste (purée)
14 oz/400 g canned chopped tomatoes
1¾ cups (14 fl oz/400 ml) beef stock
3 tablespoons chopped fresh parsley
salt and pepper

For the spice mixture
2 teaspoons pepper
1 teaspoon sea salt
1 teaspoon ground cinnamon
¼ teaspoon ground allspice
pinch of grated nutmeg

Preheat the oven to 400°F/200°C/Gas Mark 6. Toss the eggplant (aubergine) cubes with half the oil to coat, then put them onto a baking sheet. Roast for 20 minutes, then remove from the oven and set aside. Reduce the oven temperature to 325°F/160°C/Gas Mark 3. Mix together all the spices for the spice mixture in a large bowl. Dust the lamb with the flour. Heat half the remaining oil in a large flameproof casserole, add the lamb, in batches if necessary, and cook over medium heat, stirring frequently, for 8–10 minutes until evenly browned. Remove from casserole and set aside. Add the remaining oil to the casserole and heat. Add the onion and cook over low heat, stirring occasionally, for 7–8 minutes until softened lightly colored. Add the garlic and herbs and cook for 1 minute, then pour in the red wine and cook for another few minutes. Return the meat to the casserole, stir in the spice mixture, and cook 1–2 minutes until the spices release their aroma. Stir in the tomato paste (purée), tomatoes, and stock and bring to a boil. Add the eggplant cubes, cover the casserole, transfer it to the oven, and cook for 2 hours. Remove the casserole from the oven. Remove and discard the bay leaf and taste and adjust the seasoning if necessary. Stir in the chopped parsley and serve.

LAMB STEW WITH PRUNES AND APRICOTS

PHOTO PAGE 273

—

يخني لحم الغنم مع
البرقوق والمشمش

Preparation time: 30 minutes
Cooking time: 1 hour 30 minutes
Serves 4–6

1 lb 2 oz/500 g boneless lamb, diced
1 tablespoon all-purpose (plain) flour
3 tablespoons olive oil
1 onion, sliced
2 garlic cloves, chopped
1 teaspoon chopped dried thyme
1 teaspoon dried mint
1 bay leaf
scant ½ cup (3½ fl oz/100 ml) red wine
3 tablespoons tomato paste (purée)
3 cups (1¼ pints/750 ml) beef stock
5 oz/150 g prunes, pitted (stoned)
5 oz/150 g dried Blenheim apricots, pitted (stoned) and halved
3 tablespoons chopped parsley
salt and pepper

For the spice mixture
1 teaspoon pepper
1 teaspoon sea salt
1 teaspoon ground cinnamon
¼ teaspoon ground allspice
pinch of grated nutmeg

Preheat the oven to 325°F/160°C/Gas Mark 3. Mix together all the spices for the spice mixture in a large bowl. Dust the lamb with the flour. Heat 2 tablespoons of the oil in a large flameproof casserole, add the lamb, in batches if necessary, and cook over medium heat, stirring frequently, for 8–10 minutes until evenly browned. Remove from casserole and set aside. Add the remaining oil to the casserole and heat, then add the onion and cook over low heat, stirring occasionally, for 7–8 minutes until softened and lightly colored. Add the garlic, thyme, mint, and bay leaf and cook for another 2 minutes, then pour in the wine and cook for another few minutes. Return the meat to the pan, add the spice mixture, tomato paste (purée), and beef stock, and bring to a boil. Add the dried fruit, cover the casserole, transfer it to the oven, and cook for 1½ hours or until the meat is tender. sRemove the casserole from the oven. Remove and discard the bay leaf and taste and adjust the seasoning if necessary. Stir in the chopped parsley and serve immediately.

LAMB STEW WITH PRUNES AND APRICOTS

GRAPE
LEAVES

ورق عنب

Preparation time: 25 minutes
Cooking time: 2 hours
Serves 4

12 oz/350 g grape (vine) leaves
½ cup (4 fl oz/120 ml) olive oil
1 onion, finely diced
1 red bell pepper, seeded and finely diced
scant 1 cup (6 oz/175 g) long grain rice
½ teaspoon chili powder
1 teaspoon ground allspice
1 teaspoon salt
1½ tablespoons tomato paste (purée)
2 tablespoons chopped fresh parsley
¼ cup (1 oz/25 g) pine nuts

For the cooking liquid
1 tablespoon tomato paste (purée)
1 tomato, peeled and chopped
4 garlic cloves, crushed
1 teaspoon salt
½ chile
2 tablespoons lemon juice

If using fresh leaves, bring a saucepan of salted water to a boil, add the leaves, and blanch for 3 minutes. Remove from the pan and put them on a wire rack to cool. If using leaves preserved in salt solution (brine), soak them in hot water for 30 minutes, then drain, rinse thoroughly, and pat dry with paper towels. Heat the oil in a large skillet or frying pan, add the onion and bell pepper, and cook over low heat, stirring occasionally, for 5 minutes until softened. Add the rice, chili powder, allspice, salt, and tomato paste (purée) and cook, stirring occasionally, for another 10 minutes. Remove the pan from the heat, stir in the parsley and pine nuts, and transfer to a large bowl to cool. Lay out the grape (vine) leaves flat, shiny side down, and trim off any remaining stems. Put a tablespoonful of the rice mixture at the wide bottom of a leaf, fold in the sides, tuck them under, and roll up tightly into a cigar shape. Repeat with the remaining leaves and filling until all the filling has been used. Use any remaining leaves to line the base of your pan to prevent the rolls from sticking. Pack the rolls into the pan in layers as tightly as possible. Put a plate on top to weigh them down. Mix together all the ingredients for the cooking liquid in a bowl and stir in 3 cups (1¼ pints/750 ml) boiling water. Pour the mixture into the pan to covers the rolls (add more water if necessary). Bring to a boil over medium heat, then reduce the heat, cover, and cook for 1½–2 hours until the rice is tender, the leaves have softened, and the sauce has thickened slightly.

LAMB LASAGNA WITH CHEESE AND ZA'ATER CRUMB

لزانيا لحم الغنم
مع الزعتر

Preparation time: 30 minutes
Cooking time: 45 minutes
Serves 6

2 garlic cloves, chopped
¼ teaspoon grated nutmeg
½ teaspoon ground cinnamon
2 tablespoons tomato paste (purée)
5 tablespoons red wine
28 oz/800 g canned chopped tomatoes
1 teaspoon thyme leaves
1 bay leaf
8 fresh lasagna sheets
scant ½ cup (3½ oz/100 g) ricotta cheese
11 oz/300 g mozzarella cheese, torn into pieces
generous 1 cup (3½ oz/100 g) grated Parmesan cheese
4 tablespoons fresh breadcrumbs
3 tablespoons za'atar
salt and pepper

For the sauce
7 tablespoons (3½ oz/100 g) butter
¾ cup (3 oz/80 g) all-purpose (plain) flour
3 cups (1¼ pints/750 ml) whole (full-fat) milk
scant ½ cup (3½ fl oz/100 ml) heavy (double) cream
salt and pepper

Heat the oil in a large skillet or frying pan, add the lamb, and cook over medium heat, stirring frequently, for 8–10 minutes, until evenly browned, then remove from pan. Add the onion and garlic to the pan, reduce the heat, and cook, stirring occasionally, for 5 minutes. Add the nutmeg and cinnamon and cook for 2 minutes until fragrant, then stir in the tomato paste (purée) and red wine, increase the heat to high, and cook for a few minutes. Add the tomatoes, thyme, and bay leaf, season with salt and pepper, reduce the heat, and simmer for 1 hour. Meanwhile, make the sauce. Melt the butter in a saucepan over low heat, stir in the flour, and cook, stirring constantly, for 2 minutes. Gradually whisk in the milk, a little at a time, and then whisk in the cream, a little at a time. Cook, whisking constantly, until thickened. Season with salt and pepper, remove from the heat, and set aside. Preheat the oven to 375°F/190°C/Gas Mark 5. Spoon half the lamb mixture into a 12 x 6 x 2 inch/30 x 15 x 5 cm ovenproof dish. Cover with 4 lasagna noodles (sheets), then add the remaining lamb mixture, and top with the remaining lasagna noodles. Pour the sauce over the lasagna, add spoonfuls of ricotta, and sprinkle with the torn mozzarella. Mix together the Parmesan, breadcrumbs, and za'ater in a bowl, then sprinkle the mixture over the top. Bake for 45 minutes, then remove from the oven and let cool slightly before serving.

LAMB
RAGOUT

يخني لحم الغنم

3 tablespoons olive oil
14 oz/400 g boneless leg of lamb, cut into cubes
1 large onion, sliced
2 garlic cloves
3 small round eggplants (aubergines), quartered
2 teaspoons ground allspice
2 teaspoons pepper
¼ teaspoon grated nutmeg
1 cinnamon stick
14 oz/400 g canned tomatoes
4 tomatoes, cut into eighths
2 tablespoons tomato paste (purée)
2 tablespoons red wine
5 dried figs, sliced
toasted split almonds and rice vermicelli, to serve

Heat 1 tablespoon of the oil in a large heavy saucepan, add the lamb, and sear over high heat for 1 minute on each side. Remove from the pan and set aside. Reduce the heat to medium-high, add the remaining oil, the onion, garlic, and eggplants (aubergines), and cook, stirring frequently, for 5–8 minutes until the onion and eggplants have softened. Stir in the allspice, pepper, and nutmeg and add the cinnamon stick, canned and fresh tomatoes, tomatoes paste (purée), and red wine. Reduce the heat and simmer, stirring occasionally, for 30 minutes. Add the figs, cover, and cook over low heat for another 45–60 minutes until the sauce has thickened and the meat is tender. Serve sprinkled with toasted split almonds and rice vermicelli.

MOTHER'S MILK WITH LAMB

PHOTO PAGE 279

لبن أمه مع لحم
الغنم

Preparation time: 15 minutes
Cooking time: 30–40 minutes
Serves 4

½ cup (3½ oz/100 g) long grain rice
2½ cups (1 pint/600 ml) plain (natural) yogurt
1 tablespoon cornstarch (cornflour)
1½ teaspoons butter
4 garlic cloves, crushed
1 lb 2 oz/500 g ground (minced) lamb
1 small bunch of fresh mint, chopped
salt and white pepper

Put the rice into a small pan, pour in boiling water to cover, and cook for 10–15 minutes until the rice is tender and the water has been absorbed. Put the yogurt into a large pan, pour in generous 2 cups (18 fl oz/500 ml) water, and add the cornstarch (cornflour). Bring to a boil, whisking constantly, then stop stirring and cook until the yogurt starts to thicken. Meanwhile, melt the butter in a skillet or frying pan, add the garlic and cook over low heat, stirring occasionally, for a few minutes. Add the lamb, increase the heat to medium, and cook, stirring frequently, for 5–8 minutes until browned. Stir the lamb mixture into the yogurt mixture, then add the mint and rice. Cook for a few minutes more, then season to taste, and serve.

SHEPHERD'S PIE

فطيرة الراعي اللبنانية
بلحم الغنم

Preparation time: 30 minutes
Cooking time: 1 hour 30 minutes
Serves 4

1 lb 2 oz/500 g ground (minced) lamb
1 onion, chopped
1 celery stalk, diced
1 carrot, diced
1 bay leaf
1 teaspoon seven spices seasoning
½ teaspoon salt
1 teaspoon pepper
4½ cups (1¾ pints/1 liter) beef stock
4 potatoes, thinly sliced
4 tablespoons (2 oz/50 g) butter, melted
salt and pepper

Heat a skillet or frying pan, add the lamb, and cook over medium heat, stirring frequently, for 8–10 minutes until evenly browned. Add the onion, celery, and carrot and cook for 5 minutes, then stir in the bay leaf, seven spices seasoning, salt, and pepper. Pour in the stock and bring to a boil. Reduce the heat, cover, and simmer, stirring occasionally, for 1 hour, adding a little water if the mixture seems to be drying out. Meanwhile, parboil the potatoes in salted boiling water for 10 minutes, then drain. Preheat the oven to 375°F/190°C/Gas Mark 5. Spoon the lamb mixture into an ovenproof dish and top with the slices of potato. Brush with melted butter and season. Bake for 30 minutes or until the potatoes are tender and golden.

MOTHER´S MILK WITH LAMB

SHISH
BARAK

PHOTO PAGE 285

—

شيش برك

Preparation time: 40–45 minutes
Cooking time: 15 minutes
Serves 4

generous 2 cups (18 fl oz/500 ml) plain (natural) yogurt
1 egg lightly beaten
⅓ cup (2 oz/50 g) cold cooked rice
1 tablespoon olive oil
3 garlic cloves, crushed
salt and pepper
chopped fresh parsley and mint, to serve

For the dough
2 cups (8 oz/225 g) all-purpose (plain) flour, plus extra
    for dusting
pinch of salt
1 tablespoon olive oil

For the filling
1 teaspoon olive oil
6 oz/175 g ground (minced) lamb
1 onion, finely diced
4 tablespoons pine nuts, toasted
2 tablespoons chopped fresh mint
¼ teaspoon seven spices seasoning
salt and pepper

First make the dough. Sift together the flour and salt into a
bowl, add the oil and scant ½ cup (312 fl oz/100 ml) water, and
mix to a smooth soft dough. Wrap in plastic wrap (clingfilm)
and let rest in the refrigerator for 30 minutes. Make the filling.
Heat the olive oil in a saucepan, add the lamb, and cook over
medium heat, stirring frequently, for 8–10 minutes until evenly
browned. Reduce the heat, add the onion, season with salt
and pepper, and cook, stirring occasionally, for 5 minutes until
softened. Add the pine nuts, mint, and seven spices seasoning
and season with salt and pepper. Cook for 5 minutes, then
remove from the heat, and let cool completely. To make the
packages, roll out the dough on a well-floured surface to ⅛
inch/2 mm thick and stamp out 25 circles with a 3¼ inch/8
cm cutter. Take a circle and flatten it even more with your
fingers. Add 1 teaspoon of the lamb mixture and fold over the
edges to form packages. Make sure no air is trapped inside the
packages, otherwise they will break when boiled. Repeat this
until all the dough has been used. Put the yogurt and generous
2 cups (18 fl oz/500 ml) water into a large saucepan, add the
egg, and bring to a boil, stirring occasionally. Carefully add
the parcels and cooked rice, season with salt and pepper, and
cook for 5 minutes. Heat the oil in a small skillet or frying pan,
add the garlic cloves, and cook, stirring frequently, for a few
minutes until lightly golden. Add to the pan of packages. Serve
immediately garnished with chopped parsley and mint.

SHISH BARAK

STUFFED
BAKED
EGGPLANTS

محشي الباذنجان
بلحم البقر

Preparation time: 30 minutes
Cooking time: 1 hour
Serves 4

2 eggplants (aubergines), halved lengthwise
scant 1 cup (3½ oz/100 g) pine nuts, toasted
2 tablespoons chopped fresh parsley

For the filling
1 tablespoon olive oil
9 oz/250 g ground (minced) beef
1 onion, finely chopped
3 garlic cloves, sliced
1 teaspoon seven spices seasoning
salt and pepper

For the sauce
1 tablespoon olive oil
1 onion, finely chopped
2 garlic cloves, sliced
14 oz/400g tomatoes, chopped
1 teaspoon seven spices seasoning
salt and pepper

Preheat the oven to 400°F/200°C/Gas Mark 6. Put the eggplant (aubergine) halves on a baking sheet and bake for 40 minutes until softened. Meanwhile, make the filling. Heat a skillet or frying pan, add the oil and beef, and cook over medium heat, stirring frequently, for 8–10 minutes until evenly browned. Add the onion, garlic, and seven spices seasoning, reduce the heat, and cook, stirring occasionally, for another 5 minutes. Season with salt and pepper, remove from the heat, and set aside. To make the sauce, heat the oil in a saucepan, add the onion and cook over low heat, stirring occasionally, for 5 minutes until softened but not colored. Add the garlic and cook for another minute, then add the tomatoes and pour in scant 1 cup (7 fl oz/200 ml) water. Simmer for 20 minutes. Remove the eggplants from the oven and make an indentation in the softened flesh with the back of a spoon. Divide the filling into 4 equal portions and spoon into each of the eggplant halves. Pour the tomato sauce into an ovenproof dish and carefully place the eggplant halves on top. Sprinkle with the pine nuts, cover tightly with foil, and bake for another hour. Remove the eggplants from the oven, sprinkle with the chopped parsley, and serve immediately.

STUFFED BELL PEPPERS WITH RICE AND BEEF

محشي الفلفل بلحم
البقر والارز

Preparation time: 30 minutes
Cooking time: 1 hour
Serves 4

1 teaspoon olive oil
9 oz/250 g ground (minced) beef
1 onion, chopped
1 cup (7 oz/200 g) basmati or quick-cook long grain rice, rinsed
2 teaspoons seven spices seasoning
½ teaspoon dried chili flakes
1 teaspoon salt
½ teaspoon pepper
⅓ cup (1 oz/25 g) chopped parsley
3 red bell peppers, halved lengthwise and seeded
2 yellow bell peppers, halved lengthwise and seeded

For the tomato sauce
14 oz/400 g canned tomatoes
2 garlic cloves, crushed
1 cup (8 fl oz/250 ml) water
pinch of brown sugar
salt and pepper

Heat the oil in a skillet or frying pan, add the beef, and cook over medium heat, stirring frequently, for 8–10 minutes until evenly browned. Add the onion, reduce the heat, and cook, stirring occasionally, for 5 minutes until softened. Stir in the rice, seven spices seasoning, chili flakes, salt, and pepper. Pour in 1 cup (8 fl oz/250 ml) water and continue to cook for a few minutes, then add the parsley. Simmer for 5 minutes, then remove from the heat and cool. Preheat the oven to 375°F/190°C/Gas Mark 5. Carefully stuff the bell pepper halves with the beef filling and put them into an ovenproof dish. To make the tomato sauce, put the tomatoes into a pan, add the garlic, brown sugar, and water. Season with salt and pepper and cook for 10 minutes. Pour the sauce around the stuffed bell peppers, cover the dish with foil, and bake for 1 hour. Serve immediately.

MARINATED CHICKEN IN GARLIC

فروج متبل بالثوم

Preparation time: 10 mnutes, plus marinating time
Cooking time: 1 hour
Serves 4

1 x 2½-lb/1.2-kg chicken, cut into pieces
5 garlic cloves, crushed
olive oil, for drizzling
pepper

Put the chicken pieces into a bowl, sprinkle with the garlic, drizzle generously with olive oil, and season with pepper. Let marinate in the refrigerator for 1 hour. Preheat the oven to 375°F/190°C/Gas Mark 5. Tip the chicken into a roasting pan and roast for 1 hour. Remove from the oven and serve immediately.

CHICKEN AND BASIL SAUCE

دجاج بصلصة
الحبق

Preparation time: 15 minutes
Cooking time: 30–40 minutes
Serves 4

4 chicken breasts
4 tablespoons extra virgin olive oil, plus extra for brushing
2 garlic cloves
½ bunch of fresh basil
pinch of chili flakes
1 onion, chopped
salt and pepper

Preheat the oven to 350°F/180°C/Gas Mark 4. Brush the chicken breasts with olive oil and season with salt and pepper. Heat a skillet or frying pan, add the chicken breasts skin side down, and cook for about 5 minutes until golden. Turn over and cook for another 2 minutes. Remove the chicken breasts from the pan and put them into an ovenproof dish, skin side uppermost. Put the garlic, basil leaves, and oil olive into a food processor and process until nearly smooth, adding more oil if necessary. Pour the basil mixture around the chicken, add a pinch of chili flakes and the chopped onion, and roast for 30 minutes. Remove the chicken from the oven and let rest for 5 minutes before serving.

CHICKEN PHYLLO ROLLS

رقائق ملفوفة
محشوة بالدجاج

Preparation time: 30 minutes
Cooking time: 15 minutes
Serves 4

1 tablespoon olive oil
4 skinless, boneless chicken breasts, diced
1 onion, finely chopped
2 tablespoons ground sumac
pinch of chili powder
½ teaspoon cayenne pepper
2 tablespoons chopped fresh parsley
4 phyllo (filo) pastry sheets
7 tablespoons (3½ oz/100 g) butter, melted
salt and black pepper

Heat the oil in a skillet or frying pan, add the chicken, and cook over medium heat, stirring frequently, for 5–8 minutes until golden. Reduce the heat, add the onion and spices, season with salt and pepper, and cook, stirring occasionally, for 10 minutes. Remove the pan from the heat and set aside to cool slightly, then stir in the parsley. Preheat the oven to 400°F/200°C/Gas Mark 6. Line a baking sheet with wax (greaseproof) paper. Lay 1 sheet of phyllo (filo) on the work surface and brush with melted butter. Lay a second sheet on top and brush with melted butter. Repeat this for the remaining phyllo. Spoon the cooled chicken evenly along one short edge of the pastry, then roll the pastry up tightly into a sausage shape. Brush again with melted butter and cut into 1½ inch/4 cm slices. Put them on the prepared baking sheet, season with salt and pepper, and bake for 15 minutes until golden. Remove from the oven and transfer the slices to a wire rack to cool before serving.

STUFFED ZUCCHINI WITH CHICKEN AND CILANTRO

محشي الكوسا بالدجاج والكزبرة

Preparation time: 25 minutes
Cooking time: 45–55 minutes
Serves 4

4 zucchini (courgettes), halved lengthwise
1 tablespoon olive oil, plus extra for brushing and drizzling
11 oz/300 g ground (minced) chicken
2 garlic cloves, finely chopped
¼ teaspoon ground cinnamon
1 teaspoon seven spices seasoning
2 tablespoons tahini
1 cup (8 fl oz/250 ml) chicken stock
½ cup (3½ oz/100 g) basmati or quick-cook long grain rice, rinsed
2 tablespoons chopped fresh cilantro (coriander)
juice of ½ lemon
⅔ cup (¼ pint/150 ml) plain (natural) yogurt
juice and grated zest of ½ lime
4 tablespoons pine nuts, toasted
salt and pepper

Preheat the oven to 400°F/200°C/Gas Mark 6. Brush the zucchini (courgette) halves with olive oil and season with salt and pepper. Put them on a baking sheet and roast for 15–20 minutes until tender. Remove from the oven and, when cool enough to handle, scoop out the center of the zucchini, and discard. Keep the zucchini "boats" warm. Heat the olive oil in a saucepan, add the chicken, and cook over medium heat, stirring frequently, for 5 minutes until browned. Add the garlic, cinnamon, seven spices seasoning, and tahini and cook for another 1–2 minutes. Meanwhile, bring the stock to a boil in a saucepan, add the rice, and bring back to a boil. Reduce the heat, cover, and simmer for 10–15 minutes, until the rice is tender. Tip the rice into the pan with the chicken, season with salt and pepper, and mix well, then remove the pan from the heat. Divide the chicken mixture among the zucchini boats, drizzle with olive oil, and return to the oven for 5 minutes until heated through. Mix together the cilantro (coriander), lemon juice, yogurt, lime juice, and lime zest. Transfer the stuffed zucchini to serving plates, spoon the yogurt sauce over them, and top with the pine nuts.

CHICKEN WINGS WITH CHILI

اجنحة الدجاج

Preparation time: 5 minutes, plus marinating time
Cooking time: 45–50 minutes
Serves 4–6

2¼ lb/1 kg chicken wings
½ teaspoon chili flakes
2 tablespoons olive oil
salt and pepper

Put the chicken wings into a bowl, add the chili flakes and olive oil, season with salt and pepper, and toss well. Cover with plastic wrap (clingfilm) and let marinate in the refrigerator for 1 hour. Preheat the oven to 425°F/220°C/Gas Mark 7. Tip the chicken wings into an ovenproof dish and cook in the oven for 45–50 minutes. Let cool slightly before eating.

CHICKEN WINGS IN GARLIC

PHOTO PAGE 287

اجنحة الدجاج بالثوم

Preparation time: 10 minutes, plus marinating time
Cooking time: 40 minutes
Serves 4–6

2¼ lb/1 kg chicken wings
4 tablespoons olive oil
4 garlic cloves, crushed
1 teaspoon sea salt

Put the chicken wings into an ovenproof dish, pour the oil over them, and sprinkle with the garlic and sea salt. Rub into the chicken with your hands, cover with plastic wrap (clingfilm), and let marinate for 30 minutes. Preheat the oven to 400°F/200°C/Gas Mark 6. Uncover the chicken, put the dish into the oven, and cook for 40 minutes. Serve immediately.

CHICKEN LIVERS WITH LEMON AND POMEGRANATE

كبدة الدجاج مع الليمون والرمان

Preparation time: 15 minutes
Cooking time: 10 minutes
Serves 2

14 oz/400 g chicken livers
2 tablespoons all-purpose (plain) flour
corn oil, for deep-frying
3 garlic cloves, peeled
juice of 1 lemon
1 pomegranate, seeds removed
salt and pepper

Dust the chicken livers with the flour and season with salt and pepper. Heat the oil in a deep-fryer to 350°F/180°C or until a cube of bread browns in 30 seconds. Add the liver to the hot oil and cook for 10 minutes. Remove with a slotted spoon and drain on paper towels. Meanwhile crush the garlic with a pinch of salt, then mix with the lemon juice and olive oil. Put the chicken livers into a bowl, pour in the garlic and lemon mixture, and sprinkle with the pomegranate seeds. Serve immediately.

CHICKEN WINGS IN GARLIC

LEBANESE CHICKEN AND POMEGRANATE

PHOTO PAGE 289

—

دجاج على الطريقة اللبنانية
مع دبس الرمان

Preparation time: 25 minutes
Cooking time: 20–30 minutes
Serves 4

4 chicken breasts
1 tablespoon olive oil
2 scallions (spring onions), chopped
2 garlic cloves, grated
scant ½ cup (3½ fl oz/100 ml) pomegranate juice
1 tablespoon clear honey
1-inch/2.5-cm piece fresh ginger, peeled and grated
½ teaspoon ground allspice
½ teaspoon ground cinnamon
½ teaspoon grated nutmeg
pinch of ground cloves
3 tablespoons lemon juice
5 thyme sprigs
salt and pepper
pomegranate seeds and chopped fresh cilantro (coriander),
    to garnish

Preheat the oven to 375°F/190°C/Gas Mark 5. Brush the chicken with the olive oil and season with salt and pepper. Heat a skillet or frying pan, add the chicken, skin side down, and cook over medium heat for about 5 minutes until golden brown, then turn and cook for another 2 minutes. Remove the chicken from the pan and put into an ovenproof dish. Put all the remaining ingredients, except the pomegranate seeds and chopped cilantro (coriander) into a food processor and process until thoroughly combined. Pour the sauce over the chicken and cook in the oven for 20 minutes or until the chicken is cooked through. Garnish with pomegranate seeds and chopped cilantro and serve.

LEBANESE CHICKEN AND POMEGRANATE

LEBANESE CHICKEN COUSCOUS

LEBANESE CHICKEN COUSCOUS

PHOTO PAGE 290

مغربية بالدجاج

Preparation time: 25 minutes
Cooking time: 25–30 minutes
Serves 4

4 chicken breasts
1 tablespoon olive oil, plus extra for brushing
2 tablespoons (clear) honey
1 onion, chopped
2 garlic cloves, grated
½ inch/1.25 cm fresh ginger, peeled and grated
¼ teaspoon ground allspice
¼ teaspoon ground cinnamon
salt and pepper

For the couscous
scant 1 cup (5 oz/150 g) giant couscous
pinch of ground turmeric
pinch of saffron dissolved in 2 teaspoons hot water
4 scallions (spring onions), finely chopped
2 tablespoons chopped cilantro (coriander)
2 tablespoons pine nuts, toasted
salt and pepper

Preheat the oven to 400°F/200°C/Gas Mark 6. Brush the chicken with olive oil and season with salt and pepper. Heat a skillet or frying pan, add the chicken, skin side down, and cook over medium heat for about 5 minutes until golden brown, then turn and cook for another 2 minutes. Remove the chicken from the pan and place in a roasting pan, skin side up. Pour over the honey and roast in the oven for 20 minutes or until the chicken is cooked. Meanwhile, add the oil to the pan and heat. Add the onion and garlic, reduce the heat to low, and cook, stirring occasionally, for 6–8 minutes until softened and lightly colored. Cook the couscous in plenty of salted boiling water for 6–8 minutes until tender but still firm to the bite. Drain well, tip into a serving dish, and drizzle with olive oil and add the remaining ingredients. Mix well. Remove the chicken from the oven, cut the chicken into slices, and put on a serving plate, topped with caramelized onions. Pour any remaining cooking juices over the chicken and serve immediately with the couscous.

CHICKEN WITH GREEN LENTILS

PHOTO PAGE 293

—

دجاج مع العدس
الاخضر

Preparation time: 20 minutes
Cooking time: 1 hour
Serves 4

1 tablespoon olive oil
1 onion, chopped
6 garlic cloves, sliced
scant ½ cup (3½ oz/100 g) green lentils
3 cups (1¼ pints/750 ml) hot chicken stock
3 skinless, boneless chicken breasts, cut into bite-sized pieces
½ cup (3½ oz/100 g) basmati or quick-cook long grain rice, rinsed
1 teaspoon seven spices seasoning
½ teaspoon ground cumin
½ teaspoon dried thyme
salt and pepper

Heat the oil in a pan, add the onion and garlic, and cook over low heat, stirring occasionally, for 5 minutes until softened. Add the lentils, stir in the stock. Cover the pan and simmer for 30 minutes. Season the chicken, add it to the pan, and cook for another 15 minutes. About 10 minutes before the end of the cooking time add the rice, seven spices seasoning, 1 teaspoon pepper, the cumin, and thyme. Season to taste, and serve.

CHICKEN WITH CHICKPEAS AND CASHEW NUTS

—

دجاج مع الحمص
والكاجو

Preparation time: 20 minutes
Cooking time: 50 minutes–1 hour
Serves 4

3-lb/1.3-kg chicken, cut into breasts and legs
2 cinnamon sticks
5 cardamom pods, crushed
3 cloves
scant 1 cup (3½ oz/100 g) cashew nuts
2 tablespoons olive oil
2 cups (14 oz/400 g) basmati or quick-cook long grain rice, rinsed
1½ teaspoons seven spices seasoning
1½ teaspoons salt
1 teaspoon pepper
14 oz/400 g canned chickpeas, drained and rinsed
generous 2 cups (18 fl oz/500 ml) hot chicken stock
3 tablespoons chopped fresh cilantro (coriander)

Put the chicken pieces into a large pan, pour in water to cover, and bring to a boil. Reduce the heat, add the cinnamon sticks, cardamom pods, and cloves, and simmer for 30–40 minutes until the chicken is tender. Drain the chicken and let cool, then remove the skin and shred the meat. Dry-fry the cashew nuts in a small pan over medium heat for a few minutes until golden. Heat the oil in a saucepan, add the rice and cook over low heat, stirring frequently, for 1–2 minutes until all the grains are coated. Add the seven spices seasoning, salt, pepper, and chickpeas, then pour in the stock and add the chicken. Bring to a boil, then reduce the heat, cover, and cook for 10–12 minutes until the rice is tender. Turn off the heat and let stand for a few minutes. Stir in the cilantro (coriander), sprinkle with the nuts and serve.

CHICKEN WITH GREEN LENTILS

STUFFED CHICKEN WITH NUTS

STUFFED CHICKEN WITH NUTS

PHOTO PAGE 294

—

دجاج مشوي محشي
بالمكسرات مع ماء
الورد

Preparation time: 30 minutes
Cooking time: 25 minutes
Serves 4

½ cup (4 fl oz/120 ml) chicken stock
pinch of saffron threads, lightly crushed
½ teaspoon salt
½ cup (3½ oz/100 g) basmati or quick-cook long grain rice, rinsed
⅓ cup (1½ oz/40 g) shelled walnuts, finely chopped
1 tablespoon ground sumac
4 boneless chicken breasts
4 tablespoons (2 oz/50 g) butter, melted
salt and pepper
pomegranate seeds, to serve

Bring the stock to a boil in a saucepan, add the saffron, salt, and the rice, and bring back to a boil. Reduce the heat, cover, and simmer for 10–15 minutes. Remove from the heat and let cool. Mix together the walnuts, sumac, and cooled rice. Preheat the oven to 400°F/200°C/Gas Mark 6. Loosen the skin from the chicken breasts to make a pocket on each, then carefully push in the rice and nut mixture. Put the chicken breasts into an ovenproof dish, brush with melted butter, and season with salt and pepper. Cover the dish with foil. Bake for 25 minutes or until the chicken is cooked. Remove from the oven rest for 10 minutes, then sprinkle with pomegranate seeds, and serve.

CHICKEN WITH ALMONDS

—

دجاج باللوز

Preparation time: 15 minutes
Cooking time: 35–45 minutes
Serves 4

4 skinless, boneless chicken breasts
2½ tablespoons olive oil, plus extra for brushing
2 onions, chopped
2 garlic cloves, sliced
1¼ cups (9 oz/250 g) basmati or quick-cook long grain rice, rinsed
1 teaspoon seven spices seasoning
1 teaspoon ground cumin
3 cups (1¼ pints/750 ml) hot chicken stock
sunflower oil, for frying
⅓ cup (1½ oz/40 g) slivered (flaked) almonds
3 tablespoons blanched almonds
salt and freshly ground white pepper

Preheat the broiler (grill). Brush the chicken breasts with olive oil, season, and broil (grill) for 4–5 minutes on each side. Meanwhile, heat 2 tablespoons of the oil in a saucepan, add the onions and garlic, and cook over low heat for 5–8 minutes until softened. Add the rice and spices and cook, stirring constantly, for 1 minute. Pour in the hot stock, cover, and cook for 10–15 minutes until the rice is tender. Slice the chicken and stir it into the cooked rice. Heat the remaining oil in a skillet or frying pan, add the almonds, and cook over low heat, stirring frequently, for 1–2 minutes until golden. Remove the pan from the heat and add to the chicken and rice. Serve immediately.

MEAT

BRAISED CHICKEN AND POTATOES

—

دجاج مع البطاطس

Preparation time: 15 minutes
Cooking time: 2 hours
Serves 4

1 x 3¼ lb/1.5 kg chicken
3 tablespoons olive oil
1 onion, chopped
2 carrots, chopped
4¼ cups (1¾ pints/1 liter) chicken stock
2 teaspoons ground turmeric
3 potatoes, sliced
3 bay leaves
1 teaspoon ground white pepper

Preheat the oven to 350°F/180°C/Gas Mark 4. Cut the chicken into serving pieces–2 chicken breasts cut in half, 2 legs, 2 thighs, and 2 wings. Heat 2 tablespoons of the oil in a large flameproof casserole, add the chicken, skin side down, and cook over medium heat for 5–6 minutes until golden brown. Turn and cook for another few minutes. Remove the chicken from the casserole and set aside. Add the remaining oil to the casserole and heat. Add the onion and carrots and cook over low heat, stirring occasionally, for 6–8 minutes until softened and slightly golden. Return the chicken to the casserole and add the stock and turmeric. Bring to a boil and add the potatoes, bay leaves, and white pepper. Cover the casserole, transfer it to the oven, and cook for 1½ hours. Remove and discard the bay leaves and serve immediately.

ROAST CHICKEN ZA'ATAR

—

الدجاج المشوي مع الزعتر

Preparation time: 10 minutes
Cooking time: 1 hour 30 minutes
Serves 4–6

2½ lb/1.2 kg chicken
1 small onion, halved
1 tablespoon za'atar
2 tablespoons olive oil
salt and pepper

Preheat the oven 400°F/200°C/Gas Mark 6. Put the onion in the cavity of the chicken and season well with salt and pepper. Wrap the chicken in foil and put it into a roasting pan. Roast for 30 minutes, then reduce the oven temperature to 350°F/180°C/Gas Mark 4, and roast for another 50 minutes. Meanwhile mix together the za'atar and olive oil in a bowl. Remove the chicken from the oven, unwrap, and remove the foil, then brush the za'ater mixture over the chicken. Return the chicken to the oven and roast for another 10–15 minutes. Remove from the oven and serve.

CHICKEN
AND
VEGETABLE
STEW

—

دجاج مع يخني الخضار

Preparation time: 25 minutes
Cooking time: 1 hour
Serves 4

6 chicken thighs
1 tablespoon olive oil, plus extra for brushing
4 tablespoons (2 oz/50 g) butter
1 leek, sliced
2 carrots, diced
2 celery stalks, diced
⅔ cup (¼ pint/150 ml) white wine
1 tablespoon tomato paste (purée)
generous 2 cups (18 fl oz/500 ml) hot chicken stock
pinch of saffron threads, lightly crushed
¼ teaspoon ground cinnamon
½ teaspoon seven spices seasoning
juice of 1 lemon
2 garlic cloves, grated
salt and pepper

Brush the chicken thighs with the oil and season with salt and
pepper. Heat a medium saucepan, add the thighs, and cook
over medium heat, turning frequently, for 5–8 minutes until
golden all over. Remove from the pan and set aside. Add the
oil and butter to the pan and when the butter has melted,
add the leeks, carrots, and celery. Cook over low heat, stirring
occasionally, for about 10 minutes until softened. Increase the
heat, pour in the wine, and cook until reduced, then add the
tomato paste (purée) and stock, and return the thighs to the
pan. Bring to a boil, stir in the spices, Reduce the heat, cover,
and simmer for 40 minutes. Season well with salt and pepper,
add a squeeze of lemon juice and the freshly grated garlic,
and serve.

CHICKEN RICE AND TOMATO

دجاج مع الارز
والطماطم

Preparation time: 20 minutes
Cooking time: 1 hour 15 minutes
Serves 4

1½ tablespoons olive oil

1 onion, chopped

3 garlic cloves, sliced

8 oz/225 g skinless, boneless chicken breast, cut into cubes

3 cups (1¼ pints/750 ml) hot chicken stock

8 cherry tomatoes, chopped

1 teaspoon seven spices seasoning

½ teaspoon dried thyme

scant 1 cup (6 oz/175 g) basmati rice, rinsed, soaked in hot water for 30 minutes, and drained, or quick-cook long grain rice

¾ cup (3 oz/80 g) cashew nuts

salt and pepper

Heat 1 tablespoon of the oil in a saucepan, add the onion and garlic, and cook over low heat, stirring occasionally, for about 8 minutes until lightly golden. Add the chicken, increase the heat to medium, and cook, stirring frequently, for 7–8 minutes until evenly browned. Pour in the hot stock and simmer for 45 minutes. Add the tomatoes, seven spices seasoning, thyme, and rice and cook for 10 minutes or until the rice is tender and the liquid has been absorbed. Meanwhile, heat the remaining oil in a small skillet or frying pan, add the cashew nuts, and cook over low heat, stirring frequently, for 1–2 minutes. Season the chicken and rice with salt and pepper and transfer to a warm serving dish. Sprinkle with the cashews and serve immediately.

MOLOKHIA CHICKEN

PHOTO PAGE 301

———

ملوخية بالدجاج

Preparation time: 20 minutes, plus soaking time
Cooking time: 1 hour 20 minutes
Serves 4–6

2½ lb/1.2 kg chicken, cut into pieces
2 onions
8 garlic cloves
2 teaspoons salt
4 tablespoons (2 oz/50 g) butter
1 tablespoon olive oil
1 tablespoon ground coriander
juice of 1 lemon
½ teaspoon ground cinnamon
1 teaspoon pepper
7 oz/100 g molokhia (Jew's mallow) leaves, (available frozen in Middle Eastern grocery stores), or spinach thawed and soaked in boiling water for 2 hours
2 tablespoons chopped fresh cilantro (coriander)

Put the pieces of chicken into a large saucepan. Halve 1 onion, add it to the pan, and pour in boiling water to cover. Bring to a boil, skim off any scum that rises to the surface, reduce the heat, and simmer for 1 hour. Meanwhile, chop the remaining onion. Crush the garlic and add half to the chicken with the salt. Melt the butter with the oil in a skillet or frying pan, add the chopped onion, remaining garlic, and ground coriander, and cook over low heat, stirring occasionally, for 5 minutes until softened. Remove the pan from the heat. When the chicken is tender, lift the pieces out of the pan. Remove and discard the skin, pull off the meat from the bones, and shred. Set aside. Strain the cooking liquid into a clean saucepan and add the garlic and onion mixture, lemon juice, cinnamon, and pepper. Stir well, then add the molokhia (mallow) leaves. Bring to a boil over medium heat, then reduce the heat and simmer for 5 minutes. Spoon onto a serving plate, add the chicken, and sprinkle with the chopped cilantro (coriander).

MOLOKHIA CHICKEN

BAKED CHICKEN WRAP WITH SUMAC AND GARLIC DIP

BAKED CHICKEN WRAP WITH SUMAC AND GARLIC DIP

PHOTO PAGE 302

—

دجاج مسخن

Preparation time: 10 minutes, plus resting time
Cooking time: 20–25 minutes
Serves 2

1 onion, sliced
4 tablespoons ground sumac
3 skinless, boneless chicken breasts, cut into strips
4 tablespoons olive oil
juice and grated zest of ½ lemon
4 Lebanese flatbreads
salt and pepper
Garlic Dip (see page 43) and salad greens, to serve

Mix together the onion, sumac, chicken strips, olive oil, and lemon juice and zest in a bowl. Season with salt and pepper and let stand for 20 minutes. Meanwhile preheat the oven to 400°F/200°C/Gas Mark 6. Tear the flatbreads into bite-sized pieces and put two-thirds into an ovenproof dish. Spoon the chicken mixture over the bread and cover with the remaining bread. Bake for 20–25 minutes checking frequently so that if the bread starts to burn, you can cover it with foil. Serve in slices with a spoonful of Garlic Dip and salad greens.

SPICY CHICKEN SHAWARMA

—

شاورما الدجاج
الحارة

Preparation time: 10 minutes, plus marinating time
Cooking time: 30 minutes
Serves 2

13 oz/375 g skinless, boneless chicken breasts, cut into strips
3 tablespoons malt vinegar
juice of ½ lemon
1 teaspoon seven spice seasoning
pinch of chili powder
salt and pepper
rice, vermicelli, and chopped fresh cilantro (coriander), to serve

Put the chicken into a bowl, add the vinegar, lemon juice, and 3 tablespoons water, mix well, and let stand overnight in the refrigerator. Preheat the oven to 400°F/200°C/Gas Mark 6. Tip the chicken into a roasting pan, add the spices, and season with salt and pepper. Toss well, then put the pan into the oven and cook for 30 minutes. Serve the chicken with rice, vermicelli, and chopped cilantro (coriander).

CHICKEN SHAWARMA

CHICKEN SHAWARMA

PHOTO PAGE 304

—

شاورما الدجاج

Preparation time: 10 minutes, plus marinating time
Cooking time: 30 minutes
Serves 2

3 tablespoons malt vinegar
juice of ½ lemon
13 oz/375 g skinless, boneless chicken breasts, cut into strips
1 teaspoon seven spices seasoning
salt and pepper
flatbread, rice, and vermicelli, to serve

Mix together the vinegar, lemon juice, and 3 tablespoons water in a bowl, add the chicken, stir well, and let stand overnight in the refrigerator. Preheat the oven to 400°F/200°C/Gas Mark 6. Tip the chicken into a roasting pan, add the seven spices seasoning, and season with salt and pepper. Toss well, then put the pan in the oven and cook for 30 minutes. Remove the chicken from the oven and serve immediately with flatbread, rice, and vermicelli.

CHICKEN KEBABS

—

كباب الدجاج

Preparation time: 15 minutes, plus marinating time
Cooking time: 15 minutes
Serves 4

1 lb/450 g skinless, boneless chicken breasts,
    cut into 1 inch/2.5 cm cubes
4 garlic cloves, chopped
½ teaspoon paprika
½ teaspoon pepper
½ teaspoon dried thyme
½ teaspoon salt
juice of ½ lemon
3 tablespoons olive oil
flatbreads and Mixed Lebanese Salad (see page 58), to serve

Start preparing the chicken the day before you intend to serve the kebabs. Put the chicken into a bowl, add the garlic, paprika, pepper, thyme, salt, lemon juice, and olive oil, and mix well. Cover the bowl with plastic wrap (clingfilm) and let marinate overnight in the refrigerator. Preheat the broiler (grill). Tip the chicken onto a baking sheet and cook under a hot broiler, turning occasionally for 15 minutes. Remove from the broiler and serve immediately in flatbreads with Lebanese Salad.

CHICKEN SHAWARMA WITH EGGPLANT

CHICKEN SHAWARMA WITH EGGPLANT

PHOTO PAGE 306

—

شاورما الدجاج مع الباذنجان

Preparation time: 10 minutes, plus marinating time
Cooking time: 30 minutes
Serves 4

13 oz/375 g skinless, boneless chicken breasts, cut into strips
3 tablespoons malt vinegar
3 tbsp water
juice of ½ lemon
1 teaspoon seven spices seasoning
1 eggplant (aubergine), cut into cubes
salt and pepper
pomegranate seeds, rice, and vermicelli, to serve

Put the chicken into a bowl, add the vinegar, lemon juice, and 3 tablespoons water, mix well, and let stand overnight in the refrigerator. Preheat the oven to 400°F/200°C/Gas Mark 6. Tip the chicken into a roasting pan, season with salt and pepper, sprinkle with the seven spices seasoning, and add the eggplant (aubergine) cubes. Toss well, put the pan into the oven, and cook for 30 minutes. Remove the chicken from the oven and serve with pomegranate seeds, rice, and vermicelli.

CHICKEN KEBABS SHISH TAOUK

—

كباب الدجاج

Preparation time: 15 minutes, plus marinating time
Cooking time: 10 minutes
Serves 2

1 teaspoon paprika
½ teaspoon allspice
4 teaspoons tomato paste (purée)
1 tablespoon plain (natural) yogurt
2 garlic cloves, crushed
juice and grated zest of ½ lemon, plus extra juice to serve
1 tablespoon olive oil
8 skinless, boneless chicken thighs, cut in chunks
2 large pita breads
2 heaping tablespoons Garlic Dip (see page 43)

Mix together the paprika, allspice, tomato paste (purée), yogurt, garlic, lemon juice and rind, and olive oil in a large bowl. Add the chicken and rub the marinade into the flesh, then cover with plastic wrap (clingfilm) and let marinate for 4 hours at room temperature or overnight in the refrigerator. Thread the pieces of chicken onto long skewers, 6 on each skewer, leaving a small gap between each piece. Grill over a hot barbecue or cook under a preheated broiler (grill) for about 5 minutes on each side, until cooked through. Meanwhile, warm the pita breads on the side of the barbecue or in a preheated oven, 350°F/180°C/Gas Mark 4, for a few minutes. Pull off the pieces of chicken, put into the pita breads, top with garlic dip, squeeze over lemon juice, and serve.

CHICKEN
AND
RICE

ارز بالدجاج

Preparation time: 10 minutes
Cooking time: 1 hour 30 minutes
Serves 4

4 skinless, boneless chicken breasts
3 cardamom pods
4 cloves
1 cinnamon stick
scant 1 cup (3½ oz/100 g) pine nuts (optional)
1 cup (7 oz/200 g) basmati or quick-cook long grain rice, rinsed
2 tablespoons olive oil
2 oz/50 g vermicelli
1 teaspoon ground cumin
1 teaspoon seven spices seasoning
1 teaspoon salt
1 teaspoon pepper

Bring a large saucepan of water to a boil, add the chicken and whole spices, cover, and simmer for about 30 minutes until the chicken is very tender. Lift out the chicken breasts with a slotted spoon and let cool slightly. Remove and discard the spices from the cooking liquid and reserve it. Shred the chicken. Dry-fry the pine nuts in a small skillet or frying pan, stirring frequently, for a few minutes until golden. Remove from the heat and set aside. Put the rice in a bowl, pour in hot water to cover, and let soak for 10 minutes, then drain. Heat the oil in a saucepan, add the vermicelli, and cook for a few minutes, then add the rice, cumin, seven spices seasoning, salt, and pepper. Cook, stirring constantly, for 2 minutes, then pour in 3 cups (1¼ pints/750 ml) of the reserved cooking liquid and stir. Stir in the shredded chicken, cover, and cook for 45 minutes until the all the liquid has been absorbed. Remove from the heat and serve immediately.

PAN-FRIED
SQUAB
IN
GARLIC

حمام مقلي بالثوم

Preparation time: 10 minutes, plus marinating time
Cooking time: 12 minutes
Serves 2

4 squab (pigeon) breasts
3 garlic cloves
1 tablespoon olive oil
1 teaspoon white wine vinegar
4 cardamom pods, crushed
salt and pepper
rice and vermicelli, to serve

Put the squab (pigeon) breasts in a shallow dish. Crush the garlic with a little salt in a mortar with a pestle, stir in the oil and vinegar, and pour the mixture over the squab breasts. Add the cardamom pods and season well. Rub the marinade into the meat and let marinate for 2 hours in the refrigerator. Heat a skillet or frying pan, add the squab breasts, and cook for 3–6 minutes. Turn and cook for another 3–6 minutes, depending on how well you like your meat cooked. Remove from the pan and serve immediately with rice and vermicelli

CHICKEN HASHWEH WITH VEGETABLE STUFFING

دجاج بحشوة الخضار

Preparation time: 30 minutes, plus resting time
Cooking time: 2 hours
Serves 4–6

3¼ lb/1.5 kg chicken
1 tablespoon olive oil, plus extra for brushing
1 small onion, finely chopped
1 teaspoon seven spices seasoning
1¼ cups (9 oz/250 g) instant (easy-cook) rice, rinsed in boiling water and soaked in boiling water for 10 minutes.
2 teaspoons ground cumin
½ teaspoon ground cinnamon
11 oz/300g canned sweet corn kernels, drained
1 teaspoon salt
½ teaspoon pepper
¾ cup (3 oz/80 g) pine nuts, toasted
1 bunch of fresh parsley, chopped

Remove the wings from the chicken and discard, or freeze for making stock. Carefully separate the skin from the breast of the chicken with your fingers to make a pocket. Heat the oil in a skillet or frying pan, add the onion and seven spices seasoning, and cook over low heat, stirring occasionally, for 7–8 minutes until softened and lightly colored. Drain the rice and stir it into the pan, then add the cumin, cinnamon, and sweet corn. Season with the salt and pepper and cook for another 5 minutes. Pour in 1¾ cups (14 fl oz/400 ml) boiling water to cover and bring back to a boil over medium heat. Reduce the heat, cover, and simmer, stirring occasionally, for 20 minutes until the liquid has been absorbed and the rice is nearly tender. Stir in the toasted pine nuts and parsley. Remove the pan from the heat and let cool. To speed this up, you can place the pan in a bowl of ice water. Preheat the oven to 400°F/200°C/Gas Mark 6. Fill the chicken's cavity, neck, and pocket in between the skin and breast with the rice mixture, being careful not to tear the skin. Use a trussing needle and thread to sew the skin and breast together and underneath the chicken. Rub the chicken with oil, season with salt and pepper, put it into a roasting pan, and cover tightly with foil. Roast for 1½ hours, then remove the foil and continue to cook for another 30 minutes until the skin is golden brown and crisp. Remove from the oven and let rest for 10 minutes before carving and serving.

CHICKEN HASHWEH

PHOTO PAGE 311

دجاج محشو بالارز
واللحم

Preparation time: 30 minutes, plus resting time
Cooking time: 2 hours
Serves 6

1 x 3½ lb/1.5 kg chicken
9 oz/250 g ground (minced) lamb
1 small onion, finely chopped
1 teaspoon seven spices seasoning
1 teaspoon salt
½ teaspoon pepper
scant 1 cup (6 oz/175 g) instant (easy-cook) rice, rinsed in
    boiling water and soaked in boiling water for 10 minutes
2 teaspoons ground cumin
½ teaspoon ground cinnamon
¾ cup (3 oz/80 g) pine nuts, toasted
1 bunch of fresh parsley, chopped
olive oil, for brushing

Carefully remove the wings from the chicken and discard, or
freeze for making stock. Carefully separate skin from the breast
of the chicken with your fingers to make a pocket. Heat a skillet
or frying pan until hot, add the lamb, and cook over medium
heat, stirring frequently, for 8–10 minutes until evenly browned.
Reduce the heat, add the onion and seven spices seasoning, and
cook, stirring occasionally, for 5 minutes until softened. Season
with the salt and pepper. Drain the rice, add to the lamb, and
stir well, then stir in the cumin and cinnamon, and cook for
another 5 minutes. Pour in about 1¾ cups (14 fl oz/400 ml)
boiling water to cover and bring back to a boil over medium
heat. Reduce the heat, cover, and simmer, stirring occasionally,
for 20 minutes until the liquid has been absorbed. Stir in the
toasted pine nuts and parsley, then remove from the heat, and
let cool. To speed this up, you can place the pan in a bowl of ice
water. Preheat the oven to 400°F/200°C/Gas Mark 6. Fill the
chicken's cavity, neck, and the pocket in between the skin and
breast with the rice and lamb mixture, being careful not to tear
the skin. Using a trussing needle and thread, sew the skin and
breast together and underneath the chicken. Brush the chicken
with oil, season with salt and pepper, put it into a roasting pan,
and cover tightly with foil. Cook for 1½ hours, then remove the
foil and continue to cook for another 30 minutes until the skin
is golden brown and crisp. Remove from the oven and let rest
for 10 minutes before carving and serving.

CHICKEN HASHWEH

CORNISH GAME HENS AND GARLIC

CORNISH GAME HENS AND GARLIC

PHOTO PAGE 312

دجاج صغير مشوي
مع الثوم

Preparation time: 20 minutes, plus marinating and resting time
Cooking time: 25 minutes
Serves 6

2 Cornish game hens (poussins)
2 garlic cloves
½ teaspoon salt
½ teaspoon cumin seeds
2 tablespoons olive oil
Tahini Sauce (see page 200), to serve

Ask your butcher to butterfly (spatchcock) the birds. Crush the garlic with the salt and cumin seeds in a mortar with a pestle, then mix with the olive oil. Put the birds into a dish, pour the marinade over them, and use your hands to rub it into the birds. Cover the bowl with plastic wrap (clingfilm) and let marinate for at least 3 hours, preferably overnight, in the refrigerator. Remove the Cornish game hens (poussins) from the refrigerator and let stand at room temperature for 30 minutes before cooking. Use 2 skewers to secure the legs and keep each bird flat. Push the skewers through the thigh and then diagonally through the breast and wing. Heat 2 skillets or frying pans over medium heat, add the birds, skin side down, and cook for 15 minutes. Turn and cook on the other side for another 10 minutes. Remove the birds from the pans and let rest for 10 minutes before serving with the Tahini Sauce.

MEAT

TURKEY HASHWEH WITH RICE, APPLE, AND CHESTNUTS

ديك حبش محشو بالارز
واللحم

Preparation time: 30–40 minutes, plus resting time
Cooking time: 3 hours
Serves 6–8

8¾ lb/4 kg turkey
1 lb 2 oz/500 g ground (minced) lamb
1 small onion, finely chopped
1 celery stalk, finely chopped
1 large apple, grated
2 teaspoons seven spices seasoning
1 tablespoon ground cumin
1 teaspoon ground cinnamon
1 teaspoon salt
2 teaspoons pepper
generous 1 cup (8 oz/225 g) instant (easy-cook) rice, rinsed in
    boiling water and soaked in boiling water for 10 minutes
¾ cup (3 oz/80 g) pine nuts, toasted
9 oz/250 g cooked chestnuts, finely chopped
grated zest and juice of 1 lemon
2 tablespoons fresh thyme leaves
1 bunch of fresh parsley, chopped
olive oil, for brushing
salt and pepper

Remove the wings from the turkey and discard or freeze for
making stock. Carefully separate the skin from the breast of
the turkey with your fingers to make a pocket. Heat a skillet or
frying pan until hot, add the lamb, and cook over medium heat,
stirring frequently, for 8–10 minutes until evenly browned.
Reduce the heat, add the onion and celery, and cook, stirring
occasionally, for 5–10 minutes until the vegetables have
softened. Add the apple and stir in the seven spices seasoning,
cumin, cinnamon, salt, and pepper. Drain the rice, add to
the lamb, and cook for another 5 minutes. Increase the heat
to medium, pour in generous 2 cups (18 fl oz/500 ml) boiling
water to cover, and bring back to a boil. Reduce the heat,
cover, and simmer, stirring occasionally, for 20 minutes until
the liquid has been absorbed. Stir in the toasted pine nuts and
chestnuts, then stir in the lemon zest and juice, thyme leaves,
and parsley. Remove the pan from the heat and let cool.
To speed this up, you can put the pan in a bowl of ice water.
Preheat the oven to 400°F/200°C/Gas Mark 6. Fill the turkey's
cavity, neck, and pocket in between the skin and breast with the
rice and lamb mixture, taking care not to tear the skin. Use a
trussing needle and thread to sew the skin and breast together
and underneath the turkey. Brush the turkey with olive oil,
season with salt and pepper, put it into a roasting pan, and
cover tightly with foil. Roast for 2½ hours, then remove the foil
and continue to cook for 30 minutes until the skin is golden
brown and crisp. Remove from the oven and let rest for 20
minutes before carving and serving.

GRILLED FROGS' LEGS WITH GARLIC AND LEMON

ارجل الضفادع المحمرة
مع الثوم والليمون

Preparation time: 5 minutes, plus marinating time
Cooking time: 6–8 minutes
Serves 4

4 garlic cloves, finely chopped
juice 1 lemon
1 teaspoon salt
1 teaspoon pepper
12 frogs' legs
lemon wedges, to serve

Mix together the garlic, lemon juice, salt, and pepper in a large bowl, add the frogs' legs, and rub the mixture into the meat. Let marinate in the refrigerator for 1 hour. Remove the frogs' legs from the marinade and put them into a hinged wire rack. Grill over a hot barbecue for 2–3 minutes on each side until cooked through. Serve immediately with lemon wedges for squeezing.

MARINATED QUAILS IN SUMAC

MARINATED QUAILS IN SUMAC

PHOTO PAGE 316

—

سمان متبل بالسماق

Preparation time: 15 minutes, plus marinating time
Cooking time: 10–15 minutes
Serves 4

4 quails
2 garlic cloves
½ teaspoon salt
2 tablespoons olive oil
juice of ½ lemon
3 tablespoons ground sumac
1 tablespoon fresh thyme leaves

Remove the backbone from the quails and flatten the birds.
Put them in a shallow dish. Crush the garlic with the salt in a
mortar with a pestle, stir in the oil and lemon juice, and pour
the mixture over the quails. Add the sumac and thyme and
rub in with your hands. Cover with plastic wrap (clingfilm)
and let marinate for 2 hours. Preheat the oven to 400°F/200°C/
Gas Mark 6. Heat a skillet or frying pan then, when it is hot,
add the quails and seal on both sides. Transfer the quails to an
ovenproof dish and roast for 10–15 minutes. Remove from the
oven and let rest for 5 minutes before serving.

VEGETABLES

✶

الخضراوات

VEGETABLE CASSEROLE

—

طاجن الخضار

Preparation time: 30 minutes
Cooking time: 1 hour
Serves 4–6

2 tablespoons olive oil
1 onion, chopped
4 garlic cloves, sliced
1 rutabaga (swede), cut into cubes
1 parsnip, chopped
2 large carrots, chopped
1 eggplant (aubergine), cut into cubes
1 zucchini (courgette), chopped
2 tomatoes, chopped
2 cups (5 oz/150 g) white (button) mushrooms
2½ cups (600 ml/1 pint) vegetable stock
pinch of ground cinnamon
½ teaspoon paprika
½ teaspoon pepper
1 teaspoon seven spices seasoning
½ teaspoon salt

Heat the oil in a large casserole, add the onion, and cook over low heat, stirring occasionally, for 7–8 minutes until softened and lightly colored. Add the garlic and cook for another 1 minute, then add the rutabaga (swede), parsnip, carrots, eggplant (aubergine), zucchini (courgette), tomatoes, and mushrooms. Cover and cook for another 5 minutes. Increase the heat to medium, pour in the vegetable stock, add the cinnamon, paprika, pepper, seven spices seasoning, and salt, and bring to a boil. Reduce the heat, cover, and simmer for 30–40 minutes. Serve immediately.

VEGETABLE STUFFING

—

حشوة الخضار

Preparation time: 10 minutes
Cooking time: 15 minutes
Serves 4

1 cup (7 oz/200 g) basmati rice, rinsed
1 teaspoon seven spices seasoning
¼ teaspoon ground cinnamon
1 teaspoon salt
1 teaspoon pepper
1 onion, finely chopped
1 celery stalk, finely chopped
1 red bell pepper, seeded and finely chopped
1 green bell pepper, seeded and finely chopped
2 tablespoons chopped fresh parsley

Put the rice into pan, pour in 1½ cups (12 fl oz/350 ml) hot water, add the seven spices seasoning, cinnamon, salt, and pepper, and bring to a boil over medium heat. Reduce the heat, cover, and simmer for 10 minutes until the rice is nearly tender and the liquid has been absorbed. Tip the rice into a bowl and let cool, then add the onion, celery, and bell peppers, and mix well. Taste and adjust the seasoning, if necessary, and add the parsley. This stuffing can be used for any savory stuff dish.

LIMA BEAN STEW

—

يخني الفاصولياء البيضاء
العريضة

Preparation time: 15 minutes, plus soaking time
Cooking time: 1 hour 10 minutes
Serves 4

2 cups (13 oz/375 g) dried lima (butter) beans, soaked overnight
    in water to cover and drained
3 tablespoons olive oil
1 red onion, chopped
2 onions, chopped
1 garlic bulb, chopped
6 tablespoons tomato paste (purée)
1 teaspoon seven spices seasoning
1 teaspoon pepper
2 tablespoons ground flax seeds (linseeds)

Put the beans into a pan, pour in boiling water to cover, and bring back to a boil over medium heat, then reduce the heat to low. Meanwhile, heat the olive oil in a skillet or frying pan, add the onions and garlic, and cook over low heat, stirring occasionally, for 20 minutes slightly caramelized. Tip the onions and garlic into the pan of beans and cook for another 30 minutes. Stir in the tomato paste (purée), seven spices seasoning, pepper, and flax seeds (linseeds) and cook for another 15 minutes. Serve immediately.

TARO AND CRANBERRY BEANS

—

بطاطس مع حبوب
اللوبياء

Preparation time: 15 minutes, plus soaking time
Cooking time: 1 hour 40 minutes
Serves 4–6

2 tablespoons olive oil
10 taro, scrubbed and dried
2 cups (14 oz/400 g) dried cranberry (borlotti) beans, soaked
    overnight in water to cover, drained and rinsed
5 garlic cloves
1 teaspoon salt
juice of 1 lemon
4 tablespoons extra virgin oil
salt and pepper
bread, to serve

Preheat the oven to 425°F/220°C/Gas Mark 7. Put the olive oil into a roasting pan and heat in the oven. When hot, add the taro and roast, turning frequently, for about 50 minutes until tender. Meanwhile, put the beans into a large pan, pour in water to cover, and bring to a boil, then remove from the heat and drain. Return to the pan, pour in fresh water to cover, and bring to a boil. Reduce the heat and cook for 1–1½ hours until soft. Add the cooked taro, cover the pan, cook for 10 minutes. Crush the garlic with the salt in a mortar with a pestle, then stir in the lemon juice and extra virgin olive oil. Pour the garlic dressing into the pan with the beans and potatoes and cook for another few minutes. Serve this lunch time dish with bread.

BUTTERNUT SQUASH STEW

PHOTO PAGE 325

—

يخني القرع

Preparation time: 20 minutes
Cooking time: 40–50 minutes
Serves 4–6

2 tablespoons olive oil
1 onion, sliced
3 garlic cloves, chopped
2 teaspoons curry powder
1 carrot, sliced
1 butternut squash, peeled, seeded, and cut into large cubes
14 oz/400 g chopped tomatoes
generous 2 cups (18 fl oz/500 ml) vegetable stock
2 tablespoons tomato paste (purée)
1 cinnamon stick
3¾ cups (9 oz/250 g) cremini (chestnut) mushrooms, quartered
14 oz/400 g canned chickpeas, drained and rinsed
2 tablespoons chopped fresh cilantro (coriander)
salt and pepper

Heat the oil in a large pan, add the onion and garlic, and cook over low heat, stirring occasionally, for 5 minutes until softened. Stir in the curry powder and cook for 2–3 minutes until it releases its aroma. Add the carrot and butternut squash, increase the heat to medium, and stir well so that the vegetables are coated with curry powder and onion, then add the tomatoes, stock, tomato paste (purée), and cinnamon stick. Bring to a boil, then reduce the heat, cover, and simmer for 30 minutes until the squash is nearly tender. Stir in the mushrooms and chickpeas and cook for another 10 minutes. Season to taste, remove from the heat, and serve immediately sprinkled with chopped cilantro (coriander).

CHICKPEA JEDHA

—

أرز بالحمص

Preparation time: 10 minutes
Cooking time: 40–45 mnutes
Serves 4

2 tablespoons olive oil
2 onions, coarsely chopped
28oz/800 g canned chickpeas, drained and rinsed
scant ½ cup (3 oz/80 g) basmati rice
½ teaspoon ground cumin
½ teaspoon seven spices seasoning
½ teaspoon pepper
½ teaspoon salt

Heat the oil in a skillet or frying pan, add the onions, and cook over medium-low heat, stirring occasionally, for 7–8 minutes until lightly colored. Meanwhile, put the chickpeas into a pan, pour in water to cover, and cook for 15 minutes. Add the rice and cook for about 10 minutes until it is nearly tender. Add the onions and cumin, seven spices seasoning, pepper, and salt to the pan and cook for another few minutes until the rice is tender. Serve immediately.

BUTTERNUT SQUASH STEW

FENNEL, POTATO, AND LEMON SALAD

FENNEL, POTATO, AND LEMON SALAD

PHOTO PAGE 326

—

سلطة البطاطس
والشومر

Preparation time: 15 minutes
Cooking time: 10–15 minutes
Serves 4–6

7 oz/200 g new potatoes
2 fennel bulbs, thinly sliced
scant 1 cup (3½ oz/100 g) pitted (stoned) green olives
2 tablespoons chopped fresh parsley
1 teaspoon ground sumac
sea salt and pepper

For the dressing
4 tablespoons extra virgin oil
1 teaspoon whole grain mustard
juice of 1 lemon

Cook the potatoes in a pan of salted boiling water for 10–15 minutes until tender. Remove from the heat, drain, and let cool. When they are cool enough to handle, cut them in half and put into a serving bowl. Add the fennel, olives, and parsley. Whisk together all the ingredients for the dressing in a small bowl and pour it over the salad. Sprinkle with the sumac and season well with salt and pepper. Toss together and serve immediately.

SMALL POTATOES WITH TOMATOES AND PARSLEY

—

بطاطس جديدة مع
الطماطم والبقدونس

Preparation time: 10 minutes
Cooking time: 30 minutes
Serves 2

12 oz/350 g small potatoes
olive oil, for drizzling
1 teaspoon sea salt
½ teaspoon ground sumac
6 cherry tomatoes
1 teaspoon clear honey
1 rosemary sprig
2 tablespoons chopped fresh parsley

Preheat the oven to 400°F/200°C/Gas Mark 6. Halve the potatoes, put them into a bowl, drizzle generously with olive oil, and sprinkle with sea salt. Toss well, add the sumac and cherry tomatoes, and toss lightly again. Tip the vegetables into a roasting pan. Pour the honey over them and add the rosemary. Roast for 30 minutes until the potatoes are tender. Serve warm, sprinkled with the chopped parsley.

POTATO WEDGES AND SUMAC

قطع البطاطس مع السماق

Preparation time: 10 minutes
Cooking time: 55 minutes
Serves 4–6

⅔ cup (¼ pint/150 ml) sunflower oil
3 large baking potatoes
1 teaspoon sea salt
2 teaspoon ground sumac
2 tablespoons chopped fresh parsley
garlic dip, to serve

Preheat the oven to 400°F/200°C/Gas Mark 6. Pour the oil into a roasting pan and put it in the oven to heat. Cut the potatoes into wedges, put them into a pan, and pour in water to cover. Bring to a boil, then reduce the heat and cook for 10–15 minutes until nearly tender. Drain and pat dry with paper towels. Sprinkle the wedges with the sea salt and sumac and carefully tip them in to the hot roasting pan. Return the pan to the oven and roast the wedges, turning occasionally, for 30–40 minutes until golden and crispy. Transfer the wedges to a serving dish, sprinkle with chopped parsley, and serve immediately with a garlic dip.

POTATO WEDGES AND ZA'TAR

قطع البطاطس مع الزعتر

Preparation time: 10 minutes
Cooking time: 55 minutes
Serves 4–6

⅔ cup (¼ pint/150 ml) sunflower oil
3 large baking potatoes
1 teaspoon sea salt
2 teaspoons za'atar
2 tablespoons chopped fresh mint
pepper
garlic dip, to serve

Preheat the oven to 400°F/200°C/Gas Mark 6. Pour the oil into a roasting pan and put in the oven to heat. Cut the potatoes into wedges, put into a pan of cold water, and bring to a boil over medium heat. Reduce the heat and cook for 15 minutes until nearly tender, then drain, and pat dry with paper towels. Sprinkle the wedges with the sea salt and za'atar and carefully tip them into the roasting pan. Roast, turning occasionally, for 30–40 minutes until golden and crispy. Serve the wedges sprinkled with chopped mint and black pepper, accompanied by a garlic dip.

ROASTED SLICED POTATOES

شرائح بطاطس محمرة

Preparation time: 10 minutes
Cooking time: 1 hour 15 minutes
Serves 6–8

6 potatoes
olive oil, for brushing
salt

Cook the unpeeled potatoes in a pan of boiling water for 20–25 minutes until nearly tender. Remove from the heat, drain, and let cool for a few minutes. Meanwhile, preheat the oven to 375°F/190°C/Gas Mark 5. Generously brush a baking sheet with oil. As soon as the potatoes are cool enough to handle but while they are still warm, peel off the skins and slice thickly. Put the potato slices in a single layer on the prepared baking sheet and roast, turning once, for 45 minutes. Remove from the oven and drain on paper towels, then sprinkle with salt and serve.

GREEN LENTILS AND BULGUR WHEAT

البرغل بالعدس البني

Preparation time: 10 minutes
Cooking time: 25–30 minutes
Serves 4

4¼ cups (1¼ pints/1 liter) vegetable stock
scant 1 cup (7 oz/200 g) puy lentils
1¼ cups (6 oz/175 g) coarse bulgur wheat
2 teaspoons seven spices seasoning
2 tablespoons olive oil
2 onions, sliced
salt and pepper

Pour the stock into a pan, add the lentils, and bring to a boil over medium heat. Reduce the heat and simmer for 15 minutes or until the lentils are nearly tender. Stir in the bulgur wheat and seven spices seasoning and cook for another 10 minutes until the liquid has been absorbed. Meanwhile, heat the oil in a skillet or frying pan, add the onions, and cook over medium-low heat, stirring occasionally, for 8–10 minutes until golden. Tip the onions into the lentil mixture and combine, season well with salt and pepper, and serve warm.

GREEN LENTILS, RICE AND CARAMELIZED ONIONS

PHOTO PAGE 331

—

مدردرة (عدس اخضر مع بصل محمر)

Preparation time: 10 minutes
Cooking time: 30–35 minutes
Serves 4

scant 1 cup (7 oz/200 g) green lentils
4 tablespoons olive oil
5 small onions, sliced
½ cup (3½ oz/100 g) instant (easy cook) rice, rinsed
2 teaspoons salt
½ teaspoon ground cumin
½ teaspoon seven spices seasoning
½ teaspoon pepper

Put the lentils in a pan, pour in water to cover, and bring to a boil over medium heat. Reduce the heat, cover, and simmer for 20 minutes. Meanwhile, heat the oil in a skillet or frying pan, add the onions, and cook over medium heat, stirring occasionally, for 10–15 minutes until caramelized. Add the rice and salt to the pan of lentils, replace the lid, and simmer for 10–15 minutes until the rice and lentils are tender and the liquid has been absorbed. Stir in the cumin, seven spices seasoning, pepper, and caramelized onions and serve warm.

COARSE BULGUR WHEAT WITH BEANS AND ONIONS

—

برغل خشن مع الفاصولياء والبصل

Preparation time: 15 minutes
Cooking time: 30–45 minutes
Serves 4–6

2 tablespoons (1 oz/25 g) butter
2 tablespoons olive oil
3 onions, sliced
2 garlic cloves, grated
1½ cups (7 oz/200 g) coarse bulgur wheat
1 cup (8 fl oz/250 ml) hot vegetable stock
1 teaspoon seven spices seasoning
1 teaspoon ground cumin
1 teaspoon pepper
½ teaspoon salt
14 oz/400 g canned cranberry (borlotti) beans, drained and rinsed
2 tablespoons chopped fresh parsley

Melt the butter with half the olive oil in a skillet or frying pan, add the onions, and cook over low heat, stirring occasionally, for 25–30 minutes until caramelized. Meanwhile, heat the remaining oil in a pan, add the garlic, and cook over low heat, stirring frequently, for a few minutes. Add the bulgur wheat, pour in the hot stock, and simmer until all the liquid has been absorbed. Turn off the heat, stir in the seven spices seasoning, cumin, pepper, salt, and beans, cover the pan, and let stand for 15 minutes until the bulgur wheat is tender. Transfer the bulgur wheat mixture to a serving bowl, top with the caramelized onions, sprinkle with the chopped parsley, and serve immediately.

GREEN LENTIL, RICE, AND CARAMELIZED ONIONS

LEBANESE RICE

ارز على الطريقة اللبنانية

Preparation time: 15 minutes
Cooking time: 15–20 minutes
Serves 4

2 tablespoons olive oil
2¼ oz/70 g vermicelli
scant 1½ cups (10 oz/275 g) basmati rice, rinsed, soaked in hot
  water for 10 minutes, and drained
2 teaspoons ground cumin
1 teaspoon salt
scant 1 cup (3½ oz/100 g) shelled walnuts
2 tablespoons clear honey
¼ teaspoon chili flakes
¼ teaspoon ground turmeric
2 tablespoons chopped fresh parsley
scant 1 cup (3½ oz/100 g) slivered (flaked) almonds, toasted

Preheat the oven to 325°F/160°C/Gas Mark 3. Line a baking
sheet with wax (greaseproof) paper. Heat the oil in a pan,
add the vermicelli, and cook over low heat for a few minutes
until golden. Add the rice, cumin, and salt and cook for 2
minutes. Stir in 2 cups (18 fl oz/500 ml) of hot water, cover, and
cook for 10 minutes until the liquid has been absorbed. Dry-fry
the walnuts in a skillet or frying pan for 2 minutes, then add
the honey, chili flakes, and turmeric and cook for another few
minutes. Transfer the mixture to the baking sheet and put in
the oven for 10 minutes. Stir the parsley and almonds into the
rice and vermicelli, top with the walnuts, and serve.

SWISS CHARD STUFFED WITH RICE AND PEAS

محشي ورق السلق بالارز
والبازلاء

Preparation time: 30 minutes
Cooking time: 45–55 minutes
Makes 12–15 rolls

1 Swiss chard, leaves separated
¾ cup (5 oz/150 g) basmati rice, rinsed
6 cherry tomatoes, chopped
scant 1 cup (3½ oz/100 g) frozen peas, thawed
1 red onion, finely chopped
½ red bell pepper, seeded and finely chopped
1 tablespoon pesto
½ teaspoon ground cinnamon
2 tablespoons chopped parsley
olive oil, for drizzling
salt and black pepper

Blanch the leaves of the Swiss chard in boiling water for a few
minutes, then drain. Remove the stems when cool enough
to handle. Mix together the rice, tomatoes, peas, onion, bell
pepper, pesto, cinnamon, and parsley and season to taste. Put a
few of the leaves into the bottom of a pan. Put 1–2 spoonfuls of
the stuffing on the remaining leaves and roll up like a cigar. Put
the rolls into the pan so that they fit snuggly. Put a small plate
on top to keep the rolls submerged and pour in boiling water to
cover. Cover and cook for 45–55 minutes. Transfer the rolls to a
serving dish, drizzle with olive oil, and serve.

RISOTTO
WITH
MUSHROOMS

ريزوتو مع الفطر

Preparation time: 20 minutes
Cooking time: 30–40 minutes
Serves 6

5 cups (2 pints/1.2 liters) vegetable stock
1 cup (1¼ oz/35 g) dried porcini mushrooms
2½ tablespoons butter
2 teaspoons olive oil
1 onion, finely chopped
1 celery stalk, finely chopped
2 cups (14 oz/400 g) risotto rice
½ cup (4 fl oz/120 ml) white wine
1 teaspoon seven spices seasoning
pinch of grated nutmeg
3 cups (9 oz/250 g) mixed mushrooms, such as shiitake,
    cremini (chestnut), oyster, and girolle, chopped
juice of ½ lemon
1 teaspoon salt
½ teaspoon pepper
2 tablespoons chopped fresh parsley
salt and pepper
Lebanese flatbread, to serve

Pour the stock into a pan and bring to a boil, then reduce the
heat and simmer. Put the dried mushrooms into a heatproof
bowl, add hot stock to cover, and let soak. Meanwhile, melt
1 tablespoon (½ oz/15 g) of the butter with the oil in a large
pan, add the onion and celery, and cook over low heat, stirring
occasionally, for 5 minutes until softened but not colored. Add
the rice and cook, stirring constantly, for 1 minute until all the
grains are coated and glistening. Add the white wine and cook
until the liquid has been absorbed, then stir in the seven spices
seasoning, nutmeg, and soaked mushrooms. Add a ladleful
of hot stock to the pan and cook, stirring constantly, until all
the liquid has been absorbed. Continue adding the hot stock,
a ladleful at a time, stirring constantly until each addition has
been absorbed. This will take about 20 minutes. Season with
salt and pepper. Melt the remaining butter in a skillet or frying
pan, add the mushrooms, lemon juice, salt, and pepper, and
cook over medium heat, stirring occasionally, for 5–10 minutes
until the mushrooms are soft and cooked through. Stir the
parsley into the risotto and transfer to a large serving bowl. Top
with the mushrooms and serve warm with Lebanese flatbread.

ZUCCHINI OMELET

—

اومليت الكوسا

Preparation time: 10 minutes
Cooking time: 10–15 minutes
Serves 2

4 baby zucchini (courgettes), halved lengthwise
1 scallion (spring onion)
3 eggs
1 tablespoon olive oil
salt and pepper

Scoop out the flesh of from the zucchini (courgettes) and discard the shells. Chop the flesh with the scallion (spring onion). Lightly beat the eggs with salt and pepper in a bowl. Heat the oil in an omelet pan, add the zucchini mixture, and cook over medium-low heat, stirring occasionally, for 7–10 minutes until lightly colored. Meanwhile, preheat the broiler (grill). Pour the eggs into the pan and cook until set on one side. Put the pan under the hot broiler to cook the top. Turn out the omelet onto a plate, fold in half, and serve.

STUFFED BABY ZUCCHINI WITH VEGETABLES

—

محشي الكوسا بالخضار

Preparation time: 20–25 minutes
Cooking time: 35–40 minutes
Serves 4

10 baby zucchini (courgettes)
1 small onion, finely chopped
½ red bell pepper, seeded and finely chopped
1 tomato, diced
2 tablespoons chopped fresh mint
scant ¾ cup (5 oz/150 g) basmati rice, rinsed
1 teaspoon seven spices seasoning
3 tablespoons olive oil
½ large tomato, cut into 10 chunks
4¼ cups (1¼ pints/1 liter) hot vegetable stock
4½ tablespoons tomato paste (purée)
1 cinnamon stick
Salt and pepper

Trim the zucchini (courgette) and scoop out the flesh from the center of each using an apple corer. Mix together the onion, bell pepper, tomato, mint, rice, and seven spices seasoning in a bowl, stir in the olive oil, and season with salt and pepper. Mix well. Fill each zucchini with the mixture, then seal the end with a piece of tomato to stop the filling from falling out. Pour the stock into a large pan, stir in the tomato paste (purée), add the cinnamon stick, and bring to a boil over medium heat. Reduce the heat, add the stuffed zucchini, season with salt and pepper, cover, and simmer for 35–40 minutes. Serve immediately.

OKRA AND TOMATO

بامية بصلصة
الطماطم

Preparation time: 15 minutes
Cooking time: 40 minutes
Serves 4

8 oz/225g okra, trimmed
2 tablespoons olive oil, plus extra for drizzling
2 onions, sliced
4 garlic cloves, sliced
14 oz/400 g canned chopped tomatoes
1 tablespoon tomato paste (purée)
1 teaspoon seven spices seasoning
salt and pepper

Preheat the oven to 400°F/200°C/Gas Mark 6. Put the okra onto a baking sheet, drizzle with a little oil, and bake for 20 minutes. Remove from the oven and let cool. Heat the oil in a large pan, add the onions and garlic, and cook over low heat, stirring occasionally, for 5 minutes until softened but not colored. Add the tomatoes and 1⅔ cups (14 fl oz/400 ml) water and bring to a boil over medium heat. Stir in the seven spices seasoning, season with salt and pepper, reduce the heat, and simmer for 25 minutes. Add the okra to the pan and simmer for another 20 minutes until the sauce has thickened. Serve immediately.

STUFFED TOMATOES

محشي الطماطم بلحم
الغنم

Preparation time: 30 minutes
Cooking time: 40 minutes
Serves 6

6 large tomatoes
2 tablespoons olive oil, pus extra for drizzling
9 oz/250 g ground (minced) lamb
½ onion, diced
2 garlic cloves, crushed
3½ tablespoons long-grain rice
1 tablespoon tomato paste (purée)
1 teaspoon ground allspice
salt and pepper

Preheat over 350°F/180°C/Gas Mark 4. Slice off and reserve the tops of the tomatoes and scoop out and reserve the flesh with a teaspoon. Salt the tomato "shells" and set aside upside down on paper towels. Heat the oil in a large skillet or frying pan, add the lamb, and cook over medium-high heat, stirring frequently, for 8–10 minutes until lightly browned. Reduce the heat, add the onion and garlic, and cook, stirring occasionally, for minutes until the onion has softened. Stir in half the reserved tomato flesh (discard the remainder), the rice, tomato paste (purée), allspice, and 5 tablespoons water, season with salt and pepper, and cook for 5 minutes. Spoon the filling into the tomato shells until almost full and put the "lids" on top. Put them into an ovenproof dish in a single layer, drizzle with olive oil, cover with foil, and bake, basting occasionally with the cooking juices, for 40 minutes. Serve hot.

STUFFED BELL PEPPERS WITH RICE, TOMATOES, AND HERBS

STUFFED BELL PEPPERS WITH RICE, TOMATOES, AND HERBS

PHOTO PAGE 336

—

محشي الفلفل بالارز والطماطم والاعشاب

Preparation time: 20 minutes
Cooking time: 30 minutes
Serves 2–4

2 red bell peppers, halved and seeded
2 tomatoes, halved
olive oil, for drizzling
2 thyme sprigs
1 rosemary sprig
scant ½ cup (3 oz/80 g) basmati rice, rinsed
⅔ cup (¼ pint/150 ml) vegetable stock
½ teaspoon cayenne pepper
juice of 1 lemon
½ cup (2 oz/50 g) cooked peas
2 tablespoons chopped fresh mint
1 cup (1 oz/25 g) arugula (rocket)
sea salt and pepper

For the dressing
5 tablespoons extra virgin olive oil
juice of 1 lime
1 garlic clove, grated

Preheat the oven to 375°F/190°C/Gas Mark 5. Put a tomato half in each bell pepper half and put them into a roasting pan. Drizzle with olive oil and put the thyme and rosemary sprigs on top. Season with salt and pepper and roast for 30 minutes. Meanwhile, cook the basmati rice in the vegetable stock for 10–15 minutes until tender, then stir in the cayenne pepper, lemon juice, peas, and mint. Toss well and season with salt and pepper. Remove the bell peppers from the oven and put them into a serving dish. Reserve any cooking juices for the dressing. Spoon the rice over the top and add the arugula (rocket). Make the dressing by putting all the ingredients into a small bowl with the reserved cooking juices and mixing well. Pour the dressing over the arugula leaves and serve immediately.

SPAGHETTI WITH A RICH TOMATO SAUCE AND TOASTED ALMONDS

—

مكرونة سباغيتي بصلصة الطماطم مع اللوز المحمص

Preparation time: 20 minutes
Cooking time: 50 minutes
Serves 2

28 oz/800 g canned chopped tomatoes
2 tablespoons tomato paste (purée)
3 garlic cloves, grated
1 teaspoon brown sugar
1 tablespoon olive oil
pinch of ground cinnamon
pinch of ground allspice
pinch of grated nutmeg
½ teaspoon salt
pinch of pepper
7 oz/200 g spaghetti
½ cup (2 oz/50 g) slivered (flaked) almonds, toasted
2 tablespoons chopped parsley

Bring a large pan of salted water to a boil. Meanwhile, put the tomatoes, tomato paste (purée), garlic, and sugar into a pan and simmer over low heat, stirring frequently, for 30 minutes. Stir in the olive oil, cinnamon, allspice, nutmeg, salt, and pepper and cook for another 20 minutes. Add the pasta to the boiling water, bring back to a boil, and cook for 10–12 minutes until tender. Drain, reserving 3 tablespoons of the cooking liquid. Return the spaghetti and reserved cooking liquid to the pan and add the tomato sauce. Toss well, then serve in bowls sprinkled with the almonds and parsley.

SWEET POTATO AND SUMAC PHYLLO ROLLS

—

لفائف رقائق البطاطس الحلوة بالسماق

Preparation time: 1 hour
Cooking time: 12–15 minutes
Makes 12

2 sweet potatoes
juice of 1 lime
¼ teaspoon ground sumac
½ teaspoon clear honey
2 tablespoons chopped fresh cilantro (coriander)
10 oz/275 g phyllo (filo) pastry
4 tablespoons (2 oz/50 g) butter, melted
sea salt and pepper

Preheat the oven to 425°F/220°C/Gas Mark 7. Bake the sweet potatoes for 35–40 minutes until soft. Remove them from the oven, then halve and scoop out the flesh into a bowl. Add the lime juice, sumac, honey, and cilantro (coriander), season with salt and pepper, and mix well. Lay a sheet of pastry on a work surface with a wide edge toward you. Brush with melted butter and lay another pastry sheet on top. Cut into 4 equal vertical strips. Put a tablespoon of the sweet potato mixture at one end of the pastry, fold the ends in, and then roll up into a cigar shape. Seal by brushing all sides with melted butter. Repeat this process until all the sweet potato mixture has been used. Put the rolls onto a baking sheet and bake for 12–15 minutes. Serve immediately.

FASSOULIA STEW

يخنة الفاصولياء مع صلصة
الزبادي بالفلفل الحلو

Preparation time: 25 minutes
Cooking time: 3 hours
Serves 4

scant 1½ cups (9 oz/250 g) dried haricot beans, soaked
    overnight in water to cover and drained
4 tablespoons olive oil
2 onions, diced
6 garlic cloves, crushed
2 carrots, diced
2 celery stalks, diced
½ cup (3½ oz/100 g) pearl barley
14 oz/400 g canned tomatoes
2 tablespoons tomato paste (purée)
2 bay leaves
1 teaspoon dried marjoram
2 teaspoons dried oregano
2 heaping teaspoons smoked paprika
1 teaspoon chili flakes
1 cinnamon stick
salt and pepper

For the paprika yogurt
scant ½ cup (3½ fl oz/100 ml) plain (natural) yogurt
1 teaspoon smoked paprika
1 tablespoon lemon juice
salt and pepper

Put the beans into a pan, pour in water to cover, and bring
to a boil, then reduce the heat and cook for 1½–2 hours until
tender. Remove from the heat and drain. Heat the oil in a
large, heavy pan, add the onions, and cook over low heat,
stirring occasionally, for 5 minutes until softened. Add the
garlic, carrots, and celery and cook, stirring occasionally, for
another 5–7 minutes until softened. Add the beans, barley,
tomatoes, tomato paste (purée), bay leaves, marjoram, oregano,
paprika, chili flakes, and cinnamon stick and season with salt
and pepper. Simmer over low heat for 40–60 minutes until
the sauce has thickened, the beans are soft, and the barley
is cooked. Remove and discard the bay leaves. To make the
paprika yogurt, mix together the yogurt, paprika, and lemon
juice in a bowl and season to taste with salt and pepper. Serve
the stew topped with a spoonful of the paprika yogurt.

ASPARAGUS TART

تارت الهيليون

Preparation time: 30 minutes, plus chilling time
Cooking time: 50 minutes
Makes 1 x 10 inch/25 cm tart

2 eggs
1¼ cups (½ pint/300 ml) milk
1¼ cups (5 oz/150 g) grated sharp (mature) cheddar cheese
6 asparagus spears, halved
salt and pepper

For the dough
2 cups (8 oz/225 g) all-purpose (plain) flour, plus extra
    for dusting
pinch of salt
1 stick (4 oz/120 g) butter, chilled and diced

First, make the dough. Sift together the flour and salt into a
bowl, add the butter, and rub in with your fingertips rub until
the mixture resembles fine breadcrumbs. Pour scant ½ cup
(3½ fl oz/100 ml) ice water around the edge of the bowl and,
using a round-bladed knife, bring the mixture together to form
a dough. Knead for a few minutes, then shape into a ball, wrap
in plastic wrap (clingfilm), and let rest in the refrigerator for 30
minutes. Preheat the oven to 400°F/200°C/Gas Mark 6. Roll
out the dough on a lightly floured surface and use to line a 10
inch/25 cm tart pan, letting the excess overhang the edge. Prick
the bottom with a fork, then line with wax (greaseproof) paper
and pie weights (baking beans). Bake for 15 minutes. Remove
the pie weights and paper, return the pan to the oven, and bake
for another 5 minutes until the pie shell (pastry case) is golden
and firm. Remove from the oven and carefully trim off and
discard the excess pie shell while it is still warm. Let cool on a
wire rack while you make the filling. Whisk the eggs in a small
bowl, pour in the milk, season with salt and pepper, and add
the cheese. Blanch the asparagus in a pan of boiling water for
a few minutes, then drain well and pat dry with paper towels.
Arrange the asparagus spears in the cooled pie shell, pour the
milk and cheese mixture over them, and bake for 30 minutes.
Remove from the oven and let cool slightly on a wire rack, then
remove from the pan and serve.

SPINACH
AND
CHEESE PIE

—

فطيرة السبانخ بالجبنة

Preparation time: 30 minutes, plus chilling time
Cooking time: 30 minutes
Makes 1 x 8 inch/20 cm pie

2 tablespoons (1 oz/25 g) butter
14 oz/400 g baby spinach
5 cheese slices

For the dough
2 cups (8 oz/225 g) all-purpose (plain) flour, plus extra
    for dusting
1¼ sticks (5 oz/150 g) butter, diced
1 egg
2 tablespoons milk

First make the dough. Sift the flour into a large bowl, add
the butter, and rub in with your fingertips until the mixture
resembles breadcrumbs. Lightly beat the egg with the milk
in a small bowl, then gradually add to the mixture, mixing to
a dough with a round-bladed knife. Reserve any leftover egg
and milk mixture. Lightly knead the dough for a few minutes
until smooth, then wrap in plastic wrap (clingfilm) and chill
in the refrigerator for 1 hour. Meanwhile, melt the butter in a
large skillet or frying pan, add the spinach, and cook for a few
minutes until wilted. Tip into a strainer (sieve) set over a bowl
and squeeze out as much liquid as possible by pressing with the
back of a spoon, then let cool completely. Preheat the oven to
400°F/200°C/Gas Mark 6. Roll out three-quarters of the dough
on a lightly floured surface to 1/8 inch/3 mm thick and use to
line an 8 inch/20 cm pie dish, letting the excess overhang the
edge. Fill the pie shell (pastry case) with the spinach and top
with layers of sliced cheese to cover. Brush the dough edges
with the leftover egg mixture. Roll out the remaining dough
and lift on top of the pie. Press the edges together to seal. Trim
off the excess dough with a sharp knife. Brush the top of the pie
with the egg mixture and make a small hole in the top. Bake for
30 minutes or until golden. Serve warm.

SPINACH
AND
WALNUT
TARTS

PHOTO PAGE 342

——

رقاقات السبانخ مع
المكسرات

Preparation time: 20–30 minutes
Cooking time: 15–20 minutes
Makes 12 mini tarts

6 tablespoons (3 oz/80 g) butter, plus extra melted butter
    for brushing
3 tablespoons olive oil
1 onion, sliced
1 teaspoon brown sugar
1½ lb/700 g baby spinach
¼ teaspoon grated nutmeg
1 teaspoon seven spices seasoning
½ teaspoon salt
½ teaspoon pepper
9 oz/250g phyllo (filo) pastry dough, thawed if frozen
1¼ cups (½ pint/300 ml) heavy (double) cream
4 eggs, lightly beaten
½ cup (2 oz/50 g) shelled walnuts, coarsely chopped
1 teaspoon clear honey
½ teaspoon ground turmeric

Melt 1 tablespoon of the butter with 2 tablespoons of the oil in
a pan, add the onion and sugar, and cook over low heat, stirring
occasionally, for 20 minutes until caramelized. Remove from
the heat and set aside. Heat the remaining oil in a large skillet
or frying pan, add the spinach, and cook for a few minutes
until wilted, then stir in 1 tablespoon (½ oz/15 g) butter. Tip
the spinach into a colander and squeeze out the excess liquid,
then chop and put into a bowl. Add the nutmeg, seven spices
seasoning, salt, and pepper and toss well. Preheat the oven to
350°F/180°C/Gas Mark 4. Melt 1 tablespoon of the butter in a
pan over low heat or in the microwave oven and brush a 12-cup
muffin pan with it. Melt the remaining butter. Cut the sheets of
phyllo (filo) pastry dough into 8 on a clean surface, stack them,
and cover to stop them from drying out. Brush each piece
with melted butter and lay in the prepared pan, repeating this
process until there are 4–6 layers of dough in each cup. Brush
the top layer with melted butter. Spoon the spinach filling
into each pie shell (pastry case). Pour the cream in to a small
bowl, stir in the eggs, and season with salt and pepper. Pour
a little of this mixture into each pie shell, then bake for 15–20
minutes until the filling is set and the pastry is golden brown.
Meanwhile, dry-fry the nuts in a skillet or frying pan, then stir
in the honey and turmeric. Remove from the heat and set aside
in a warm place. When the spinach pies are cooked, remove
from the oven and let cool on a wire rack. Serve topped with
the caramelized onions and nuts.

SPINACH AND WALNUT TARTS

SHEESH BARAK SPINACH, ONION AND CHEESE DUMPLINGS

فطيرة عجينة الكنافة
بالجبنة والسبانخ

Preparation time: 30 minutes
Cooking time: 15 minutes
Serves 4–6

For the dough (makes about 40)
1½ cups (6½ oz/190 g) all-purpose (plain) flour, plus extra
    for dusting
1 teaspoon salt
1 tablespoons olive oil

For the spinach and onion filling (makes about 40)
1 tablespoon olive oil
1 onion, finely chopped
14 oz/400 g baby spinach
1 teaspoon seven spices seasoning
½ teaspoon pepper

For the cheese filling (makes about 40)
1⅓ cups (11 oz/300 g) soft cheese, such as ricotta
2 teaspoons za'atar

For the cheese, spinach, and pine nut filling (makes about 40)
1 tablespoon olive oil
11 oz/300 g baby spinach
1¼ cups (5 oz/150 g) grated mozzarella cheese
½ cup (2 oz/50 g) pine nuts, toasted
1 teaspoon seven spices seasoning
pinch of grated nutmeg
½ teaspoon salt
½ teaspoon pepper

For the sauce
2¼ lb/1 kg plain yogurt
2 tablespoons cornstarch (cornflour)
½ teaspoon ground cumin
½ teaspoon white pepper
1 teaspoon salt

To serve
2 garlic cloves
1 teaspoon salt
2 tablespoons chopped mint or cilantro (coriander)
1 tablespoon butter
generous ½ cup (4 oz/120 g) basmati rice, cooked and drained

First, make the dough. Sift together the flour and salt into a bowl. Mix the oil with 2/3 cup (1/4 pint/150 ml) water in a small bowl, gradually pour the mixture into the dry ingredients, and mix to a smooth dough. Add extra flour if the dough is too wet. Wrap in plastic wrap (clingfilm) and chill in the refrigerator.

For the spinach and onion filling, heat the oil in a pan, add the onion, and cook over low heat, stirring occasionally, for 5 minutes. Add the spinach and cook for another few minutes until wilted. Squeeze out and drain off any excess liquid, then stir in the seven spices seasoning and pepper. Remove from the heat and let cool, then chop.

For the cheese filling, mix together the cheese and za'atar in a bowl and set aside.

For the cheese, spinach, and pine nut filling, heat the oil in a skillet or frying pan, add the spinach, and cook for a few minutes until wilted. Remove from the heat, let cool, and drain off any excess liquid. Chop the spinach and mix with the mozzarella and pine nuts in a bowl. Add the seven spices seasoning, nutmeg, salt, and pepper.

Roll out the dough on a lightly floured surface to ⅛ inch/2 mm thick. Stamp out rounds with a 1½ inch/4 cm cutter, then stretch them slightly with your hands. Put a teaspoon of your chosen filling on each round, then fold over to form a half-moon, and seal. Put onto a baking sheet and chill in the refrigerator. Pour the yogurt into a pan, add scant 1 cup (7 fl oz/200 ml) water, and bring to a boil, whisking constantly. Mix the cornstarch (cornflour) to a paste with 4 tablespoons water and add to the pan, whisking constantly until thickened. Stir in the cumin, pepper, and salt, then add the dumplings and rice and cook for 15 minutes. Crush the garlic with the salt in a mortar with a pestle, then add the chopped mint or cilantro (coriander). Melt the butter in a pan, add the garlic and herb mixture, and cook, stirring occasionally, for a few minutes. Remove from the heat and stir the mixture into the yogurt sauce. Serve immediately.

CHEESE AND ONION KONAFAH PIE

فطيرة عجينة الكنافة
بالجبنة والسبانخ

Preparation time: 20 minutes
Cooking time: 30–40 minutes
Serves 6

12 oz/350 g kadaifi pastry
2¼ sticks (9 oz/250 g) butter, melted
generous 1 cup (9 oz/250 g) ricotta cheese
1 red onion, finely chopped
2 tablespoons milk
1¼ cups (7 oz/200 g) grated mozzarella cheese
salt and pepper

Preheat the oven to 350°F/180°C/Gas Mark 4. Shred the kadaifi pastry, put it into a bowl, and pour the melted butter over it. Divide the pastry in half and put one half into a 10 inch/25 cm square cake pan. Beat the ricotta with a fork in a bowl until smooth, then stir in the onion and milk. Season well with salt and pepper. Spread the ricotta mixture over the pastry layer, then add the grated mozzarella. Cover with the remaining pastry and bake for 30–40 minutes.

MOUSSAKA

MOUSSAKA

PHOTO PAGE 346

مسقعة

Preparation time: 20 minutes, plus soaking time
Cooking time: 1 hour
Serves 2–4

2 large eggplants (aubergines), sliced lengthwise
4 potatoes, cut into ¼ inch/5 mm thick slices
4 tomatoes , cut into ¼ inch/5 mm thick

For the cheese sauce
2 tablespoons (1¼ oz/30 g) butter
1/3 cup (1¼ oz/30 g) all-purpose (plain) flour
2½ cups (1 pints/600 ml) milk
1¼ cups (5 oz/150 g) grated cheddar cheese
salt and pepper

Preheat the oven to 400°F/200°C/Gas Mark 6. Soak the eggplant (aubergine) slices in salted water for 30 minutes, then drain, and pat dry. Make a layer of potato slices in an ovenproof dish, add a layer of eggplant slices, and then a layer of tomato slices. Repeat the layers until all the potatoes, eggplant, and tomatoes have been used. To make the sauce, melt the butter in a pan, add the flour, and cook, stirring constantly, for 1 minute. Remove the pan from the heat and stir in the milk a little at a time. Stir until all the milk has been added, then return the pan to the heat, and cook, stirring constantly, until thickened. Stir in half the cheese and season generously with salt and pepper. Pour the sauce over the vegetables, sprinkle with the remaining cheese, and bake for 50–60 minutes. Remove from the oven and let cool slightly before serving.

BROILED CHEESE WITH SUMAC AND PEAR

PHOTO PAGE 349

—

جبنة حلوم مشوية مع الكمثرى

Preparation time: 10 minutes
Cooking time: 10–15 minutes
Serves 4

7 oz/200 g halloumi cheese, sliced
3 tablespoons olive oil
2 garlic cloves, grated
1 teaspoon ground sumac
¼ cup (3 oz/80 g) shelled walnuts, halved
1 teaspoon brown sugar
1½ teaspoons butter
2 pears, peeled, cored, and quartered
1 romaine or cos lettuce, shredded
juice of 2 limes
2 tablespoons chopped fresh parsley

Preheat the broiler (grill) to hot. Put the cheese into shallow ovenproof dish, pour the olive oil over it, add the garlic and sumac, and toss well. Broil (grill) for 8 minutes, until golden, turning the cheese halfway through the cooking time. Meanwhile, put the walnuts, sugar, and butter into a skillet or frying pan and cook over medium-low heat, tossing the pan frequently, for 3–4 minutes. Tip out onto a sheet of wax (greaseproof) paper and let cool. Mix together the pears, lettuce, and lime juice in a salad bowl and toss well. Add the cheese, sprinkle with the walnuts and parsley, and serve.

VEGETARIAN MOTHER'S MILK

—

لبن أمه نباتي

Preparation time: 15 minutes
Cooking time: 15–20 minutes
Serves 2–4

½ cup (3½ oz/100 g) long grain rice
generous 2 cups (18 fl oz/500 ml) plain (natural) yogurt
1 tablespoon cornstarch (cornflour)
1½ teaspoons butter
4 garlic cloves, crushed
1 small bunch of fresh mint leaves, chopped
salt and freshly ground white pepper

Put the rice into a small pan, pour in boiling water to cover, and bring back to a boil over medium heat. Reduce the heat and cook for 10–15 minutes until the rice is tender and the water has been absorb. Pour the yogurt into a large pan, add 2½ cups (1 pint/600 ml) water and the cornstarch (cornflour), and bring to a boil, whisking constantly. Once boiling, stop stirring and let the yogurt start to thicken. Meanwhile, melt the butter in a small skillet or frying pan, add the garlic, and cook, stirring frequently, for a few minutes. Stir the garlic, mint, and rice into the yogurt mixture, cook for another few minutes, season with salt and pepper, and then serve.

VEGETABLES

BROILED (GRILLED) CHEESE WITH SUMAC AND PEAR

BREADS
AND
PASTRIES

✴

الخبز والمعجنات

WHOLE WHEAT BREAD

PHOTO PAGE 357

خبز اسمر

Preparation time: 40 mnutes, plus resting time
Cooking time: 30 minutes
Makes 1 loaf

3⅔ cups (1 lb 2 oz/500 g) whole wheat (wholemeal) flour
1 teaspoon salt
1 tablespoon instant milk powder
1 envelope active dry (fast-action) yeast
1⅓ cups (11 fl oz/325 ml) lukewarm water
2 tablespoons olive oil
all-purpose (plain) flour, for dusting
low-fat spray, for misting

Sift together the whole wheat (wholemeal) flour, salt, and milk powder into a bowl. Put the yeast into a small dish, pour in a little of the water, and let stand for a few minutes. Make a well in the center of the dry ingredients and pour in the yeast mixture, olive oil, and remaining water. Mix together with a wooden spoon to form a dough. Bring the dough together with your hands, then turn out onto a lightly floured surface and knead for at least 10 minutes until smooth and elastic. Shape the dough into a ball, put it into a clean, lightly oiled bowl, cover with plastic wrap (clingfilm) or a damp dishtowel, and let stand in a warm place for at least 1 hour or until doubled in size. Mist a loaf pan with low-fat spray and dust with flour. Uncover the dough and punch down (knock back), then knead for another 5 minutes. Shape into a loaf and put into the prepared pan. Cover with a dish towel and let stand in a warm place for another hour until almost doubled in size. Preheat the oven to 400°F/200°C/Gas Mark 6. Dust the top of the loaf with a little more flour and bake for 30 minutes or until golden. Turn out of the pan and let cool on a wire rack.

KNOUBZ BREAD

الخبز العربي

Preparation time: 20 minutes, plus resting time
Cooking time: 10 minutes
Makes 10

5 tablespoons (2½ oz/65 g) butter, melted,
    plus extra for greasing
2¾ cups (11 oz/300 g) hard (strong) white bread flour
scant 1 cup (3½ oz/100 g) whole wheat (wholemeal) flour
1 envelope active dry (fast-action) yeast
½ teaspoon salt
1¼ cups (½ pint/300 ml) lukewarm water

Preheat the oven to 425°F/220°C/Gas Mark 7 and lightly grease a baking sheet with butter. Sift both kinds of flour into a bowl and add the yeast and salt. Make a well in the middle of the flour and pour in the melted butter, then gradually pour in the water. Bring together the flour and liquid to form a dough and knead for a few minutes in the bowl. Keep the dough in the bowl, cover with a dish towel, and let stand in a warm place for 1 hour until doubled in size. Divide the dough into 10 pieces and roll each one out to a thin circle. Bake the bread in batches of 4 on a baking sheet for 10 minutes. Cool slightly and serve.

WHOLE WHEAT BREAD

WHOLE WHEAT ROLLS

WHOLE WHEAT ROLLS

PHOTO PAGE 358

—

كرات الخبز الاسمر

Preparation time: 20 minutes, plus resting time
Cooking time: 20–25 minutes
Makes 4

1 envelope active dry (fast-action) yeast
1 teaspoon clear honey
scant ½ cup (3½ fl oz/100 ml) lukewarm water
1½ cups (7 oz/200 g) whole wheat (wholemeal) flour
¾ cup (3½ oz/100 g) hard (strong) white bread flour
1 teaspoon salt
5 tablespoons lukewarm milk
vegetable oil, for oiling
semolina flour, for dusting

For the topping (optional)
1 egg lightly beaten with 1 tablespoon water
1 tablespoon toasted sesame seeds and poppy seeds

Stir the yeast and honey into the lukewarm water in a bowl and let stand for 10 minutes until frothy. Mix together both kinds of flours and the salt in a large bowl, then gradually stir in the yeast mixture and milk with a wooden spoon. Once the dough has come together, turn out onto a work surface lightly dusted with semolina flour and knead for at least 10 minutes until smooth and elastic. Shape the dough into a ball, put it into a clean, lightly oiled bowl, cover with plastic wrap (clingfilm) or a damp dish towel, and let stand in a warm place for about 1 hour until doubled in size. Meanwhile, lightly oil a baking sheet and dust with semolina flour. Turn out the dough onto a work surface lightly dusted with semolina flour. Divide it into 4 and shape each piece into a ball. Put the dough balls on the prepared baking sheet, cover, and let stand for another 30–40 minutes until the rolls have puffed up to almost double in size.

Preheat the oven to 425°F/220°C/Gas Mark 7. Uncover and dust the rolls with a little more semolina flour or brush with egg wash and sprinkle with the seeds. Bake for 20–25 minutes until golden brown and the rolls sound hollow when you tap the underside. Transfer to a wire rack to cool.

BREADS AND PASTRIES

OLIVE
BREAD

خبز بالزيتون

Preparation time: 15 minutes, plus resting time
Cooking time: 30 minutes
Makes 1 loaf

4 cups (1 lb 2 oz/500 g) whole wheat (wholemeal) flour
1 envelope active dry (fast-action) yeast
1 teaspoon salt
¾ cup (3 oz/80 g) green pitted (stoned) olives, halved
2 tablespoons olive oil
1⅓ cups (11 fl oz/325 ml) lukewarm water
all-purpose (plain) flour, for dusting

Mix the flour, yeast, and salt in a large bowl. Stir in the olives, then add the oil and gradually stir in the water with a wooden spoon to form a dough. Turn out onto a floured work surface and knead for 10 minutes until smooth and elastic. Dust a loaf pan with flour, put the dough into it, sprinkle with a little more flour, and score the top. Cover with plastic wrap (clingfilm) and let stand in a warm place for 1 hour until doubled in size. Preheat the oven to 450°F/230°C/Gas Mark 8. Uncover the loaf and bake for 30 minutes until golden. Cool, then serve.

SEEDED
BREAD

خبز بالبذور

Preparation time: 30 minutes, plus retsing time
Cooking time: 10 minutes
Makes 4

1 envelope active dry (fast action) yeast
1¼ cups (½ pint/300 ml) lukewarm water
1¾ cups (9 oz/250 g) hard (strong) white bread flour,
    plus extra for dusting
scant ½ cup (2 oz/50 g) whole wheat (wholemeal) flour
⅓ cup (2 oz/50 g) cornmeal
1 tablespoon salt
⅓ cup (1½ oz/40 g) sunflower seeds, toasted
⅓ cup (1½ oz/40 g) pumpkin seeds, toasted
3 tablespoons (1½ oz/40 g) sesame seeds, toasted

Dissolve the yeast in the water in a bowl. Mix together both types of flour, the cornmeal, and salt in a mixing bowl. Gradually add the yeast mixture and bring together the ingredients into a dough with a wooden spoon. Turn out onto a lightly floured surface and knead for at least 10 minutes until the dough is smooth and elastic. Put the dough in bowl, cover with plastic wrap (clingfilm), and let stand in a warm place for about 1 hour until doubled in size. Turn out the dough onto a lightly floured surface and punch down (knock back). Press the dough down and push the seeds into the center, pulling the corners back over to the center to enclose them. Knead the dough to distribute the seeds. Divide into 4 and shape into circles, cover with a damp dish towel, and let stand for 40 minutes, until they have puffed up. Preheat the oven to 450°F/230°C/Gas Mark 8. Roll out each ball into an 8 inch/ 20 cm circle, transfer to a baking sheet, brush lightly with water, and bake for 7–9 minutes until the breads are golden. Serve warm.

PITA BREAD

PITA BREADS

PHOTO PAGE 362

خبز البيتا

Preparation time: 25 minutes, plus retsing time
Cooking time: 10 minutes
Makes 6

1 envelope active dry (fast-action) yeast
²⁄₃ cup (¼ pint/150 ml) lukewarm water
1 tablespoon clear honey
3⅓ cups (1 lb/450 g) hard (strong) white bread flour,
    plus extra for dusting
1½ teaspoons fine sea salt
scant ½ cup (3½ fl oz/100 ml) lukewarm milk

Dissolve the yeast in 3 tablespoons of the lukewarm water
in a small bowl and stir in the honey. Sift together the flour
and salt into large mixing a bowl, add the yeast mixture, and
gradually add the remaining water and lukewarm milk, mixing
with a wooden spoon until all the ingredients are thoroughly
combined. Turn out the dough onto a lightly floured surface
and knead for at least 10 minutes until smooth and elastic.
Shape the dough into a ball, put it into a bowl, cover with
plastic wrap (clingfilm) or a damp dish towel, and let stand in a
warm place for about 1 hour until doubled in size. Preheat the
oven to 450°F/230°C/Gas Mark 8. Uncover the dough, turn it
out, and divide into 6 balls. Roll out each ball into an 8 inch/20
cm circle. Put the circles on baking sheets, brush with a little
water, and bake for 7–9 minutes until golden. Serve warm.

WHOLE WHEAT PITA BREADS

خبز البيتا الاسمر

Preparaion time: 25 minutes, plus resting time
Cooking time: 10–15 minutes
Makes 14

3²⁄₃ cups (1 lb 2 oz/500 g) whole wheat (wholemeal) flour
4½ cups (1 lb 2 oz/500 g) all-purpose (plain) flour,
    plus extra for dusting
2 envelopes active dry (fast-action) yeast
1½ teaspoons salt
4 tablespoons extra virgin olive oil, plus extra for brushing
2½ cups (1 pint/600 ml) lukewarm water

Mix together both types of flour, the yeast, and salt in a large
bowl, then add the oil and gradually add the water to form
a dough. You may need a little less or more water to bring
together the dough. Turn out the dough onto a lightly floured
work surface and knead for at least 10 minutes until smooth
and elastic. Shape the dough into a ball, return it to the bowl,
and lightly dust with flour. Cover with plastic wrap (clingfilm)
and let stand in a warm place for 1 hour. Preheat the oven
to 450°F/230°C/Gas Mark 8. Brush 2 baking sheets with oil.
Uncover the dough and punch down (knock back), then make
golf ball-size balls with your hands, and lightly flour each one.
Roll out each dough ball into a thin circle and place on the
prepared baking sheets. Bake for 10–15 minutes. Serve warm.

SAVORY BLESSED BREAD

—

خبز معروك مالح

Preparation time: 30–35 minutes, plus resting time
Cooking time: 20–15 minutes
Makes 12

4 cups (1 lb 2 oz/500 g) all-purpose (plain) flour,
    plus extra for dusting
1 teaspoon salt
3 tablespoons grated Parmesan cheese
1 envelope active dry (fast-action) yeast
⅔ cup (¼ pint/150 ml) lukewarm water
⅔ cup (¼ pint/150 ml) lukewarm milk
3 tablespoons olive oil, plus extra for brushing

Sift together the flour and salt into a large bowl and stir in the Parmesan. Put the yeast into a small dish, pour in a little of the warm water and milk, and let stand for a few minutes. Make a well in the center of the dry ingredients and pour in the olive oil, yeast mixture, and remaining liquid. Mix with a wooden spoon to form a dough. Bring together the dough with your hands, then turn out onto a floured surface and knead for at least 10 minutes until smooth and elastic. Lightly dust a clean bowl with flour, shape the dough into a ball, and put it into the bowl. Cover with a dish towel and let stand in a warm place for at least 1 hour until doubled in size. Brush a baking sheet with oil. Uncover the dough and punch down (knock back), then knead for another 5 minutes. Shape into 12 small rolls, put them onto the baking sheet, and cover with a dish towel. Let stand for 1 hour until risen. Preheat the oven to 400°F/200°C/Gas Mark 6. Uncover the rolls and bake for 20 minutes until golden. Remove from the oven and transfer to a wire rack to cool.

CHEESE STRAWS

—

جدائل بالجبن

Preparation time: 20 minutes
Cooking time: 10–15 minutes
Makes 12

1¾ cups (8 oz/225 g) all-purpose (plain) flour,
    plus extra for dusting
1 stick (4 oz/120 g) butter, chilled and diced
½ cup (2 oz/50 g) grated sharp (mature) cheddar cheese
1 teaspoon paprika
vegetable oil, for brushing
salt

Sift the flour into a bowl, add the butter, and rub in with your fingertips until the mixture resembles breadcrumbs. Stir in the cheese, paprika, and a pinch of salt. Pour in ¼ cup (2 fl oz/50 ml) water and, working quickly, bring together to form a dough. Knead lightly for 1 minute, then wrap in plastic wrap (clingfilm) and chill in the refrigerator for 1 hour. Preheat the oven to 400°F/200°C/Gas Mark 6. Brush a baking sheet with oil. Roll out the dough to ¼ inch/5 mm thick on a lightly floured surface. Cut into ¾ x 8 inch/2 x 20 cm strips and twist. Put the twisted strips onto the prepared baking sheet and bake for 10–15 minutes. Remove the cheese straws from the oven and transfer to a wire rack to cool. Serve with mezza dishes.

SWEET BLESSED BREAD

خبز معروك حلو

Preparation time: 30–35 minutes
Cooking time: 20–25 minutes
Makes 12

4¾ (1 lb 5 oz/600 g) all-purpose (plain) flour,
    plus extra for dusting
½ cup (3½ oz/100 g) superfine (caster) sugar
1 envelope active dry (fast-action) yeast
1 tablespoons mahlab
7 tablespoons (3½ oz/100 g) butter, melted,
    plus extra for greasing
⅔ cup (¼ pint/150 ml) lukewarm water
⅔ cup (¼ pint/150 ml) lukewarm milk

Sift the flour into a large bowl and stir in the sugar, yeast, and mahlab. Mix the melted butter with the lukewarm water and milk in a small bowl. Make a well in the center of the dry ingredients and pour in the warm liquid. Mix together with a wooden spoon to form a dough. If necessary, add a little more water or flour. Use your hands to bring together the dough, then turn out onto a lightly floured surface, and knead for at least 10 minutes until smooth and elastic. Lightly dust a clean bowl with flour, shape the dough into a ball, and put it into the bowl. Cover with a dish towel and let stand in a warm place for at least 1 hour until doubled in size. Grease a large baking sheet with butter. Uncover the dough, punch down (knock back), and knead for another 5 minutes. Shape into 12 small rolls, put them onto the prepared baking sheet, cover with a dish towel, and let stand for another hour more until risen. Preheat the oven to 400°F/200°C/Gas Mark 6. Uncover the rolls and bake for 20–25 minutes until golden. Remove from the oven and transfer to a wire rack to cool.

LEBANESE
LOAF

—

رغيف الخبز اللبناني

Preparation time: 10–15 minutes, plus resting time
Cooking time: 15 minutes
Makes 1 loaf

1 envelope active dry (fast-action) yeast
scant 2 cups (16 fl oz/450 ml) lukewarm water
4¾ cups (1 lb 5 oz/600 g) unbleached hard (strong) white
  bread flour
1 heaping teaspoon fine sea salt
semolina flour, for dusting

Dissolve the yeast in 1 tablespoon of the water in a small bowl. Sift together the flour and salt into a bowl, make a well in the center, and add the yeast mixture. Gradually add the remaining water, using your fingers to work it into the flour at a little a time. Work out any lumps with your fingers and knead for another 2–3 minutes. The dough will be very wet, almost like a thick batter. Cover the bowl with plastic wrap (clingfilm) and let stand in a warm place for 4–6 hours until the dough has doubled in size. Preheat the oven to 425°F/220°C/Gas Mark 7 and put a baking sheet into the oven. Once the baking sheet is hot, sprinkle it with semolina flour. Gently roll out the dough onto the baking sheet and dust with a little more semolina flour. Bake for 15 minutes, then lower the oven temperature to 400°F/200°C/Gas Mark 6 and bake for another 30 minutes. Lift the bread off the baking sheet onto the middle shelf of the oven and bake for another 15 minutes until crisp on the underside. Transfer to a wire rack to cool completely before slicing.

BULGUR
BREAD
WITH
ZA'ATAR

PHOTO PAGE 367

—

خبز البرغل مع الزعتر

Preparation time: 10 minutes, plus resting time
Cooking time: 20–25 minutes
Makes 1 loaf

½ cup (3 oz/80 g) bulgur wheat, washed in warm water
  and squeezed in a cheesecloth (muslin) cloth
1 cup (4 oz/120 g) all-purpose (plain) flour,
  plus extra for dusting
1 cup (4 oz/120 g) whole wheat (wholemeal) flour
1 envelope active dry (fast-action) yeast
6 tablespoons olive oil, plus extra for brushing
1 teaspoon salt
⅔ cup (¼ pint/150 ml) lukewarm water
4 tablespoons za'atar

Put the bulgur wheat, both types of flour, the yeast, 1 tablespoon of the olive oil, and the salt into a bowl, pour in the water, and bring together the dough in the bowl. Cover with a dish towel and let stand in a warm place for 1 hour. Preheat the oven to 400°F/200°C/Gas Mark 6. Brush a 12 x 16 inch/30 x 40 cm baking sheet with oil. Uncover the dough and punch down (knock back), then tip out onto a floured work surface. Roll the dough into a rectangle the size of the baking sheet, lift it onto the sheet. Prick it all over with a fork. Mix the za'atar with the remaining olive oil in a bowl, then spread the mixture over the dough. Bake for 20–25 minutes and serve warm.

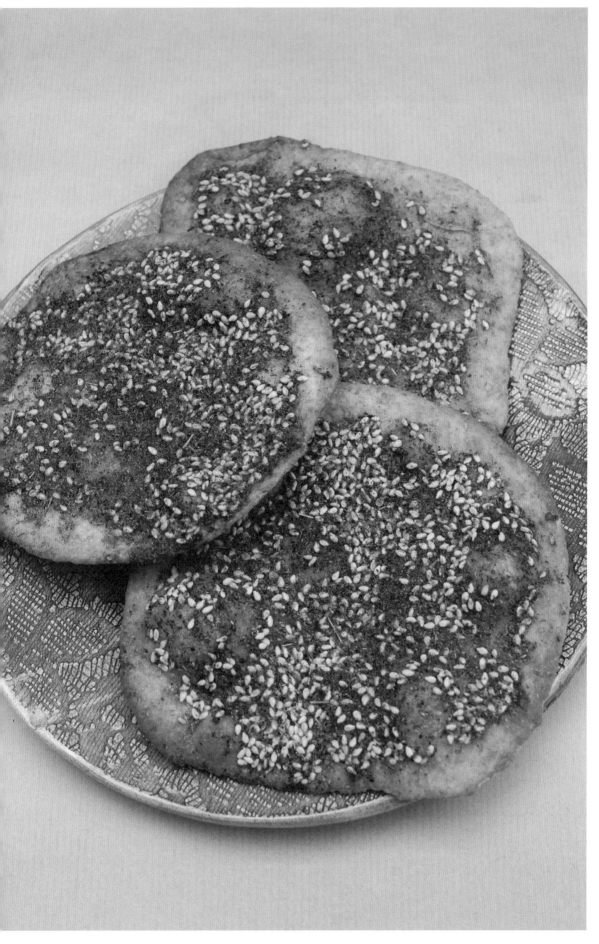

BULGUR BREAD WITH ZA´ATAR

CHICKEN AND ZA'ATAR FLATBREAD

خبز مسطح بالدجاج
والزعتر

Preparation time: 15 minutes, plus marinating and resting time
Cooking time: 30–40 minutes
Serves 4

2 teaspoons active dry (fast-action) yeast
2 cups (450 ml/16 fl oz) lukewarm water
4 cups (1 lb 2 oz/500 g) hard (strong) white bread flour,
    plus extra for dusting
1 teaspoon baking powder
2 teaspoons salt
4 tablespoons (50 g/2 oz) butter, diced
2 tablespoons evaporated milk
olive oil, for brushing

For the topping
2 skinless, boneless chicken breasts
1 small red onion, chopped
1 garlic clove, crushed
2 tablespoons olive oil
½ lemon, thinly sliced
1 teaspoon salt
1 teaspoon pepper
½ teaspoon ground allspice
½ teaspoon ground cinnamon
½ tablespoon ground sumac
2 tablespoons za'atar
4 tablespoons toasted pine nuts
2 tablespoons chopped fresh parsley

Start preparing the topping. Put the chicken, onion, garlic, olive oil, lemon, salt, pepper, allspice, cinnamon, and sumac into a large bowl. Rub the spices into the chicken and let marinate in the refrigerator for 2 hours. Dissolve the yeast in the lukewarm water in a small bowl. Sift together the flour, baking powder, and salt into a bowl and add the butter and evaporated milk. Gradually add the yeast mixture, working it in with a wooden spoon until a dough forms. Turn out onto a lightly floured work surface and knead at least 10 minutes until smooth and elastic. Shape the dough into a ball, put it in a lightly oiled bowl, and cover with plastic wrap (clingfilm) or a damp dish towel. Let stand in a warm place for about 1 hour until the dough has doubled in size. Preheat the oven to 400°F/200°C/Gas Mark 6. Transfer the chicken with the marinade to a roasting pan, sprinkle with the za'atar, and roast for 20–30 minutes until cooked through. Remove the chicken from the oven and let cool, then shred the meat with 2 forks. Increase the oven temperature to 450°F/230°C/Gas Mark 8. Turn out the dough onto a lightly floured surface and divide it into 4 equal pieces. Roll out each piece into an 8 inch/20 cm circle. Put the circles on a baking sheet, cover, and let stand for about 20 minutes until the dough has puffed up. Brush the dough circles with olive oil and top with the chicken mixture and the pine nuts. Bake for 7–9 minutes until the dough is golden brown and cooked through.

THYME AND SUMAC BREADS

—

فطائر الزعتر والسماق

Preparation time: 40 minutes, plus resting time
Cooking time: 10 minutes
Makes 14

1¾ cups (7 oz/200 g) hard (strong) whole wheat
   (wholemeal) bread flour
1½ cups (6 oz/175 g) all-purpose (plain) flour,
   plus extra for dusting
1 1/8 teaspoons dry (fast-action) yeast
2½ teaspoons salt
1 cup (8 fl oz/250 ml) extra virgin oil, plus extra for brushing
1¼ cups (½ pint/300 ml) lukewarm water
scant ½ cup (¾ oz/20 g) dried thyme
½ teaspoon toasted sesame seeds
1 teaspoon ground sumac

Put both kinds of flour, the yeast, and 1½ teaspoons of the
salt into a bowl and mix well, then add 1 tablespoon of the
oil, and gradually add the lukewarm water, mixing in the dry
ingredients to form a dough. You may need a little less or more
water to bring the dough together. Knead for 10 minutes, then
return the dough to the bowl and dust lightly with flour. Cover
the bowl with plastic wrap (clingfilm) and let stand in a warm
place for 1 hour until doubled in size. Meanwhile, mix together
the thyme, sesame seeds, sumac, the remaining salt, and the
remaining olive oil in a bowl. Preheat the oven to 450°F/230°C/
Gas Mark 8. Brush 2 baking sheets with oil. Punch down
(knock back) the dough and then make golf ball-sized dough
balls with your hands. Lightly flour each one and roll out into
thin circles. Put the dough circles onto the prepared baking
sheet. Spread 2 teaspoons of the thyme and sumac mixture over
the dough and bake for 10 minutes. Serve warm.

FLATBREAD
WITH
TOMATO
AND
ONION

—

خبز مسطح مع الطماطم
والبصل

Preparation time: 30–35 minutes, plus resting time
Cooking time: 10 minutes
Makes 4

1¾ cups (9 oz/250 g) hard (strong) white bread flour,
  plus extra for dusting
1 teaspoon fine sea salt
½ teaspoon active dry (fast-action) yeast
⅔ cup (¼ pint/150 ml) lukewarm water
2 tablespoons olive oil

For the topping
1 onion, halved
2 large tomatoes, peeled and diced
1 tablespoon ground sumac, plus extra for sprinkling
1 teaspoon salt
2 tablespoons olive oil

Sift together the flour and salt into large bowl. Dissolve the yeast in the lukewarm water and gradually add to the dry ingredients, mixing it in with a wooden spoon. Once the dough has come together, turn out onto lightly floured work surface and knead for at least 10 minutes until smooth elastic. Shape the dough into a ball, put it into a bowl, and cover with plastic wrap (clingfilm) or a damp dish towel. Let stand in a warm place for about 1 hour until it has doubled in size. Meanwhile, make the topping. Dice half the onion and slice the other half. Put the diced onion and the tomatoes into a bowl, sprinkle with the sumac and salt, drizzle with 1 tablespoon of the oil, and squash together with your fingers. Preheat the oven to 425°F/220°C/Gas Mark 7. Turn out the dough onto a lightly floured surface and divide into 4. Shape each piece into a ball and then roll out each ball into an ⅛ inch/3 mm thick circle. Brush with the remaining olive oil, divide the tomato topping among the circles, and top with the sliced onion. Bake for 7–9 minutes until the bread is crisp and golden and crispy. Remove from the oven and sprinkle with a little extra sumac.

WALNUT BREAD

PHOTO PAGE 376

خبز بالجوز

Preparation time: 30–35 minutes, plus resting time
Cooking time: 20–25 minutes
Makes 2 loaves

¾ teaspoon active dry (fast-action) yeast
4 tablespoons lukewarm water
1 tablespoon (clear) honey
1⅔ cups (7 oz/200 g) whole wheat (wholemeal) flour
¾ cup (3½ oz/100 g) hard (strong) white bread flour
1 teaspoon fine sea salt
¾ cup (6 fl oz/175 ml) lukewarm milk
4 tablespoons coarse semolina flour
½ cup (2 oz/50 g) shelled walnuts, toasted and coarsely
   chopped

Put the yeast into a bowl and stir in the lukewarm water until
the yeast dissolves. Add the honey. Put both types of flour and
the salt into a bowl, make a well in the center, and add the yeast
mixture, then gradually work the lukewarm milk into the dough
with your hands or a wooden spoon until fully incorporated.
Turn out onto a work surface sprinkled with 1 tablespoon
of the semolina flour and knead for about 10 minutes until
smooth and elastic. Halve the dough and roll into balls. Flatten
each ball and divide the walnuts between them, placing them
in the center of each round. Pull in the sides of the dough to
enclose the nuts completely. Turn over so that the smooth
sides are on the top and shape into circles, about ¾ inch/2 cm
thick and 4½–5½ inches/12–14 cm in diameter. Sprinkle a
baking sheet with 1 tablespoon of the semolina flour, put the
loaves onto the sheet, cover with plastic wrap (clingfilm) or a
damp dish towel, and let stand in a warm place for 2–4 hours
until almost doubled in size. Preheat the oven to 425°F/220°C/
Gas Mark 7. Uncover the loaves and sprinkle the remaining
semolina flour over them. Bake for 20–25 minutes until golden
and the loaves sound hollow when tapped on the underside.
Remove from the oven and let cool on a wire rack.

WALNUT AND ONION BREAD

خبز بالجوز والبصل

Preparation time: 30–35 minutes
Cooking time: 20–25 minutes
Makes 2 loaves

1 onion, diced
½ teaspoon ground allspice
½ teaspoon ground cinnamon
½ cup (2 oz/50 g) shelled walnuts, toasted and coarsely
    chopped
¾ teaspoon active dry (fast-action) yeast
4 tablespoons lukewarm water
1 tablespoon honey
1⅔ cups (7 oz/200 g) whole wheat (wholemeal) flour
¾ cup (3½ oz/100 g) hard (strong) white bread flour
1 teaspoon fine sea salt
¾ cup (6 fl oz/175 ml) lukewarm milk
4 tablespoons coarse semolina flour, for dusting

Heat the oil in a skillet or frying pan, add the onion, and
cook over low heat, stirring occasionally, for 5 minutes until
softened. Stir in the allspice and cinnamon and cook for
another minute, then remove from the heat, tip into a bowl,
and let cool. When the mixture is cold, stir in the walnuts. Put
the yeast in a small bowl and stir in the lukewarm water until
the yeast has dissolved, then stir in the honey. Put both types
of flour and the salt in a bowl, make a well in the center, and
add the yeast mixture, then gradually work the lukewarm milk
into the dough with your hands or with a wooden spoon. Turn
out the dough onto a work surface lightly dusted with semolina
flour and knead for at least 10 minutes until smooth and elastic.
Halve the dough and roll into 2 balls. Flatten each ball and
divide the onion and walnut mixture between them, placing it
in the center of each circle and pulling in the sides of the dough
to enclose the filling. Turn over so that the smooth side is on
the top and shape into a neat circle, about ¾ inch/2 cm thick
and 4½–5½ inches/11–14 cm in diameter. Sprinkle a baking
sheet with 1 tablespoon of the semolina flour, put the loaves on
the sheet, cover with plastic wrap (clingfilm) or a damp dish
towel, and let stand in a warm place for 2–4 hours until almost
doubled in size. Meanwhile, preheat the oven to 425°F/220°C/
Gas Mark 7. Sprinkle the remaining semolina flour over the
loaves and bake for 20–25 minutes until they sound hollow
when tapped on the underside. Remove from the oven and let
cool on a wire rack before serving.

SESAME RINGS WITH CORIANDER AND CUMIN

PHOTO PAGE 377

كعك حلقات بالسمسم مع
الكزبرة والكمون

Preparation time: 25 minutes
Cooking time: 25 minutes
Makes 12

olive oil, for brushing
2 cups (9 oz/250 g) all-purpose (plain) flour,
    plus extra for dusting
2 teaspoons baking powder
½ teaspoon ground cumin
½ teaspoon ground coriander
2 tablespoons sesame seeds
1 egg
⅔ cup (¼ pint/150 ml) milk

Preheat the oven to 375°F/190°C/Gas Mark 5. Brush a baking sheet with a little oil. Sift together the flour, baking powder, and spices into a large bowl and add the sesame seeds. Whisk the egg in a small bowl, add the milk, and mix. Make a well in the center of the dry ingredients and gradually pour in the milk and egg mixture, a little at a time, bringing together the flour and liquid to form a dough. (You probably won't need all the liquid, so reserve about 4 teaspoons for glazing.) Divide the dough in 12 equal balls and then roll each one in to a sausage shape on a lightly floured work surface. Bring the ends of each "sausage" together to form a circle. Put the sesame rings on the prepared baking sheet, allowing plenty of space between them. Brush with the remaining egg and milk mixture and bake for 25 minutes. Remove from the oven, transfer the rings to a wire rack, and let cool.

SESAME RINGS WITH CORIANDER AND CUMIN

HALLOUMI STUFFED SESAME LOAF

رغيف بالسمسم محشو
بجبنة حلوم

Preparation time: 25 minutes, plus resting time
Cooking time: 30 minutes
Makes 1 loaf

3 envelopes active dry (fast-action) yeast
scant ½ cup (3½ fl oz/100 ml) lukewarm water
3⅔ cups (1 lb 2 oz/500 g) hard (strong) white bread flour,
    plus extra for dusting
1 tablespoon salt
6 tablespoons lukewarm milk
6 tablespoons olive oil, plus extra for oiling
5 oz/150 g halloumi cheese, cubed
1 tablespoon dried mint

For the topping
1 egg, lightly beaten
2 tablespoons toasted sesame seeds

Dissolve the yeast in the lukewarm water in a small bowl.
Sift together the flour and salt into a bowl and gradually add
the yeast mixture, milk, and olive oil, gradually incorporating
the dry ingredients with a wooden spoon to form a dough.
Turn out onto a floured work surface and knead for at least
10 minutes until the dough becomes soft and elastic. Shape the
dough into a ball and put it into a lightly oiled bowl. Cover with
plastic wrap (clingfilm) or a damp dish towel and let stand in
a warm place for about 1 hour until doubled in size. Preheat
oven 450°F/230°C/Gas Mark 8. Lightly brush a small round loaf
pan with oil. Mix together the cheese and dried mint in a bowl.
Punch down (knock back) the dough, flatten slightly, and press
the cheese into the middle. Pull each corner of the dough back
to part cover the cheese. Repeat this with each corner of the
dough and press them together in the middle. Turn the dough
over so the smooth round side is on top, shape into a large ball,
and put into the prepared pan. Cover with a damp cloth and let
rise for another 20–30 minutes until the dough has puffed up.
Brush with the beaten egg and sprinkle with the sesame seeds.
Bake for 30 minutes until golden brown and loaf sounds hollow
when tapped on the underside. Turn out to cool on a wire rack.
Do not slice until the loaf has cooled.

SPINACH TURNOVERS

فطائر السبانخ

Preparation time: 45 minutes, plus resting time
Cooking time: 20 minutes
Makes about 20

1½ cups (7 oz/200 g) hard (strong) whole wheat
   (wholemeal) flour
1⅓ cups (6 oz/175 g) all-purpose (plain) flour,
   plus extra for dusting
1⅛ teaspoons active dry (fast-action) yeast
1½ teaspoons salt
2 teaspoons extra virgin olive oil
1¼ cups (½ pint/300 ml) lukewarm water
butter, for greasing
1 egg lightly beaten with 2 tablespoons water

For the filling
5 tablespoons extra virgin olive oil
1 leek, thinly sliced
4 small onions, finely diced
1 tablespoon ground sumac
1 teaspoon seven spices seasoning
juice of 1 lemon
9 oz/250g baby spinach, coarse stems removed
salt and pepper

Sift together both kinds of flour into a bowl, then tip in the
bran from the sifter (sieve) and add the yeast and salt. Make a
well in the middle of the dry ingredients and add the oil, then
gradually add the water and mix to a dough. You may need a
little less or more water to bring together the dough. Knead
for 10 minutes, then return the dough to the bowl and dust
lightly with flour. Cover the bowl with plastic wrap (clingfilm)
and let stand in a warm place for 1 hour. Meanwhile, make
the filling. Heat the oil in a saucepan, add the leek and onions,
and cook over low heat, stirring occasionally, for 5–8 minutes,
until softened. Add the sumac, seven spices seasoning, and
lemon juice and cook for another minute. Add the spinach
and cook for a few minutes until wilted. Season with salt and
pepper, remove from the heat, and let cool. Preheat the oven to
450°F/230°C/Gas Mark 8. Grease 2 baking sheets with butter.
Punch down (knock back) the dough and knead again for a few
minutes. Use your hands to make golf ball-sized dough balls
and dust them lightly with flour. Thinly roll out each dough ball
into a circle, put a little of the spinach filling into the middle,
dampen the edges of the dough, and bring up the sides to seal
to form a turnover. Put the turnovers onto the prepared baking
sheets and brush with the egg wash. Bake for 10–15 minutes
until golden. Serve immediately.

FISH
AND
PEA
TURNOVERS

فطائر السمك والبازلاء

Preparation time: 45 minutes, plus resting time
Cooking time: 20 minutes
Makes about 20

1½ cups (7 oz/200 g) hard (strong) whole wheat
    (wholemeal) bread flour
1⅓ cups (6 oz/175 g) all-purpose (plain) flour
1⅛ teaspoons active dry (fast-action) yeast
1½ teaspoons salt
2 teaspoons extra virgin olive oil, plus extra for brushing
1¼ cups (½ pint/300 ml) lukewarm water
1 egg, lightly beaten with 1 tablespoon water

For the filling
juice of 1 lemon
1 garlic clove, crushed
½ teaspoon ground cumin
½ teaspoon ground coriander
½ teaspoon paprika
2 teaspoons salt
1 teaspoon pepper
11 oz/300 g cod loin
3 tablespoons olive oil
½ cup (2¾ oz/70 g) shelled or thawed frozen peas
1 tablespoon chopped fresh dill
2 tablespoons chopped fresh cilantro (coriander)

Sift together both kinds of flour into a bowl, then tip in the
bran from the sifter (sieve) and add the yeast and salt. Make
a well in the middle of the dry ingredients and add the oil, then
gradually add the water and mix to a dough. You may need
a little less or more water to bring together the dough. Knead
for 10 minutes, then return the dough to the bowl and dust
lightly with flour. Cover the bowl with plastic wrap (clingfilm)
and let stand in a warm place for 1 hour. Meanwhile, make the
filling. Mix together the lemon juice, garlic, cumin, coriander,
paprika, salt, and pepper in a large bowl, add the fish, and rub
in the flavorings. Heat the olive oil in a large skillet or frying
pan, add the cod and juices, and cook 5 minutes on each side.
Break the fish into small chunks, add the peas, and cook for
another few minutes. Stir in the herbs and remove the pan from
the heat. Taste the fish and adjust the seasoning if necessary.
Preheat the oven to 450°F/230°C/Gas Mark 8. Brush 2 baking
sheets with oil. Uncover the dough, punch down (knock back),
and knead again for a few minutes. Use your hands to make
golf ball-sized dough balls and lightly dust them with flour.
Thinly roll out each dough ball into a circle, put a little of the
cod filling into the middle, dampen the edges of the dough, and
bring up the sides to seal to form a turnover. Put the turnovers
onto the prepared baking sheets and brush with the egg wash.
Bake for 10–15 minutes until golden. Serve immediately.

LAMB MANAKISH

بيتزا بلحم الغنم

Preparation time: 20–25 minutes, plus resting time
Cooking time: 10–15 minutes
Makes 20

1½ cups (7 oz/200 g) hard (strong) whole wheat
    (wholemeal) bread flour
1⅓ cups (6 oz/175 g) all-purpose (plain) flour,
    plus extra for dusting
1⅛ teaspoons active dry (fast-action) yeast
1½ teaspoons salt
2 teaspoons extra virgin olive oil, plus extra for brushing
1¼ cups (½ pint/300 ml) lukewarm water

For the topping
1 teaspoon olive oil
9 oz/250 g ground (minced) lamb
1 small onion, chopped
½ teaspoon seven spices seasoning
12 cherry tomatoes, chopped
3 tablespoons chopped fresh mint
salt and pepper

Put both types of flour, the yeast, and salt into a large bowl and mix well. Add the oil, then gradually add the lukewarm water and mix to a dough. You may need a little less or more water to bring together the dough. Turn out onto a lightly floured work surface and knead for at least 10 minutes until smooth and elastic. Shape the dough into a ball, return it to the bowl, and dust with a little flour. Cover with plastic wrap (clingfilm) and let stand in a warm place for 1 hour until doubled in size. Meanwhile, for the topping, heat the oil in a skillet or frying pan, add the lamb and onion, and cook over medium heat for 5–8 minutes until the meat is evenly browned. Add the seven spices seasoning and season well with salt and pepper. Stir in the tomatoes and mint. Remove from the heat and let cool. Preheat the oven to 450°F/230°C/Gas Mark 8. Brush 2 baking sheets with oil. Uncover the dough and punch down (knock back), then make golf ball-sized balls with your hands and lightly dust each with flour. Roll out the dough balls into thin circles and put them on the prepared baking sheets. Spread the lamb mixture over the dough and bake for 10–15 minute. Remove from the oven and serve immediately.

LAMB
AND
SUMAC
TURNOVERS

PHOTO PAGE 384

—

فطائر لحم الغنم
والسماق

Preparation time: 45 minutes
Cooking time: 30 minutes
Makes about 20

1½ cups (7 oz/200 g) hard (strong) whole wheat
  (wholemeal) flour
1⅓ cups (6 oz/175 g) all-purpose (plain) flour,
  plus extra for dusting
1¼ teaspoons active dry (fast-action) yeast
1½ teaspoons salt
2 teaspoons extra virgin olive oil
1¼ cups (½ pint/300 ml) lukewarm water
butter, for greasing
1 egg, lightly beaten with 2 tablespoons water

For the lamb and sumac filling
9 oz/250 g ground (minced) lamb
1 onion, chopped
¼ cup (1 oz/25 g) pine nuts, toasted
1 teaspoon ground sumac
salt and pepper

Sift together both kinds of flour into a bowl, then tip in the
bran from the sifter (sieve) and add the yeast and salt. Make
a well in the middle of the dry ingredients and add the oil, then
gradually add the water and mix to a dough. You may need a
little less or more water to bring together the dough. Knead
for 10 minutes, then return the dough to the bowl and dust
lightly with flour. Cover the bowl with plastic wrap (clingfilm)
and let stand in a warm place for 1 hour. Meanwhile, for the
filling, heat a skillet or frying pan, add the lamb, and cook
over medium heat, stirring frequently, for 5–8 minutes until
evenly browned. Reduce the heat, add the onion, pine nuts,
and sumac, season well with salt and black pepper, and cook,
stirring occasionally, for 15 minutes. Remove the pan from the
heat and let cool. Preheat the oven to 450°F/230°C/Gas Mark
8. Grease 2 baking sheets with butter. Punch down (knock
back) the dough and knead again for a few minutes. Use your
hands to make golf ball-sized dough balls and dust them lightly
with flour. Thinly roll out each dough ball into a circle, put a
little of the lamb filling into the middle, dampen the edges of
the dough, and bring up the sides to seal to form a turnover.
Put the turnovers onto the prepared baking sheets and brush
with the egg wash. Bake for 10–15 minutes until golden. Serve
immediately.

DESSERTS

✦

الحلويات

APPLE
AND
BLACKBERRY
CAKE
WITH CRUMB TOPPING

—

كعكة التفاح والعليق مع
زينة مقرمشة

Preparation time: 25 minutes
Cooking time: 2 hours
Makes 1 8 inch/20 cm cake

2 large tart apples, peeled, cored, and chopped
2 tablespoons granulated sugar
pinch of ground cinnamon
pinch of grated nutmeg
1¾ sticks (7 oz/200 g) butter, softened
1 cup (7 oz/200 g) superfine (caster) or granulated sugar
3 eggs
1 tablespoon apple juice
2 cups (9 oz/250 g) all-purpose (plain) flour
4 teaspoons baking powder
drop of vanilla extract
1¼ cups (5 oz/150 g) blackberries
2 tablespoons slivered (flaked) almonds
confectioners' (icing) sugar, for dusting

For the crumb topping
1¼ cups (5 oz/150 g) all-purpose (plain) flour
7 tablespoons (3½ oz/100 g) butter, chilled and diced
⅓ firmly packed cup (3 oz/80 g) brown sugar

Preheat the oven to 350°F/180°C/Gas Mark 4. Line an 8 inch/ 20 cm round loose-bottom cake pan with parchment paper. Put the apples, granulated sugar, cinnamon, and nutmeg into a saucepan, add 3–4 tablespoons water, and cook over low heat for 15–20 minutes until softened. Remove from the heat and let cool. Meanwhile, beat the butter with the superfine (caster) sugar with an electric mixer until light and creamy. Add the eggs, one at a time, beating well after each addition. Sir in the apple juice. Sift together the flour and baking powder into the cake batter and gently fold in with a metal spoon. Finally, fold in the vanilla extract, apples, and blackberries. Pour the batter into the prepared pan and set aside while you make the crumb topping. Sift the flour into a bowl, add the butter, and rub in with your fingertips until the mixture resembles coarse breadcrumbs. Stir in the brown sugar. Spoon the topping over the batter and bake for 1 hour. Remove the cake from the oven and sprinkle with the almonds, then return to the oven and bake for another hour. Remove the cake from the oven and let cool in the pan for 10 minutes before turning out onto a wire rack. Dust with confectioners' (icing sugar) before serving.

DATE CAKE

—

كيكة التمر

Preparation time: 20–25 minutes
Cooking time: 30 minutes
Makes 1 10-inch/25-cm cake

7 oz/200 g date paste, cut into chunks, or 1⅓ cups finely
    chopped pitted (stoned) dried dates
1 teaspoon baking (bicarbonate of) soda
1¼ cups (5 oz/150 g) all-purpose (plain) flour
2 teaspoons baking powder
1 teaspoon ground cinnamon
7 tablespoons (3½ oz/100 g) unsalted butter at
    room temperature
scant 1 cup (6 oz/175 g) sugar
2 eggs, lightly beaten

Preheat the oven to 350°F/180°C/Gas Mark 4. Line a 10-inch/
25-cm springform cake pan with parchment paper. Bring 1 cup
(8 fl oz/250 ml) water to a boil in a pan, add the date paste or
chopped dates and baking (bicarbonate of) soda, and stir for 5
minutes until thickened. Set aside. Meanwhile, sift together the
flour, baking powder, and cinnamon into a bowl. Beat together
the butter and sugar in another bowl until fluffy. Gradually
beat in the eggs until the mixture is smooth, then fold in the
dry ingredients. Finally, fold in the date mixture. Pour the
batter into the cake pan and bake for 35 minutes. (Test after
30 minutes by inserting a cocktail stick into the center.) The
cake should be moist and almost gooey, so be careful not to
overcook. Remove the cake from the oven and let stand in the
pan for 30 minutes before turning out. Serve warm or cold.

DRIED FRUIT HONEY CAKE

—

كيكة الفواكه المجففة
والعسل

Preparation time: 15–20 minutes
Cooking time: 40 minutes
Makes 1 loaf

4 tablespoons olive oil
¾ cup (5 oz/150 g) superfine (caster) or granulated sugar
4 eggs
⅔ cup (¼ pint/150 ml) plain (natural) yogurt
2 cups (9 oz/250 g) all-purpose (plain) flour
4 teaspoons baking powder
¾ cup (3½ oz/100 g) golden raisins (sultanas)
scant 1 cup (3½ oz/100 g) shelled walnuts, chopped
2 apples, peeled and grated
4 teaspoons (clear) honey

Preheat the oven to 350°F/180°C/Gas Mark 4. Line a 9 x 5 x 3
inch (2 lb/900 g) loaf pan with wax (greaseproof) paper. Beat
the olive oil and sugar with an electric mixer until light and
creamy. Beat in the eggs, one at a time. Mix in the yogurt. Sift
the flour and baking powder over the mixture, add the dried
fruit, nuts, and grated apple, and gently fold in with a metal
spoon. Spoon the batter into the pan s and bake for 40 minutes.
Remove and turn out onto a wire rack. Pierce holes over the
top of the cake with a skewer. Warm the honey in a saucepan
over low heat, then pour it over the cake and let cool.

BANANA CAKE

PHOTO PAGE 391

—

كعكة الموز

Preparation time: 10–15 minutes
Cooking time: 1 hour 40 minutes
Makes 1 8 inch/20 cm square cake

1½ sticks (6 oz/175 g) unsalted butter, softened
1¾ cups (12 oz/350 g) superfine (caster) or granulated sugar
4 eggs
3⅔ cups (1 lb/450 g) all-purpose (plain) flour
1½ tablespoons baking powder
1 teaspoon baking soda (bicarbonate of soda)
4 large bananas, mashed
1 cup (4 oz/125 g) shelled walnuts, lightly crushed
½ cup (4 oz/125 g) candied (glacé) cherries, chopped

Preheat the oven to 350°F/180°C/Gas Mark 4. Line an 8 inch/20 cm square cake pan with parchment paper. Beat the butter and sugar with an electric mixer until fluffy. Add the eggs, one at a time, and continue to beat for 5 minutes. Sift together the flour, baking powder, and baking soda (bicarbonate of soda) and beat until combined. Fold in the bananas, walnuts, and cherries. Spoon the batter into the pan and bake for 1 hour 40 minutes. Remove and let the cake cool before turning it out.

ORANGE AND COCONUT CAKE

—

كعكة البرتقال وجوز
الهند

Preparation time: 15–20 minutes
Cooking time: 30 minutes
Makes 1 9½ inch/24 cm cake

1½ sticks (6 oz/175 g) unsalted butter, softened
scant 1 cup (6 oz/175 g) superfine (caster) or granulated sugar
3 extra large (uk large) eggs
1⅓ cups (6 oz/175 g) all purpose (plain) flour
1 tablespoon baking powder
¾ cup (3 oz/80 g) dry unsweetened (desiccated) coconut
1 teaspoon vanilla extract
2 tablespoons orange flower water
grated zest of 1 orange

For the topping
7 tablespoons (3½ oz/100 g) butter, softened
1 teaspoon orange flower water
scant 1 cup (3½ oz/100 g) confectioners' (icing) sugar
1 tablespoon milk
grated zest of 1 orange
2 tablespoons dry unsweetened (desiccated) coconut

Preheat the oven to 350°F/180°C/Gas Mark 4. Line a 9½ inch/24 cm loose-bottom cake pan with wax (greaseproof) paper. Beat the butter and sugar with an electric mixer until creamy, add the eggs, one at a time. Sift the flour and baking powder into the bowl and fold in with a metal spoon. Fold in the coconut, vanilla, orange flower water, and zest. Spoon into the pan and bake for 30 minutes. Remove and let cool in the pan, then turn out. For the topping, beat the butter with the orange flower water and sugar until smooth, then mix in the milk and zest. Spread over the cake and sprinkle with the coconut.

BANANA CAKE

FRUIT LOAF

رغيف الفاكهة

Preparation time: 10 minutes, plus resting time
Cooking time: 1 hour
Makes 1 loaf

1¼ cups (8 oz/225 g) mixed dried fruit
½ firmly packed cup (4 oz/125 g) brown sugar
⅔ cup (¼ pint/150 ml) freshly made tea
vegetable oil, for brushing
1¾ cups (8 oz/225 g) all-purpose (plain) flour
2¾ teaspoons baking powder
1 egg, lightly beaten

Combine the fruit and sugar in a bowl and pour the warm tea over them. Let soak overnight. Preheat the oven to 350°F/180°C/Gas Mark 4. Brush a 2½ cup (1 pint 600 ml) loaf pan with oil. Sift the flour and baking powder into a large bowl, add the soaked fruit, and mix well. Add the egg and mix well again. Pour the batter into the prepared pan and a bake for 1 hour or until a toothpick or cocktail stick inserted into the middle of the loaf comes out clean. Remove from the oven and turn out onto a wire rack to cool.

PISTACHIO AND YOGURT CAKE

PHOTO PAGE 393

كعك الفستق والزبادي

Preparation time: 15 minutes
Cooking time: 1 hour 10 minutes
Makes 1 8 inch/20 cm cake

1½ cups (11 oz/300 g) superfine (caster) or granulated sugar
3⅔ cups (1 lb/450 g) all-purpose (plain) flour, sifted
1½ tablespoons baking powder
⅔ cup (¼ pint/150 ml) plain (natural) yogurt
⅔ cup (¼ pint/150 ml) sunflower oil
3 eggs, lightly beaten
1 vanilla bean (pod), seeds removed
grated zest of 1 orange
1¾ cups (7 oz/200 g) shelled pistachio nuts, coarsely chopped
confectioners' (icing) sugar, for dusting

Preheat the oven to 350°F/180°C/Gas Mark 4. Line an 8 inch/20 cm cake pan with wax (greaseproof) paper. Combine the superfine (caster) sugar, flour and baking powder in a bowl, pour in the yogurt and oil, and mix well. Add the eggs and beat together all the ingredients for a few minutes. Scrap in the seeds from the vanilla bean (pod) and add the orange zest and nuts. Gently fold together until combined, then spoon the batter into the prepared pan. Bake for 1 hour 10 minutes, then remove form the oven and let cool in the pan on a wire rack before turning out. Dust with confectioners' (icing) sugar before slicing and serving.

PISTACHIO AND YOGURT CAKE

WALNUT AND PISTACHIO CAKE

كيكة الجوز والفستق
الحلبي

Preparation time: 20 minutes
Cooking time: 35–40 minutes
Makes 1 loaf

⅔ cup (4 oz/120 g) superfine (caster) or granulated sugar
1 stick (4 oz/120 g) unsalted butter, softened
2 eggs
1⅓ cups (6 oz/175 g) all-purpose (plain) flour
1 tablespoon baking powder
scant 1 cup (3½ oz/100 g) shelled pistachio nuts, chopped
¾ cup (3 oz/80 g) shelled walnuts, chopped
grated zest and juice of 1 lemon

Preheat the oven to 350°F/180°C/Gas Mark 4. Line a 9 x 5 x 3 inch (2 lb/900 g) loaf pan with wax (greaseproof) paper. Set aside ½ teaspoon of the sugar. Put the butter and remaining sugar in the bowl of an electric mixer and beat until light and creamy. Add the eggs, 1 at a time, and continue to beat for 5 minutes. Sift together the flour and baking powder and gently fold in with a metal spoon. Gently fold in all the nuts and the lemon zest. Spoon the batter into the prepared loaf pan and bake for 35–40 minutes until a cocktail stick inserted into the middle comes out clean. Remove the cake from the oven and let cool slightly in the pan, then make small holes all over the top with a skewer. Heat the lemon juice with the reserved sugar, stirring until the sugar has dissolved. Remove the saucepan from the heat and pour the mixture over the cake. Let stand for 10 minutes, then turn out and put on a wire rack to cool completely.

CHOCOLATE AND DATE BROWNIES WITH ALMONDS

براوني الشوكولا والتمر
مع اللوز

Preparation time: 30 minutes
Cooking time: 40 minutes
Serves 8–10

11 oz/300 g dark chocolate, broken into pieces
2¾ sticks (11 oz/300 g) unsalted butter
1½ cups (11 oz/300 g) superfine (caster) or granulated sugar
4 eggs
1 teaspoon vanilla extract
1⅓ cups (6 oz/175 g) all-purpose (plain) flour
1 teaspoon baking powder
generous 1 cup (7 oz/200 g) chopped dried dates
scant 1 cup (3½ oz/100 g) blanched almonds,
    toasted and coarsely chopped

Preheat the oven to 325°F/160°C/Gas Mark 3. Line an 8 inch/ 20 cm square cake pan with wax (greaseproof) paper. Melt the chocolate and butter in a heatproof bowl set over a pan of simmering water, then stir well. Remove from the heat and let cool slightly. Beat the sugar and eggs with an electric mixer until light and creamy. Gradually fold in the chocolate mixture and add the vanilla extract. Sift in the flour and baking powder. Fold all the ingredients together, then add the dates and almonds. Pour the batter into the pan and bake for 40 minutes. Let cool in the pan on a wire rack, cut into squares, and serve.

SEMOLINA
AND
ALMOND
CAKE

—

كعك السميد مع اللوز

Preparation time: 10 minutes
Cooking time: 40–50 minutes
Makes 1 8 inch/20 cm round cake

tahini, for brushing
½ cup (2 oz/50 g) blanched almonds
2 cups (12 oz/350 g) semolina
½ cup (3½ oz/100 g) superfine (caster) or granulated sugar
1 teaspoon baking powder
1 teaspoon baking soda (bicarbonate of soda)
½ cup (4 fl oz/120 ml) milk
7 tablespoons (3½ oz/100 g) butter, melted

For the syrup
⅔ cup (4 oz/120 g) superfine (caster) or granulated sugar
juice of 1 lemon
1 lemon leaf
1 teaspoon rose water

Preheat the oven to 350°F/180°C/Gas Mark 4. Brush an
8 inch/20 cm loose-bottom round cake pan with tahini and
arrange the almonds in concentric circles on the bottom of
the pan. Put the semolina, sugar, baking powder, and baking
soda (bicarbonate of soda) into the bowl of an electric mixer
and stir to combine. Add the milk, melted butter, and ½ cup
(4 fl oz/120 ml) water and beat until a creamy batter forms.
Carefully pour the batter into the prepared cake pan without
disturbing the almonds. Bake for 40 minutes or until a
toothpick or cocktail stick inserted into the middle of the cake
comes out clean. Meanwhile, make the syrup. Put the sugar,
lemon juice and leaf, and rose water into a saucepan, pour in
½ cup (4 fl oz/120 ml) water, and stir over medium heat until
the sugar has completely dissolved. Increase the heat, bring to
a boil, and boil, without stirring, until syrupy. Remove from the
heat and let cool slightly. Remove the cake from the oven and
turn out onto a wire rack with a tray underneath. Make holes
all over the top of the cake with a skewer and pour over the
syrup. Spoon up any syrup in the tray and pour it back over the
cake. Serve warm or cold.

DATE COOKIES

PHOTO PAGE 396

بسكويت بالتمر

Preparation time: 15 minutes, plus chilling time
Cooking time: 10 minutes
Makes 20

scant ½ cup (3½ oz/100 g) butter, softened
⅓ cup (3 oz/80 g) superfine (caster) or granulated sugar
1 egg
1¾ cups (8 oz/225 g) all-purpose (plain) flour,
    plus extra for dusting
1½ tablespoons baking powder
generous ¾ cup (4 oz/125 g) chopped, pitted dried dates
1½ teaspoons ground anise seed (aniseed)

Beat together the butter and sugar with an electric mixer until light and fluffy. Add the egg and continue to beat. Sift together the flour and baking powder and gently fold in with a spoon. Fold in the dates and anise seed (aniseed). Tip the mixture onto a piece of plastic wrap (clingfilm), wrap into a ball, and chill in the refrigerator overnight. Preheat the oven to 350°F/180°C/Gas Mark 4. Line 2 baking sheets with wax (greaseproof) paper. Remove the dough from the refrigerator, unwrap, and knead lightly. Roll out to ½ inch/1 cm thick on a lightly floured surface. Using a 2 inch/5 cm plain cutter, stamp out 20 cookies and place on the prepared baking sheets, spaced well apart. Bake for 10 minutes until golden brown. Remove from the oven and carefully transfer to a wire rack to cool.

SESAME COOKIES

كعك السمسم

Preparation time: 20 minutes, plus resting time
Cooking time: 20 minutes
Makes about 25

2¼ cups (9 oz/250 g) all-purpose (plain) flour,
    plus extra for dusting
½ teaspoon baking powder
1½ sticks (6 oz/175 g) butter, diced
3 tablespoons sesame seeds, plus extra for sprinkling
⅓ cup (3 oz/80 g) superfine (caster) or granulated sugar
1 egg, lightly beaten

Preheat the oven to 180°C/350°F/Gas Mark 4. Sift the flour and baking powder into a large bowl, add the butter, and rub in with your fingertips until the mixture resembles breadcrumbs. Stir in the sesame seeds and sugar. Add half the beaten egg and bring together the mixture to form a dough. Let stand for 15 minutes. Roll out the dough on a lightly floured work surface to ½ inch/1 cm thick. Stamp out circles with a 1½-2 inch/4-5 cm cutter. Put the cookies onto a baking sheet, spaced well apart, and brush with the remaining beaten egg. Bake for 20 minutes until golden. Remove from the oven and transfer the cookies to a wire rack to cool.

SESAME AND COCONUT BARS

اصابع السمسم والعسل

Preparation time: 10 minutes, plus chilling time
Makes 16

scant 1 cup (3½ oz/100 g) granola (muesli)
⅔ cup (2 oz/50 g) dry unsweetened (desiccated) coconut
2½ cups (2¾ oz/70 g) crisped rice breakfast cereal
2 tablespoons sesame seeds
1½ sticks (6 oz/175 g) unsalted butter
2 tablespoons smooth peanut butter
½ cup (3½ oz/100 g) superfine (caster) or granulated sugar

Put the granola (muesli), coconut, breakfast cereal, and sesame seeds into a large bowl and mix well. Put the butter, peanut butter, and sugar into a saucepan and heat gently, stirring until thoroughly combined. Pour the mixture over the dry ingredients and mix well. Line a 10 inch/25 cm square cake pan with wax (greaseproof) paper. Spoon the mixture into the pan, pressing it down well. Chill in the refrigerator overnight. When set, turn out and cut into 16 slices. Store in an airtight container.

ANISE COOKIES

PHOTO PAGE 399

بسكويت اليانسون

Preparation time: 15 minutes
Cooking time: 20 minutes
Makes 20

1¼ sticks (5 oz/150 g) unsalted butter, plus extra for greasing
⅔ cup (4½ oz/130 g) superfine (caster) or granulated sugar
1 egg, lightly beaten
4 tablespoons milk, plus extra for brushing
2 cups (11½ oz/330 g) all-purpose (plain) flour, plus extra for dusting
pinch of salt
1½ teaspoons ground anise seed (aniseed), ground star anise, or Pernod
2 teaspoons baking powder

Preheat the oven to 350°F/180°C/Gas Mark 4. Grease 2 baking sheets with butter. Beat together the butter and sugar with an electric handheld mixer until light and fluffy. Add the egg and milk and beat for another few minutes. Sift the flour into the bowl and add the salt, ground anise seed (aniseed), if using, and baking powder. Using a metal spoon gently fold in the dry ingredients. Fold in the Pernod, if using. Tip out the dough onto a lightly floured surface and divide it in half. Roll each piece into a sausage shape and cut into 1¼ inch/3 cm slices. Put the cookies onto the prepared baking sheets spaced well apart. Brush with a little milk and bake for 20 minutes. Remove the baking sheets from the oven and transfer the cookies to a wire rack to cool, then store in an airtight container.

ANISE COOKIES

MA'MOOL COOKIES

MA'MOOL COOKIES

معمول

Preparation time: 1 hour, plus resting time
Cooking time: 40 minutes
Makes 40

4½ sticks (1 lb 2 oz/500 g) unsalted butter
6 cups (2¼ lb/1 kg) coarse semolina
3 tablespoons superfine (caster) or granulated sugar
2 tablespoons mahleb
2¼ cups (10 oz/275 g) all-purpose (plain) flour,
    plus extra for dusting
1¼ teaspoons active dry (rapid rise dried) yeast
2 tablespoons rose water

For the date filling
11 oz/300 g dried pitted dates
1 teaspoon apple pie (mixed) spice

For the walnut filling
scant 1 cup (3½ oz/100 g) shelled walnuts
1 teaspoon superfine (caster) or granulated sugar
1 tablespoon orange flower water
1 tablespoon rose water

For the pistachio filling
¾ cup (3 oz/80 g) shelled pistachio nuts
4 tablespoons superfine (caster) or granulated sugar
1 tablespoon rose water
1 tablespoon orange flower water

Melt the butter in a large pan, then stir in the semolina, sugar, and mahleb. Push the mixture down into the pan, cover, and remove from the heat. Let stand for at least 3 hours or overnight at room temperature. To make the date filling, put the dates in a microwave-proof bowl, add 1 tablespoon water, and cook on high for 2 minutes. Mash with a fork and add the spice. Roll the mixture into about 14 small balls. To make the walnut filling, put all the ingredients into a blender and process to fine crumbs. To make the pistachio filling, put the nuts and sugar into a blender and process to coarse crumbs. Tip into a bowl and stir in the rose water and orange flower water. Return the pan of semolina mixture to low heat for a few minutes to loosen, then tip the mixture into a bowl. Add the flour, yeast, rose water, and 2 tablespoons water. Knead the mixture in the bowl, adding 1–2 tablespoons more water if required, for about 15 minutes until a dough forms. Preheat the oven to 325°F/160°C/Gas Mark 3. To make the ma'moul, take a handful of dough and dust with flour, then flatten into a patty. Put 1 tablespoon walnut filling, or 1 tablespoon pistachio filling, or 1 date ball in the middle of the patty, then wrap the dough around the filling. Roll in flour and press into a ma'moul mold. Tap the mold on the work surface to release the cookie and put it onto a baking sheet. If you don't have the molds, use an individual gelatin (jelly) mold or cut a decorative shape with a ravioli cutter. Repeat the filling and shaping until all the dough and filling mixtures have been used. Bake for 30–40 minutes until golden. Remove from the oven and transfer the cookies to a wire rack to cool. Store in an airtight container.

401

DESSERTS

PISTACHIO COOKIES

PHOTO PAGE 403

بسكويت بالفستق

Preparation time: 20 minutes
Cooking time: 20–25 minutes
Makes 18

2¼ cups (10½ oz/285 g) all-purpose (plain) flour,
   plus extra for dusting
½ teaspoon baking powder
2¾ sticks (11 oz/300 g) butter, chilled and diced
scant 1 cup (6 oz/175 g) superfine (caster) or granulated sugar
1 egg, lightly beaten
¾ cup (3 oz/80 g) shelled pistachio nuts, coarsely chopped
1 tablespoon orange flower water

Preheat the oven to 325°F/160°C/Gas Mark 3. Line a baking sheet with wax (greaseproof) paper. Sift the flour and baking powder into a large mixing bowl, add the butter, and rub in with your fingertips until the mixture resembles fine breadcrumbs. Stir in the sugar. Gradually stir in the egg, add the orange flower water, and bring together the mixture to form a smooth dough. Don't overwork the dough because this will make the cookies spread. Roll out the dough on a lightly floured surface to ¼ inch/5 mm thick. Stamp out circles with a 3¼ inch/8 cm cutter and put them on the prepared baking sheet. Bake for 20–25 minutes, then remove from the oven and transfer to a wire rack to cool.

ALMOND AND PISTACHIO BARS

اصابع اللوز والفستق

Preparation time: 10–15 minutes
Cooking time: 25 minutes
Makes 12

6 tablespoons (3 oz/80 g) butter
⅓ cup firmly packed (3 oz/80 g) brown sugar
4 tablespoons light corn (golden) syrup
scant 1 cup (3½ oz/100 g) jumbo oats
1 cup (1 oz/25 g) crispy rice cereal
½ cup (1½ oz/40 g) dry unsweetened (desiccated) coconut
3 tablespoon chopped dried apricots
½ cup (2 oz/50 g) blanched almonds
½ cup (2 oz/50 g) shelled pistachio nuts

Preheat the oven to 325°F/160°C/Gas Mark 3. Line the bottom and sides of an 8 inch/20 cm square cake pan with parchment paper. Put the butter, sugar, and syrup into a large saucepan and heat gently, stirring occasionally until the butter and sugar have melted. Remove from the heat and stir in the remaining ingredients. Spoon the dough into the prepared pan and press down firmly. Bake for 25 minutes until golden around the edges. Remove from the oven and let cool completely in the pan, then turn out and cut into 12 small bars. Store in the refrigerator.

PISTACHIO COOKIES

SWEET COOKIES WITH RICOTTA CREAM AND ROSE PETAL JELLY

PHOTO PAGE 405

كعكة محلاة مع الكريما
ومربى تويجات الزهر

Preparation time: 30–40 minutes, plus chilling time
Cooking time:15–20 minutes
Makes 12

2⅓ cups (11 oz/300 g) all-purpose (plain) flour,
    plus extra for dusting
2¼ sticks (9 oz/250 g) butter, chilled and diced
⅓ cup (2¾ oz/70 g) superfine (caster) or granulated sugar
1 egg
2 tablespoons milk
generous 1 cup (9 oz/250 g) ricotta cheese
3 tablespoons heavy (double) cream
1 teaspoon confectioners' (icing) sugar
6 teaspoons rose petal jelly or jam

Preheat the oven to 350°F/180°C/Gas Mark 4. Sift the flour into a large bowl, add the butter, and rub in with your fingertips until the mixture resembles breadcrumb. Stir in the superfine (caster) or granulated sugar. Beat the egg with the milk and gradually pour half the mixture into the bowl. Bring the mixture together to form a dough and knead for 1 minute until smooth. Wrap the dough in plastic wrap (clingfilm) and chill in the refrigerator for 30 minutes. Roll out the dough on a lightly floured surface to ⅛ inch/2 mm thick. Stamp out 24 circles with a 2½ inch/6 cm cutter. Put 12 circles on a baking sheet and bake for 15–20 minutes. Meanwhile, put the remaining circles on another baking sheet and stamp out the centers with a ¾ inch/2 cm cutter. Discard the centers. Bake the circles for 15–20 minutes. Remove from the oven and transfer the cookies to a wire rack to cool. Beat the ricotta with the cream, then stir in the confectioners' (icing) sugar. Spoon the mixture into a pastry (icing) bag fitted with a plain tip (nozzle). Spread out the whole cookies on a work surface and pipe the cream around the edge. Top each with a perforated cookie, pressing down gently to let the cream squeeze through. Add a little more cream to the middle of each cookie, then spoon ½ teaspoon of rose petal jelly or jam into the center of each one.

SWEET COOKIES WITH RICOTTA CREAM AND ROSE PETAL JELLY

MA'KAROON FRITTERS

حلوى ماكرون مقلية

Preparation time: 15–20 minutes, plus resting time
Cooking time: 5 minutes
Makes 40

generous 1 cup (7 oz/200 g) coarse semolina
3¼ cups (14 oz/400 g) all-purpose (plain) flour
3 tablespoons brown sugar
1 envelope (¼ oz/7 g) dried yeast
¼ teaspoon ground cinnamon
pinch of salt
2 tablespoons sunflower oil
1⅔ cups (14 fl oz/400 ml) Sugar Syrup (see page 33)
vegetable or sunflower oil, for deep-frying

Put the semolina, flour, sugar, yeast, cinnamon, and salt into a bowl and mix well. Pour in the oil and 1¼ cups (½ pint/300 ml) of water and mix until a dough forms. Knead the dough in the bowl until smooth, then cover with a dish towel and let stand in a warm place for 1 hour until risen. Take 2 tablespoons of the dough and roll into an oval ball between the palms of your hands. Continue making balls in this way until all the dough has been used. Pour the Sugar Syrup into a saucepan and keep warm over low heat. Heat the oil in a deep fryer to 350°F/180°C or until a cube of bread browns in 30 seconds. Deep-fry the ma'karoons, in batches, until golden. Gently remove with tongs, transfer to the pan of sugar syrup, and let soak for 2 minutes. Transfer the ma'karoons to paper towels to drain, then serve warm.

SWEET BREAD DONUTS

دونات (خبز محلى)

Preparation time: 30–40 minutes, plus resting time
Cooking time: 4 minutes
Makes 16–18

2 cups (9 oz/250 g) all-purpose (plain) flour
½ teaspoon baking soda (bicarbonate of soda)
1¼ teaspoons active dry (rapid rise dried) yeast
2 teaspoons superfine (caster) or granulated sugar,
    plus extra for dusting
5 tablespoons milk
1 teaspoon vanilla extract
dash of rose water
corn oil, for deep-frying

Put the flour, baking soda (bicarbonate of soda), yeast, and sugar in a bowl and stir to mix. Pour the milk into a small pan, add 5 tablespoons water, and heat gently until tepid. Remove the pan from the heat and pour the mixture into the bowl. Add the vanilla and rose water, and mix well. Knead the dough for 5–10 minutes. Shape the dough into a ball and cover with plastic wrap (clingfilm). Let stand in a warm place for at least 1½ hours until risen, then turn out and knead again. Heat corn oil in a deep-fryer to 350°F/180°C. Meanwhile, shape the dough into 16–18 balls. Fry 4 dough balls, turning once, for 3–4 minutes until golden. Remove and briefly drain on paper towels. Cook the remaining dough balls in batches of 4 in the same way. Dust the cooked donuts with sugar and serve.

PINK TURKISH DELIGHT

PHOTO PAGE 409

—

راحة الحلقوم التركية
الزهرية

Preparation time: 5–10 minutes, plus chilling time
Cooking time: 45 minutes
Makes 20 pieces

4 tablespoons powdered gelatin
2¼ cups (1 lb/450 g) superfine (caster) or granulated sugar
½ cup (2 oz/50 g) cornstarch (cornflour)
4 teaspoons rose water
few drops of liquid pink food coloring
vegetable oil, for brushing

To decorate
½ cup (2 oz/50 g) confectioners' (icing) sugar
¼ cup (1 oz/25 g) cornstarch (conrflour)

Put the gelatin, superfine (caster) sugar, cornstarch (cornflour), and rose water into a large saucepan, pour in 3½ cups (1½ pints/850 ml) of water, and gradually bring to a boil over low heat, stirring constantly. Boil, without stirring, for 45 minutes. Add a few drops of food coloring and mix until thoroughly combined. Remove the pan from the heat. Brush a 6 x 6 x 1 inch/15 x 15 x 2.5 cm baking pan with oil and pour the warm Turkish delight into it. Let cool, then put in the refrigerator for 24 hours until set. Sift together the confectioners' (icing) sugar and cornstarch into a bowl. Cut the Turkish delight into pieces and coat with the mixture. Store in an airtight container.

WHITE TURKISH DELIGHT

—

راحة الحلقوم التركية
البيضاء

Preparation time: 5–10 minutes, plus chilling time
Cooking time: 20 minutes
Makes 20 pieces

vegetable oil, for brushing
generous 2½ cups (1 lb/450 g) superfine (caster) or granulated sugar
4 tablespoons powdered gelatin
½ cup (2 oz/50 g) cornstarch (cornflour)
2 teaspoons rose water
½ cup (2 oz/50 g) shelled pistachio nuts, toasted and coarsely chopped
½ cup (2 oz/50 g) confectioners' (icing) sugar

Brush an 8 x 10 inch/20 x 25 cm baking pan with oil. Put the superfine (caster) sugar into a saucepan, add 1 cup (8 fl oz/250 ml) water, and stir over low heat until the sugar has dissolved, then bring gently to a boil. Mix together the gelatin, half the cornstarch (cornflour), and scant ½ cup (3½ fl oz/100 ml) water and add to the pan. Stir constantly until the gelatin has dissolved, then continue to simmer very gently for 20 minutes until thickened. Remove from the heat and add the rose water and pistachios and pour into the baking pan. Let stand for 24 hours until set. Cut the Turkish delight into pieces and coat in the confectioners' (icing) sugar and remaining cornstarch. Store in an airtight container.

PINK TURKISH DELIGHT

CHOCOLATE COATED DATES AND ALMONDS WITH COCONUT

PECAN BAKLAVA

بقلاوة جوز البقان

Preparation time: 20–25 minutes
Cooking time: 30–40 minutes
Serves 8

1¼ cups (5 oz/150 g) pecans, toasted
3½ tablespoons superfine (caster) or granulated sugar
1¾ sticks (7 oz/200 g) butter, melted
9 oz/250 g phyllo (filo) pastry

For the sugar syrup
¾ cup (5 oz/150 g) sugar
150 g water
1 tablespoon orange flower water
1 lemon leaf

Put the nuts and sugar into a food processor and process until coarsely ground, then tip into a bowl. Make the sugar syrup. Put the sugar into a saucepan, pour in ⅔ cup (¼ pint/150 ml) of water, and stir over low heat until the sugar has dissolved. Increase the heat to high and boil until syrupy. Remove the pan from the heat, stir in the orange flower water, add the lemon leaf, and let cool completely, then stir the syrup into the pecan mixture. Discard the lemon leaf. Preheat the oven to 350°F/180°C/Gas Mark 4. Brush an 8 x 12 inch/20 x 30 cm rectangular loose-bottom cake pan with melted butter. Lay a sheet of pastry in the bottom of the pan, brush with melted butter, add another sheet, brush again with butter, then spread thinly with some of the nut and syrup mixture. Repeat this process 5 times. Score the pastry into rectangles and bake for 30–40 minutes. Let cool completely before slicing.

CHOCOLATE COATED DATES AND ALMONDS WITH COCONUT

PHOTO PAGE 410

لوز وتمر مغلف بالشوكولاتة
مع جوز الهند

Preparation time: 30 minutes
Makes 10

14 oz/400 g semisweet dark (plain) chocolate, broken into pieces
scant 1 cup (7 fl oz/200 ml) heavy double cream
5 dates, pitted (stoned)
5 almonds
dry unsweetened (desiccated) coconut, for coating

Put half the chocolate and the cream into a pan and heat gently, stirring until chocolate has melted and mixture is smooth. Remove from the heat and beat with an electric mixer until cool and thick. Let stand for 15 minutes until firm, then roll into 10 balls. Stuff a date or almond into the middle of each ball and roll smooth. Melt the remaining chocolate in a heatproof bowl set over a saucepan of simmering water. Dip the chocolate balls into the chocolate, then remove, let cool slightly, and roll in coconut to coat.

BAKLAVA

BAKLAVA

PHOTO PAGE 412

بقلاوة

Preparation time: 20–25 minutes
Cooking time: 30–40 minutes
Serves 8

2¼ cups (9 oz/250 g) shelled pistachio nuts
scant ½ cup (3 oz/80 g) superfine (caster) or granulated sugar
melted butter, for brushing
9 oz/250 g phyllo (filo) pastry dough, thawed if frozen

For the sugar syrup
1 cup (7 oz/200 g) superfine (caster) or granulated sugar
few drops of rose water
few drops of orange flower water
1 lemon leaf

Process the pistachio nuts and sugar into a food processor until coarsely ground. Make the sugar syrup. Put the sugar into a saucepan and pour in 1 cup (8 fl oz/250 ml) of water. Stir over low heat until the sugar has dissolved, then increase the heat to high, and bring to a boil. Boil without stirring until the mixture has a syrupy consistency. Remove the pan from the heat and add a few drops of rose water and orange flower water and the lemon leaf. Let the syrup cool. Preheat the oven to 350°F/180°C/ Gas Mark 4. Brush an 8 x 12 inch/20 x 30 cm loose-bottom rectangular cake pan with melted butter. Carefully take a sheet of pastry and lay it on the bottom of the pan. Brush with melted butter and repeat this process to make 5 layers. Spoon the pistachio nut mixture over the dough and pour over the syrup. Add another 5 layers of pastry dough, brushing each with melted butter. Score the dough into diamond shapes and then bake for 30 minutes until golden. Remove the pan from the oven and let cool completely before slicing.

BANANA FRITTERS

فطائر الموز المقلية

Preparation time: 15 minutes, plus resting time
Cooking time: 25 minutes
Serves 10

1¼ cups (5 oz/150 g) all-purpose (plain) flour,
    plus extra for dusting
1 envelope active dry (fast-action) yeast
1 egg
scant ½ cup (3½ fl oz/100 ml) milk
corn oil, for deep-frying
10 medium bananas
sugar, for coating

Sift the flour into a large bowl, stir in the yeast, and make a well in the center. Add the egg, milk, and scant ½ cup (3½ fl oz/100 ml) to the well and mix with a wooden spoon, then use an electric mixer to form a smooth batter. Cover and let stand in a warm place for 1 hour. Heat the oil in a deep-fryer to 350°F/180°C. Peel the bananas and dust with flour, then dip in to the batter. Add them to the hot oil, 2 at a time, and cook for 5 minutes or until crispy and golden. Coat in sugar and let cool before serving.

WALNUT BAKLAVA

بقلاوة الجوز

Preparation time: 20–25 minutes
Cooking time: 30–40 minutes
Serves 8

1¼ cups (5 oz/150 g) walnuts, toasted
3½ tablespoons superfine (caster) or granulated sugar
1¾ sticks (7 oz/200 g) butter, melted
9 oz/250 g phyllo (filo) pastry

For the sugar syrup
¾ cup (5 oz/150 g) sugar
1½ teaspoons rose water
1½ teaspoons orange flower water

Put the walnuts and sugar into a food processor and process until coarse. Make the sugar syrup. Put the sugar into a pan, add ⅔ cup (¼ pint/150 ml) water, and stir over low heat until the sugar has dissolved. Increase the heat to high and boil until syrupy. Remove the pan from the heat, stir in the rose water and orange flower water, and let cool, then stir the syrup into the nut mixture. Preheat the oven to 350°F/180°C/Gas Mark 4. Brush an 8 x 12 inch/20 x 30 cm rectangular loose-bottom cake pan with melted butter. Lay a sheet of pastry in the bottom of the pan, brush with melted butter, add another sheet, brush again with butter, then spread thinly with some of the nut mixture. Repeat this process 5 times. Score the pastry into rectangles and bake for 30–40 minutes. Cool before slicing.

ALMOND BAKLAVA

بقلاوة اللوز

Preparation time: 20–25 minutes
Cooking time: 30–40 minutes
Serves 8

1¼ cups (5 oz/150 g) shelled almonds, toasted
3½ tablespoons superfine (caster) or granulated sugar
1¾ sticks (7 oz/200 g) butter, melted
9 oz/250 g phyllo (filo) pastry

For the sugar syrup
¾ cup (5 oz/150 g) sugar
1½ teaspoons rose water
1½ teaspoons orange flower water

Put the almonds and sugar into a food processor and process until coarse. Make the sugar syrup. Put the sugar into a pan, pour in ⅔ cup (¼ pint/150 ml) of water, and stir over low heat until the sugar has dissolved. Increase the heat to high and boil until syrupy. Remove the pan from the heat, stir in the rose water and orange flower water, and let cool, then stir the syrup into the almond mixture. Preheat the oven to 350°F/180°C/Gas Mark 4. Brush an 8 x 12 inch/20 x 30 cm rectangular cake pan with melted butter. Lay a sheet of pastry in the bottom of the pan, brush with melted butter, add another sheet, brush again with butter, then spread thinly with some of the nut and syrup mixture. Repeat this process 5 times. Score the pastry into squares and bake for 30–40 minutes. Cool before slicing.

KONAFAH

كنافة

Preparation time: 15 minutes
Cooking time: 25 minutes
Makes 1 10 inch/25 cm round cake

1 stick (4 oz/120 g) butter, melted, plus extra for greasing
9 oz/250 g konafah pastry or phyllo (filo) pastry
generous 1 cup (9 oz/250 g) mascarpone cheese
2 tablespoons confectioners' (icing) sugar
1 tablespoon rose water
1 tablespoon of orange flower water

For the sugar syrup
½ cup (3½ oz/100 g) superfine (caster) or granulated sugar
1 teaspoon lemon juice
1 lemon leaf

Preheat the oven to 350°F/180°C/Gas Mark 4. Generously grease a 10 inch/25 cm round cake pan with butter. Briefly process the pastry in a food processor because this will make it easier to line the pan. Transfer it to a bowl and toss with the melted butter using your hands. Beat the mascarpone with the confectioners' (icing) sugar in another bowl until smooth, then stir in the rose water and orange flower water. Divide the pastry in half. Spread one half in the cake pan, packing it in tightly and making a rim around the edge. Spread the mascarpone mixture over it. Cover with the remaining konafah pastry. Bake for 25–30 minutes. Meanwhile, make the sugar syrup. Put the sugar, lemon juice, and 5 tablespoons water into a small pan and add the lemon leaf. Stir over low heat until the sugar has dissolved. Increase the heat and bring to a boil, then boil, without stirring, until syrupy. Remove and discard the leaf and remove the pan from the heat. Remove the konafah from the oven and pour the syrup over it. Serve warm, cut into slices.

NUT
AND CINNAMON
PHYLLO
PASTRIES

رقائق بالمكسرات
والقرفة

Preparation time: 20 minutes
Cooking time: 8–10 minutes
Makes 8

scant 1 cup (3½ oz/100 g) unsalted shelled pistachio nuts
3½ tablespoons superfine (caster) or granulated sugar
pinch of ground cinnamon
1 teaspoon rose water
2 sheets of phyllo (filo) pastry
4 tablespoons (2 oz/50 g) butter, melted
confectioners' (icing) sugar, for dusting

Preheat the oven to 400°F/200°C/Gas Mark 6. Line a baking sheet with wax (greaseproof) paper. Put the nuts, sugar, and cinnamon into a food processor and process until ground, then tip into a bowl. Cut each pastry sheet into 4 squares. Brush a square of pastry with butter and put a tablespoonful of nut filling in the middle. Fold the edges to the middle form a package, brush with butter, and put on the baking sheet. Repeat until all the squares of pastry have been used. Bake for 8–10 minutes, until golden and crisp. Let cool on a wire rack.

FIG TART
WITH
ALMONDS

PHOTO PAGE 417

تارت التين مع اللوز

Preparation time: 40 minutes, plus chilling time
Cooking time: 1 hour 20 minutes
Serves 8

1¼ sticks (5 oz/150 g) unsalted butter, softened
¾ cup (5 oz/150 g) superfine (caster) or granulated sugar
2 eggs
1½ cups (5 oz/150 g) ground almonds
2 tablespoons all-purpose (plain) flour
12 figs, cut into quarters
2 tablespoon slivered (flaked) almonds
1 tablespoon demerara or other raw sugar
confectioners' (icing) sugar, for dusting

For the sweet pastry dough
1¼ cups (5 oz/150 g) all-purpose (plain) flour,
    plus extra for dusting
pinch of salt
6 tablespoons (3 oz/80 g) unsalted butter, chilled and diced,
    plus extra for greasing
¾ cup (3 oz/80 g) confectioners' (icing) sugar
1 egg yolk

First, make the dough. Sift together the flour and salt into a bowl, add the butter, and rub in with your fingertips until the mixture resembles fine breadcrumbs. (This can also be done in a food processor.) Stir in the sugar, then add the egg yolk, and mix to a smooth dough, adding 1 tablespoon of water if necessary. Wrap in plastic wrap (clingfilm) and chill in the refrigerator for 1 hour. Preheat the oven to 350°F/180°C/Gas Mark 4. Lightly grease a loose-bottom 9½ inch/24 cm tart pan. Roll out the dough on a lightly floured work surface to ⅛ inch/3 mm thick. Carefully line the prepared pan, letting a little of the dough overhang the edge. Chill in the refrigerator for 20 minutes. Prick the bottom of the pie shell (pastry case) with a fork, line with wax (greaseproof) paper, fill with pie weights (baking beans or dried beans), and bake for 20 minutes. Remove the paper and weights, return the pie shell to the oven, and bake for another 5–10 minutes until the pastry is golden. Let stand on a wire rack to cool. Reduce the oven temperature to 300°F/150°C/Gas Mark 2. To make the filling, beat the butter with the superfine (caster) sugar until light and creamy, then gradually beat in the eggs. Add the ground almonds and flour and mix well. Spread the almond mixture over the bottom of the pie shell, then press the figs into it. Sprinkle with the slivered (flaked) almonds and demerara sugar and bake for 1 hour 20 minutes. Remove the tart from the pan, dust with a little confectioners' (icing) sugar, and serve warm or cold.

FIG TART WITH ALMONDS

PLUM AND ORANGE FLOWER WATER TART

PLUM AND ORANGE FLOWER WATER TART

PHOTO PAGE 418

تارت البرقوق مع ماء الزهر

Preparation time: 40 minutes, plus chilling time
Cooking time: 1 hour
Serves 8

1¼ sticks (5 oz/150 g) unsalted butter, softened
¾ cup (5 oz/150 g) superfine (caster) or granulated sugar
2 eggs
2 tablespoons orange flower water
1½ cups (5 oz/150 g) ground almonds
8 plums, pitted (stoned) and cut in quarters
2 tablespoons slivered (flaked) almonds
1 tablespoon demerara or other raw sugar
1 tablespoon confectioners' (icing) sugar

For the sweet pastry dough
1¼ cups (5 oz/150 g) all-purpose (plain) flour,
    plus extra for dusting
pinch of salt
6 tablespoons (3 oz/80 g) unsalted butter, chilled and diced,
    plus extra for greasing
¾ cup (3 oz/80 g) confectioners' (icing) sugar
grated zest of ½ lemon
1 egg yolk

First, make the dough. Sift together the flour and salt into a
bowl, add the butter, and rub in with your fingertips until the
mixture resembles fine breadcrumbs. (This can also be done
in a food processor.) Stir in the sugar and lemon zest, then add
the egg yolk and mix to a smooth dough, adding 1 tablespoon
of water, if necessary. Wrap in plastic wrap (clingfilm) and chill
in the refrigerator for 1 hour. Preheat the oven to 350°F/180°C/
Gas Mark 4. Lightly grease a loose-bottom 9½ inch/24 cm tart
pan. Roll out the dough on a lightly floured work surface to ⅛
inch/3 mm thick. Carefully line the prepared pan, letting a little
of the dough overhang the edge. Chill in the refrigerator for 20
minutes. Prick the bottom of the pie shell (pastry case) with
a fork, line with wax (greaseproof) paper, fill with pie weights
(baking beans or dried beans), and bake for 20 minutes.
Remove the paper and weights, return the pie shell to the oven,
and bake for another 5–10 minutes until the pastry is golden.
Let stand on a wire rack to cool. Reduce the oven temperature
to 300°F/150°C/Gas Mark 2. To make the filling, beat the butter
with the superfine (caster) sugar until light and creamy, then
gradually beat in the eggs. Add the orange flower water and
ground almonds and mix well. Spread the almond mixture
over the bottom of the pie shell, then press the plums into it.
Sprinkle with the slivered (flaked) almonds and demerara sugar
and bake for 1 hour. Remove the tart from the pan, dust with a
little confectioners' (icing) sugar, and serve warm or cold.

ORANGE
AND
LEMON
CUSTARD
TARTS

—

تارت الكاسترد
بالليمون والبرتقال

Preparation time: 35–40 minutes
Cooking time: 5 minutes, plus chilling time
Makes 24

1½ tablespoons (¾ oz/20 g) butter, melted
9 oz/250 g phyllo (filo) pastry
scant 1 cup (3½ oz/100 g) shelled pistachio nuts,
    toasted and ground

For the custard
1½ cups (12 fl oz/350 ml) heavy (double) cream
⅔ cup (¼ pint/150 ml) whole (full-fat) milk
1 vanilla bean (pod), halved lengthwise
½ cup (3½ oz/100 g) superfine (caster) or granulated sugar
3 eggs
2 egg yolks
juice of 1 lemon
finely grated zest of 1 orange

Preheat the oven to 375°F/190°C/Gas Mark 5. Brush two
12 cup muffin pans with melted butter. Cut the pastry sheets
into 4 inch/10 cm squares and keep them covered to prevent
them from drying out. Line each muffin cup with 4 layers of
pastry, brush the top layer with melted butter, and bake for
5 minutes. Remove the muffin pans from the oven, turn the pie
shells (pastry cases) upside down, and return to the oven for
2 minutes to dry out the undersides. Remove from the oven
and let cool in the pans on wire racks. To make the custard,
pour the cream and milk into a pan, scrap in the vanilla seeds,
and add the bean (pod). Bring just to a boil, remove from the
heat cover, and let steep for 10 minutes. Remove and discard
the bean. Meanwhile, beat the sugar with the eggs and egg
yolks until light and creamy. Bring the cream and milk mixture
back to a boil, then gradually whisk into the egg mixture. Pour
into the pan, return to the heat, and whisk constantly until
thickened. Remove from the heat and stir in the lemon juice
and orange zest, strain into a small bowl, and let cool. When
the custard is cold, pour it into the pie shells and chill in the
refrigerator until set. Meanwhile, put the ground pistachios
into a saucepan, pour in the sugar syrup and lemon juice, and
heat for 1–2 minutes. Remove from the heat, spoon a little onto
each of the custard tarts, and serve.

APPLE CRISP

كعكة التفاح
المقرمشة

Preparation time: 20–25 minutes
Cooking time: 30 minutes
Serves 4

4 large tart apples, peeled, cored, and diced
4 tablespoons brown sugar
¾ cup (5½ oz/165 g) superfine (caster) or granulated sugar
5 cloves
1¾ cups (8 oz/225 g) all-purpose (plain) flour
7 tablespoons (3½ oz/100 g) butter, chilled and diced
½ cup (2 oz/50 g) ground almonds
1 tablespoon slivered (flaked) almonds
cream or ice cream, to serve

Put the apples, brown sugar, 4 tablespoons of the superfine (caster) sugar, and the cloves into a pan. Cook over low heat until the apples are soft and the sugar has dissolved. Remove the pan from the heat and let cool slightly. Preheat the oven to 400°F/200°C/Gas Mark 6. Sift the flour into a bowl, add the butter, and rub in with your fingertips until the mixture resembles breadcrumbs. Stir in the remaining sugar and the ground almonds. Remove and discard the cloves from the apples and put them into an ovenproof dish. Spoon the crumb mixture over the top and sprinkle with the slivered (flaked) almonds. Bake for 30 minutes. Serve warm with cream or ice cream.

BAKED STUFFED APPLES

تفاح محشو محمص

Preparation time: 15 minutes
Cooking time: 30 minutes
Serves 4

4 large apples
scant ½ cup (2 oz/50 g) raisins
⅓ cup (2 oz/50 g) chopped dried apricots
½ cup (2 oz/50 g) blanched almonds, coarsely chopped
½ teaspoon ground cinnamon
¼ teaspoon grated nutmeg
1 tablespoon (½ oz/15 g) butter
scant 1 cup (7 fl oz/200 ml) apple juice
scant ½ cup (3½ fl oz/100 ml) Sugar Syrup (see page 33)
2 tablespoons pomegranate seeds
2 tablespoons slivered (flaked) almonds, toasted
grated zest of 1 lemon

Preheat the oven to 350°F/180°C/Gas Mark 4. Core the apples and put them into an ovenproof dish so they fit snuggly in a single layer. Combine the raisins, apricots, blanched almonds, cinnamon, and nutmeg and divide the mixture among the cavities in the center of the apples. Add a little butter to each one and then pour the apple juice and scant 1 cup (7 fl oz/200 ml) of water into the dish. Bake for 30 minutes, basting with the cooking juices halfway through the cooking time. Meanwhile, heat the Sugar Syrup in a small saucepan. Remove the apples from the oven and transfer to a shallow dish. Drizzle with the Sugar Syrup, decorate with the pomegranate seeds, slivered (flaked) almonds, and lemon zest, and serve.

APPLE
AND
WALNUT
BUNDLES

لفافات التفاح
والجوز

Preparation time: 30 minutes, plus chilling time
Cooking time: 10–15 minutes
Makes 16

6 crisp sweet apples, peeled, cored, and diced
4 tablespoons superfine (caster) or granulated sugar
1 teaspoon apple pie (mixed) spice
½ cup (2 oz/50 g) chopped walnuts
1 lb 2 oz/500 g ready-to-bake puff pastry dough (2 sheets)
all-purpose (plain) flour, for dusting
1 egg, lightly beaten with 1 tablespoon water

Put the apples and sugar into a saucepan, set over medium heat, and cook, stirring gently, until the sugar has dissolved and the apples are nearly tender. Stir in the spice and walnuts, then remove from the heat and let cool completely. Put the dough sheets on a lightly floured work surface and cut them into 16 equal squares. Put a small mound of cooled apple filling in the middle of each square. Brush the egg wash around the edges of a dough square and bring each corner to the middle. Brush the surface with egg wash and place on a baking sheet. Repeat this process until all 16 bundles are made. Chill the bundles in the refrigerator for 30 minutes. Meanwhile, preheat the oven to 400°F/200°C/Gas Mark 6. Bake the bundles for 10–15 minutes until the pastry is golden brown and puffed up. Serve hot or cold as a light snack or for breakfast.

APPLE
PACKAGES

رقائق التفاح الملفوفة

Preparation time: 30–40 minutes
Cooking time: 10 minutes
Makes 8

3 apples, peeled, cored, and diced
4 tablespoons superfine (caster) or granulated sugar
¼ teaspoon ground cinnamon
⅓ cup (2 oz/50 g) golden raisins (sultanas)
8 sheets phyllo (filo) pastry dough
7 tablespoons (3½ oz/100 g) butter, melted

Put the apples, sugar, cinnamon, and golden raisins (sultanas) into a saucepan and cook over low heat, stirring occasionally, for 10–15 minutes, until the apples are very tender. Remove from the heat and let cool. Lay the pastry dough on a work surface and cut into 4 x 10 inch/10 x 25 cm strips. Keep the dough covered to prevent it from drying out. Preheat the oven to 400°F/200°C/Gas Mark 6. Put 2 strips of dough, 1 on top of the other, horizontally on a work surface and brush the top with melted butter. Put 2 more strips vertically, 1 on top of the other, to make an L shape and brush with melted butter. Put a spoonful of apple filling on the corner of the L shape and fold the pastry over to form a package. Brush with melted butter and put the package on a baking sheet. Make 7 more packages in the same way. Bake for 10 minutes until the pastry is golden and crisp. Remove from the oven, transfer to a wire rack, and let cool.

CREPES
WITH
PISTACHIO
FILLING
AND SYRUP

—

كريب مع الفستق
الحلبي والقطر

Preparation time: 20 minutes
Cooking time: 2 minutes
Makes 7

2 eggs
1¼ cups (½ pint/300 ml) milk
1¾ cups (8 oz/225 g) all-purpose (plain) flour
2¾ teaspoons baking powder
1 teaspoon baking soda (bicarbonate of soda)
2 tablespoons superfine (caster) or granulated sugar
butter, for greasing
Homemade Yogurt (see page 28), to serve

For the sugar syrup
1¼ cups (9 oz/250 g) superfine (caster) or granulated sugar

For the filling
½ cup (2 oz/50 g) shelled pistachio nuts, crushed
2 tablespoons superfine (caster) or granulated sugar
1 tablespoon orange flower water

Whisk the eggs in a bowl, then gradually whisk in the milk. Add the flour, baking powder, baking soda (bicarbonate of soda), and sugar and beat until combined. Let stand for 30 minutes. Meanwhile, make the sugar syrup. Put the sugar into a saucepan, pour in 1 cup (8 fl oz/250 ml) of water, and stir over low heat until the sugar has completely dissolved. Increase the heat slightly and bring to a boil. Boil, without stirring, until syrupy. Remove the pan from the heat, pour the syrup into a small bowl and let cool, then chill in the refrigerator. To make the filling, combine the crushed pistachios, sugar, and orange flower water in a bowl, then set aside. When you are ready to cook, heat a 6 inch (15 cm) nonstick skillet or frying pan and grease lightly with butter. Stir the batter and add a ladleful to the pan, tilting and turning the pan so that it spreads evenly. Cook for about 45 seconds until the underside is golden. Shake the pan to loosen the crepe, then flip it over with a frosting spatula (palette knife) and cook the other side for about 30 seconds until golden. Slide out onto a plate and repeat until all the batter has been used. Stack the cooked crepes interleaved with wax (greaseproof) paper. Add a spoonful of the pistachio filling to the middle of each crepe, then fold over and seal by pinching together. Serve immediately, generously drizzled with the sugar syrup and accompanied with Homemade Yogurt.

APRICOTS
WITH
POMEGRANATE
SYRUP

PHOTO PAGE 427

—

مشمش مشوي مع شراب
الرمان

Preparation time: 10 minutes
Cooking time: 10 minutes
Serves 8

8 apricots, halved and pitted (stoned)
4 tablespoons (2 oz/50 g) butter
3 tablespoons light demerara or other raw sugar
scant 1 cup (7 fl oz/200 ml) pomegranate juice
scant ½ cup (3½ fl oz/100 ml) Sugar Syrup (see page 33)
grated zest of 1 lemon
¼ cup (1 oz/25 g) unsalted shelled pistachio nuts, ground
plain (natural) yogurt, to serve

Preheat the broiler (grill) to hot. Put the apricot halves into a flameproof dish, fitting them snuggly in a single layer, add a little butter to each, and sprinkle with the sugar. Put under the hot broiler for 5 minutes or until the sugar starts to brown and caramelize. Remove from the heat and let cool slightly. Meanwhile, pour the pomegranate juice and sugar syrup into a saucepan and bring to a boil. Add the lemon zest and boil until reduced by half. Remove from the heat and drizzle the pomegranate syrup over the apricots. Sprinkle with the ground pistachios and serve immediately with the yogurt.

PEARS
POACHED
IN
ARAK

—

كمثرى مسلوق مع
العرق

Preparation time: 10 minutes
Cooking time: 30 minutes
Serves 4

2 tablespoons arak or other anise-flavored liqueur
generous ½ cup (4 oz/120 g) sugar
thinly pared zest of 2 lemons, cut into slivers
½ vanilla bean (pod), split lengthwise and seeds scraped
4 pears, peeled
scan 1 cup (5 oz/150 g) pomegranate seeds

Pour 3½ cups (1½ pints/850 ml) of water into a deep saucepan, add the arak, sugar, half the lemon zest, and the vanilla seeds and bean (pod), and heat gently until the sugar has dissolved. Increase the heat and bring to a boil. Add the pears, making sure that they are completely covered with the cooking liquid and adding more water if necessary. Reduce the heat to low and poach for 30 minutes until the pears are tender. Lift out the pears and set aside. Strain the cooking liquid and return it to the pan with the vanilla bean. Bring to a boil and boil rapidly until syrupy and reduced by half. Add the pomegranate seeds and remaining lemon zest. To serve, cut a thin slice from the bottom of the pears so that they stand up and put them on shallow plates. Pour the pomegranate and lemon syrup over them and serve.

APRICOTS WITH POMEGRANATE SYRUP

ROASTED FIGS AND ALMONDS

PHOTO PAGE 429

—

تين محمص مع اللوز

Preparation time: 10 minutes
Cooking time: 10 minutes
Serves 4

12 figs, halved lengthwise
6 tablespoons pomegranate juice
2 tablespoons demerara or other raw sugar
finely grated zest of 1 orange
⅓ cup (1½ oz/40 g) blanched almonds
⅔ cup (¼ pint/150 ml) plain (natural) yogurt
clear honey, to serve

Preheat the oven to 400°F/200°C/Gas Mark 6. Put the fig halves, cut side uppermost, on a baking sheet, pour the pomegranate juice over them, and sprinkle with the sugar. Sprinkle with the orange zest, put 1 almond on each fig, sprinkling the remainder around the sides. Roast for 10 minutes until soft and juicy. Serve immediately with the yogurt and a drizzle of honey.

DRIED FRUIT COMPOTE

—

كومبوت الفواكه
المجففة

Preparation time: 10 minutes, plus resting time
Serves 10

generous 1⅔ cups (7 oz/200 g) chopped prunes
generous 1⅔ cups (7 oz/200 g) chopped dried apricots
generous cup (5 oz/150 g) chopped dried mango
⅓ cup (2 oz/50 g) raisins
⅓ cup (2 oz/50 g) golden raisins (sultanas)
generous 2 cups (18 fl oz/500 ml) apple juice
1¼ cups (½ pint/300 ml) orange juice
2 cinnamon sticks
8 cloves
juice and grated zest of ½ lemon
3 tablespoons (clear) honey

Put all the dried fruit into a bowl. Pour the apple juice into a saucepan and heat to simmering point, then pour it over the fruit. Let stand overnight. Pour the orange juice and generous 2 cups (18 fl oz/500 ml) of water into a large saucepan, add the cinnamon sticks, cloves, lemon juice and zest, and honey, and bring to a boil. Add the fruit, reduce the heat, and simmer, stirring occasionally, for 45 minutes until the liquid has thickened. Serve immediately or let cool and store, covered, in the refrigerator for up to 2 or 3 days.

LEMON, ROSE WATER, AND CARDAMOM BRÛLÉE

—

كريم بروليه بالليمون
وماء الزهر

Preparation time: 20–25 minutes
Cooking time: 20–25 minutes
Serves 6

1½ cups (12 fl oz/350 ml) heavy (double) cream
⅔ cup (¼ pint/150 ml) whole (full-fat) milk
1 vanilla bean (pod), halved lengthwise
4 cardamom pods
½ cup (3½ oz/100 g) superfine (caster) or granulated sugar
3 eggs
2 egg yolks
juice of 1 lemon
1 teaspoon rose water
demerara or other raw sugar, to decorate

Preheat the oven to 300°F/150°C/Gas Mark 2. Pour the cream and milk into a saucepan, scrape the seeds from the vanilla bean (pod) into the pan, and add the pod. Add the cardamom pods and bring just to a boil, then remove from the heat, cover, and let steep for 10 minutes. Meanwhile, beat the sugar with the eggs and egg yolks in a bowl until light and creamy. Remove and discard the vanilla bean and cardamom pods from the cream, return it to low heat, and bring back to a boil. Remove it from the heat and gradually whisk it into the egg mixture. Strain the custard into a small bowl and then pour into 6 ramekins. Put the ramekins into a roasting pan and pour in enough hot water to come halfway up the sides. Put the pan in the oven and bake for 20–25 minutes or until the custards are nearly set. Remove from the roasting pan and let cool. When ready to serve, sprinkle the demerara sugar evenly over the custards and caramelize either with a cook's blow torch or by placing briefly under a preheated broiler (grill). Serve immediately.

SWEET CHEESE PUDDING

—

مهلبية بالجبن الحلو

Preparation time: 10–15 minutes, plus chilling time
Serves 6–8

3½ oz/100 g crushed graham crackers (digestive biscuits)
7 tablespoons (3½ oz/100 g) butter, melted
generous 1 cup (9 oz/250 g) ricotta cheese
2 heaping teaspoons confectioners' (icing) sugar
2 tablespoons orange flower water
3 tablespoons ground pistachio nuts

Put the graham cracker (digestive biscuit) crumbs into a bowl, pour in the melted butter, and mix well. Spoon the mixture into a 6 inch/15 cm loose-bottom cake pan and press down firmly. Chill in the refrigerator for 1 hour. Meanwhile, beat the ricotta with the confectioners' (icing) sugar and orange flower water until smooth. Spoon this mixture over the crumb layer and smooth the top. Decorate with ground pistachios and chill until to ready to serve.

DONUTS
WITH
ROSE PETAL
JELLY

دونات مع مربى تويجات
الزهر

Preparation time: 20–25 minutes, plus resting time
Cooking time: 5–7 minutes
Makes 12–15

3¼ cups (14 oz/400 g) all-purpose (plain) flour,
    plus extra for dusting
1 envelope active dry (fast-action) yeast
3 tablespoons instant milk powder
3 tablespoons sunflower oil, plus extra for brushing
    and deep-frying
3 tablespoons rose petal jelly or jam, or strawberry jelly or jam
sugar, for dusting

Sift the flour in to a bowl, stir in the yeast and milk powder,
and make a well in the center. Pour the oil and 1¼ cups
(½ pint/300 ml) of lukewarm water into the well and bring
together the flour with your hands to form a dough. Add a little
more water if the dough seems too dry. Knead the dough for 10
minutes until it is smooth and elastic. Put it into a clean, lightly
floured bowl, cover with a dish towel, and let stand in a warm
place for 1 hour until doubled in size. Punch down (knock
back) the dough, turn out onto a lightly floured work surface,
and knead for 1 minute. Divide the dough into 15 balls, the size
of golf balls. Flatten a ball with your fingers, add ½ teaspoon
of jelly or jam to the middle, and roll the dough back into a
smooth ball, enclosing the jam completely. You may need a little
water to help the dough seal. Repeat this with all the dough
balls. Lightly brush a baking sheet with oil, put the donuts on
it, and cover with a dish towel. Let stand for 30 minutes to rise.
Heat the oil in a large deep-fryer to 350°F/180°C or until a cube
of day-old bread browns in 30 seconds. Add the donuts to the
hot oil, in batches, and cook, turning once with a long-handled
slotted spoon, for 5–6 minutes. Lift out, drain on paper towels,
and dust with sugar. Serve warm.

Varieties of donut
To make ring donuts, simple flatten the dough ball with your
finger and cut out the middle with a small cutter. Let rise again
and then deep-fry for 5 minutes, turning once. Dust in sugar
and serve warm. Don't throw away the middle piece of dough,
just re-roll in to a small ball, let rise, and then deep-fry for 3
minutes. Dust with sugar and serve.

MUHALLABIEH

MUHALLABIEH

PHOTO PAGE 432

مهلبية

Preparation time: 5 minutes, plus chilling time
Cooking time: 15 minutes
Serves 4

3 heaping tablespoons cornstarch (cornflour)
5 cups (2 pints/½ litres) milk
1 tablespoon rose water
2 heaping tablespoons sugar
½ cup (2 oz/50 g) shelled pistachio nuts, ground
4 teaspoons rose jelly or jam (optional)

For the syrup
generous 1½ cups (11 oz/300 g) sugar
1 lemon leaf
1 lemon slice
juice of ½ lemon

Mix the cornstarch (cornflour) to a paste with a little of the milk. Pour the remaining milk into a saucepan and bring to a boil over low heat. Gradually stir the cornstarch paste into the milk with a wooden spoon and cook, stirring constantly, until the mixture has thickened. Add the rose water and sugar and stir for a few minutes until the sugar has dissolved. Remove the pan from the heat and carefully ladle the mixture into 4 individual serving dishes. Let cool completely and then chill in the refrigerator for at least 3 hours or overnight. Meanwhile, make the syrup. Put the sugar into a heavy saucepan, pour in ⅔ cup (¼ pint/150 ml) of water, and stir over medium heat until the sugar has dissolved. Add the lemon leaf, slice, and juice and bring to a boil. Boil gently, without stirring, until syrupy, then remove from the heat. Pour the syrup into a small bowl, let cool, and then chill in the refrigerator. To serve, pour the syrup over the top of the chilled desserts, sprinkle with the ground pistachios, and add 1 teaspoon of rose jelly, if using.

SEMOLINA PUDDING

حلاوة السميد بماء الزهر

Preparation time: 5 minutes
Cooking time: 15–20 minutes
Serves 4

3¾ cups (1½ pints/900 ml) milk
scant 1 cup (5 oz/150 g) semolina
¾ cup (5 oz/150 g) superfine (caster) or granulated sugar
2 teaspoons orange flower water
fresh fruit, to serve

Put the milk, semolina, and sugar into a saucepan and bring to a boil, stirring constantly. Cook, stirring, until smooth and thickened. Stir in the orange flower water. Remove the pan from the heat and divide the mixture among 4 individual serving bowls. Let cool completely, then chill in the refrigerator. Serve topped with fresh fruit.

HELLOEL JEBBEN
(SEMOLINA PUDDING)

—

حلاوة الجبن (حلاوة
السميد مع جبنة الموزاريلا)

Preparation time: 15 minutes
Cooking time: 20 minutes
Serves 4

¾ cup (5 oz/150 g) superfine (caster) or granulated sugar
7 oz/200 g mozzarella cheese, diced
1 tablespoon rose water
juice of ½ lemon
¾ cup (4½ oz/130 g) semolina
crushed shelled pistachio nuts, to decorate

For the syrup
1 cup (7 oz/200 g) superfine (caster) or granulated sugar
1 tablespoon rose water
juice of 1 lemon

Put the sugar into a large saucepan, pour in 1¼ cups (½ pint/ 300 ml) of water, and bring to a boil, stirring until the sugar has completely dissolved. Add the mozzarella and stir until melted, then stir in the rose water and lemon juice. Add the semolina and cook, stirring constantly, until thickened. Remove the pan from the heat. Make the syrup. Put the sugar into a saucepan, pour in 4 tablespoons of water and stir over medium heat until the sugar has completely dissolved. Add the rose water and lemon juice, increase the heat to high, and bring to a boil. Boil without stirring until the mixture has a light syrupy consistency. Remove from the heat and let cool. Pour a little of the cooled syrup onto a work surface and tip the semolina onto it. Using a rolling pin, roll out to ½ inch/1 cm thick. Break into pieces and place in a bowl. Pour over the remaining syrup and sprinkle with crushed pistachios.

ORANGE FLOWER MILK PUDDING

—

بودينغ بالحليب
وماء الزهر

Preparation time: 15 minutes, plus chilling time
Serves 6

5 cups (2 pints/1.2 liters) milk
¾ cup (4 oz/120 g) rice flour (ground rice)
⅔ cup (4 oz/120 g) superfine (caster) or granulated sugar
2 tablespoons orange flower water
¾ cup (3 oz/80 g) unsalted shelled pistachio nuts,
    coarsely ground
rose petal jelly or jam, to serve

Pour the milk into a saucepan and bring to a boil, then add the rice and cook, stirring constantly, until it starts to thicken. Stir in the sugar and cook, stirring constantly, until dissolved. Remove the pan from the heat, stir in the orange flower water, and divide among 6 serving dishes. Let cool, then chill in the refrigerator. Serve sprinkled with the ground nuts and a little rose petal jelly.

RICE
PUDDING

ارز بالحليب مع التوابل

Preparation time: 5–10 minutes
Cooking time: 40–50 minutes
Serves 4

⅔ cup (5 oz/150 g) short grain (pudding) rice
3¾ cups (1½ pints/900 ml) milk
3 tablespoons superfine (caster) or granulated sugar
dash of orange flower water
½ cantaloupe melon, seeded and cut into cubes
1 cup (4 oz/120 g) shelled pistachio nuts, crushed
Sugar Syrup (see page 33), to serve

Put the rice, milk, and sugar into a saucepan and bring to a boil, stirring until the sugar has dissolved. Simmer, stirring occasionally, for 40 minutes until the rice is tender. Remove the pan from the heat and let cool. Stir in orange flower water to taste. Divide the rice pudding among 4 individual serving dishes and chill in the refrigerator. To serve, top with the diced melon and pistachio nuts and drizzle with sugar syrup.

ORANGE
FLOWER
WATER
AND
PISTACHIO
YOGURT

زبادي بماء الزهر
والفستق

Preparation time: 30 minutes, plus resting time
Cooking time: 30 minutes
Makes 1 lb 2 oz/500 g

2 cups (1 lb/450 g) plain (natural) set yogurt
2½ cups (1 pint/600 ml) whole full-fat milk
1 tablespoons orange flower water
1 vanilla bean (pod), halved lengthwise

For the sugar syrup
⅓ cup (2½ oz/65 g) sugar
1 teaspoon rose water
¾ cup (3 oz/80 g) shelled pistachio nuts, coarsely chopped

Put the yogurt into a bowl and set aside. Pour the milk in to a saucepan and heat gently until a froth forms on the top, then remove from the heat and let cool slightly for 5–10 minutes. Gradually stir the hot milk into the yogurt, cover with plastic wrap (clingfilm), cover with a dish towel, and let stand overnight in a warm place. (It is very important not to move the pan or remove the towel.) The following day, add the orange flower water and the seeds from the vanilla bean (pod), stir only once, and put the pan in the refrigerator for 1 day to set. Make the syrup. Dissolve the sugar in 5 tablespoons of water in a saucepan and set over medium heat until it turns syrupy. Add the rose water and pistachio nuts. Serve the orange flower water yogurt topped with syrup pistachio nuts.

SPICED RICE PUDDING

SPICED RICE PUDDING

PHOTO PAGE 436

—

بودنغ الأرز

—

Preparation time: 10 minutes
Cooking time: 40 minutes
Serves 4

generous ¾ cup (6 oz/175 g) short grain (pudding) rice
scant 1 cup (6 oz/175 g) superfine (caster) or granulated sugar
1¼ cups (1 pint/600 ml) whole (full-fat) milk
1 cinnamon stick
¼ teaspoon grated nutmeg
1 tablespoon rose water
1 teaspoon ground cinnamon
3 tablespoons slivered (flaked) almonds, toasted

Put the rice and sugar into a saucepan, pour in the milk, and bring to a boil. Reduce the heat, add the cinnamon stick, stir in the nutmeg, and simmer, stirring occasionally, for 40 minutes until the rice is tender. Remove the pan from the heat. Remove and discard the cinnamon stick and set the rice aside to cool. Add the rose water and stir well. Spoon the rice pudding into a large dish. Sprinkle with the ground cinnamon and almonds and serve hot or cold.

CINNAMON AND HONEY YOGURT PUDDING

—

مهلبية الزبادي بالقرفة
والعسل

Preparation time: 10 minutes, plus chilling time
Serves 4

1 vanilla bean (pod), split lengthwise
2 cups (1 lb 2 oz/500 g) plain (natural) yogurt
⅓ cup (3 oz/80 g) superfine (caster) or granulated sugar
1 tablespoon orange flower water
1 teaspoon (clear) honey
pinch of ground cinnamon
1 envelope gelatin powder
grated zest of 1 orange

Scrap the vanilla seeds into a bowl, add the yogurt, sugar, orange flower water, honey. and cinnamon, and beat until the sugar has dissolved and the mixture is creamy. Put the gelatin into a small heatproof bowl and pour in 4 tablespoons of hot water. Once the gelatin has dissolved, pour it into the yogurt mixture and mix well. Divide the mixture among 4 dishes and chill in the refrigerator for 2 hours. You can serve the desserts in their dishes or dip the bottom of the dishes into hot water to loosen and then turn out the desserts onto a plates. Whichever way you choose, decorate with the grated orange zest.

WHEAT BERRY DESSERT

PHOTO PAGE 438

—

عصيدة حب القمح
بتوت البيري

Preparation time: 5 minutes
Cooking time: 1 hour 10 minutes
Serves 6

2 cups (14 oz/400 g) whole wheat berries,
    soaked in cold water for 24 hours
2 cinnamon sticks
4½ tablespoons (1 oz/25 g) anise seeds (aniseeds)
2 tablespoons rose water
½ cup (3 oz/100 g) superfine (caster) or granulated sugar
scant 1 cup (3½ oz/100 g) shelled walnuts

Drain and rinse the wheat, put it into a saucepan, pour in
5 cups (2 pints/½ liters) of water, and bring to a boil. Add the
cinnamon sticks and anise seeds (aniseeds), reduce the heat,
and simmer for 50 minutes. Stir in the rose water, sugar, and
walnuts and simmer for another 10–15 minutes. Serve warm.

CHOCOLATE COFFEE MOUSE

—

موس الشوكولا بالقهوة

Preparation time: 30 minutes, plus chilling time
Serves 4

3½ oz/100 g semisweet dark (plain) chocolate,
    broken into pieces
3½ oz/100 g milk chocolate, broken into pieces
5 oz/150 g white chocolate, broken into pieces
2 tablespoons Lebanese Coffee with Cardamom (see page 451)
scant 1 cup (7 fl oz/200 ml) heavy (double) cream
4 egg whites
3 tablespoons superfine (caster) or granulated sugar
3 tablespoons ground pistachio nuts

Put the chocolate into 3 separate heatproof bowls and melt
each over a separate saucepan of simmering water. Stir half
the coffee into the semisweet (plain) chocolate and half into
the milk chocolate. Let the chocolate cool slightly. Whisk the
cream until soft peaks form. Stiffly whisk the egg whites in
another bowl, then gradually whisk in the sugar. Divide the
cream among the bowls of chocolate and fold in. Divide the
egg whites among the bowls and fold in. Spoon the semisweet
chocolate mixture evenly into 4 glass dishes, add the milk
chocolate mixture, and top with the white chocolate mixture.
Chill in the refrigerator until ready to serve. Serve decorated
with the ground pistachio nuts.

WHEAT BERRY DESSERT

ZALABIYEH

—

زلابية

Preparation time: 30–40 minutes
Cooking time: 15 minutes
Serves 10

⅔ cup (¼ pint/150 ml) whole (full-fat) milk
5 tablespoons (2½ oz/65 g) butter
2¾ cups (12 oz/350 g) all-purpose (plain) flour,
    plus extra for dusting
scant ¼ cup (1½ oz/40 g) superfine (caster)
    or granulated sugar
1 envelope active dry (fast-action) yeast
1⅔ cups (7 oz/200 g) confectioners' (icing) sugar

Pour the milk in small pan, add the butter, and heat until the butter has melted. Remove from the heat and let cool. Sift the flour into a large bowl, stir in the sugar and yeast, and make a well in the middle. Pour the liquid into the well and bring together to form a dough. Knead for 10 minutes until smooth and elastic. Put the dough into a lightly floured bowl, cover with a dish towel, and let rest in a warm place for 1 hour until doubled in size. Punch down (knock back) the dough and knead for a few minutes, then roll into a long sausage shape on a lightly floured work surface. Divide the dough into 10 pieces and roll each one into small sausage shapes. Score with 5–6 lines and put onto a lightly floured baking sheet. Let stand in a warm place for 30 minutes until risen. Meanwhile preheat the oven to 425°F/220°C/Gas Mark 7. Bake the zalabiyeh for 15 minutes, then transfer to a wire rack. Mix the confectioners' (icing) sugar with 4 tablespoons of water in a large bowl. Dip the zalabiyeh into the mixture, then put them on a wire rack.

PALACE PUDDING

—

حلوى بودينغ القصر

Preparation time: 15 minutes, plus chilling time
Cooking time: 15 minutes
Serves 4

4 thick (¾ inch/2 cm) slices white bread, crusts removed
1⅔ cups (14 fl oz/400 ml) Sugar Syrup (see page 33)
1½ cups (12 fl oz/350 ml) whole (full-fat) milk
3 tablespoons cornstarch (cornflour)
2 tablespoons superfine (caster) or granulated sugar
1¼ cups (½ pint/300 ml) heavy (double) cream
¼ cup (1 oz/25 g) shelled pistachio nuts, finely ground
    candied (glacé) cherries, to decorate

Toast the bread on both sides. Lay the toasted bread in an 8 inch/20 cm square dish. Pour the Sugar Syrup over the bread and set aside to be absorbed while you make the sauce. Pour the milk into a pan and stir in the cornstarch. Heat gently, stirring constantly with a wooden spoon. When it comes to a boil, add the sugar and simmer, stirring constantly, until thick enough to coat the back of the spoon. Pour the sauce over the bread, let cool, and chill in the refrigerator until set. Whip the cream in a bowl with an electric mixer. Spoon it into a pastry (piping) bag and pipe on top of the dessert. Sprinkle with ground pistachios and cherries. Chill until ready to serve.

VANILLA ICE CREAM

ايس كريم الفانيلا

Preparation time: 30–40 minutes, plus freezing time
Makes 2½ cups (1 pint/600 ml)

1 cup (8 fl oz/250 ml) whole (full-fat) milk
1 cup (8 fl oz/250 ml) heavy (double) cream
1 vanilla bean (pod), split lengthwise
6 egg yolks
⅔ cup (4 oz/120 g) superfine (caster) or granulated sugar

Pour the milk and cream into a saucepan, scrape the vanilla seeds into the pan with the point of a knife, and add the bean (pod). Bring just to a boil, then turn off the heat and let steep for 30 minutes. Beat the egg yolks with the sugar in a bowl until pale and creamy. Remove the vanilla bean from the pan and discard. Bring the mixture just back to a boil, then strain it into the egg yolk mixture, stirring constantly. Pour the custard into a clean saucepan and stir constantly over medium heat until it starts to thicken and thinly coats the back of a wooden spoon. Remove from the heat, pour into a bowl, and let cool, then chill in the refrigerator for at least 30 minutes before churning in an ice cream maker until almost frozen. Transfer to a freezerproof container and store in the freezer until required.

VANILLA AND PISTACHIO ICE CREAM

آيس كريم الفانيلا والفستق

Preparation time: 45 minutes, plus freezing time
Makes 2½ cups (1 pint/600 ml)

1 cup (8 fl oz/250 ml) whole (full-fat) milk
1 cup (8 fl oz/250 ml) heavy (double) cream
1 vanilla bean (pod), split lengthwise
6 egg yolks
⅔ cup (4 oz/120 g) superfine (caster) or granulated sugar
scant 1 cup (3½ oz/100 g) unsalted shelled pistachio nuts,
    coarsely chopped

Pour the milk and cream into a saucepan, scrape the vanilla seeds into the pan with the point of a knife, and add the bean (pod). Bring just to a boil, then turn off the heat and let steep for 30 minutes. Beat the egg yolks with the sugar in a bowl until pale and creamy. Remove the vanilla bean from the pan and discard. Bring the mixture just back to a boil, then strain it into the egg yolk mixture, stirring constantly. Pour the custard into a clean saucepan and stir over medium heat until it starts to thicken and thinly coats the back of a wooden spoon. Remove from the heat, pour into a bowl, and let cool. Chill in the refrigerator for at least 30 minutes before churning in an ice cream maker until almost frozen. Gently fold in the pistachios. Transfer to a freezerproof container and store in the freezer until required.

PISTACHIO AND ROSE WATER ICE CREAM

PISTACHIO AND ROSE WATER ICE CREAM

PHOTO PAGE 442

آيس كريم ماء الزهر
والفستق

Preparation time: 30 minutes, plus freezing time
Makes 2½ cups (1 pint/600 ml)

1¼ cups (5 oz/150 g) unsalted shelled pistachio nuts
⅔ cup (4 oz/120 g) superfine (caster) or granulated sugar
4 egg yolks
1 cup (8 fl oz/250 ml) whole (full-fat) milk
1 cup (8 fl oz/250 ml) heavy (double) cream
1 tablespoon rose water

Put half the nuts and half the sugar in a food processor and process until very fine. Coarsely chop the remaining nuts. Beat the egg yolks with the remaining sugar until pale and creamy. Pour the milk and cream into a saucepan, add the pistachio mixture, and bring almost to a boil. Remove from the heat and strain into the egg yolk mixture, stirring constantly. Pour the custard back into a clean saucepan and stir over medium heat until it starts to thicken and just coats the back of a wooden spoon. Remove from the heat, pour into a bowl, and let cool. Stir in the rose water, then chill in the refrigerator for at least 30 minutes before churning in an ice cream maker until almost frozen. Gently fold in the chopped pistachio nuts, transfer to a freezerproof container, and store in the freezer until required.

STRAWBERRY AND PISTACHIO ICE CREAM

آيس كريم الفراولة
والفستق

Preparation time: 15 minutes, plus freezing time
Makes 2½ cups (1 pint/600 ml)

3 cups (1 lb 2 oz/500 g) sliced strawberries
1¼ cups (½ pint/300 ml) heavy (double) cream
1¼ cups (5 oz/150 g) confectioners' (icing) sugar
scant 1 cup (3½ oz/100 g) unsalted shelled pistachio nuts, coarsely chopped

Process the strawberries in a food processor to a smooth puree. You should have 2 cups (16 fl oz/450 ml). Pour the puree into a bowl, add the cream and sugar, and whisk until thoroughly combined. Chill in the refrigerator for at least 30 minutes before churning in an ice cream maker until almost frozen. Gently fold in the chopped pistachios, transfer to a freezerproof container, and store in the freezer until required.

WATERMELON AND ORANGE FLOWER WATER SORBET

HONEYCOMB ICE CREAM WITH PISTACHIOS AND ROSE PETALS

ايس كريم العسل بشهده مع
الفستق وبتلات الزهر

Preparation time: 30–40 minutes, plus freezing time
Makes 2½ cups (1 pint/600 ml)

butter, for greasing
⅓ cup (3 oz/80 g) superfine (caster) or granulated sugar
2 tablespoons light corn (golden) syrup
2 tablespoons baking soda (bicarbonate of soda), sifted
1 quantity Vanilla Ice Cream (see page 441) made without the vanilla bean (pod) and using only 4 eggs
scant 1 cup (3½ oz/100 g) unsalted shelled pistachio nuts, coarsely chopped
2⅔ cups (2 oz/50 g) candied rose petals

Make the honeycomb toffee (sponge candy). Grease and line a shallow baking pan. Put the sugar and syrup into a pan and heat gently until the sugar has dissolved, then increase the heat and cook until a golden brown caramel forms. Immediately remove the pan from the heat and stir in the baking soda (bicarbonate of soda) and pour into the prepared pan. Let cool. After churning the ice cream base, break the honeycomb toffee into small pieces and gently fold them into the almost frozen mixture together with the pistachios and rose petals. Transfer to a freezerproof container and store in the freezer until required.

WATERMELON AND ORANGE FLOWER WATER SORBET

PHOTO PAGE 444

مثلجات البطيخ الاحمر
ووماء الزهر

Preparation time: 15 minutes, plus freezing time
Makes 2½ cups (1 pint/600 ml)

6½ cups (2¼ lb/1 kg) cubed watermelon flesh (seeds removed)
⅔ cup (4 oz/120 g) superfine (caster) or granulated sugar
1 teaspoon orange flower water

Put the watermelon flesh into a food processor and process until smooth. You should have 2 cups (16 fl oz/450 ml) watermelon puree. Put the sugar into a saucepan, pour in 1¼ cups (½ pint/300 ml) of water, and stir over medium heat until the sugar has dissolved. Increase the heat and bring to a boil, then boil, without stirring, for 5 minutes until slightly syrupy. Remove from the heat and let cool, then stir in the watermelon puree and orange flower water. Chill in the refrigerator for a least 30 minutes, then churn in an ice cream maker until almost frozen. Alternatively, pour the cooled mixture into a shallow freezerproof container and freeze until firm, whisking every hour with a fork to stop ice crystals from forming.

LEMON SORBET

—

مثلجات الليمون

Preparation time: 10 minutes, plus freezing time
Makes 2½ cups (1 pint/600 ml)

1 cup (7 oz/200 g) superfine (caster) or granulated sugar
1¼ cups (½ pint/300 ml) strained lemon juice
    (about 6 large lemons)
finely grated zest of 1 lemon

Put the sugar into a saucepan, pour in 1¼ cups (½ pint/ 300 ml) of water, and stir over low heat until the sugar has dissolved. Increase the heat and bring to a boil, then boil, without stirring, for 5 minutes until slightly syrupy. Remove from the heat and let cool, then stir in the lemon juice and lemon zest. Chill in the refrigerator for at least 30 minutes, then churn in an ice cream maker until almost frozen. Alternatively, pour the cooled mixture into a shallow freezerproof container and freeze until firm, whisking every hour with a fork to stop ice crystals from forming.

ROSE WATER ICE CREAM

—

ايس كريم ماء الورد

Preparation time: 30–40 minutes, plus freezing time
Makes 2½ cups (1 pint/600 ml)

1 quantity Vanilla Ice Cream, made without the vanilla bean
    (pod) (see page 441)
1 teaspoon rose water

When the ice cream has been chilled in the refrigerator, stir in the rose water and churn in an ice cream maker for 30 minutes until almost frozen. Transfer to a freezerproof container and store in the freezer until required.

ORANGE AND GINGER SORBET

—

مثلجات البرتقال
والزنجبيل

Preparation time: 10 minutes, plus freezing time
Makes 2½ cups (1 pint/600 ml)

¾ cup (5 oz/150 g) superfine (caster) or granulated sugar
1¼ cups (½ pint/300 ml) strained orange juice
    (about 3 oranges)
1 teaspoon grated fresh ginger

Put the sugar into a saucepan, pour in 1¼ cups (½ pint/300 ml) of water, and stir over low heat until the sugar has dissolved. Increase the heat and bring to a boil, then boil, without stirring, for 5 minutes until slightly syrupy. Remove from the heat and let cool, then stir in the orange juice and ginger. Chill in the refrigerator for at least 30 minutes, then churn in an ice cream maker until almost frozen. Alternatively, pour the cooled mixture into a shallow freezerproof container and freeze until firm, whisking every hour with a fork to stop ice crystals from forming.

DRINKS

✴

المشروبات

WHITE COFFEE
WITH ORANGE FLOWER WATER

—

القهوة اللبنانية البيضاء
مع ماء الزهر

Preparation time: 5 minutes
Makes 1 small pot (rackwa) for 4–6

4 heaping teaspoons Lebanese coffee
scant 1 cup (7 fl oz/200 ml) whole (full-fat) milk
1 tablespoon orange flower water

Put the coffee in the pot and pour in boiling water to fill it within 1 inch/2.5 cm from the top. Bring the coffee to a boil, then remove from the heat, and stir. Repeat this 4–5 times until the coffee no longer froths but boils smoothly. Pour the milk into a small saucepan and bring just to a boil. Add the orange flower water and remove from the heat. Divide the milk equally among 4 cups and add the freshly brewed coffee. Mix together and serve immediately.

BLACK COFFEE
WITH ORANGE FLOWER WATER

—

القهوة اللبنانية مع
ماء الزهر

Preparation time: 5 minutes
Makes 1 small pot (rackwa) for 4–6

4 heaping teaspoons Lebanese coffee
2 tablespoons orange flower water

Put the coffee in the pot and pour in boiling water to fill it within 1 inch/2.5 cm from the top. Bring to a boil, then remove from the heat and stir. Repeat this 4–5 times until the coffee no long froths but boils smoothly. Stir in the orange flower water and serve.

LEBANESE COFFEE

PHOTO PAGE 453

—

القهوة اللبنانية

Preparation time: 5 minutes
Makes 1 small pot (rackwa) for 4–6

4 heaping teaspoons Lebanese coffee

Put the coffee in the pot and pour in boiling water to fill it within 1 inch/2.5 cm from the top. Bring to a boil, then remove from the heat and stir. Repeat this 4–5 times until the coffee no long froths but boils smoothly, then serve.

LEBANESE COFFEE

LEBANESE COFFEE
WITH
CARDAMOM

—

القهوة اللبنانية مع الهال

Preparation time: 5 minutes
Makes 1 small pot (rackwa) for 4–6

4 heaping teaspoons Lebanese coffee
8 cardamom pods, lightly crushed

Put the coffee in the pot and pour in boiling water to fill it within 1 inch/2.5 cm from the top. Bring to a boil, then remove from the heat and stir. Repeat this 4–5 times until the coffee no longer froths but boils smoothly. Add the cardamom pods and let steep over low heat for 5 minutes, then remove the pods and serve.

MINT TEA

—

شاي النعناع

Preparation time: 5 minutes
Serves 2

1 tea bag
2 fresh mint sprigs, plus extra to decorate
clear honey, for drizzling

Put the tea bag into a teapot and pour in 2 cups (16 fl oz/ 450 ml) of boiling water. Let stand, stirring occasionally, for 30 seconds, then remove the bag. Add the mint sprigs and let steep for 5 minutes. Strain the tea into heatproof glasses, add a drizzle of honey to each, decorate with mint leaves, and serve.

ROSE PETAL
TEA

PHOTO PAGE 455

—

شاي بتلات الزهر

Preparation time: 10 minutes
Serves 2

4 tablespoons dried rose petals, plus extra to decorate
thinly pared zest of 1 lemon
2 tablespoons clear honey
lemon wedges, to serve

Put the rose petals, lemon zest, and honey into a tea pot, pour in generous 2 cups (18 fl oz/500 ml) of boiling water, and let stand for 5 minutes. Strain the tea into heatproof glasses, decorate with lemon wedges and rose petals, and serve.

ROSE PETAL TEA

ANISE SEED TEA

—

شاي حب اليانسون

Preparation time: 10 minutes
Serves 2

1 teaspoon anise seeds
1 tea bag
2 lemon slices, to serve

Put the anise seeds into a heatproof jug, pour in 1 cup (8 fl oz/250 ml) of boiling water, and let steep for 10 minutes. Put the tea bag into a pot, pour in generous 2 cups (18 fl oz/500 ml) of boiling water, and let brew for 3 minutes. Strain the anise seed-flavored liquid into the pot of tea, pour into cups, and serve with a slice of lemon.

POMEGRANATE LEMONADE

PHOTO PAGE 457

—

ليمونادة الرمان

Preparation time: 10 minutes, plus chilling time
Serves 6–8

thinly pared zest and juice of 4 lemons
½ cup (3½ oz/100 g) superfine (caster) or granulated sugar
generous 2 cups (18 fl oz/500 ml) pomegranate juice
ice, to serve

Put the lemon zest and juice into a heatproof jug, add the sugar, and pour in 3 cups (1¼ pints/750 ml) of boiling water. Set aside and let cool and steep, stirring occasionally. Once cold, strain into another jug, stir in the pomegranate juice, and serve over ice.

POMEGRANATE LEMONADE

APPLE, MINT, GINGER, AND LIME LEMONADE

CLOUDY
LEMONADE

—

شراب الليمونادة
الغائمة

Preparation time: 10 minutes, plus chilling time
Serves 8–10

thinly pared zest and juice of 8 lemons
generous 1 cup (8 oz/225 g) superfine (caster)
     or granulated sugar
ice, to serve

Put the lemon zest and juice into a heatproof jug, add the
sugar, and pour in 6¼ cups (2½ pints/1.5 liters) of boiling
water. Set aside and let cool and steep, stirring occasionally.
Once cold, strain and serve over ice.

APPLE, MINT,
GINGER,
AND
LIME
LEMONADE

PHOTO PAGE 460

—

ليمونادة التفاح والنعناع
والزنجبيل

Preparation time: 10 minutes, plus chilling time
Serves 6

thinly pared zest and juice of 6 lemons
thinly pared zest and juice of 2 limes
¾ cup (5 oz/150 g) superfine (caster) or granulated sugar
2 inch/5 cm piece of fresh ginger, peeled and sliced
20 fresh mint leaves
generous 2 cups (18 fl oz/500 ml) apple juice
lime wedges, to serve

Put the lemon and lime zest and juice into a heatproof jug,
add the sugar, ginger, and mint leaves, and pour in 4¼ cups
(1¾ pints/1 liter) of boiling water. Set aside and let cool and
steep, stirring occasionally. Once cold, strain into another
jug, stir in the apple juice, and serve in glasses with a wedge
of lime.

PINEAPPLE,
MINT,
AND
GINGER
LEMONADE

—

ليمونادة الأناس والنعناع
والزنجبيل

Preparation time: 10 minutes, plus chilling time
Serves 6–8

thinly pared zest and juice of 8 lemons
scant ¾ cup (5 oz/150 g) superfine (caster) or granulated sugar
2 inch/5 cm piece of fresh ginger, peeled and sliced
20 fresh mint leaves
1¼ cups (½ pint/300 ml) pineapple juice
1 lime, cut into wedges

Put the lemon zest and juice into a heatproof jug, add the
sugar, ginger, and mint leaves, and pour in 4½ cups
(1¾ pints/1 liter) of boiling water. Set aside and let cool and
steep, stirring occasionally. Once cold, strain into another
jug, stir in the pineapple juice, and serve in glasses decorated
with a wedge of lime.

YOGURT
DRINK

شراب الزبادي المحلى

Preparation time: 5 minutes
Serves 2

1 cup (8 fl oz/250 ml) plain (natural) yogurt
1¼ cups (½ pint/300 ml) whole (full-fat) milk
1 vanilla bean (pod), split and seeds removed
clear honey, to taste
pomegranate seeds, to decorate

Put the yogurt, milk, honey, and vanilla seeds into a blender and process until smooth and thoroughly combined. Pour into glasses and decorate with a drizzle of honey and a few pomegranate seeds.

STRAWBERRY
AND
HONEY YOGURT
DRINK

شراب اللبن الزبادي
بالفراولة والعسل

Preparation time: 10 minutes
Serves 2

3 cups (14 oz/400g) hulled and quartered strawberries
generous 2 cups (18 fl oz/500 ml) plain (natural) yogurt
1¼ cups (½ pint/300 ml) milk
juice of 1 lime
clear honey, to taste
⅓ cup (2 oz/50 g) sliced strawberries

Put the strawberries, yogurt, and milk into a blender and process until smooth and thoroughly combined. Pass through a nylon strainer (sieve) into a jug and add the lime juice and honey to taste. Pour in to glasses, add the sliced strawberries, and serve immediately.

SAHLAB

PHOTO PAGE 462

سحلب

Preparation time: 10 minutes
Serves 2

4¼ cups (1¾ pints/1 liter) milk
1 teaspoon sahlab powder or cornstarch (cornflour)
pinch of ground cinnamon
pinch of grated nutmeg
4 tablespoons coarsely chopped pistachio nuts

Mix together a little of the milk and the sahlab powder in a small bowl to a smooth paste. Heat the remaining milk in a saucepan, stir in the paste, cinnamon, and nutmeg. Simmer over low heat, stirring consistently, for 10 minutes until thickened. Pour into heatproof glasses and top with the pistachios. Serve immediately.

JALLAB JUICE

عصير جلاب

Preparation time: 5 minutes
Serves 2–4

ice
6 tablespoons jallab syrup
4 tablespoons raisins
1 tablespoon pine nuts

Fill a jug with ice, pour in the jallab syrup, add 2½ cups
(1 pint/600 ml) of water, and mix well. Pour into glasses, top
with raisins and pine nuts, and serve.

LICORICE JUICE

شراب السوس

Preparation time: 10 minutes, plus resting time
Serves 6

2 tablespoons licorice powder

Put the licorice powder into a bowl, add 5 tablespoons of water,
and mix to a paste. Let stand for 30 minutes. Pour 4¼ cups
(1¾ pints/1 liter) of water into a heatproof jug. Put the licorice
paste into a piece of cheesecloth (muslin) and tie securely with
kitchen string. Put the cheesecloth bag into the jug and chill in
the refrigerator until required. Lift the cheesecloth bag out of
the jug and squeeze out. Pour the licorice juice into glasses
and serve.

MULBERRY SYRUP

شراب التوت

Preparation time: 10–15 minutes
Cooking time: 10 minutes
Makes 4¼ cups (1¾ pints/1 liter)

6½ cups (2¼ lb/1 kg) mulberries
10 cups (4½ lb/2 kg) superfine (caster) or granulated sugar

Wear plastic or latex gloves to protect your hands from stains.
Press the berries through a food mill over a large bowl.
Alternatively, put the berries into a cheesecloth (muslin) bag
and press the juice from them into a large bowl. Discard the
seeds and skins. Press the juice through a strainer to remove
any remaining pieces of flesh. Measure the juice and pour it
into a large saucepan. Add 2 cups (14 oz/400 g) of sugar for
every 1 cup (8 fl oz/250 ml) of juice and stir over low heat until
the sugar has completely dissolved. Increase the heat to high
and bring to a boil, stirring constantly until syrupy. Remove
from the heat and let cool, then store in a sterilized bottle in the
refrigerator. To use, stir 1 tablespoon syrup or to taste into
a glass of water. Add ice and serve.

NONALCOHOLIC POMEGRANATE WINE

نبيذ الرمان المتبل الخالي من الكحول

Preparation time: 50 minutes
Serves 6–8

4¼ cups (1¾ pints/1 liter) pomegranate juice
2 tablespoons pomegranate molasses
juice of 2 oranges
generous 2 cups (18 fl oz/500 ml) apple juice
4 cloves
2 cinnamon sticks
5 juniper berries
pinch of freshly grated nutmeg

Put all the ingredients into a saucepan, set over medium heat, and simmer for 40 minutes so the flavors can develop. Remove from the heat, strain, and serve warm.

ROSE WATER DAIQUIRI

كوكتيل الرام وماء الورد

Preparation time: 5 minutes
Serves 1

½ cup (2¾ oz/70 g) strawberries
crushed ice
4 tablespoons white rum
2 teaspoons Strawberry and Rose Water Jam (see page 475)
1 teaspoon Sugar Syrup (see page 33)
juice of 1 lime

Put the strawberries into a food processor and process to a puree, then pass through a nylon strainer (sieve) into a bowl. Put the crushed ice, strawberry puree, rum, rose water jam, Sugar Syrup, and lime juice into a cocktail shaker, fasten the lid, and shake until a frost forms on the outside. Strain into a chilled cocktail glass and serve immediately.

VODKA AND ORANGE FLOWER WATER COCKTAIL

كوكتيل الفودكا وماء الزهر

Preparation time: 5 minutes
Serves 2

cracked ice
scant ½ cup (3½ fl oz/100 ml) vodka
2 teaspoons orange flower water
2 teaspoons Sugar Syrup (see page 33)
juice of 1 orange
1¼ cups (½ pint/300 ml) club soda (soda water)
rose petals, to decorate
thinly pared slivers of zest of ¼ orange

Put the cracked ice, vodka, orange flower water, Sugar Syrup, and orange juice into a cocktail shaker and shake well until a frost forms on the outside of the shaker. Strain into chilled glasses, fill with club soda (soda water), and decorate with rose petals and slivers of orange zest. Serve immediately.

PICKLES
AND
JAMS

*

المربيات والمخللات

APPLE JAM

مربى التفاح

Preparation time: 20 minutes
Cooking time: 1 hour
Makes 4 medium jars

2¼ lb/1 kg (about 9) apples, peeled, cored, and sliced
2½ cups (1 lb 2 oz/500 g) sugar
2 lemon leaves
juice of ½ lemon

Put the apples, sugar, lemon leaves, and lemon juice into
a large stainless steel saucepan, bring to a boil, and cook
for 1 hour. Remove the pan from the heat and let cool, then
discard the lemon leaves. Ladle the jam into sterilized jars,
leaving a ¼ inch (5 mm) head space, cover, and seal. Store
in the fridge for up to 1 month.

APRICOT JAM

مربى المشمش

Preparation time: 15 minutes, plus resting time
Cooking time: 1 hour 30 minutes
Makes 1 medium jar

1 lb 2 oz/500 g (about 12) apricots, halved and pitted (stoned)
1¼ cups (9 oz/250 g) sugar
3 lemon leaves

Put the apricots into a stainless steel saucepan, sprinkle with
the sugar, and let stand overnight. The next day, put the pan
over medium heat, add the lemon leaves, and bring to a boil.
Partially cover with a lid, reduce the heat, and simmer for
1½ hours. Remove the pan from the heat, ladle the jam into
sterilized jars, leaving a ¼ inch (5 mm) head space, and
let cool. Cover, seal, and store in the fridge for up to 1 month.

ORANGE MARMALADE WITH ROSE WATER AND ALMONDS

—

مربى قشور البرتقال مع ماء الورد واللوز

Preparation time: 10 minutes, plus resting time
Makes 6 medium jars

2¼ lb/1 kg (about 7) oranges
5 cups (2¼ lb/1 kg) sugar
scant ½ cup (3½ fl oz/100 ml) lemon juice
4 tablespoons rose water
scant 1 cup (3½ fl oz/100 g) slivered (flaked) almonds, toasted

Cut the oranges in half and reserve the juice in a bowl. Cut each orange half, including the pith, into ¼ inch/5 mm strips, put them into the reserved juice, and add 4½ cups (1¾ pints/1 liter) of water. Let stand for 2 hours or overnight to draw out the pectin. Put the oranges and their soaking liquid into a heavy stainless steel saucepan, bring to a boil, and boil for 2 hours or until the liquid is reduced by two-thirds. Reduced the heat, add the sugar and lemon juice, and stir until the sugar has dissolved. Increase the heat and boil rapidly for 25 minutes or until the temperature registers 220°f/104.5°c on a candy (sugar) thermometer and setting point is reached. (If you don't have a candy thermometer, test for setting point by removing the pan from the heat and putting a teaspoonful of the marmalade on a chilled saucer. Let it cool, then push the surface with your finger. If it crinkles, setting point has been reached.) Remove the pan from the heat and let cool for 10 minutes. Stir in the rose water and almonds, then ladle into 6 sterilized jars, leaving a ½ inch (1 cm) head space, let cool, cover, and seal. Store in the fridge for up to 1 month.

BLACKBERRY, RASPBERRY, AND HONEY COMPOTE

—

كومبوت العليق والتوت الاسود والعسل

Preparation time: 5 minutes
Cooking time: 5–10 minutes
Makes 2 medium jars

scant ½ cup (3½ fl oz/100 ml) honey
1 tablespoon pomegranate molasses
2½ cups (12 oz/350 g) blackberries
3 cups (12 oz/350 g) raspberries

Pour the honey into a stainless steel saucepan, add scant ½ cup (3½ fl oz/100 ml) of water, and heat gently to dissolve the honey. When the syrup comes to simmering point, add the pomegranate molasses and the berries and remove the pan from the heat. Let the compote cool, then pour into a sterilized 1 pint (18 fl oz/500 ml) jar, leaving a ½ inch (1 cm) head space, let cool, cover, and seal. Store in the fridge for up to 1 month.

SEVILLE ORANGE PRESERVE

محفوظ البرتقال الاشبيلي

Preparation time: 10 minutes, plus resting time
Cooking time: 2 hours 30 minutes
Makes 6 medium jars

2¼ lb/1 kg (about 7) Seville oranges
scant 7½ cups (3¼ lb/1.5 kg) sugar
scant ½ cup (3½ fl oz/100 ml) lemon juice

Cut the oranges in half and reserve the juice in a large bowl. Slice each orange half, including the pith, into ¼ inch/5 mm strips. Put them into the bowl with the juice, pour in 5 cups (3½ pints/2 liters) of water and let stand for 2 hours or overnight to draw out the pectin. Put the oranges and the soaking liquid into a heavy stainless steel saucepan and bring to a boil. Boil for 2 hours or until the liquid has reduced by two-thirds. Reduce the heat, add the sugar and lemon juice, and simmer until the sugar has dissolved. Increase the heat and boil rapidly for 25 minutes or until the temperature registers 220°f/104.5°c on a candy (sugar) thermometer and setting point is reached. (If you don't have a candy thermometer, test for setting point by removing the pan from the heat and putting a teaspoonful of the preserve on a chilled saucer. Let it cool, then push the set surface with your finger. If it crinkles, the setting point has been reached.) Remove from the heat and let cool for 10 minutes. Ladle into 6 sterilized jars, leaving a ½ inch (1 cm) head space, let cool, cover, and seal. Store in the fridge for up to 1 month.

FIG JAM

PHOTO PAGE 473

مربى التين

Preparation time: 5 minutes
Cooking time: 1 hour
Makes 1 medium jar

½ cup (3½ oz/100 g) sugar
2 lemon leaves
1¼ cups (9 oz/250 g) quartered dried figs
¾ cup (3 oz/80 g) blanched almonds

Pour 1 cup (250 ml/8 fl oz) of water into a heavy stainless steel saucepan, add the sugar, and heat gently until the sugar dissolves. Add the lemon leaves and figs. Bring to a boil and cook for 20 minutes, then add the almonds and continue to cook for another 30 minutes. Remove the pan from the heat, ladle the jam into sterilized jars, leaving a ¼ inch (5 mm) head space, let cool, cover, and seal. Store in the fridge for up to 1 month.

FIG JAM

SOUR
CHERRY
JAM

—

مربى الكرز الحامض

Preparation time: 5 minutes, plus resting time
Cooking time: 1 hour
Makes 4 medium jars

2¼ lb/1 kg sour cherries
7½ cups (3¼ lb/1.5 kg) sugar
thinly pared zest and juice of 1 lemon

Put half the cherries in a bowl and sprinkle them with half the
sugar. Let stand overnight to draw out the pectin. Meanwhile,
cut the lemon zest into thin strips. Transfer the cherry and
sugar mixture to a heavy stainless steel saucepan and bring
to a boil. Turn off the heat and let the mixture cool. Add the
remaining cherries, the remaining sugar, and the strips of
lemon zest and bring to a boil. Turn off the heat and let the
mixture cool again. Finally, bring to a boil again, add the lemon
juice, and boil for 20 minutes. Remove the pan from the heat
and let the jam cool for 10 minutes. Ladle into warm sterilized
jars, leaving a ¼ inch (5 mm) head space, let cool, cover, and
seal. Store in the fridge for up to 1 month.

FIG
AND
SESAME
SEED
JAM

—

مربى التين والسمسم

Preparation time: 5 minutes, plus resting time
Cooking time: 30 minutes
Makes 4 medium jars

2¼ lb/1 kg (about 20) figs
5 cups (2¼ lb/1 kg) sugar
½ cup (4 oz/120 g) sesame seeds, toasted

Put the figs into a heavy stainless steel saucepan and sprinkle
the sugar over them. Let stand for 10 minutes, then set over low
heat until the sugar has dissolved. Increase the heat and bring
to a boil. Cook until the mixture has a syrupy consistency.
Remove the pan from the heat, stir in the sesame seeds and
ladle the jam into sterilized jars, leaving a ¼ inch (5 mm)
head space, and let cool. Cover and seal the jam, and store in
the fridge for up to 1 month.

STRAWBERRY AND ROSE WATER JAM

—

مربى الفراولة بماء الورد

Preparation time: 20 minutes, plus resting time
Cooking time: 30 minutes
Makes 3 medium jars

5 cups (1½ lb/700 g) strawberries, hulled and halved
2½ cups (1 lb 2 oz/500 g) sugar
scant ½ cup (3½ fl oz/100 ml) lemon juice
4 tablespoons rose water

Put 2 cups (11 oz/300 g) of the halved strawberries and ½ cup (3½ oz/100 g) of the sugar into a bowl, mix gently, and let stand for 2 hours or overnight to draw out the pectin. Put the strawberry and sugar mixture into a heavy stainless steel pan and set over low heat. When it becomes warm, add the remaining strawberries and remaining sugar and heat gently to dissolve the sugar. Add the lemon juice, increase the heat, and boil for about 15 minutes or until the temperature registers 220°f/104.5°c on a candy (sugar) thermometer and setting point is reached. (If you don't have a candy thermometer, test for setting point by removing the pan from the heat and putting a teaspoonful of the marmalade on a chilled saucer. Let it cool, then push the set surface with your finger. If it crinkles, the setting point has been reached.) Remove the pan from the heat, skim off any scum from the surface of the jam, and stir in the rose water. Ladle into sterilized jars, leaving a ¼ inch (5 mm), head space, let cool, cover, and seal. Store in the fridge for up to 1 month.

PLUM, PEACH, AND ROSE WATER COMPOTE

—

كومبوت البرقوق والدراق
مع ماء الورد

Preparation time: 10 minutes
Cooking time: 20 minutes
Makes 1 medium jar

1 cup (7 oz/200 g) superfine (caster) or granulated sugar
6 plums, halved and pitted (stoned)
2 tablespoons rose water
4 peaches, halved and pitted (stoned)

Pour scant 1 cup (7 fl oz/200 ml) of water into a stainless steel saucepan, stir in the sugar, and heat gently until it has dissolved the sugar. Bring to simmering point, add the plums, and poach for 10 minutes. Add the rosewater and peaches and poach for another 5 minutes. Remove the pan from the heat and let the fruit cool in its syrup for 10 minutes. Spoon the fruit into a sterilized 1 pint (18 fl oz/500 ml) jar and pour in the syrup to cover, leaving a ½ inch (1 cm) head space. Let cool, cover, and seal. Store in the fridge for up to 1 month.

QUINCE PRESERVE

PHOTO PAGE 477

محفوظ السفرجل

Preparation time: 20 minutes
Cooking time: 2 hours
Makes 1 medium jar

thinly pared zest of 7 limes, cut into strips
14 oz/400 g quinces, cored and cut into ½ inch/1 cm cubes
1 cup (7 oz/200 g) superfine (caster) or granulated sugar
4 tablespoons freshly squeezed lime juice

Put the lime zest into a small stainless steel saucepan and pour in water to cover. Bring to a boil and boil for 20 minutes, then drain and set aside. Put the quinces into a separate stainless steel saucepan and pour in water to cover. Bring to a boil, reduce the heat, and simmer for 1 hour. Add the sugar and the lime zest and cook over low heat for 30 minutes. Crush some of the quince with a back of a fork and cook, stirring occasionally, for another 30 minutes. The preserve is ready when the quinces have turned a deep copper color. Stir in the lime juice, remove the pan from the heat, and let cool for 10 minutes. Ladle into a sterilized jar, leaving a ½ inch (1 cm) head space, let cool, cover, and seal. Store in the fridge for up to 1 month.

DATE AND HONEY JAM

مربى التمر والعسل

Preparation time: 10 minutes
Cooking time: 25–30 minutes
Makes 1 large jar

1¼ cups (½ pint/300 ml) honey
1 lb 2 oz/500 g dates, pitted (stoned) and chopped
scant ½ cup (3½ fl oz/100 ml) lemon juice
scant ¾ cup (2¾ oz/70 g) pecan nuts, chopped

Pour generous 2 cups (18 fl oz/500 ml) of water into a heavy stainless steel saucepan, add the honey, and heat gently until it has dissolved. Add the dates and cook for 20 minutes or until they have cooked down into a homogeneous mass. Add the lemon juice and nuts and cook for another 2 minutes. Remove from the heat and let cool for 10 minutes, then ladle into a sterilized 4¼ cup (1¾ pint/1 liter) jar, leaving a ¼ inch (5 mm) head space, let cool, cover, and seal. Store in the fridge for up to 1 month.

QUINCE PRESERVE

DATE PRESERVE

DATE PRESERVE

PHOTO PAGE 478

محفوظ التمر

Preparation time: 20 minutes
Cooking time: 2 hours
Makes 4 medium jars

1 tablespoon coriander seeds
1 teaspoon black peppercorns
1 teaspoon cumin seeds
2 inch/5 cm piece fresh ginger
1½ cups (9 oz/250 g) chopped pitted (stoned) dried dates
1 lb 5 oz/600 g (about 5) tart apples, cored and diced
2 onions, diced
¾ cup (3½ oz/100 g) dried apricots, chopped
⅓ cup (2 oz/50 g) golden raisins (sultanas)
1½ firmly packed cups (11 oz/300 g) brown sugar
generous 2 cups (18 fl oz/500 ml) apple (cider) vinegar

Cut a square piece of cheesecloth (muslin), put the coriander seeds, peppercorns, cumin seeds, and ginger in the center, and tie securely with kitchen string to make a bag. Put all the ingredients and the spice bag into a heavy stainless steel saucepan and heat gently until the sugar dissolves. Cook for 2 hours or until the mixture is sufficiently reduced. Test by drawing a wooden spoon across the bottom of the pan; when it is ready, the mixture will stay apart and reveal the bottom of the pan for a few seconds. Remove the pan from the heat and ladle the preserve into sterilized jars while it is still warm. Stir with a sterilized knife to make sure there are no air pockets at the bottom, and leave a ½ inch (1 cm) head space. Let cool, cover, and seal. Store in the fridge for up to 1 month.

ONION MARMALADE

مرملاد البصل

Preparation time: 10 minutes
Cooking time: 1 hour 15 minutes
Makes 2 medium jars

8 onions, thinly sliced
1 stick (4 oz/120 g) butter, clarified
1 teaspoon fenugreek seeds, toasted and crushed
1 teaspoon ground turmeric
⅓ cup (2 oz/50 g) golden raisins (sultanas)
2 tablespoons sugar
salt and pepper

Melt the butter in a large stainless steel saucepan, and add the fenugreek and turmeric, and cook over low heat, shaking the pan occasionally, for a few minutes until the spices release their aroma. Add the onions, season with salt and pepper, cover the onions with parchment paper, and cook over very low heat for 30 minutes. Add the golden raisins (sultanas) and sugar, cover the onions again, and cook for another 15 minutes. Uncover the onions and cook for another 30 minutes or until they become a deep dark brown color. Remove from the heat and let cool slightly, then ladle into sterilized jars, leaving a ½ inch (1 cm) head space. Let cool, cover, and seal. Store in the fridge for up to 1 month.

PRESERVED PEARS

PHOTO PAGE 481

محفوظ الاجاص

Preparation time: 15 minutes
Cooking time: 30 minutes
Makes 1 large jar

1⅔ cups (14 fl oz/400 ml) apple (cider) vinegar
1¾ cups (12 oz/350 g) superfine (caster) or granulated sugar
2 cinnamon sticks
2 teaspoons coriander seeds
2 teaspoons ground allspice
large pinch of saffron threads, lightly crushed
6 Bosc (Conference) pears, peeled with the stem intact

Pour the vinegar and scant ½ cup (3½ fl oz/100 ml) of water into a heavy stainless steel saucepan, add the sugar, and heat gently to dissolve the sugar. When the liquid comes to a simmer, add the cinnamon, coriander seeds, saffron, and pears, and poach for about 20 minutes or until they become soft but still hold their shape. Remove the pan from the heat and let the pears cool in the poaching liquid for 10 minutes. Put the pears into a sterilized 1-quart (1¾ pint/1 liter) jar, ladle in the poaching liquid to cover, leaving a ½ inch (1 cm) head space, let cool, cover, and seal. Store in the fridge for up to 1 month.

EGGPLANT RELISH

مشهي الباذنجان

Preparation time: 15 minutes
Cooking time: 20–25 minutes, plus chilling time
Makes 1 medium jar

2 eggplants (aubergines), cut into ½ inch/1 cm dice
4 tablespoons olive oil
2 shallots, diced
1 cinnamon stick
4 large garlic cloves, chopped
3 green chiles, diced
2 teaspoons chopped fresh ginger
2 tablespoons superfine (caster) or granulated sugar
4 tablespoons white wine vinegar
2 tablespoons chopped parsley
salt and pepper

Preheat the oven to 400°f/200°c/Gas Mark 6. Put the eggplant (aubergine) dice into a roasting pan, pour 3 tablespoons of the oil over them, season with salt and pepper, and toss well. Roast, turning them occasionally, for 20 minutes or until evenly browned. Meanwhile, heat the remaining oil in a skillet or frying pan, add the shallots and cinnamon stick, and cook over low heat, stirring occasionally, for 5–8 minutes until the shallots are starting to brown slightly. Stir in the garlic, chiles, and ginger and cook for another 2 minutes, then season with salt and pepper and stir in the sugar and 2 tablespoons of the vinegar. Cook until slightly reduced. Remove the pan from the heat and gently fold the diced eggplants. Let cool completely, then chill in the fridge. Stir in the remaining vinegar and the chopped parsley, ladle into a sterilized ¾ pint (12 fl oz/350 ml) jar, leaving a ½ inch (1 cm) head space, let cool, cover, and seal. Store in the fridge for up to 1 week.

PRESERVED PEARS

PRESERVED LEMONS

PRESERVED LEMONS

PHOTO PAGE 482

—

محفوظ الليمون

Preparation time: 10 minutes
Makes 1 large jar

6 unwaxed lemons
6 tablespoons coarse sea salt
6 fresh bay leaves
2 tablespoons pink peppercorns, lightly crushed
juice of 7 lemons

Cut a deep cross in the lemons, leaving the quarters attached at the tip. Stuff each lemon with 1 tablespoon salt, 1 bay leaf, and 1 teaspoon peppercorns. Pack them into a sterilized 1 quart (1¾ pint/1 liter) jar. Cover with lemon juice, and seal. Store in the fridge for at least 1 month before eating.

PICKLES

—

مخللات

Preparation time: 5 minutes
Cooking time: 10 minutes
Makes 2 medium jars

1½ lb/700 g pickling cucumbers (fresh gherkins)
3 tablespoons salt
1 tablespoons white wine vinegar

Put the cucumbers (gherkins) into sterilized jars. Bring 5 cups (2 pints/1.2 liters) water to a boil, then remove from the heat. Stir in the salt and vinegar cool. Pour the cooled liquid into the jars, leaving a ½ inch (1 cm) space, cover, and seal. Store in the fridge for up to 3 months, but wait for 2 weeks before eating.

STUFFED EGGPLANTS WITH NUTS AND PARSLEY IN OLIVE OIL

—

باذنجان محشو
بالمكسرات والبقدونس
بزيت الزيتون

Preparation time: 15 minutes, plus resting time
Cooking time: 1 minute
Makes 1 large jar

3 small eggplants (aubergines)
1 cup (4 oz/120 g) shelled walnuts, finely chopped
3 garlic cloves, crushed
2 tablespoons white wine vinegar
2 tablespoons coarse sea salt
1 tablespoon superfine (caster) or granulated sugar
1 small bunch of fresh parsley, chopped
1 cup (8 fl oz/250 ml) olive oil

Put the eggplants (aubergines) into a stainless steel pan, pour in water to cover, and bring to a boil. Simmer for 1 minute, then drain. Cut a slit along each eggplant, put them in a baking pan, cover with plastic wrap (clingfilm), and put something heavy on top to weight them down and draw out the moisture. Let stand overnight. The next day, mix together the walnuts, garlic, vinegar, salt, sugar, parsley, and 1 tablespoon of the olive oil in a bowl. Stuff each eggplant with the mixture and pack them into a sterilized 1 quart (1¾ pint/1 liter) jar. Pour in the oil to cover, leaving a ½ inch (1 cm) head space, cover, and seal. Store in the fridge for up to 1 week.

RED BELL PEPPER PUREE

PHOTO PAGE 485

—

معجون الفلفل الاحمر

Preparation time: 10–15 minutes
Cooking time: 40–50 minutes
Makes 1 medium jar

grated zest and juice of 1 orange
pinch of saffron threads
6 Romano bell peppers
10 garlic gloves, unpeeled
3 tablespoons olive oil, plus extra for packing
2 teaspoons sugar
2 teaspoons sea salt
2 teaspoons pepper

Preheat the oven to 400°f/200°c/Gas Mark 6. Pour the orange juice into a bowl, add the orange zest and saffron threads, and let soak. Meanwhile, put the bell peppers and garlic into a roasting pan, pour the oil over them, and toss well. Tuck the garlic under the bell peppers so that it doesn't dry out and roast for 20 minutes or until the bell peppers are charred and the garlic is soft. Remove the pan from the oven and, when they are cool enough to handle, peel off the skins from the bell peppers and garlic and discard. Put the bell peppers, garlic, orange juice mixture, olive oil, sugar, salt, and pepper into a food processor or blender and process until smooth and combined. Scrape the puree into a saucepan and reduce over high heat for about 20 minutes, then remove from the heat and let cool. Spoon the puree into a sterilized 1½ cup (12 fl oz/350 ml) jar and carefully pour a film of olive oil on top, leaving a ¼ inch (5 mm) head space. Cover, seal, and store in the fridge for up to 1 month. Cover and seal, then store in a cool, dark place.

PICKLED TURNIPS

—

مخلل اللفت

Preparation time: 15 minutes, plus resting time
Cooking time: 10 minutes
Makes 4 medium jars

2 lb/900 g turnips, cut into ¼ inch/5 mm slices
2 uncooked beets (beetroots), peeled and sliced
1 tablespoon pickling salt
1 tablespoon sugar

Put the turnips and beet (beetroot) slices into a bowl, add the salt, and toss well. Let stand for 2 hours. Meanwhile, bring 6¼ cups (2½ pints/1.5 liters) of water to a boil in a saucepan, then remove from the heat and let cool. Stir in the sugar. Pack the vegetables into sterilized jars, pour in the sweetened water to cover, leaving a ½ inch (1 cm) head space, then cover, and seal. Store in the fridge for 1 week before eating, and use within 3 months.

RED BELL PEPPER PUREE

MARINATED OLIVES

GARLIC AND CHILI OIL

زيت بالفلفل الحار
والثوم

Preparation time: 10 minutes
Cooking time: 15–20 minutes
Makes 1 medium jar

10 garlic cloves, peeled and sliced
10 red chiles, sliced
1 cup (8 fl oz/250 ml) olive oil

Put the garlic, chiles, and oil into a saucepan and bring to a boil over medium heat, then reduce the heat and simmer for 10 minutes until the garlic starts turning brown. Remove the pan from the heat and let cool. When cool, pour into a sterilized ¾ pint (12 fl oz/350 ml) jar, leaving a ½ inch (1 cm) head space, cover, and seal. Store in the fridge and use within 1 week.

MARINATED OLIVES

PHOTO PAGE 486

الزيتون المتبل

Preparation time: 10 minutes
Makes 4 small jars

4 cups (14 oz/400 g) green olives
6 thyme sprigs, leaves only
2 garlic cloves, thinly sliced
1 lemon, cut into 8 2 long red chiles, halved lengthwise
1 cup (8 fl oz/250 ml) olive oil

Mix the olives with thyme and garlic in a bowl. Pack into 4 ½ pint (8 fl oz/250 ml) jars, adding 2 pieces of lemon and half a chile to each jar. Pour in the oil to cover, leaving a ½ inch (1 cm) gap. Cover the jars and seal, then store in the fridge.

PICKLED CAULIFLOWER

مخلل القرنبيط

Preparation time: 10–15 minutes, plus resting time
Cooking time: 25 minutes
Makes 1 medium jar

1 cup (4 oz/120g) cauliflower florets
½ cup (4 fl oz/120 ml) white wine vinegar
1 tablespoon sugar
1 tablespoon sea salt
3 star anise
1 teaspoon juniper berries
1 teaspoon black peppercorns
1 teaspoon mustard seeds
½ teaspoon cloves
5 garlic cloves, peeled
salt

Put cauliflower into a strainer (sieve), sprinkle with salt, and let stand for 1 hour. Pour scant ½ cup (3½ fl oz/100 ml) of water and the vinegar into a saucepan, add the salt and sugar, and heat until the sugar has dissolved. Add all the spices to the liquid and simmer for 20 minutes. Rinse the cauliflower and pack into a sterilized ¾ pint (12 fl oz/350 ml) jar with the garlic cloves. Pour the hot brine over them, leaving a ½ inch (1 cm) gap, let cool, then seal. Store in the fridge for up to 3 months.

GUEST CHEFS

✶

ضيف الطهاة

GREG MALOUF

Greg Malouf has inspired
a generation of young
chefs and transformed the
Australian restaurant scene
with his passion for the
flavors of the Middle East
and North Africa. Drawing
on his cultural heritage and
European training, Greg
has forged a unique style
of cooking that combines
Middle Eastern tradition with
contemporary flair.

CHICKPEA-BATTERED ZUCCHINI FLOWERS STUFFED WITH GOAT CHEESE AND MINT

Preparation time: 20 minutes
Cooking time: 5–10 minutes
Serves 4

For the chickpea batter
13 fl oz (375 ml) beer
1¼ cups (5 oz/150 g) gram (chickpea) flour
2¼ cups (9 oz/250 g) self-rising flour
½ cup (2 oz/50 g) cornflour
½ teaspoon cumin
1 pinch baking (bicarbonate of) soda
salt

4 oz/120 g goat cheese
1 teaspoon dried mint
1 teaspoon fresh parsley, chopped
2 tablespoons extra-virgin olive oil
12 baby zucchini (courgettes) with flowers attached
generous 2 cups (18 fl oz/500 ml) olive oil and vegetable oil
    blend, for deep frying
½ cup (2 oz/50 g) all-purpose (plain) flour, for dusting
salt

First make the batter. Pour the beer into a mixing bowl and
whisk the gram (chickpea) flour, self-rising flour and cornflour.
Add the cumin, salt and baking (bicarbonate of) soda and then
set aside for half and hour before using. Mash the cheese with
the mint, parsley and extra virgin olive oil. Carefully open each
zucchini (courgette) flower and pinch out the stamen. Roll a
lump of the cheese stuffing into a thumb-sized sausage shape
between the palms of your hands and gently stuff it into the
flower. Twist the top of the flower to seal. Heat the olive oil
and vegetable oils to 400°F/200°C (when a blob of batter will
sizzle to the surface and color within 30 seconds). Hold the
zucchini and carefully dust each flower in the flour and then
the chickpea batter. Carefully place in the oil, cooking no more
than four at a time, until the batter turns crisp and golden.
Remove and drain on kitchen paper. Season with salt and
serve immediately.

Preparation time: 30 minutes, plus cooling time
Cooking time: 1 hour 10 minutes
Serves 4

6 squab (pigeons)
scant ½ cup (3½ fl oz/100 ml) olive oil
2 medium onion, finely chopped
2 garlic cloves, finely chopped
½ teaspoon ground ginger
12 threads saffron, lightly roasted and crushed
1 teaspoon cinnamon
1 teaspoon ground cumin
1 bullet chile, seeded and finely chopped
scant ¼ cup (2 fl oz/50 ml) sherry
1 pint 7 fl oz/800 ml chicken stock
4 eggs
5 tablespoons fresh parsley, chopped
5 tablespoons fresh cilantro (coriander), chopped
11 sheets phyllo (filo) pastry
1¼ sticks (5 oz/150 g) butter, melted
scant 1 cup (3½ oz/100 g) flaked almonds,
    fried in vegetable oil and drained
scant 1 cup (3½ oz/100 g) confectioners' (icing) sugar,
    sifted with 1 tablespoon ground cinnamon
salt and pepper

Wash the squab and pat them dry with kitchen paper. Remove the legs and breasts, and season with salt and pepper. Heat half the oil in a heavy pan and sauté the squab until golden brown. Add the onions, garlic, ginger, saffron, cinnamon, cumin and chile, adding more oil if necessary. Stir so the squab is well coated with spices. Add the sherry and stock, bring to a boil, then lower heat and simmer for 45-50 minutes, or until the squab is tender. When cool enough, remove the meat from the squab, discarding skin and bones, and shred it finely. Reduce the poaching liquid by half and then add the eggs and whisk until well combined. Pour this mixture into a small saucepan, season and scramble over gentle heat until creamy and nearly set. Stir in the parsley and cilantro, then allow the mixture to cool completely. Stir the meat into the egg mixture and refrigerate until ready to use. To make the pies, work with one sheet of pastry at a time. Lay one sheet on the work surface and brush with melted butter. Fold in half then with another sheet repeat the same. Brush one sheet with butter and lay the other sheet across to form a cross. Place the phyllo (filo) cross in the base of an oiled small pan pushing the phyllo into the sides. Scatter with 2 teaspoons of fried almonds then spoon on the meat-egg mixture till it is level with the top of the pan. Brush the top of the pastry with melted butter and then bring the surrounding pastry sides up and over the filling to make a flat surface. Refrigerate until ready to bake. Place the pan in the centre of an oven, preheated to 350°F/180°C/Gas Mark 4 and bake for 15-18 minutes until golden brown. Remove from the oven and turn out the pie from the pan to a plate and sprinkle with cinnamon dust.

Preparation time: 10 minutes
Cooking time: 5 minutes
Serves 4

For the dukkah
8 tablespoons sesame seeds, lightly toasted
4 tablespoons coriander seeds, roasted and crushed
3 tablespoons cumin seeds, roasted and crushed
scant ⅓ cup (2 oz/50 g) hazelnuts, toasted, peeled & crushed

4 eggs
1 teaspoon sea salt
½ teaspoon white pepper
all-purpose (plain) flour, for dusting
vegetable oil, for deep frying

First make the dukkah. Roast each ingredient separately, and rub away as much of the brown skin from the hazelnuts as you can. Pound the seeds using a mortar and pestle or whiz them carefully in a spice or coffee grinder. When you grind the sesame seeds and hazelnuts be careful not to over grind them as they will disintegrate into an oily paste. Soft boil the eggs for 3 minutes. Cool down under running water and peel carefully. Season with salt and pepper, dust them in flour and then deep fry each egg for 1-1½ minutes, or until golden brown. Remove from the oil and immediately roll them in dukkah.

BLOOD ORANGE AND STRAWBERRY SALAD WITH PINENUT
PRALINE ICE CREAM AND ORANGE BLOSSOM CARAMEL

Preparation time: 1 hour, plus freezing time
Cooking time: 15–20 minutes
Serves 4

For the pine nut praline
150 g superfine (caster) sugar
2 tablespoons water
scant 2 cups (7 oz/200 g) pine nuts

For the pine nut praline ice cream
scant 2¼ cups (9 oz/250 g) superfine (caster) sugar
scant 1 cup (7 fl oz/200 ml) water
8 egg yolks
1 pint 7 fl oz/800 ml thickened cream
1 vanilla pod, split lengthways and scraped
½ cup (4 oz/120 g) pine nut praline

For the orange blossom caramel
½ cup (3½ oz/100 g) caster (superfine) sugar
generous ½ cup (¼ pint/150 ml) strained orange juice
2 tablespoons orange blossom water
4 blood oranges, peeled and cut into segments
2 punnets strawberries, hulled and cut in half
1 punnet blueberries

Place the sugar and water in a pan and heat slowly to dissolve
the sugar. Bring to the boil and cook for five minutes until the
syrup reaches the thread stage at around 225°F/110°C. Stir in
the pine nuts, which will make the sugar mixture crystallize
as the oils come out of the nuts. Turn the heat down a little
and stir gently until the crystallized sugar re-dissolves to
a caramel. This will take around 10–15 minutes. Carefully
pour onto a baking tin lined with greased foil. Smooth with
the back of a fork and allow to cool down and harden. When
cold, bash it with a rolling pin to break into chunks and then
pound to crumbs in mortar and pestle. The praline should
be the consistency of breadcrumbs. Put the water, sugar
and vanilla pod in a pan and bring to the boil, stirring so the
sugar is dissolved. Lower the heat and simmer for 5 minutes.
Meanwhile, place the egg yolks in an electric mixer and whisk
for 5 minutes until they are fluffy. Reduce the speed of the
mixer and pour over the syrup. Then add the cream and whisk
quickly to incorporate, then turn off the motor. Pour the
mixture into your ice cream machine and churn according to
the manufacturer's instructions. Just before it is ready to be
transferred to the freezer, add the praline and let the machine
work it through the mixture. Firm up in the freezer before
serving. In a pan slowly boil ½ cup (3½ oz/100 g) superfine
(caster) sugar with half the orange juice. Once the sugar has
caramelized add the remaining orange juice. Allow to cool
before adding orange blossom water. Place the oranges,
strawberries and blueberries in a large bowl. Scoop ice-cream
onto the fruits. Drizzle with caramel and sprinkle with praline.

KAMAL
MOUZAWAK

—

*Kamal Mouzawak is the
founder of Souk el Tayeb,
Lebanon's first farmers'
market. Through his work
at the market and its sister
restaurant, Tawlet, both in
Beirut, Kamal is seeking to
protect Lebanon's culinary
heritage, raise awareness
of local producers, and
create a forum for them
to sell their wares.*

Tawlet, Chalhoub building,
22 ground floor, Nahar
Street 12, Beirut, Lebanon

VEGETABLE FREEKEH

Preparation time: 15 minutes
Cooking time: 50 minutes
Serves 6

3 onions
5 carrots
6 zucchini (courgettes)
4 tablespoons olive oil
2 cups (12 oz/350 g) freekeh
7 oz/200 g broccoli
7 oz/200 g cauliflower
1 tablespoon ground coriander
salt and pepper

Peel and dice fine the onions, carrots and zucchini (courgettes).
Heat the olive oil and sauté the onions and the carrots. Wash
the freekeh, drain well, and add to the onions. Season with salt
and pepper and cook over a low flame for 40 minutes, until the
freekeh is cooked. Add the broccoli and the cauliflower, and
cook for 5 minutes more. Serve hot.

KEBBET BATATA

Preparation time: 10 minutes
Cooking time: 20 minutes
Serves 4

2¼ lb/1 kg new potatoes, peeled
2 scallions (spring onions)
2 marjoram sprigs
2 basil sprigs
1 cup (6 oz/175 g) fine bulgur wheat, soaked in water for
    10 minutes and squeezed out in cheesecloth (muslin)
salt

Place the potatoes in a pan of boiling water and cook until
tender. Finely chop the scallions (spring onions) in a blender
or mini food processor, then add the basil and marjoram and
process briefly. Add the bulgur wheat and process for 1 minute
more; the bulgur should be well combined with the herbs and
have taken on a green color. Mash the potato with a fork and
combine with the bulgur wheat mixture. Serve immediately.

STUFFED SQUID

Preparation time: 10 minutes
Cooking time: 45–60 minutes
Serves 6

1 large squid, around 2¼ lb/1 kg in weight
2 tomatoes, diced
1 onion, chopped
1 bunch of fresh cilantro (coriander), chopped
1 cup brown rice, cooked
2 tablespoons olive oil
juice of 2 lemons
salt and pepper

Preheat the oven to 400°F/200°C/Gas Mark 6. Clean the squid under cold running water. Combine the tomato, onion, cilantro (coriander), rice, olive oil, and lemon juice. Season with salt and pepper and mix well. Stuff the cavity of the squid with mixture. Put in an ovenproof dish, add ½ cup/125 ml of water and cook in the oven for 45–60 minutes, until the squid is cooked and lightly browned. Cut into slices and serve.

SIYADIEH

Preparation time: 15 minutes
Cooking time: 30 minutes
Serves 4

vegetable oil, for frying
2 sea bass, filleted, head and bones retained
5 onions, sliced
½ cup (2 oz/50 g) pine nuts
1 tablespoon ground cumin
generous 1½ cups (11 oz/300 g) long grain rice
1 tablespoon cornstarch (cornflour)
juice of 1 lemon
salt

Heat the oil in a deep-fryer to 350°F/180°C or until a cube of bread browns in 30 seconds. Salt the sea bass fillets, then deep-fry in the hot oil until golden. Drain on kitchen paper. Deep-fry the onion in batches, until golden. Drain on kitchen paper. Fry the pine nuts in 1 tablespoon of vegetable oil until golden. Drain on kitchen paper. Bring 5 pints/3 liters of water to a boil in a pan, add the fish head and bones, ⅔ of the fried onions, the cumin, and ½ teaspoon of salt. Simmer for 20 minutes, then pass through a strainer (sieve) and set aside. Put the rice in a pan and pour in enough of the fish stock to cover. Cook the rice over a low heat until it has absorbed all of the liquid. Meanwhile, bring the remainder of the fish stock to a boil in a small pan. Dilute 1 tablespoon of cornstarch (cornflour) in 3 tablespoons of water and stir into the stock. Stir until the stock has thickened, then add the lemon juice and season. Serve the rice hot, topped with the fish, the rest of the fried onions, the roasted pine nuts, and the sauce on the side.

JOE BARZA

Born in Tyr, Lebanon, Joe Barza was first influenced by traditional Lebanese cuisine as a child in his mother's kitchen. After a successful career culminating in positions at some of Lebanon's finest restaurants, Joe has gone on to host a number of television shows and to run his own culinary consultancy.

Joe Barza Culinary Consultancy, Hoshar building, ground floor, Horsg Kfoury, Badaro, Beirut, Lebanon

FREEKEH WITH FRESH OCTOPUS

Preparation time: 15 minutes
Cooking time: 20 minutes
Serves 4

1 tablespoon olive oil
1 onion, finely chopped
1 garlic clove, peeled and finely chopped
2 tablespoon fresh cilantro (coriander) finely chopped
3½ oz/100 g octopus, cooked and cut into cubes
generous 1 cup (7 oz/200 g) freekeh, soaked in cold water
    for 24 hours and drained
2 cups (18 fl oz/500 ml) fish stock
1 teaspoon lemon juice
1 tablespoon pine nuts, roasted
1 tablespoon sesame seeds, roasted
sliced lemon, to serve
salt and pepper

Heat the olive oil in a medium pan and cook the onion, garlic, cilantro (coriander) for 5 minutes until softened. Add the octopus and season with salt and pepper. Add the freekeh to the pan and cook until it becomes translucent. Pour in a small amount of the fish stock and cook, stirring occasionally, until all of the liquid is absorbed. Keep adding small amouts of fish stock until the freekeh is cooked. Add the lemon juice and a dash of olive oil. Remove from the heat and place in a serving dish. Scatter over the pine nuts and sesame seeds, and garnish with sliced lemon. Serve immediately.

LEBANESE FATTOUSH
WRAPPED IN AKKAOUI CHEESE

Preparation time: 10 minutes
Serves 4

For the fattoush
3½ cups (7 oz/200 g) romaine lettuce, shredded
2 tablespoons fresh parsley, chopped
3 tablespoons purslane leaves
2 thyme sprigs
½ green bell pepper, chopped
4 tomatoes, chopped into quarters
2 radishes, finely chopped
1 scallion (spring onion), sliced
1 tablespoon fresh mint, chopped

For the dressing
1 teaspoon lemon juice
1 teaspoon red wine vinegar
1 garlic clove, crushed
4 teaspoons olive oil
pinch of sumac
salt and pepper

4 slices of Akkaoui cheese
4 grissini sticks

Combine all of the fattoush ingredients in a large bowl. Whisk all of the dressing ingredients together in a small bowl. Season with salt and pepper to taste. Pour the dressing over the fattoush and mix well. Distribute the cheese slices between 4 serving plates and place a spoonful of fattoush on each one. Roll up each slice of cheese to form a wrap. Garnish each wrap with a grissini stick and serve.

FISH MOGHRABIEH WITH SAFFRON

Preparation time: 10 minutes
Cooking time: 30 minutes
Serves 4

1½ cups (9 oz/250 g) giant couscous
1¾ pints/1 liter fish stock
pinch saffron
1 tablespoon of olive oil
2 tablespoons butter
½ onion, finely chopped
2 oz/50 g canned chickpeas, drained
1 teaspoon lemon juice
1 tablespoon fresh cream
pinch lemon zest
pinch salt
1 tablespoon fresh cilantro (coriander), finely chopped
pinch dried coriander
1 tablespoon Parmesan cheese, grated
1 teaspoon white wine
pinch dried cumin
9 oz/250 g sea bass fillet, sliced

For the sauce
½ pint/300 ml fish stock
1 tablespoon cornstarch (cornflour)
pinch saffron
1 tablespoon pinenuts, roasted
20 g fresh cilantro (coriander) leaves

Preheat the oven to 275°F/140°C/Gas Mark 1. Place the giant couscous in a large pan over a medium heat and add the fish stock. Add the saffron and simmer over a low heat until the couscous is almost cooked. Drain the couscous, reserving the fish stock, and set aside. Heat the olive oil and butter in a skillet or frying pan, add the onions and cook until softened. Add the couscous to the onions and stir to combine. Add a small amount of the reserved fish stock and cook, stirring occasionally, until the liquid is fully absorbed. Continue adding small amounts of fish stock until the couscous is cooked. Add the chickpeas, lemon juice, cream, lemon zest, salt, cilantro (coriander), dried coriander, Parmesan, white wine, and a pinch of cumin and stir. Remove from heat and set aside. Place the fish in an ovenproof dish with any remaining fish stock and cook in the preheated oven for 20 minutes. Make the sauce. Put the fish stock, cornstarch (cornflour), and saffron into a pan and cook over a low heat until thickened. Divide the couscous between 4 serving bowls and place the poached fish on top. Garnish with roasted pinenuts and cilantro (coriander). Pour the sauce around the couscous and serve.

JAD
YOUSSEF

*Jad Youssef and his partner
Aga Ilska opened the first
Yalla Yalla, in Green's Court,
Soho in late 2008. The
restaurant was an instant
hit, and a second restaurant
opened early in 2010. The
template for informal Lebanese
cuisine has provided Jad and
Aga with the eagerness to
spread the Yalla Yalla concept
even further, and they are
actively looking for additional
restaurant sites in London.*

Yalla Yalla, 12
Winsley Street
London, W1W 8HQ

*Preparation time: 10 minutes, plus marinating time
Cooking time: 40 minutes
Serves 6*

1 bunch fresh thyme
4 tablespoons olive oil
7 tablespoons pomegranate molasses, plus extra to drizzle
4 tablespoons red wine vinegar
18 lamb cutlets
salt and pepper

For the dip:
5 baby eggplants (aubergines)
1 red bell pepper, diced
½ bunch fresh parsley, finely chopped
3 scallions (spring onions), chopped
1 garlic clove, grated
olive oil
2 tablespoons lemon juice
salt
pomegranate seeds, to decorate

To make the marinade, chop the thyme finely and mix with the olive oil, pomegranate molasses and red wine vinegar. Season the marinade with salt and black pepper and pour over the lamb cutlets. Leave to marinate in the fridge for at least 6 hours. Broil (grill) the eggplant (aubergine), either under a preheated broiler (grill) or in a ridged griddle pan, for 25–30 minutes, until the skin has blackened all over. Peel the black skin off and finely chop the flesh. Mix the eggplant with the diced red bell pepper, chopped parsley, scallions (spring onions), and grated garlic. Add the olive oil, lemon juice and salt. Chargrill the lamb cutlets for 3 minutes on each side, until cooked through. Serve the lamb with the eggplant dip, drizzled with pomegranate molasses and pomegranate seeds.

Preparation time: 25 minutes
Cooking time: 40 minutes
Serves 6

1½ tablespoons ground cumin
1 tablespoon extra virgin olive oil, plus extra for frying
6 sea bass fillets
zest of 2 lemons
zest of 2 oranges
zest of 1 lime
2¼ lb/1 kg basmati rice
2 onions, chopped
3 garlic cloves, grated
2 red bell peppers, chopped
1 red chile
4 tomatoes, chopped
1 bunch cilantro (coriander)
3 limes, to garnish
salt and pepper

Combine 1 tablespoon of the cumin, the olive oil and a pinch of salt and pepper in a small bowl. Place the sea bass fillets in a flat dish and pour the cumin and oil mixture over, rubbing it into the fish with your hands. Set aside. Heat a splash of olive oil in a pan and cook the lemon, orange and lime zests for 1–2 minutes. Add the rice, season with salt and add 2½ pints/ 1.5 liters water. Bring to a boil and simmer the rice, covered, for 20 minutes until fluffy. Meanwhile, heat a little olive oil in a skillet or frying pan over a low heat. Add the onion and garlic to the pan and cook for 5 minutes, until softened but not colored. Add the red bell pepper and chile and cook, stirring occasionally, for 7–8 minutes. Add the chopped tomatoes and cook over a low heat for 20 minutes. Add the cilantro (coriander) and season with salt, pepper and the remaining cumin. Preheat the broiler (grill). Broil (grill) the sea bass, skin side up for about 5 minutes, until cooked. Serve the fish on a bed of the citrus-scented rice, with the spiced tomato and cilantro sauce on the side. Garnish with a half lime.

ROLAND SEMAAN

Roland Semaan has an array of hospitality experience, from the Intercontinental Hotel in Beirut, Lebanon, to Great Performances, B.R. Guest Restaurant Group, and Hilton Hotels in New York. Desiring to open a neighborhood restaurant, Roland created Balade, an authentic Lebanese Pitza and Grill in Manhattan's East Village.

Balade, 208 First Avenue, New York, NY 10009

LABNEH WITH GARLIC

Preparation time: 10 minutes, plus resting time
Serves 6

9 cups (4½ lbs/2 kg) plain (natural) yogurt
1 tablespoon dried mint
½ tablespoon salt
4 garlic cloves, crushed
Lebanese bread, to serve

Line a strainer (sieve) with a double thickness of cheesecloth (muslin) and set over a large bowl. Pour in the yogurt and let strain for about 6 hours, until the water has drained off. Add the mint, salt and garlic and stir to combine. Serve with Lebanese bread.

MOUHAMMARA

Preparation time: 15 minutes
Serves 6

2 red bell pepper, finely chopped
generous 2 cups (9 oz/250 g) walnuts
1 tablespoon salt
2 tablespoons ground cumin
2 teaspoons cayenne pepper
5 tablespoons pomegranate seeds
juice of 1 lemon
8 tablespoons olive oil
Lebanese bread, to serve

Process the bell pepper in a food processor until smooth. Press the pepper into a strainer (sieve) to remove any excess water. Process the walnuts in a food processor until coarsely ground. Combine the bell pepper, walnuts, salt, cumin, cayenne pepper, pomegranate seeds, lemon juice and olive oil in a bowl. Serve with Lebanese bread.

ANISSA HELOU

Anissa Helou is a writer, journalist, broadcaster and blogger. Born and raised in Beirut, Lebanon, she knows the Mediterranean as only a well-traveled native can. Helou is the author of numerous award-winning cookbooks, owns a cooking school in London and runs culinary tours to Lebanon, Turkey, Morocco and other Mediterranean countries.

Anissa's School
www.anissas.com

HUMMUS KHAWALI

Preparation time: 10 minutes
Serves 4

14 oz/400 g canned chickpeas
7 tablespoons tahini
juice of 1 lemon
1 tablespoon Aleppo pepper paste
½ tablespoon pomegranate syrup
¼ teaspoon ground cumin
fine sea salt
Aleppo pepper
extra virgin olive oil, to drizzle
pita bread, to serve

Drain and rinse the chickpeas and put in a food processor. Add the tahini, lemon juice, pepper paste and pomegranate syrup and process until very smooth. Transfer to a mixing bowl. Add the cumin and salt to taste. Mix well. If the hummus is too thick, loosen it by adding a little water or lemon juice. Taste and adjust the seasoning. Spoon the hummus into a shallow serving dish and, with the back of a spoon, spread it across the dish, raising it slightly at the edges and in the centre, so that you create a shallow groove. Sprinkle a little Aleppo pepper over the raised edges and the middle. Drizzle a little olive oil in the groove. Serve with pita bread.

FATAYER BI S'BANEGH
BAKED TRIANGLES

Preparation time: 1 hour
Cooking time: 15–25 minutes
Makes 28

1 medium onion, finely chopped
sea salt
½ teaspoon finely ground black pepper
2 tablespoons sumac
14 oz/400 g spinach, thinly sliced
2 tablespoons pine nuts
juice of 1 lemon
2 tablespoons extra virgin olive oil
1 x 14 oz/400 g packet phyllo (filo) pastry
4 oz/120 g unsalted butter, melted

Put the chopped onion into a small bowl. Add a little salt, the pepper and sumac and, with your fingers, rub the seasonings into the onion to soften it. Put the chopped spinach in a large bowl and sprinkle with a little salt. Rub the salt in with your hands until the spinach is wilted. Squeeze the spinach to remove any liquid. Transfer the spinach to a clean mixing bowl and separate the leaves. Add the onion to the spinach, together with the pine nuts, lemon juice and olive oil. Mix well. Taste and adjust the seasoning if necessary – the filling should be strongly flavored. Place the filling in a strainer (sieve) to remove any excess liquid. Lay one sheet of phyllo (filo) pastry on a work surface. Brush it with butter and fold in half lengthways, then brush it with butter again. Place 2 tablespoons of filling at the top end corner nearest to you and fold the other corner over the filling to make a triangle. Carefully pick up the triangle and fold it over, and over, again and again, keeping to the triangle shape, until you have reached the end. Brush with butter every two or three folds. Trim any loose ends. Brush with butter on both sides and place on a nonstick baking sheet, loose side down. Cover with cling film and finish making the triangles following the same method. You should end up with 28 triangles. Preheat the oven to 425°F/220°C/Gas Mark 7. Bake the triangles in the preheated oven for 15–25 minutes, or until crisp and golden brown all over. Let cool on a wire rack before serving.

LAMB STEWED IN YOGURT

Preparation time: 15 minutes
Cooking time: 1 hour 10 minutes
Serves 4

2¼ lb/1 kg lamb from the shank end of the leg, boned and cut
    into medium-sized pieces
1 tablespoon coarse sea salt
16 baby onions, peeled
2 tablespoons unsalted butter
1 bunch fresh cilantro (coriander), finely chopped
7 garlic cloves, crushed
4½ cups (2¼ lb /1 kg) Greek style yogurt
1 egg, whisked
vermicelli rice, to serve

Put the meat and 2 pints/1.25 liters water in a large saucepan. Place over a medium heat. As the water is about to boil, skim the surface clean, then simmer, covered, for 45 minutes. Add the salt, and onions and simmer for 15 minutes more, or until the onions and meat are cooked. Melt the butter in a skillet or frying pan over a medium heat. Add the chopped cilantro (coriander) and crushed garlic and cook for 1–2 minutes, or until the cilantro is softened, but not browned. Take off the heat. Put the yogurt in a large pan. Add the whisked egg and mix well. Place over a medium heat and bring to a boil, stirring constantly to prevent the yogurt from curdling. When the yogurt has come to a boil, reduce the heat to low and simmer for 3 minutes, still stirring. With a slotted spoon, remove the meat and onions and drop into the yogurt. Add the garlic and coriander mixture and mix well. Keep gently stirring until both meat and onions are as hot as the yogurt sauce. Serve with vermicelli rice.

MOHAMMED ANTABLI

*Al Waha has long been
established as one of London's
finest Lebanese restaurants.
Owner and head chef,
Mohammed Antabli, presents
authentic, fresh food from
his native Lebanon with an
extensive and varied menu.*

Al Waha, 75 Westbourne
Grove, London W2 4UL

GRILLED EGGPLANTS WITH SESAME PASTE
AND LEMON JUICE

Preparation time: 10 minutes
Cooking time: 35–40 minutes
Serves 4

2 eggplants (aubergines)
5 tablespoons tahini
5 tablespoons plain (natural) yogurt
2 tablespoons lemon juice
1 teaspoons salt
1½ tablespoons pomegranate paste (optional)
paprika, to garnish
3 tablespoons fresh parsley, chopped
3 tablespoons pomegranate seeds
walnuts, to garnish

Place the eggplants (aubergines) onto skewers and cook them
over an open flame of a gas stove; this is the best way to obtain
a smoky flavor. You could also cook the eggplants under the
broiler (grill) if you prefer. Cook the aubergines, turning
frequently, until the skin is blackened all over and the skin is
soft to the touch. Remove the eggplants from the heat and
place in a bowl of cold water for a few minutes. Discard the
burnt skin, put the flesh in a (sieve) strainer and place in the
fridge to remove any excess liquid. Cut the aubergines into
small pieces and then pound to a rough pulp. Add the tahini
and yogurt and stir to combine. Next, add the lemon juice and
season with salt to taste. Place the mixture in a dish and garnish
with paprika, parsley leaves, pomegranate seeds and walnuts.
Finish off with a dash of olive oil.

LAMB, ONIONS, AND PARSLEY
GRILLED ON SKEWERS

Preparation time: 20 minutes
Cooking time: 15 minutes
Serves 4

1 large onion, finely chopped
1 green bell pepper, finely chopped
1 red bell pepper, finely chopped
1 bunch fresh parsley, finely chopped
2¼lb/1 kg ground (minced) lamb
pinch of cinnamon
salt and pepper
rice, Lebanese bread and salad, to serve

In a large bowl, combine the onions, green and red bell peppers
and parsley. Once they are well mixed, squeeze all excess water
out of the mixture with your hands. Add the ground (minced)
meat and cinnamon, and season with salt and pepper. Knead
the mixture until all of the ingredients are well combined. Take
a golf ball-size handful of the mixture and spread it around a
skewer, squeezing it out to make a sausage shape. Cook the
skewers on a hot barbecue or under a preheated broiler (grill)
for 10–15 minutes, until cooked through. Serve with rice,
Lebanese bread and salad.

Author Acknowledgements
The author would like to dedicate this book to her
family, especially her son Joe, and her grandchildren.
She would also like to thank Hannah, Kate, Marisa
and Matt for all their hard work.

Phaidon Press Limited
Regent's Wharf
All Saints Street
London N1 9PA

Phaidon Press Inc.
180 Varick Street
New York, NY 10014

www.phaidon.com

© 2012 Phaidon Press Limited

ISBN 978 0 7148 6480 8

A CIP catalogue record for this book is available
from the British Library.

Commissioning Editor: Emilia Terragni
Project Editor: Daniel Hurst
Production Controller: Laurence Poos

Photographs by Toby Glanville
Designed by Astrid Stavro
Introductory text by Maureen Abood

The Publisher would like to thank Theresa
Bebbington, Vanessa Bird, Carol Blinman, Kate
Blinman, Linda Doeser, Kali Hamm, Olia Hercules,
Marisa Viola, and Troy Willis for their contributions
to the book.

Printed in China

Note on the recipes
Some recipes include uncooked or very lightly
cooked eggs, fish or meat. These should be
avoided by the elderly, infants, pregnant women,
convalescents and anyone with an impaired
immune system.